1) Nina was born in **L'vov,** Poland and remained there until her escape from Janowska Labor Camp in the spring of 1941.

2) Soon after her escape into the woods, Nina encounters partisans who eventually agree to recruit her for work under the new identity of Maria Kvasigroich. She is sent to find employment within the units supporting German troops fighting in Russia. She gains a position forwarding mail to Nazi soldiers in the Russian city of **Dnepropetrovsk.** While working with this unit she smuggles travel papers to the partisans whenever possible.

NINA'S WARTIME JOURNEY THROUGH EUROPE (1938-39)

SOVIET UNION

POLAND

Vinnica
4

Dnepropetrovsk
2

5 Ghivan

3

6

Zaporozje

Zmerinka

ROMANIA

3) Nina's unit moves to accommodate the troops throughout the war. In October of 1943 Dnepropetrovsk is liberated by the Allies, causing her German employers transport their entire operation further south to **Zaporozje.**

4) Once again Nina's unit is forced to relocate, this time to the town of **Vinnica.**

5) After several months, Nina's unit follows behind German troops to nearby **Ghivan**, a town close to the Romanian border.

6) Nina flees from her German employers in the middle of the night on December 31, 1943, escaping across the Romanian border to the city of **Zmerinka.** She eventually finds employment with a mobile medical unit operated by the liberating Soviet army. It is in Zmerinka that she meets her future husband, Josef Morecki.

7) Nina's unit moves with Soviet troops as the Nazis retreat further west. In the fall of 1944 she eludes the watchful eyes of her Russian employers, escaping to **L'vov** when the medical unit passes close to her hometown.

8) Unsuccessful in her attempts to find any surviving family members, Nina travels to the city of **Katowice** in order to register with the United Nations Relief and Rehabilitation.

9) Nina and Josef reunite, and by the summer of 1945 travel to **Warsaw** to marry. Josef then organizes a band of fellow Jews for the exodus toward the American Allies occupying Austria.

10) Nina and her small group of expatriates make their way west, ultimately arriving in **Vienna,** Austria. There they are housed and protected by American troops.

11) By 1946 the Moreckis are living as "Displaced Persons" in **Salzburg,** Austria. While Nina struggles to regain her health compromised by a series of illnesses, Josef arranges for their immigration to America.

12) The Moreckis leave on March 19, 1947 from the port of **Bremen,** Germany to begin a new life in America. They arrive at Ellis Island in New York City on May 6, 1947.

THROUGH THE EYES *of a* SURVIVOR

THROUGH
THE EYES
of a
SURVIVOR

COLETTE
WADDELL

Top
Cat
PRESS

CARPINTERIA, CA

1072 Casitas Pass Road, Suite #245
Carpinteria, CA 93013
www.topcatpress.com

Publishers Cataloging-in-Publication

Waddell, Colette.
    Through the eyes of a survivor : a living history of Nina Morecki from pre-World War II Poland to modern America / Colette Waddell.
    --1st ed. --Carpinteria, CA : TopCat Press, 2007.

    p. ; cm.

    ISBN-13: 978-0-9791518-0-4, cloth
    ISBN-10: 0-979-1518-0-5, cloth

    1. Morecki, Nina. 2. Holocaust survivors--Poland--Biography.
3. World War, 1939-1945--Poland. 4. World War, 1939-1945--
Personal narratives. 5. Holocaust, Jewish (1939-1945)--Poland.
6. Holocaust, Jewish (1939-1945)--Personal narratives. 7. Poland--
History--1918-1945. I. Title.

DS135.P63 M67 2007   2006910285
940.53/18/092--dc22   CIP

Cover photo by Douglas Fogelson
Cover and interior design by Dotti Albertine
Content editing by Ilene Segalove
Copyediting by Catherine Viel
Production proofing by Brookes Nohlgren
Book consulting by Ellen Reid

Recent photos of Nina, photos of the author and photo restoration by Deedee Degelia. Pre-war and post-war photos courtesy of Jewish Federation of Greater Santa Barbara, California. ("Portraits of Survival" exhibition, August 2006)

This book is printed on acid-free paper and manufactured in the United States of America by Sheridan Books, a member of the Green Press Initiative, www.greenpressinitiative.org.

Dedication

To all the young people of the world:
May you learn from the past; for you are the future.
—NINA MORECKI

To my mother, Carrie Cline-Pike,
a woman of grace and strength.
—COLETTE WADDELL

Contents

Foreword

LITERALLY TENS OF THOUSANDS of Holocaust survivors have been interviewed about their life stories, and many thousands more have written and published accounts of their experiences during the human extermination campaigns of the World War II era. The question arises: Why another memoir? What does this story contribute to our understanding of the most highly organized genocide in human history?

There are several answers to this question. Of course every story adds information to the historical record, and each one contains its share of unique experiences and events. Also, the diversity of the narrators and events should to some extent mirror the diversity of interests among possible audiences, since the feelings of people of each age and gender, and ethnic, religious, educational and national background will resonate more deeply with some life stories than others. And a diversity of literary styles will render some narratives more appealing to some people than others. This memoir, the story of a young woman who was sucked into the maelstrom of World War II in Poland at age 18, who climbed miraculously unscathed out of a huge grave after a mass execution, who worked for Polish partisans in a Nazi post office, is more than justified for all of those reasons. But it is also truly unique in other important ways.

First, its scope encompasses much more than Nina Grütz-Morecki's Holocaust experiences. The narrative contextualizes Nina's Holocaust odyssey within a family history from her grandparents in the late nineteenth century to her grandchildren in the late twentieth and early twenty-first. Second, it recounts how Nina came to tell her story more than fifty years later, in the 1990s. This second story is no mean feat, since it encompasses the process we call the "construction of meaning"—how individuals take the chance events of their life, develop a set of values out of them, and carry those values into society at large. Finally, even more than merely retracing that process, Nina's account of her life is accompanied by the unpretentious but incisive commentary of one of the students inspired by her story.

Soon after hearing Nina speak in a college classroom, Colette Waddell became fast friends with the small, venerable woman whose grandmotherly demeanor belied the brutality she had endured decades earlier. A gifted writer blessed with extraordinary empathy, Colette wanted to document Nina's life in writing as a personal gift. Insights Colette gleaned from dozens of hours of interviewing, followed by hundreds of hours of research and writing, are interspersed throughout Nina's first-person narrative in italicized passages. Nina's multi-layered first-person narrative—a biography before, during and after the Holocaust, as well as a story of the construction of meaning from it—thus has embedded within it another layer: Colette's nuanced account of the process of writing this oral history. As a teacher of oral methods who has read many dozen oral histories, I know how rare it is to find an account that so seamlessly integrates into a biography the story of the preparation, interpretative challenges, and rewards of weaving the diverse strands of a human life into a compelling analytical narrative.

I am sure other readers will be as fascinated and rewarded by reading Colette's and Nina's stories as I have been.

—HAROLD MARCUSE, PROFESSOR OF HISTORY
UNIVERSITY OF CALIFORNIA, SANTA BARBARA

Preface

I am speaking to you as one of the few survivors of a horrible chapter in human history. The setting for my story is the city of L'vov, Poland, in Eastern Europe, during World War II.

The German regime under Hitler's Nazi rule was a world power determined to expand its boundaries at any cost. Its leaders had another diabolical plan in mind: the extermination of the Jewish people, whom they believed to be an inferior and undesirable race that polluted the superior white Aryan nation they believed themselves to be.

Six million Jewish people and five million others (including those who opposed the Nazis and of course those who helped Jews) were systematically removed from European societies and murdered over the course of the war. Eleven million people were swept up in the wave of Nazi hatred. Many innocent people watched as a mother, father, sister, brother, grandparent, friend, teacher or doctor, disappeared one by one. In my case, almost every single person I cared for was murdered. Can anyone imagine how life would change in such circumstances?

This story will sometimes be difficult to read, but I feel it is important to share my experience with others. Like many young people today, as a young woman I really had no idea what the future would bring. Before the war I was like any other student, with hopes and expectations of a great life. In my wildest dreams I would never have imagined the course it took.

I will let my readers be the judge of whether or not something may be learned from what happened to me. The only thing I know for certain is that, for better or worse, the experience has left me forever changed.

—NINA MORECKI

Introduction

I MET NINA GRÜTZ-MORECKI in 1999 when she came to speak at my undergraduate course on German history and the Holocaust at the University of California, Santa Barbara. From a very young age I had been drawn to the subject of World War II, and in particular to the event known as the Holocaust. Although I was intensely curious about the Jewish victims who lived through the war, I had never actually met a survivor. I cannot exactly say why, nor can I clearly articulate the feelings that washed over me when I heard Nina speak. I was repulsed by the sheer madness of the assaults she had been forced to bear. Yet I also felt compelled to catch every nuance of her story.

I studied her face while she spoke. What had it been like to survive such an ordeal? How had it changed this woman? What went on in Nina's head and heart as she battled the onslaught of Nazi brutality? How had she managed to evade the capture and execution that completely wiped out her friends and family? Indeed, what motivation did she have to go on when those she held so dear one by one fell from her sight? I craved details and more. In Nina I saw living history, and at the end of class I found it difficult to see such a resource walk away.

As luck would have it, Nina, and her history, walked toward me. While we collected our books and backpacks, our professor asked if anyone could provide Nina a ride into town. I was one of the "mature" students, meaning my car was relatively clean and in no danger of breaking down. So I had the honor of transporting our guest to her home. The appeal of engaging Nina in conversation was compounded by the fact that I genuinely liked this lady. She reminded me of my mother—polite, yet feisty; demure, but nobody's fool. Getting to know Nina would be beyond interesting, so when asked to play taxi driver, I happily obliged.

As we approached my BMW, however, my companion froze. She lightly touched my sleeve in a gesture I would come to recognize as a way of gently getting my attention.

"You know, dahlink," she murmured in her faint Polish accent, "I very much appreciate the ride, but normally I do not have anything to do with products manufactured in Germany."

At first confused, I suddenly realized that this was one of the few ways in which this woman could protest what the German nation had done to her years ago.

"Well, Nina," I ventured, "the Nazi regime is dead, and here you are telling others how they attempted to exterminate you and everyone you loved. So wouldn't you say that, in a way, a Jew riding in a German car could be looked at as a sort of victory?"

A shade of doubt crossed her face, but she graciously allowed me to help her into the vehicle.

"Besides," I continued to reason, "it's a used car."

"Yes, dear," Nina softly explained as I helped her into her seat, "but the point is, those bastards nearly killed me."

"Well," I sighed, putting the high performance automobile into gear, "you're here now."

So began a relationship with a woman I came to regard as both friend and mentor, and a journey that changed us both in ways we could never have imagined.

FOUR YEARS after that first meeting I began work on Nina's story. I had recently graduated with a Bachelor's degree in history and anthropology, abandoning graduate school in order to raise four stepchildren. The task of writing Nina's biography came at the best and the worst of times. My stepchildren were still quite young and in need of care, yet I had a strong desire to put my education to use. Compiling Nina Morecki's memoirs offered me an opportunity to do just that.

As our friendship grew, Nina revealed more about her past and her desires for the future, her greatest aspiration being to reach young people with a message of tolerance. She hoped that by putting her story in book form she would then have access to a larger audience.

I was never entirely clear as to why Nina chose me for this task. After many intimate conversations, I could only conclude that Nina simply felt comfortable with me. I wondered if I were up to the

Nina, with author Colette Waddell

adventure of reliving with this woman her turbulent past. I had not yet been published. Could I create from her words a moving and meaningful text? I brushed aside my doubts because I knew that turning down Nina's offer would have been a foolishly missed opportunity.

Sensing that she felt there was a lot at stake, I reminded Nina that I was not Jewish. Would a *shiksa* have the appropriate amount of passion to produce a book about the Holocaust?

"Don't worry, honey," she assured me. "There should be other people besides Jews reading my story. I need someone to write it who can see things through a different pair of eyes." I did not anticipate the exhausting task of examining the brutal details of Nina's life; instead, I took a deep breath, and set about the process of gleaning memories, both good and bad, from my willing accomplice.

My interviews with Nina Morecki took place from April, 2002, to March, 2005. By the time of our first interview, Nina had moved closer to her youngest daughter in Pomona, California. For me this meant traveling close to three hours each way, "schlepping," as she would say, all of my equipment and necessities in order to work for at least two days at a time.

My ritual of driving straight through to Pomona, powered by talk radio or blaring classical music, would end with Nina answering my buzz at the gate of her senior apartment complex. Each meeting would begin with exclamations of, "Sweetheart, I am so happy to see you!"

As I wrote the date on each little cassette tape, Nina set out for my pleasure the inevitable offerings of cookies, crackers, and candies. These were always accompanied by endless cups of coffee. Whenever I prepared for my drive back home she would make sure my backpack was laden with cookies and lollipops for the children, along with the bags of bread she had stockpiled: a habit left over from the war. Our beginning ritual never took long, however, as Nina wished to start working as soon as decently possible. Our approach to the interview process followed a particular pattern. We would catch up on each other's news as I politely fastened the microphone to her smart sweater or blouse. Then, after arranging my list of questions, we settled in for hours of discussion.

I ATTEMPTED to record Nina's life in a chronological fashion, but our minds rarely work in such a way. If an event from her childhood triggered memories of raising her own children, I quietly accepted this, redirecting Nina back to the previous question when appropriate. Even as her story unfolded, I continually questioned my own tactics. Was I getting enough detail, or bothering with too much? I tried to gauge Nina's emotions at every turn of topic. At times I felt I might be pushing too hard for particulars regarding the loss of her mother, the Nazi labor camp, or her own brushes with death.

But I needn't have worried about my friend's emotional or physical stamina. A typical interview lasted from mid-morning to very late at night, and she never seemed to run out of energy. When we finished for the day Nina always offered me her spare room. There she kept boxes of memorabilia collected over the years. "Thank You" notes from schoolchildren, and students' posters, collages, and piles of letters, were all lovingly saved. Her hospitality was sincere, but I was reluctant to impose. I also felt that, after spending hours deeply engaged in what was, at times, a disturbing conversation, I needed to be alone with my thoughts, or to think nothing at all.

With each interview I was transported, lulled by a string of memories that pulled me into a time before computers, sitcoms, and terrorists. Together we pushed aside the gossamer cloak of time. At the beginning of each meeting Nina would sit demurely, hands folded, her face a calm mask. As the interview wore on, however, she became more animated. Speaking of the Nazis brought a defiant lift to her chin, while her finger punctuated on the glass table every crime they committed. I was always reluctant to break the spell of our conversations, taking breaks only to stretch both body and mind. We relieved ourselves of the coffee. We would talk about ordinary things, then return to our places and step back in time once more.

Guiding Nina through the nightmare of her past was a profound and horrifying experience. Every scene from her life played out like pieces of a dramatic film. Nina's story grabbed at my heart and begged me to witness and then direct each cinematic sequence. It took me some time to shake off the feeling that I had been living someone else's life. After each meeting with Nina I was left with a residual vibe of melancholy and elation. Speeding along on the Los Angeles freeways, I was often surprised to find myself half-way home before I was pulled from the dream-like state created by listening to her story. Working with my friend was exhausting, yet at the same time I became invigorated by its purpose.

It seemed that Nina and I embarked on a journey that changed us both, and "the work" became a shared priority. Not satisfied with a previous interpretation, Nina sometimes telephoned me to rehash some episode she had mulled over during the night. Through it all, my friend showed me how a woman can be at once strong and vulnerable, and how one's limits are often self-imposed. I prayed that my visits allowed her to re-examine the war's effect on her, and to forgive herself for outliving those she loved.

In between these meetings I gathered research that might back up, contrast, or frame the many facets of her story. I immersed myself in literature on topics ranging from nineteenth century Polish Jews, to Jewish working women in the twentieth century, and anything available regarding World Wars I and II. I had already been exposed to a good amount of this sort of reading. Reliving the accounts of survivors such as Nina was nevertheless difficult and emotionally exhausting. The more I learned about these victims, the more I questioned. Why did some victims fare better than others? Certainly there had been no formula for survival, yet those most successful in emerging from their wartime experience seemed to have healthy portions of stubbornness, ingenuity, and good old-fashioned luck.

No matter how much I delved into the material, I was never fully satisfied with what were supposed to be the answers behind survival. Along with carrying the burden of misplaced guilt at having outlived their loved ones, the survivors themselves remained mystified about their personal victories over death. I desperately wanted to treat Nina's story with the respect it deserved, yet facing piles of tapes from hours of interviews, I was often discouraged. I admit that the process of weaving the pieces of our conversations into cohesive chapters proved daunting. I decided that if our work provided only a personal history for Nina's family, it would have been worth the time we spent compiling it.

Much of the Holocaust literature I read as a student left me asking, "…and then what happened?" I wondered how years of exposure to violence and death had affected survivors in their post-war lives. Nina's testimony offers a more complete survival story—one that covers her young life, the six hellacious years of World War II, her experience as an American immigrant, and the challenges she faced not only as a Jewish survivor but also as a working woman in twentieth century America who finally finds her voice and a purpose in life through public speaking.

I transcribed some sixty hours of taped interviews; all the while, Nina's multi-dimensional personality revealed itself to me. She has been a Pole, a Jew, a hopeful student, obedient daughter, escapee, partisan, rebel, survivor, lover, wife, mother, advocate, and finally a role model. By seeing to it that others are more informed about the Holocaust, Nina wages her own personal war against the genocide that continues throughout our world.

How did Nina Morecki survive the war while those around her perished? Like many victims of the Holocaust, this very question plagued her long after war's end. Nina saw her wartime self as a scrawny young woman, frightened and alone. Suicide often seemed a welcome alternative to Nina both during and after the war. Thankfully, she lived to see her children and grandchildren thrive in relative peace, free from the hatred she had experienced, in a country where they could be proud of their religious and ethnic background.

Would it have been better for Nina to put the past behind her, and enjoy the life she built with her husband after liberation and immigration to the United States? Upon hearing the litany of the hardships and heartache she endured, anyone would agree that Nina deserves to live and to live well. She has a right to enjoy the family and freedom denied her from 1939 to 1945. She remains uncomfortable with that freedom, however, deriving solace instead by reaching out to others with her story. Retelling her Holocaust experience creates a sort of memorial to the family Nina lost, and perhaps in some ways it helps to exorcise the demons still lingering from those dark days.

During my study of history I have seen the myriad ways women were demoted throughout the ages for political, religious, and paranoid reasons. Today's woman continues to maneuver around the murky territory that allows her to present herself as both independent and feminine. This is why Nina is to me a visage of power and strength. She would laugh at the idea, and remind me she had only survived by making snap decisions with no courage involved. The truth is, however, that as diminutive, feminine, and unassuming as my dear friend is, Nina has proved to be more powerful than the Nazis, fiercer than the prejudice and hatred that encompassed her young life, and stronger than the sorrow that threatened to overwhelm her in the post-war years. I discovered myself while writing Nina's story, and it has been her gift to me.

Our work together brought moments of laughter and tears, but never once did Nina flinch from answering even the most intimate questions. Her experiences fostered strong opinions about racism, injustice, and the Jewish faith. Nina has done her best to understand what occurred during World War II, and together we explored the roots of the anti-Semitism so deeply entrenched within the Polish mind. Her anger over the loss of family and friends, and the senseless torture inflicted upon her and others by the Nazis, has somewhat subsided. In its place Nina resolves to use as a weapon her memory, and so conquer those Nazis who disrupted her life.

Each time I sat down with my friend I experienced a part of her anguish and desperate fight for sanity and survival. Each time I went away wondering how this woman could maintain the open-hearted grace she carries with her today. Her story was a blessing to me as it addressed the human desire to endure, and to seek love in the face of hopelessness and despair. Perhaps this has been Nina's intent all along.

—COLETTE WADDELL

PART ONE

Beginnings

CHAPTER I

Nina's Homeland

(1880-1935)

MY FIRST TASK in telling Nina's story involved describing the world she knew before World War II. Providing the Grütz family background was more than a starting point, however. Because all of her loved ones were eliminated at the hands of the Nazis, it seemed appropriate to return to them the history of their lives. By doing so I also hoped to give readers a sense of Nina's life, before the war intruded with all of its painful repercussions.

All through our conversations I felt pushed and pulled by emotions brought on by my friend's revelations. Documenting family history was my first attempt at taking my readers' hands and leading them through the odyssey of Nina's life.

The Grütz ancestral history stretches back many generations in Poland. Both Nina's mother's and her father's side of the family became successful in business, and were respected members of their community even among the non-Jewish population. The family followed a strict tradition of charitable work as well as the pursuit of higher education. Nina's earliest recollections concern stories about her grandparents and nineteenth century life in Poland.

The Grütz family was part of a Jewish population that thrived at a time when almost three-quarters of the Jews in Europe called Poland home. According to historians, the Jews flourished between the two world wars, their communities within Poland were the largest in Europe: the main cultural and religious centers of the Jewish dispersion.[1]

Nina had not seen her immediate family since they were effectively erased during the war, but she was still able to recall in detail stories about those loved ones who had played such profound roles in her life.

I suppose the time has come for me to open the door to my heart. For so many years my friends asked about my life in Poland, but I wouldn't speak of it. "Nina," they would say, shaking their heads, "you are like a closed book." I knew what they said was true, but life made me that way, for better or worse. To be honest, I think that the first person I really opened up to was my friend Colette, who helped me write this story.

All that I speak of happened so long ago. I moved to America in the late 1940's when I was only twenty-three or so, and I wanted to discuss the war way back then. I had already gone through so much. I desperately wished to express my sorrow and tell my family in America how the war had affected me. But this sort of thing was discouraged at the time, especially by the Jewish community. Everybody wanted to put the miserable past behind and get on with their lives in their new country.

Now that I am finally speaking out, people might say that it never really happened. They might say to themselves, "Oh, this Nina Morecki got a date wrong, so it's all fiction…it's all in her mind." I admit that sometimes I forget exact dates or how the name of a place should be spelled, but I assure you that every bit of it happened as I tell it. I wish it were not true, because so much of my story is so tragic. I wish that I had not learned firsthand how people can become monsters during a war, yet at the same time, I am happy to say I came across a few real saints in my struggle to survive.

I have told this personal story to Colette for many reasons. I want people to understand what happened during World War II, to know what was done to us Jews for no reason at all, other than that we happened to be Jewish. I also want young people to learn from the things I did in my life that allowed me to survive. But my greatest hope in sharing this story is so that my parents and other family members did not die in vain. I truly believe that telling others about their murders and speaking out against genocide, racism, and hatred can and will make a difference.

I feel the time has come to write it all down at last. I am in my eighties and the clock is ticking.

I will begin by telling what I remember about my family. I was born on December 24th, 1920. By the time I came on the scene I already had two older sisters—Lina, who was nine years older than me, and Helena, who was eight years older. I never really knew my grandparents on my mother's side because they died while I was still a baby. What I know about my maternal grandmother I learned through my mother, Rosa, who told me countless stories about this woman who was a very kind and caring person. Everybody she came in contact with respected her for her charitable work. They used to call her "Mama Libbi," or *Libichka*, though her full name was Elizabeth Roth. If a family was in need, or a woman was busy having a baby, my grandmother was always there with food to make certain everybody was fed, and if needed she would wash up the children. When my grandmother died everybody in the area came to pay respects. My mother told me it was really quite amazing, but then my mother was loved for her generosity of spirit in the same way.

WHENEVER SPEAKING of her mother, a shadow of quiet sadness ultimately crossed Nina's face and the atmosphere grew somber. Their relationship was tragically cut short by the war, and remembering "Mama" caused Nina's voice to become wistful, and our conversation would stall. Then I would draw Nina out of her reverie and ask what she remembered about the rest of her family.

As a young girl I spent very little time with my grandmother from my father's side. She was not very pleasant and I was afraid of her. I don't even remember her name, but I recall that she was small, skinny, and wore a babushka. She complained quite a bit and continually asked my father to support her other grown children, my father's siblings. However, it seemed to me that nothing he ever did for them was enough. My father, Viktor, was quite wealthy compared to the rest of his family, but he had worked hard for every penny. It always struck me as ironic that one of my father's unsuccessful brothers had a son who eventually became a millionaire!

As I grew up, I could see that this grandmother was not nice to Mama, and because of this I disliked visiting her. What child wants to be around a grouchy old lady? I remember like in a dream when this relative died. We were not Orthodox Jews, but we were very traditional. It is a custom that after somebody very close to the family dies, you cover all of the mirrors. We call it "sitting Shiva," and it is a time when the family of the deceased stays home to receive visitors expressing their condolences.

When Mama covered our beautiful mirror in the foyer I couldn't understand why they would go to such trouble for a woman who had been so unkind. I suppose it was a little precocious of me, but I actually objected to having that mirror covered. I loved to glance at myself in it while passing by. My parents explained to me that they were honoring the memory of my grandmother, but I would have none of it. I don't remember going to my grandmother's funeral, but I know that I did not shed one tear when she passed away.

My grandfather on my mother's side had four children from his first wife: three daughters and one son, David. When his first wife died he married my grandmother. They had together three daughters and one son. The son worked as a pharmacist until he was drafted and killed in the First World War. That was a terrible tragedy for my grandmother because it was her only son. She had an older daughter, Betka, who lived about two hours from my hometown of L'vov, Poland. I had another aunt named Erna who was sent to New York in order to marry a man the family arranged for her. Her fiancé's name was Messing, and his family was very wealthy from a large bakery business. Anyway, Erna came back to Poland when she was pregnant with her first child, Miriam, who was born in Poland, and she was only three months old when they returned to America. All three of the sisters were very close.

Mama was born in 1889. Like me, my mother was the youngest girl in her family, and as the youngest child she was the last one to marry. Consequently, as the last child living at home she became like a very good friend to her mother. My grandmother had been a working mother, so I suppose it made sense that at some point my mother also would become a businesswoman.

My mother's family owned and operated a soap factory along with an attached store where our products were sold to the locals. My grandmother looked after the store and taught my mother the business, and as she grew up she eventually managed the whole place herself. When Mama took over running the store they didn't even have a cash register to ring up sales. Everything was figured by hand, so my mother of course was very good with mathematics. She was always careful to bring each day's sales home for her mother to count up and re-total. Every night she used to bring this money, saying to her mother, "Mama, come over. Count up today's sales." My grandmother, who never learned how to read and write, was still very intelligent. She diligently counted the cash, but she knew what Mama was up to. She would say, "You know…my dear child, I know why you're doing this. You don't need me to count the money. But you want me to feel that I am still active in business." This was true, but they continued the ritual until Grandma Libbi died.

Once or twice a year my mother visited the local hospital where my grandmother volunteered. My mother helped make lunch there. They could have one hundred people at this hospital during the same day, yet they helped to feed every patient. They never mentioned who they were, however, and Mama continued this practice of volunteering anonymously. She just brought the food, helped to arrange it, served them all, then quietly left without a word. When she came home I would ask her, "Mama, why don't you let the people know who you are so they can thank you for all your volunteer work?" But she always shook her head, saying to me, "It would serve no purpose for people to know who I am. The point is they need help, and we should all do our part to assist them. After all, look how we have been so blessed."

I came to understand that my mother was not volunteering to improve her standing in society, but because she had been raised by her mother to help others. This was how I came to know my grandmother, through my mother's stories of her and her similar acts of kindness. Mama always told me, "I am trying to help out because this is what my mother did, and I want to carry on her work."

DURING THE EARLY TWENTIETH CENTURY it was uncommon for upper-class Jewish women to seek employment outside the home. Many Jewish wives and mothers, given the luxury of leisure time, preferred to focus on volunteer and social work that benefited their neighborhoods. Those who chose to work did so within closely monitored boundaries in positions that offered less than equal pay to their male counterparts. In his *Social and Political History of the Jews in Poland*, Marcus wrote: "Jewish women were even more strictly kept out of public employment than Jewish men. In general, women, although at each level of employment better educated than men, had to content themselves with inferior grading and, consequently, lower remuneration for equal jobs."[2]

Grandmother Libbi's unique situation may be attributed to the fact that her family owned and operated a soap factory that had been established in L'vov as early as the eighteenth century. The Roth family was participating in a wave of entrepreneurial activity taking place among Polish Jews at the time. Though traditionally active in commerce, it was noteworthy that many Jewish businesses prospered in a country that had been industrially underdeveloped for centuries. The Polish farmer struggled with conditions that were inadequate for growing a surplus of produce, while aristocratic Poles engaged in literary pursuits or other activities they deemed acceptable to their station, yet which proved unproductive for the country's economy. Unfettered by cultural and social dictates that led the Polish elite to the misuse of capital, Polish Jews were able to produce goods that met economic demands of the time.[3] While her family enjoyed this period of Jewish economic independence, Nina's mother was raised in the traditions of her time.

I recall only a little bit of what my mother told me about her childhood. She grew up in the house situated close to the factory. My mother, her brother, and her two sisters were well cared for and happy, but my grandmother wanted her girls to have some sort of education. This was unusual for the day, and my mother's father of course would not have approved.

My grandfather Chaim was something of a big shot in the Jewish community. Even the neighboring Poles respected him because he was a good businessman and a fine person. But I must say that this man did not see things the way my grandmother did. My mother had a pleasant childhood in Poland. At that time most probably there was anti-Semitism, but Mama's family did not feel it so much because they had a business that was important to the community. Jews and Poles alike wanted to buy my grandfather's soap, and they had a very good relationship with all of their neighbors. Most of the people in town lived modestly. My grandfather also maintained a fairly simple lifestyle, even though they could have afforded fancy things. This modest living kept him in good standing within the community. His Polish neighbors did not resent him for his wealth.

Unfortunately, though my grandfather was a fine man, he also had a terrible temper. My grandmother was his second wife, and he truly loved her, but according to my mother she sometimes had to work around his anger. Altogether they had nine children. He had four kids, two sons and two daughters from the first wife. Then he had four or five children with my grandmother. He was the head of this big family, and consequently the authority figure. As the man of this family he expected his wife and children to be obedient. When something angered my grandfather, right away he would raise his voice. He easily became agitated so no one dared to disturb him.

My mother claimed that the house remained very quiet because grandfather liked it this way. When something did occur that upset him, well, grandmother somehow managed to ease the situation. She had a way about her, and she could always settle him down. She could put her arm around my grandfather and say, "Calm down, dear. Raising your voice will only make you hoarse." Mama remembered grandmother speaking quietly in Yiddish, and this seemed to have a remarkable effect on grandfather. Only for her would he become more reasonable. I suppose he liked the attention, and I believe my mother acquired the same skills that helped her to deal effectively with my father. What is it they say? "You catch more flies with honey…"

My mother said that her father could also be very rough with her and the other children. However, during most of his outbursts grandmother was clever enough to keep her girls out of his way. She also managed to keep him oblivious to the fact that his daughters were busily attending school. Like most men of his culture and generation, my grandfather didn't think that going to school was useful to a girl. Reading and writing were all right, but the higher education of *gymnasium (the European equivalent of high school)*, or college, would be frivolous and a waste of time. If boys were not occupied with learning a trade, well then college might be helpful, but certainly not for girls! Boys needed schooling in order to go into business, but higher education might distract a young woman from marriage.

My grandfather sensed my mother's intelligence, and it worried him. "You're going to be smarter than the boys you're supposed to marry," he told her, "that's no good! This can only lead to trouble! You'll drive all of the boys from the good families away." He made it very clear that he didn't want his girls educated beyond basic grammar school. Even so, my grandmother pulled my mother and her sisters aside and whispered, "Well, of course you have to have some sort of education to get by. We'll just make it our secret how much you acquire. Your father doesn't need to know every little thing."

When her husband went to attend to the family business, grandmother arranged for her girls to slip away. She waited until the coast was clear, then she threw the school books over the fence, where they could be collected by her daughters on the other side before running off to school! They had to leave early, directly after their father went to work, then race home before he returned. When grandfather came into the house at the end of the day he sometimes saw my mother having a late dinner. He never knew that she had been working on school assignments all afternoon. He would ask, "What are you doing eating again? You're going to become very plump." Grandfather just assumed that Mama had also enjoyed the dinner his children routinely ate together at an earlier hour. Grandmother played it pretty cool, and she just shooed him away, saying, "Leave the child alone, she just loves to eat."

While at school the girls in my mother's family learned a little bit of Jewish education, but they studied Polish as well. I believe they all knew Yiddish and sometimes spoke it at home, but they always spoke the native language with neighbors. Mama and her sisters were very fortunate to attend gymnasium. In those days it was the only real education a young woman might receive. Today it would be considered a little less than schooling of a high school level. Mama made the most of it and became very accomplished in mathematics.

NINA'S MOTHER benefited from schooling that had only recently become available to young girls of her status. Most Jews valued education to the point of making it compulsory for boys up to sixteen years of age.[4] Yet anything beyond instruction of a domestic nature was deemed unnecessary and perhaps even harmful for Jewish girls.[5] This was particularly true for those girls whose families were economically well off. By the time she reached a marriageable age, a young Jewish woman typically had acquired some practical skills. Most were literate enough to run a household, and had a working knowledge of basic mathematics. Study of the Talmud, writings considered sacred to the Jews, was pursued only by Jewish males, and few women completed secondary school. The majority of Eastern European schools were parochial; therefore, both Christian and Jewish children attended strictly according to their faith. By the second half of the nineteenth century, however, a shift occurred that allowed a small number of Jewish children living within the boundaries of Polish towns to integrate into secondary schools of a secular nature. Jewish private schools remained open to those females wishing to attend, but orthodox schools continued as the primary domain of young Jewish males.[6]

For girls living between the nineteenth and twentieth centuries, still more change was on the horizon. According to Paula Hyman, who researched Jewish women of this period, there was a definite swing toward challenging traditional roles for those living in Germany as well as countries further east. While these conservative Jewish women resisted complete assimilation, they consciously selected religious traditions that allowed for a more active public life. This included providing their daughters with a better education than they themselves had received. Ms. Hyman wrote that middle-class Jewish women in particular established creative methods that "...challenged their exclusion from higher education, the professions, and political life..."[7]

With her mother's help, the young Rosa Roth quietly made use of the increase in educational opportunities. Meanwhile, life went on as usual for a Jewish family of her class. Her father remained the head of the family and dictated how his children's lives played out.

Even though my grandfather was unimpressed with university education, he was very much educated in Jewish matters. This sort of knowledge could be very helpful. An education in Jewish law, for example, could be very worthwhile as a way of understanding law in general. Even now if one were to study as a rabbi it would have some advantages. Naturally, people today wouldn't understand everything there is to know in the Jewish religion, but if it were applied correctly a person really could use it as an all-around education.

This sort of education also provided a way of regarding life—a sort of philosophy in its own way. One could, for instance, review Jewish law in order to properly run a business. It's a combination of a lot of little things that, if you're smart enough and know how to apply it, can act as a tool in making decisions. Back in my grandmother's day every Jew knew that a great deal might be achieved with such knowledge. For grandfather, Jewish law was a natural thing to pursue because his family had always been very religious. It helped matters when Mama married my father. He came from the same line of business, that being the manufacture of soap, though his family operated on a smaller scale and came from a smaller town, Zloczow. Even now it's not as large as L'vov. In comparison one could say L'vov was as important a place as Chicago or Los Angeles is now. It was the third largest city in territory and population after Warsaw, the capital of Poland. My mother's entire family came from L'vov, and it was where I was brought up.

Mama finished school by sixteen or so, but with the way things were in those days right away she had to get married. This was pre-arranged. Young people could not date as they do now. All right…she met my father to look him over, but it was all arranged through a matchmaker. Grandfather decided when Mama should get married, and he chose the man for her. As most fathers did at the time, he was looking for particular things in a husband for his daughter. He actually loved my mother very much, and he knew that there were certain qualities that would ensure a secure future for her and his grandchildren.

He also wanted somebody who could take over the family business. My mother's dowry was quite substantial, and this enabled them to choose somebody responsible from a good family. They wanted an exceptional young man that maybe Mama might even like. Grandfather looked for someone who was smart, capable, Jewish…God forbid otherwise, and he wanted somebody who was fairly religious, from a kosher home.

I don't know how he found my father, who I believe was born around 1885, but fortunately for Mama her fiancé was very good-looking. My mother was a pretty girl too, but as a child she developed an infection in her tooth. At that time they didn't have penicillin or other sophisticated medicine, so there was no real cure for her ailment. Grandfather took her to Vienna in order to receive the best medical advice, and the doctors were successful in treating her, but the procedure left a scar on the side of Mama's face. The poor thing was only about ten years old when this occurred, but she learned to deal with it. As for my sisters and me, we couldn't imagine her any other way. She really was pretty in spite of her little flaw.

When my father married Mama half of the factory belonged to her already, as well as the family home. The other half of the business was divided among her siblings, however, by 1916; my father was running the business for my mother's family in every way. They gave him permission to do so because he was smart, and he worked very hard to make the business profitable.

Since father was doing so well with the business, he eventually purchased the entire business from Mama's family. As the sole owner of the property he maintained everything, and he even added on to the compound, expanding it all shortly after the First World War. My mother's parents created the soap business, and they also sold soap to locals in a store next to the factory. Grandmother was involved with the smaller store until Mama was old enough to take it over. There the family could sell retail to peddlers from neighboring towns. The soap was made into long bricks, and in Polish the brand name was *Mydto Kogueikiem*, which essentially means, "Soap Rooster." Isn't that funny to name soap after a chicken? But it was very popular, and that rooster was imprinted in the bricks, that I remember very well.

When Mama first married my father she did not work with him in the factory. She was only taking care of the little store in front to help out my grandmother, but she eventually took it over completely. My mother knew all the clients, and she made a real effort to serve those from out of town. I remember her saying, "Oh, Mr. Musha comes in from such and such town and so we have to pack for him eight to ten packs of soap." She knew exactly how much to prepare and what was needed from the factory. Deliveries were made by horse-and-buggy back then, but if someone wanted something by the pound she arranged it. The soap was cut like cheese with a sharp sort of string.

I suppose Mama and grandmother weren't your typical girls. Back then a woman might occasionally have a job as a servant or a typist, but I don't think many of these working-women were Jewish. Initially my parents lived in the family cottage located close to the factory. They were quite prepared when my older sister, Lina, was born there, and they immediately put her in a little cradle that had been passed down from the family. Sometimes you see these contraptions on television. They are built in the old style in which the cradle may be rocked back and forth. Pietrus, the family dog, was trained how to rock this thing! My mother spoke to him, "Pietrus, the baby's crying. Rock the cradle for us," and so he pushed it with his nose!

When my family moved out of the cottage my sister was a year old, maybe less. This was when my parents were doing so well they could afford to give the cottage to my uncle and move into a large apartment in the city. Even so, they had no place to keep a dog. Instead they left the dog with friends, but it must have made the animal very lonely because soon after he died. This happened very, very soon after! My mother could never forgive herself. She was the one who decided that they could not take the dog, and she believed that the poor animal died of a broken heart. At the time it made sense to leave the dog with friends. It never would have been happy in an apartment. But Mama always blamed herself for abandoning the family pet.

After her simple life in the cottage it was a big adjustment for my mother to move into such elegant quarters. Living in this beautiful place was very different from her previous life. All the furniture in her new home came from Vienna, and the rooms were very large. Before this time, life for my mother had been quiet and modest. She was accustomed to the old style of things and got by very well without luxuries, so she felt a little uncomfortable living in what she saw as extravagant conditions.

She was also distracted with raising a toddler and was expecting another baby very soon. This would be my middle sister, Helena. Mama managed very well, but I think it was difficult for her to keep up with her new life. This place where my parents moved before I was born was in a very exclusive neighborhood on Kopernika Street. This street was named after the astrologer, Copernicus, and our building's address was number ten. Our place was not in any way small like some apartments. It was more like a private home. As a three-story building it was considered really quite fine. It was situated right on the corner where the views were best. We lived on the upper floor and used about ten rooms in all. There was a large formal entrance as well as a servant's entryway. The salon had four gorgeous windows with a beautiful balcony just off my father's study. In this room he had built-in cabinets filled with books just like a real library.

Our kitchen was very spacious with all the latest appliances. The countertops were made of marble imported from Italy. The dining room had what you would call a "china hutch." The top of that was marble as well. We had a regular coal stove, and alongside that were separate electric burners to make coffee or a little breakfast meal. There were two large gas burners for heat, so we were never cold in the wintertime. There was also a faucet with running water which was quite a luxury back then.

A lawyer resided on the second floor, and downstairs there were little shops. The courtyard of our apartment had a pretty little garden with some greenery and seasonal flowers. Along with the businesses downstairs there were shops across the street. Next to those little stores there was a very famous movie theatre called the "Kopernik." It's still there but is being used for some other purpose. A lot of things were destroyed during the war because of the bombing, and of course many businesses that had been around for generations reverted to other things when Poland became a Communist country. Still, I clearly remember this theatre building because it was so pretty.

AS SHE SEARCHED her memory, Nina had an amusing habit of muttering to herself in Polish. This occurred whenever she became immersed in recalling her life in Poland. I could feel myself slipping into Nina's past as she shared the memories of a homeland she once dearly loved.

So my family settled into the new apartment and this was where I was born. Later on my father purchased land in the countryside, but most Jews lived together in the city of L'vov. This was done as a way of protecting ourselves. If Jews lived anywhere outside the main part of the city they might be harmed or their property stolen. The factory and cottage where my mother and her parents lived was not a Jewish neighborhood, so it was a little unusual at the time. The family was well respected and admired, so unlike other Jews who might attempt living in the suburbs or country, we were never harassed or disturbed. My parents carried on this unusual way of life, because even the area where we lived in the apartment was not a Jewish neighborhood. We never felt any threat there before the war, and my memories of this time are good ones.

BETWEEN 1918 AND 1919 a wave of pogroms, one of the bloodiest of which occurred in L'vov, had indeed forced many Jews to seek protection within the less isolated towns and cities of Poland.[8] The late nineteenth century ushered in a period of economic struggle for the Polish middle class. A study done by the Yivo Institute for Jewish Research found that "...The relatively young Polish trading class was not able to overcome Jewish competition by means of economic activity alone. The small Jewish traders and craftsmen took advantage of their low standard of living. Jewish merchants adhered to the principle of high turnover and low profit, which was greatly to the advantage of the economy as a whole and to the consumer in particular, but was injurious to polish business interests. Thus seeds favorable to anti-Semitism were sown among the Polish middle classes."9

The direct result of this animosity was a Jewish flight into urban areas within Poland. While the majority of the Polish population engaging in agriculture remained in small villages, Jews chose to reside in areas that would better ensure their safety. Studying this phenomenon caused author Joseph Marcus to note that "…In sharp contrast to the remainder of the population—indeed, in reverse proportions—the Jews in Poland mostly lived in towns and their occupations were predominantly urban ones."10

Certainly one must consider the fact that not every Jew in Poland feared for his or her life whenever venturing into the unprotected countryside. Nevertheless, more pogroms against Jews were indeed taking place, forcing many Jews to seek safety in numbers. This made Nina's family somewhat remarkable in that they managed to avoid the brunt of anti-Semitic violence sweeping the Polish nation at the time. Perhaps the Grütz family was not so much an anomaly as they were one of a privileged few Jewish families that had successfully assimilated into Polish life. Nina's clan operated within the Gentile community to such an extent that they had less to fear than the average Polish Jew. Nina's young life reflected this rather privileged position.

A feeling of normalcy permeates throughout her childhood recollections. In spite of the fact that anti-Semitic views were gaining popularity throughout Poland, Nina and her family lived alongside their Polish neighbors without incident. The peacefulness she enjoyed during her young life made the chaos that followed all the more disturbing. In hindsight, this part of Nina's story might easily be seen as the calm before the storm. As a child, however, Nina had every reason to believe that the love and protection her family provided was eternally secure. At the center of this blissful life was Nina's mother.

My mother was a very conscientious businesswoman, but when it came time for lunch she would always try to come home. It wasn't as if she had to keep up with domestic things at the house. By the time I was a young girl we had servants working for us to cook and to clean, but mother treated them so well. When she arrived home for lunch she would always check on how things were going with the ladies who worked for us. She made certain that they had eaten lunch themselves. Sometimes the ladies would try to convince my mother to simply enjoy her lunch break, since she would soon be returning to work. They would say, "Oh, first I'll make you something." But Mama would have none of it, saying, "No! You first sit down. You've worked already four or five hours this morning."

One year we had a cleaning woman who came from a small town, and she used to really look forward to going to visit her parents and her family. To help her out, my mother would prepare two big suitcases full of clothes to give away as a thank you for all that she did. Mama truly appreciated all of our domestic staff because in the early days she was frequently at work. During this time she came to rely on our wonderful cook, who helped us keep a kosher home.

Although my parents were what one would call cosmopolitan people, they still tried to keep the Jewish traditions as best they could. This meant that foods such as dairy and meat were never served on the same plate together, and that meat was purchased from a special rabbi. This kind of commitment took time and although Mama tried to prepare meals on occasion, it was difficult when she was at the store all day. Today it is common for mothers to work outside the home, but at this time it was unusual. To tell the truth, my mother only knew how to cook one main dish very well, and that was gefilte fish. They usually serve it for Passover, and nobody in my family likes it now but me. It is made from chopped fish that are formed into patties and served with sauce. Anyway, even this she didn't cook that much because she was working at the business most of the time.

THE EARLY TWENTIETH CENTURY feminism that brought about change in other parts of the world had not quite reached Eastern European society. In Mrs. Grütz's time upper-class Polish women were not known to work outside the home. According to historian Joseph Marcus, both Poles and Jews alike possessed "…the traditional unwillingness to let their womenfolk become wage-earners outside the home."[11] Among Jews of any class, however, it had become acceptable for a wife to work alongside her husband in the family business. This arrangement benefited the lower and middle class Jews in the past because they could strive toward the same goal of advancing family interests in a safe environment. The idea that wives were merely working as their husbands' helpmates allowed a tenuous social compromise, and permitted Jewish women to gain an economic foothold in parts of Poland.

Author Paula Hyman noted that: "By the beginning of the twentieth century, bourgeois gender divisions had become less rigid, and middle-class German Jewish women, like other women in Germany, used their pre-scribed moral sensibilities to engage in public welfare activity that brought new ideas of women's equality into communal discourse."[12]

Still, Rosa Grütz could be seen as somewhat unique in that she was an upper-class Jewish woman participating at least part time in the family busi-ness. That this business had originated with her family, and not her husband's, may have been a factor involved in Mrs. Grütz's decision to work. She also had the strong example set by her own working mother. As a wealthy woman of some standing in Jewish society, Rosa might not have been so inclined to immerse herself in philanthropic work to such an extent as expressed by Nina. Perhaps it was her dual role as businesswoman and mother that caused Nina's mother to empathize with the less fortunate women in her community.

This remained a period of struggle for most women in Poland seeking employment, and Jewish women were not spared when it came to inequality in the workplace.[13]

Nina respected her mother's compassion towards others. As a young girl, Rosa taught Nina the value of giving back to the community, and she cherished the moments they shared doing volunteer work.

When Mama was eventually able to stay at home with us she became more settled into her life. In her spare time she liked to crochet. She also loved to write letters and read. She was also very charitable with her time. She cared for people in L'vov that she didn't even know. On Sundays she patched up clothes for children in need, making up little gift packages that included new things as well. She would tell me, "This really isn't enough, but I can at least give them things we no longer wear. I have to mend them first because some of these mothers may not have needle and thread. Besides, they may not have time to mend because they're always working. I'll fix, wash and iron these things so they won't have to." She never gave away something torn or unusable.

My mother's volunteer work included going to homes for the elderly. Like her mother, she never wanted to give her name because the point was to help, not to get recognition for it. After helping to serve lunch she always had sweets to hand out wrapped in her famous little packages. People were always surprised to find in them a little money and some candy. She gave the best candy because next to our store was a neighbor who made wonderful chocolate. It was delicious, and this was the only place you could get it. I know that I am making my mother sound like a saint, but quite frankly there were plenty of people back then who would have said this about her.

Before I was born my parents went through the First World War. When I think back on how my mother reacted to the Second World War, I can understand now that her behavior was directed by previous experience. I remember that my mother could never muster the same sense of urgency I had when the Russians, and then the Germans, invaded Poland. It was very frustrating for me because I knew that our lives would be drastically changed. But Mama believed the war I was dealing with would simply be a repeat of the First World War, which my parents managed to weather quite well. Because she had such hope for a similar outcome, this second war was difficult for Mama to comprehend. She could never really grasp what was happening.

I remember hearing that during the first war our business had been threatened by the Russians. The violence eventually forced my parents to flee with my sisters to Vienna. These were the years when pogroms against Jews were not uncommon. Cossacks would get drunk and rile up the local populace against us. Some Jews were injured or even killed when these groups decided to smash up a storefront or a Jew's home.

My mother told me that during the first war a young Gentile man protected the family shop that was next to our factory. It's funny the things you remember in bits and pieces. I even remember that the address of our factory was Zamarsoska, number twenty-eight. You wouldn't recognize it now, but at the time it was a thriving business. As the Russians advanced on Poland, the Bolsheviks apparently told Polish locals they could vandalize whatever Jewish business they liked. A young Polish man who knew my father stood in front of our little store and said, "You are not going to harm this place! The people who own it are decent human beings. If you try to take one thing it will be over my dead body!"

That mob would have looted and burned our store for sure if that young man had not been there. It was a very kind gesture on his part. He was the son of Mr. Ravitsky, a man who had done business with my father for years. My parents always said that they were very grateful to this young man, who Mama said looked very much like Mr. Ravitsky: tall, handsome, and aristocratic.

We didn't visit the Ravitsky home because Jews and Polish Gentiles really did not socialize in that way. But Mr. Ravitsky and my father respected each other very much. Each man understood and admired the other's business sense. Mr. Ravitsky eventually took his family's business over and added the manufacture of candles just as my father did. My father considered him a friend and respected associate.

One thing was for certain, Mr. Ravitsky liked and admired my father, but he absolutely loved my mother for her commitment to charitable work. Because she was always doing for others, Mr. Ravitsky always assured her that if we were ever the ones in need, then we should feel free to come to him for help. As it turned out, his offer became a blessing for me during the war.

My parents' business had been spared, but before the first war became too bad, they got their affairs in order and left Poland to wait things out. It was safer in Vienna, and if a family had money it was possible to travel there quickly. That first war brought minimal hardship to my family, and Jews were not threatened with extermination. My parents had enough to get by, and though they weren't living in luxury they survived well enough to return home and resume their lives after World War I ended. My father was very efficient about getting the business running again.

As she went through the first war my mother devoted her time to her little girls, and this kept her spirits up. She didn't seem outwardly affected by the experience, but strangely enough she hardly ever spoke of it. I never did ask my mother about those years because I sensed that, even though they got by, maybe it was something she would like to forget. I would go through a similar experience after the second war.

THE FIRST WORLD WAR affected Poles and Jews alike. The Armistice brought to Nina's country inflation, a shortage of goods, and restrictions that were enforced by the conquering allies.[14] As stated by Joseph Marcus, "The average Jew in Poland during the inter-war years was by western urban standards a poor man."[15] But with prudence and a bit of foresight Nina's father had been able to secure his assets before the war, then resume his manufacturing endeavors directly afterwards. His business acumen allowed the Grütz family to quickly resume a prosperous life in Poland.

M y father believed that it was best to have diverse financial holdings, but as a Jew he had to keep most of them quiet. Our Polish neighbors never knew of our real estate holdings, or about the buildings we owned in Berlin. My father even had sixty or more cows imported from Holland for our estate in the country, but it was kept very low key. I recall that we had one bull that was used by all of the locals for breeding purposes. This was one happy bull let me tell you! My father never boasted about his success or wealth. He didn't want to risk the resentment of our Polish neighbors.

I have to say that, until 1935, families like ours had it pretty good. Centuries before, after the Spanish Inquisition, the Jews were invited to settle in Poland by the king. Naturally there were certain restrictions, and only specific areas where Jews could live, but most of them prospered in Poland and became model citizens. The Poles benefited because many of the Jews studied medicine and became physicians, or they became involved in commerce.

Over time, however, I suppose jealousy and suspicion brought about an element of distrust. By the time we purchased our country estate, the relationship between Jews and Poles was a bit shaky. My father even hired a Gentile to manage the property in order to remain discreet. During that time Poles believed that once a Jew was given the opportunity to become successful, well then every Jew for miles around would be better off than any Pole. So not only our religion caused problems, but our ambition and work ethic as well.

Priests in our town actually preached that it was the Jews who killed Jesus. This was very manipulative because many Polish peasants were illiterate and relied on the Church for their education. These clergymen forgot to mention that Jesus himself was a Jew, and that the Romans took part in his death as well. It just always seemed that the Catholics hated us, particularly the Ukrainian Catholics. I suppose there was a kind of tradition of violence against us with them. All of this brewed under the surface, however, and although there were occasional pogroms against us, Jews weren't truly persecuted until the Germans came.

NINA WAS CORRECT in her evaluation of the attitudes of her countrymen regarding Jews both before and after the reign of Marshal Josef Pilsudski. In his inauguration speech accepting the position of Prime Minister, Pilsudski stated that his aim was "to grant the Jews equal rights," claiming that relations between Christians and Jews could develop in harmony.[16]

Although Pilsudski did not necessarily embrace his Jewish countrymen, the Prime Minister's gesture promoted the idea of a more unified Poland, and he briefly became known as "the Protector of the Jews." It was Pilsudski who first understood that Poland could only gain economic recovery by accepting the valid contribution of Jewish entrepreneurs and tradesmen.[17] Unfortunately, upon his death in May of 1935 a more authoritarian government took hold, and Jews once again became victims of anti-Semitic policies.[18]

Nina's childhood had to this point remained untarnished by the anti-Semitism growing among the Polish peasant class; however, feelings of distrust and envy toward Jews continued to fester within the poorer rural communities. Conflict between Jews and Christian Poles increased almost immediately after the First World War. Marcus illuminated the post war atmosphere, stating: "...the fundamental weakness of the (Polish) economy was agriculture. Historically this had always been unable to produce enough food to sustain the peasantry at a reasonable standard of living. Poland's farm production was largely confined to cereals, and in the inter-war period the peasants, although mostly self-sufficient in absolute necessities, lived at a level so low, that it is difficult for West Europeans to imagine."[19]

In order to fully grasp the Ukrainian hatred toward Jews one must understand that Ukrainians were not only considered a minority in Poland themselves, but were largely an agrarian class. In considering the Polish peasant, research indicates a correlation between suspicion of the Jewish population and economic differences. Landless Ukrainian and Belarusian peasants, as well as small Polish landholders, made up seventy percent of the population that subsisted on agriculture. In this climate of economic struggle it was tempting for an impoverished peasant to look toward the successful Jewish tradesman or shopkeeper as an opportunist, or, even worse, the sole reason for the peasant's economic hardship.[20] The fact that the majority of peasants, Polish and Ukrainian alike, were of the Catholic faith only helped to cement feelings of distrust toward the foreign Jewish "other" living in their midst. As stated by author Joshua Fishman: "We should not overlook the deeply-rooted religious prejudices and the mighty influence of the Catholic clergy over large portions of the Polish masses."[21]

In her studies of the Jewish image in Polish folk culture, author Alina Cala noted that the average Polish farmer's view of Jews as strange and alien was fed by his own religious upbringing. Christian myth dating from medieval times continued to play a part in Gentile perceptions of Jews. As late as 1984, Cala surveyed Polish villagers who claimed to have witnessed Jews using the blood of Christians to make matzoth (matzo).[22] This kind of fear and ignorance might not have been as prevalent among the more cosmopolitan citizens of L'vov, but the residue of suspicion toward their Jewish neighbors must certainly have found its way into the hearts and minds of Poles living in Nina's hometown.

Though surrounded by Catholic Poles with no particular love for Jews, Nina remained unaware of any real difference between herself and her non-Jewish peers. Her family managed to shield their youngest child from any extreme displays of anti-Semitism by leading a quiet and unpretentious lifestyle. Mr. Grütz managed his businesses in a way that was fair and honest to his customers. This behavior, along with Mrs. Grütz's quiet charitable work, earned the family a good amount of respect among Poles in their community. Although Nina would later encounter Catholics who were antagonistic toward Jews, there were no early encounters with these or other anti-Semitic groups.

Her young life was, for the moment, serene and secure. Days revolved around school and family for the young Nina. Although her parents avoided flaunting their wealth, as upper class Jews, the Grützes did have access to goods and services considered luxuries to even middle-class Poles at the time. Mrs. Grütz remained, as ever, the center of Nina's world. To her daughters she was the very symbol of style and grace.

When Mama was working she always managed to look neat and professional. Then there were the occasions when she and my father went out together for the evening. Oh, she was so elegant, and next to my handsome father they really were an attractive couple.

Each occasion required a completely different look. For business she wore certain outfits that were stylish, but practical. These clothes were understated and allowed her to move about the store with ease. The effect was that of a woman very much in charge. Her evening gowns, however, were made to enhance her lovely skin and figure. Obtaining clothes like this was not an easy matter. There were simply no big department stores like they had in America, not even in a city like L'vov. All of our dresses were made by a tailor, and if you were well off you had a few really good ones who did work for the entire family. Dressmakers made clothes for business, and clothes for going out, and even clothes for staying home for instance on a Saturday.

My mother had three different dressmakers, and she arranged to have one for both of my sisters, while I had a separate tailor who specialized in children's clothes. I wore a school uniform that made things simple. But there were even three different kinds of these uniforms: one for regular class, one for national holidays, and yet another for special occasions connected to the school. We also wore little caps with the school's insignia embroidered on.

Getting things done took more time back then and, because of this, the pace of life was much slower. It wasn't as if you could go out and just buy what was needed in one or two places. There were no malls or "superstores." To obtain food we went to the baker, the butcher, and to the open market for vegetables. In order to dress appropriately one had to visit all kinds of stores. Even accessories were purchased at very particular places. You could buy things like handbags and perfumes imported from Italy at a local specialty store, as well as fine fabrics. My father's suits were all made from English material, which even now is very expensive.

To make things easier craftsmen came to your home to perform services. A tinker showed up once a month to repair tools, for instance, and of course the tailor would come for a visit whenever it was needed. We had catalogues and big journals of patterns to choose from, and the dressmaker copied these designs. Even the coats that allowed us to get through the cold Polish winters were handmade.

It was such a different world, and I don't believe that people today could understand the changes that have occurred over time. Now you can live in a mansion in Montecito, yet feel comfortable going out in jeans and a tee shirt, and those you can purchase at some large store where they sell clothing next to the power tools! When I was growing up people would consider wearing blue jeans a poor reflection on your position in society. Even the girls from struggling families had one decent dress and coat. Their parents made sure of this, and women didn't wear pants at all. In the wintertime there were only woolen stockings to keep our legs warm, and they itched terribly. It was unbearable and I would plead with my mother to let me take them off, to no avail.

NINA'S FATHER was a strong figure in young Nina's life. At that time Viktor Grütz represented all that was stable and disciplined. A bright and ambitious man, his striking, aristocratic looks allowed many of his Polish neighbors to simply forget his Jewish background. Nina inherited these physical features from her father, and in the war to come this advantage would allow her to avoid the Nazis by blending in with other Poles. In the eyes of her Polish countrymen, Nina, like her father, did not "look Jewish." During the early 1920s the Grütz family had little concern regarding their Jewish blood. Nina's parents at this time were every bit the dignified, successful Polish family quietly maintaining their Jewish traditions.

My father was a handsome man, blond with blue eyes and a beautiful nose. He looked like the typical Polish aristocrat or officer. Nobody would have ever guessed he was Jewish because he didn't have those dark features, just the bluest of eyes. My youngest daughter inherited such eyes from him. People in America don't often consider such things because there are so many different nationalities here, but in Poland everyone made a point of recognizing race. While I admit my father was handsome, I must say that he was not perfect. I recall that he was a rather selfish person. He used to walk out of the house like a lord wearing those fine English suits, and my mother catered to him in every way. But I remember him as a good and honest man during those years, and an extremely bright businessman.

Father loved us all, but he had a special place in his heart for my oldest sister Lina, who grew to become a beautiful lady. She looked completely different from Helena and me. Her dark hair was worn long, and she never even trimmed it for her wedding. She had blue-black eyes, a beautiful nose, and was very intelligent, which seemed to please my father.

I suppose he loved each of us in his way, but back then people didn't talk about things like love. I assume that, although my parents' marriage was arranged, they fell in love with each other. I know that my father tried his best to be a good husband and provider. He traveled quite a bit on business, at least twice a year going to Berlin to buy raw material for the factory. Relatives from my mother's family would often whisper to Mama, "Why do you let Viktor go off to a different country without you? Aren't you afraid something's going on?" They teased that he might have a woman on the side, but this never seemed to bother my mother. She was secure in her marriage and always said, "I trust my husband, and if he did enjoy somebody else's company who am I to deny him?" She was making a joke of course, but Mama was sophisticated in this way. She was also very smart and knew how to handle my father.

Mama had her first child in 1911 when she was in her early 20's. I was born in 1920. I don't have my birth certificate or any papers at all. Very few Jews who survived the war have such documents. I did manage to retrieve some family photographs, but that story comes later. I was very close to my eldest sister, Lina, who made such a strong impression on me as a child. If I were told today that I had to die in order to see Lina for one day, well then I would take up on that offer.

With my middle sister things were a little different. I loved her, but we had less of a bond. She was very creative, yet she never knew how to apply that creativity, and she really didn't know what she wanted from life. Helena was also a little difficult for my parents to manage during her teenaged years. She was seventeen when she asked to quit school to pursue a career in modeling. She had beautiful long legs and a nice figure, so maybe she would have been good at it, but my mother would never allow such a thing. Maybe it was Lina's wonderful character that caused me to see her as the real beauty in our family. I hoped to grow up looking more like her. She was also a good student, while Helena struggled a bit and jumped from one interest to another. My parents insisted that Helena complete her schooling, though even after doing so she never showed any real ambition. I wouldn't say that she was spoiled, because my mother would never have permitted any of us to become in the least bit pampered. She was a business lady and didn't have the time or patience for indulging her girls. But Mama couldn't do much about the fact that Helena was a bit wilder than Lina and I.

There used to be in my country certain ladies who we called "market women." They were always yelling from their stalls trying to sell you something. They were considered crass and a little pushy. My mother always told us to be well behaved or we would end up like the market women. "You should have absolutely nothing to do with girls who are rude or unkind," she would instruct us, "and always conduct yourselves like ladies so people will respect you." As we all grew older I thought that my sisters were both very ladylike and I admired them so much. I tried hard to be like them and of course we all wanted to please Mama. We were fortunate to attend the most prestigious private schools, and when needed private tutors were provided to help with our studies. Unlike girls during my mother's childhood, it was expected that my sisters and I would go on to university. This meant hard work during the school year, but our summers were fun and adventurous.

When Lina and Helena got older my parents could afford to send them to different resorts in the summertime. In central Poland we didn't have the ocean to enjoy on a regular basis, so the big treat for Lina and Helena was going to the Baltic Ocean. As for me, we would take one of our servants and go away to our estate in Soluki. This was the property where my father raised milk cows and horses. It was in a town not far from L'vov, about fourteen kilometers away, but for me it was a paradise. My parents believed that by owning the estate as well as the apartment property we would always have a comfortable home somewhere. Mama used to tell me, "Whatever we have will one day be divided up for the other two daughters, but Soluki will be just for you." This made me feel secure because I loved the countryside so much, and our estate encompassed a lot of property. I imagined that I would live there as a grownup and enjoy the same fun activities. There was dense forest around the estate at the time, and we traveled through it no matter what the weather. On many occasions we went out for air, hitching up two pairs of horses to ride in a sleigh. In the warm days of summer we enjoyed this *ofilerska briczka*, the open carriage made of a beautiful dark wood and gold trim, complete with comfortable leather seats.

For my father, the estate in Soluki was more than a vacation home; it was an investment. The sixty cows imported from Holland produced the finest milk. Father spent a good deal of money on these particular milk cows, and he liked to keep an eye on any operations concerning them. He became knowledgeable about grain, and soon was raising a few crops. Eventually he started up a mill nearby in order to make better use of the grain.

Milk was transported every single day to the city along with any extra produce grown on our land. Back then we still used horses to work the different crops, which included quite a bit of corn. I remember that lots of workers were needed in the fields, and we also employed local peasants to help in my father's mill. The mill was very well-run and became an important service to people living in the area. Everyone for miles around used the mill to grind grain for flour, so it was constantly in operation, sometimes twenty-four hours. It required a tremendous amount of work. My father got one of my cousins to take care only of the mill. This man lived there with his wife and his daughter. We also had a couple with three children who worked at the estate, and their sole function was to care for the cows. They got up at around four-thirty every single morning to organize the women who milked, and to make certain the milk made it into town. There were maybe fifty or sixty big milk barrels that had to be delivered to customers every single day along with a little sour cream.

My father eventually had to become less involved with the operation of this land. He only collected the money from the renters. It was simply too much work as he got older. When I speak of the life we had, I certainly don't mean to imply that we were the wealthiest people in our city. There were quite a few families that were doing as well as we were or even better. I am not listing all of the advantages we had as a way of bragging, and I don't want people who read my story to think that I was some sort of princess. As I said, my mother would never have allowed such behavior. Both of my parents were very hard working, and my sisters and I were expected to work hard on our schoolwork as well. I am only trying to explain how different our life was in the beginning from what it would become once the war started. I cannot talk about what life was like for other people before the war because I was not in their shoes. I only want to say that the estate and the fine apartment and the clothes, all of these things were part of my life and to me felt quite natural. We lived better than a middle class family, there's no doubt about that. But we were brought up to appreciate the advantages our parents provided. We tried never to take them for granted.

I was sometimes permitted to bring a friend to our estate so I shouldn't be lonely, but I also had friends among the local workers' kids for companionship. I often wandered over to the small settlement nearby that contained maybe twenty families. I thought they were tremendous fun and they always included me in their games. They spoke Ukrainian, not the Polish I had grown up speaking, but we managed to communicate the way children do. I used to love going to their family weddings. Because I was a playmate of the farmers' kids, I was always invited along to join in on their family events. These were typically in the summertime and out in the open air. And who do you think was dancing the most at every wedding? I was! I danced with all the peasant boys. They whirled me around until I thought I would drop from becoming dizzy. Naturally this was acceptable only because we were all so young, and because they knew me pretty well, but it was such fun! The summer felt like one big party to me, and I was never lonely. The parents usually invited me to have borsht with them because our playing lasted until dusk.

Another highlight on our estate was the big lake that we plunged into during the hot summer days. In the middle of this lake a wooden float was moored, and we used to swim out to it countless times, drying off in the sun then jumping from it into the water again. I was perfectly comfortable with the local children. The boys were wonderful about including me. Since they had grown up around the property they were able to show me the best places to play. It was good to have friends to play with, because my mother was often away visiting a resort for her health. There was always someone at the estate to keep an eye on me, but before long I was left to my own devices for much of every summer. Mama could never have known how much I played with the local boys. Perhaps she would not have approved of it, but our friendship was harmless. All of us played together in an equal way so that nobody was left out. Without my friends at Soluki I might never have learned how to swim and climb trees.

———

As I said, Mama often traveled in the summer to a sanitarium called *Karlsbad Marienbad*. She had a gallstone ailment, so she traveled there to recuperate. It was very well run, and my mother's doctor would personally accompany her to dinner to ensure that she ate properly. I suppose I should have been disappointed not to spend more time with my parents during the summer, but I was a rather independent child. To be perfectly honest, I loved that summers were reserved for my buddies and me. Soluki really held a special place in my heart as I was growing up and every season when my parents sent me there with the maid I just had a ball.

IT WOULD NOT HAVE BEEN UNUSUAL for Nina to know a few words of her peasant friends' language. Many Jews by this time showed competency in two or three languages in addition to their own Yiddish. Although her parents frequently conversed in this language of their ancestors, Nina, in fact, spoke no Yiddish at all, and this coincidence was one of many that saved her life during the coming war.

Nina's parents most certainly would have become well versed in whatever dialect was favored by the patrons of their store. For centuries the importance of effectively communicating with their customers led many Polish Jews engaged in business to become acquainted with any number of languages. This led to a curriculum in Jewish schools that concentrated on those dialects a child might encounter within Eastern Europe. These included German, Ukrainian, possibly Hungarian, and Russian, with a strong emphasis on Polish grammar. By the eighteenth century the number of Jews literate in the Polish language exceeded those of Poles, proportionately speaking.[23] It is possible that Nina's parents insisted on her learning to speak perfect Polish as a way of assimilating their daughter into the local population, therefore sparing her the pain and danger of Polish anti-Semitism.

In part of his study of pre-war Poland, author Leo Cooper recognized businessmen such as Nina's father as a very distinct group of traditional Jews who ultimately wished to be recognized as Poles. Cooper wrote that: "As early as in the first half of the nineteenth century there had come into existence a new group of Jewish merchants, bankers, industrialists, publishers and professional men who had absorbed the Polish culture and who regarded themselves as 'Poles of the Old Testament persuasion.' They were the forerunners of a new trend within the Jewish community of total assimilation."[24]

The ability to blend in with the Polish population would have facilitated more effective business dealings, and in general made life less precarious for Jewish families like Nina's. Short of converting to the Catholic faith, this was the best way a man such as Nina's father could ensure the safety and success of his family. Perhaps it was this ability to assimilate that gave Viktor Grütz the confidence to own and maintain property in the countryside. Many Jews would have felt far too vulnerable taking on such an endeavor.

Yet the Grütz family felt perfectly safe on their country estate far from the more secure confines of the city. Nina herself spoke of only one moment of danger she experienced at her beloved Soluki. This involved not an anti-Semitic Pole…but a dog.

I have some memories here and there of early childhood, but one day in particular comes to mind as being rather traumatic. I was about eight years old, and my parents were actually present with me at our country estate. That day I was trying to amuse myself with the cleaning ladies who were busily working around the house. I became bored and ventured outside. Our villa was situated on a little hill with a large veranda wrapping around it. As I walked to the back I could see the yard below where a big dog was fenced in among the outbuildings. He was not really a family dog, but more for protection against strangers who might trespass. This particular day I had the bright idea to let this dog out to play with me. The one servant left to watch me was doing laundry down by the lake, so there was no one to stop me as I lifted the latch on his pen. I loved the idea of having my very own pet, and now that he was free I believed that it was up to me to take care of him. I went to the kitchen and found a potato, which I peeled and cooked. It tasted delicious and I thought the dog would love it too.

Well, when I brought it to him, he showed no interest in it at all! Of course the potato was still very warm, and a dog will generally avoid hot food as a way of protecting itself from burn. Unfortunately, I failed to understand this message, and I attempted to put it directly into the poor animal's mouth. I assumed that once my new friend had a taste he would appreciate my little gift. Can you imagine? You can't feed a dog a hot potato, but all I was thinking at the time was that it would be good nourishment.

What did I know? Well, eventually the dog had enough, and soon he became angry and jumped on me. He put his two paws on my chest and lunged at me. I threw up my hands in an effort to protect my face but he bit my palms. This caused me to scream, and luckily for me one of our workers came upon the scene. He was carrying a yoke with two buckets of water from our well. When he saw what was going on in the yard he ran to help. He dropped the buckets and began to beat the dog with the yoke in order to get him off of me. I was soon rescued, bleeding and crying from the brief but terrifying ordeal.

My parents calmed me down and Mama tended to my wounds. That afternoon they telephoned my cousin, the physician who suggested they bring me to his office in the city for care. He gave me some injections right away to prevent rabies. I was bandaged up, but for the longest time the deep tooth marks in my palms were very apparent. I still have the scars. I only found out later that the dog was killed, shot because they were afraid he might attack somebody else. I naturally blamed myself for his death. After all it was my fault for letting him out and forcing him to eat, but for the longest time I was very afraid of dogs. I cried a lot about the attack even after I had recuperated. This was the very first event in my life that really frightened me. I wish that I could say it was the worst thing to happen, but of course life had other many more horrible things in store.

After the dog attack I stayed in the city until school started. I loved school, and I was doing well in every one of my subjects. I was earnestly preparing for gymnasium, but one year really set me back. I was about eleven years old when I became very, very sick. I remember the day very clearly because it was a beautiful, clear Sunday afternoon. We had endured a very strong winter, but that day was turning out to be bright and sparkling. The outdoors beckoned me, so I told my mother, "Mama, I want to go for a walk. Won't you come with me?" She agreed that it was too pretty outside to stay home, so we walked all the way to the park and back again. By the time we approached our apartment building I began to feel a terrible pain in my left knee. I went slowly up the stairs with Mama and tried to hide the pain, which was getting worse. I didn't want to worry my mother because lately she had been very busy at the family store. I didn't want to take her from work just to fuss over me.

I decided to be strong and hoped the pain would go away. The next day I went to school as usual, but by the time I came home from school I was limping very badly. When she came home from work my mother noticed my discomfort and asked, "What's wrong? Why aren't you moving normally?" I said, "Mama, it has been hurting me to walk." She asked, "Why didn't you say something?" I suppose that besides not wanting to worry her I also didn't want to go to the doctor. I liked to play and stay active, and I knew that doctors often insisted their patients stay at home.

My mother made me go see the doctor, however, and as it turned out I had somehow contracted an infection in the knee that began to affect my other joints as well. I don't know what this illness would be called in English, and I don't remember the medical term my cousin our doctor used to describe it. When he examined me he said that my heartbeat didn't sound right. After a thorough check-up he told my mother, "Auntie, we need a doctor who specializes in this sort of thing. We will get one to see this child right away."

Off they took me to visit a couple of these special doctors, and sure enough they put me to bed immediately. I was tremendously sick and they didn't know what to do with me at first. I remember being under the supervision of a very good doctor. In those days physicians were known as "professors of medicine." Every morning my cousin put some kind of an ointment directly onto my chest. When he first wanted to open my nightgown I yelled, "No!" I was very shy, so of course I didn't want to undress for anybody. I don't know what I was worried about; I didn't really have breasts at the time! It's funny now to think about how shy I was, but it was a little unnerving to have all of these doctors poking at me from all directions. I eventually began to recuperate but it took some months. Strangely enough, in all the years since, my heartbeat has never been anything but perfect.

THE PHYSICAL PROBLEMS Nina described could have been the result of any number of ailments, the most probable being rheumatic fever. The migrating joint pain she felt is one of the most apparent symptoms of this condition, and in most cases affects children from the age of five to fifteen. Antibiotics now ward off this type of fever, but in Nina's youth any treatment would have included weeks or months of bed rest and a close watch on the patient's heart. The prognosis was good for a patient's recovery if the heart remained strong.[25] Because Nina's family had the ability to call upon the best doctors available to care for their daughter, she experienced a complete recovery. This took time, however, and nothing could have been more boring for a very young and impatient Nina.

I spent almost a whole year in bed because this virus had affected my heart as well as my joints. In the beginning of my illness I was too sick to concentrate, so schoolwork was put aside for awhile. I received treatment three times a day from my cousin, and a specialist came once a week. I wasn't too badly off, but I had to stay calm and quiet in order to protect my heart from overworking while my infection healed. I was in bed for six months before I began to get a little better.

It was around springtime before I finally got out of bed to walk again. It was a very frustrating time for me, and I was bored and angry at myself for becoming sick. I wanted to just jump out of bed and play with my friends. Instead I had to follow orders and even eat specific foods to improve my stamina. Our wonderful cook always tried to keep us well-fed, but in those days that sometimes meant eating things that might be considered unhealthy by today's standards. She created the most incredible strudel and cake. She also made different kinds of meats and soups, but they were different from what people eat today. Even our soups were quite rich. We didn't eat very much produce because we didn't realize how good it was to eat fruit and vegetables. To make matters worse, Poland has very strong winters so certain things, such as oranges, were very hard to get, a real luxury and so they were imported.

When I became sick with this virus the doctors prescribed a steady flow of oranges for me, because I needed the vitamin C. Unfortunately the only oranges available were imported from Hungary. That country has a certain climate that allows them to grow, and my parents managed to purchase them for me in that way. I must admit, I looked forward to those oranges. It was really the only good thing about being in bed and sitting idle all the time. I lay there eating oranges and didn't go to school for almost that entire year. Before long, I was ready to start catching up on my schoolwork. Like most children in my neighborhood, I was about six years old when I entered the local public school, and I had always enjoyed my classes. I hated the idea of falling behind in my schoolwork because of my illness. Luckily, I had a very nice teacher who helped me to pass. She became my private tutor hired especially for me, and by the end of my illness I was able to pass the final exam. I really was very ambitious in my studies because I didn't wish to lose the entire year.

AS NINA RECUPERATED from her illness and studied for her eventual entry into gymnasium, the world continued to change around her. By 1929 the anti-Semitism that had been percolating just beneath the surface of Polish life began to erupt into more frequent and brutal pogroms. One such incident occurred in Nina's hometown of L'vov that involved a Catholic procession in honor of Corpus Christi. Poles accusing some Jewish girls of being disrespectful during the parade attacked the students and destroyed their college.[26] Like other Jewish children of her class Nina had remained relatively untouched by this sort of violence. Innocent in many ways, she was often taken by surprise by the realities of life as she grew to be a young adult.

It seems to me now that my life before the war was so very happy and full. My own little world was regulated and small, but this was how my parents raised me and it felt very secure. I had a good family life, I loved my sisters, and I even began to spend time with boys in a social way. We did not go out on dates like young people do today, but spent time in groups with relatives or other adults present.

Though I had a normal girlhood I didn't know about the facts of life. One thing in particular that would now be considered common knowledge by most girls really threw me. Maybe I shouldn't speak of this, because I'll have to hide under the table from everyone after I do! It happened while I was still recuperating from my illness. As I began to feel better my mother saw to it that some of my classmates brought me work from school so that I could visit with them as well as keep up with my education. Mama still worked a bit, and my elder sister often kept an eye on me while I was sick.

Lina was there at the house because she had just finished gymnasium. She was bookish and a homebody, so she simply checked in on me from time to time and spent the rest of her time reading. I believe she was only eighteen then, so she was preparing on going to university very soon. She wanted to major in philosophy, and she had to study a number of subjects in order to be ready. One had to work hard in preparation for college, and it was important to stay motivated. A student was on his own in those days, and quite a bit of studying had to be done to obtain a higher education. Lina was concentrating on her Greek and Latin that spring. She even stopped dating at that time because she had to study so hard. By dating of course I mean introductions that were arranged by my parents. So Lina and I quietly studied and kept each other company. Things would not remain peaceful for long, however, because this was the time I experienced my first menstruation.

I knew nothing about puberty and what to expect. At that time mothers didn't sit their girls down and talk to them about personal topics relating to their bodies. I really don't know how one usually found out about these things back then. I have no idea to this day how I learned anything about babies except to say that I learned bits and pieces from my girlfriends. It was only when my eldest sister got married and had a child that I began to get an inkling of how a woman's body might work. I confess that for the longest time I had no idea about how a woman became pregnant. I always thought to myself, "Well, a woman has to get fat and then somehow the baby is brought to the home." Believe it or not this is what I actually thought, and most of my girlfriends were as clueless as I. Luckily, Lina was an educated lady by the time she married. That was after she had finished university, and her husband was a doctor for goodness' sake. But for very young ladies the idea of giving any instruction about the changes that occurred in their bodies was unthinkable at the time. It was very much in the closet.

As I lay in bed trying to recuperate that day I began to feel a little funny in my stomach. I felt different somehow, and eventually realized that something was going on with my body. I reached down to feel the sheets and saw that I was a little bit wet. When I looked to find out why I could see that my nightie was stained with blood! I was horrified. I couldn't understand why I was bleeding. I said to myself, "I am in bed all the time! When did I hurt myself?" Our servant girl walked in right after I had discovered my new and frightening condition. She wondered why I was crying, because I was not a crybaby in the slightest. I told her that I found blood in my underpants and that I must have been injured somehow. The girl was so embarrassed that she ran straight to Lina who immediately came into my room. I took one look at my sister and screamed, "Do you know what happened to me?"

My beautiful Lina tried to be reassuring and said, "Don't get panicky. When you get older your body does this every month. There's nothing you can do about it and nothing to worry about. This is simply the way it should be."

I could only scream, "What are you talking about? This cannot possibly be a normal situation." My poor sister did her best to calm me down, and she explained a little about how a woman matures. I would have none of it, however. I yelled, "I'm not a woman yet! I'm not even married!" But eventually I had to come to terms with this new and very unpleasant condition. I thought that it really was so unfair. This was around 1930 and I was preparing to enter gymnasium. I wondered how I would deal with going to school while coping with this new affliction!

In our apartment building there lived a few other kids besides me, including two brothers and their sister. We were all very good friends and we always played together. One of the boys, Juneg Dzunek, used to come to visit me after school, and he would stay to play cards or a quiet game if I were not too sick. A day or so after I became a young woman he came for his usual visit. The first thing I said to him was, "You know what happened to me today? I got this illness where I bleed for no reason! Are you getting it too?" He didn't know what I was talking about, and of course I still didn't know much about menstruation, let alone that boys didn't get it. I eventually frightened him so badly talking about it that he ran from the room. How naïve we all were! I remained relatively innocent until the late 1940s when I got married.

UP TO THIS POINT Nina's young life had been serene. Her parents ensured their daughter remain unaffected and nearly ignorant of the anti-Semitism that was increasing in Poland and throughout Eastern Europe. Through her parents' hard work Nina and her sisters enjoyed a life of affluence. For her part Mrs. Grütz made certain to raise her children to be polite and disciplined young ladies, and it is to her credit that she directed the girls toward higher education.

By the early twentieth century a university degree was one privilege that continued to elude all but the wealthiest of women. Even with their resources and good marks, the Grütz sisters would be subject to a quota restricting all Jews from most of the universities in their native Poland. With this in mind, Nina set her sights on schools abroad that might be available to her. She began to consider entering the medical profession, and to her parents' dismay, gave no thought to marriage.

Nina enjoyed her friends, worked hard at school, and dreamed of the day she would leave Poland to pursue a career. There was no shortage of suitors for the attractive and outgoing young lady. Social events, however, remained carefully chaperoned with groups consisting of schoolmates, cousins, and neighborhood friends gathering in each other's homes as young Jews had done for years. Never realizing a war was snapping at their heels, Nina and her companions enjoyed their last days of real freedom.

CHAPTER II

A Strange Foreboding

(1935-1939)

WITH HER GYMNASIUM EDUCATION now underway, the young Nina began to view the world as a much broader place, brimming with opportunity. These last years before the war would, unfortunately, be marred by Nina's first real experiences with racism. Subtle reminders of her countrymen's hatred for the Jewish minority in Poland gave way to more direct confrontations that both angered and mystified the young Nina Grüß. Her exclusion from Polish society loomed just on the horizon, but for the vivacious pre-teen life held endless possibilities.

It was some time after I entered gymnasium that my parents and I moved to a very nice apartment on *Platz strzelecky*. It was still a very large place that required us to hire a cook and a cleaning woman. This new place was a little smaller than the one on Kopernick, however. My mother wasn't working as much and I suppose she and my father wanted to simplify things a little bit. Both of my sisters were married, so we really didn't need such a big place as we had before.

We continued to spend summers at the family estate. I still loved Soluki, but I grew out of the desire to be there. As I got older I wanted to go to different places and experience the world. That summer I went instead with my sisters to the mountains. They alternated between summers there and at the Baltic Sea, while my mother accompanied me to Soluki. After I had been so sick they didn't want me staying at the estate where I was often unsupervised, and I admit to feeling very grown up about accompanying my sisters on their young ladies' holiday. By this time I was becoming stir-crazy from the strict orders of rest. I was still a little weak from my illness, but I was so bored. I couldn't go swimming or even for a walk. How excited I was to learn of my new adventure! A servant was sent along to keep an eye on me, and my parents brought me out to get me settled in. They rented two rooms with a kitchen, so we were all very comfortable.

It was a pleasant vacation, but it turned out not to be the excitement I was looking for. How could I have known that these were the days I should have been cherishing as my last of real freedom? Boring routine spent with my family would, in the years to come, become only a dream to look back on with hunger. But I was young and impatient, and of course I could not possibly know that I would soon lose my family. I spent my days lounging poolside, trading stories with an elderly man who was also recuperating from an illness. The summer days passed in a painfully slow way, and in the fall we all went back to our normal life in the city. It actually took me about a year and a half to completely heal from the virus I had contracted. My heart was perfectly fine in the end and, after all, I had made the big transition from staying at Soluki to vacationing at the mountain resort like my sisters.

We continued to visit the estate whenever possible, but the majority of our time as a family was spent in the city of L'vov. I eventually learned that it was a little unusual for a family to have such an estate so far from the city. I once asked my Jewish friends in gymnasium why none of them lived out there. Many could certainly afford it. There was also a beautiful park outside L'vov where quite a few Jewish families certainly could have afforded to buy a home, but none of them ever did. My Jewish companions set me straight, saying that Jewish people felt much safer in their own neighborhoods. These places were always in the city where they could be secure in numbers. There in the city the synagogues were close by, and this was essential because Jews didn't travel on Saturdays and most had all their businesses in the city as well. We all had to be realistic about the anti-Semitism that existed and was beginning to grow. Jews could easily be robbed or beaten in places as isolated as the countryside. To complicate things, most people didn't have automobiles back then, so it wasn't as if you could run for help if trouble came. Many chose not to even have private homes at this time, and instead lived in apartment buildings with other Jews.

Even people like my cousin, a successful doctor, lived in an apartment. As for my family, well, we had horses and a carriage to get to Soluki, and my father was well-liked in the area where our estate was located, so surprisingly we were all right there for the most part. I thought it a little sad that Jews couldn't live where they liked simply because Poles didn't see us as ordinary citizens. But it was a hard fact that Poles never liked or trusted Jews completely. This feeling was, as one would say, inbred. They were brought up believing Jews were different.

Most of the people my family knew were fortunately not as openly hostile toward us before the war. We had many Gentile acquaintances who I doubt even gave a second thought to the fact that we were Jewish. We might have had more trouble if my father hadn't looked like a Polish aristocrat. Because both of my parents spoke Polish perfectly, they never had the Yiddish accent that gave Jews away, and that probably helped as well. No, as a family we were fortunate, and never really experienced much racism or discrimination. That all changed just before the war.

In the meantime life went on, and over time my sisters were introduced to gentlemen who they might like enough to marry. Lina eventually became the wife of Bernard Tanne, a physician, in 1931. Around three years after that Helena met and married an attorney by the name of Leopold Frostig. When my two older sisters got married and moved away, I became more of a friend than a daughter to my mother. She revealed to me a lot of things that occurred years before in the family history. My eldest sister once said, "How do you know all these things about our family? You tell stories about people who have long since passed away. When did you learn about them?" I simply responded that maybe it was just because I had time to listen to these tales.

In truth, I loved hearing about our ancestors. I could spend hours and hours listening to Mama relate our history. She was quite intelligent, and besides speaking Polish beautifully she also spoke perfect German. Her ideas were very, as one would say, ahead of her times. All these ideas of equality and fairness that she had were a little revolutionary. This was a time when others around her were so caught up in where they belonged within society. Although we did have servants Mama always treated them with the utmost respect. We had always at least two women working for us, one to clean the rooms and one to cook, but to Mama they were like family. Our servants stayed with us until they got married, and when that time came my mother opened her home for their weddings. She would arrange everything for them as if they were her own daughters.

Although you didn't usually hear of a Jewish girl doing domestic work, we did have the one Jewish servant who was our cook. Apparently she needed the extra money so she simply went to work doing what she did best, and that was cooking. I tell you that woman knew how to cook just about everything! She did an especially nice job for my sisters' weddings. Naturally my mother helped, but our cook did the majority of the preparation, along with some extra staff. The ceremonies were in our home because we had such a big place. We put all the furniture out on the balconies in order to make room for dancing afterwards. We could never imagine a better place to have a wedding.

One of the first weddings we had in our home was for Lina. She married the young doctor chosen for her by my parents. Although his name was Bernard we called him "Buzho" *(the Polish spelling is Buzio)*, and he became a very successful physician. Buzio and Lina worked hard to provide a nice home for themselves, and they eventually had a child. They always seemed very happy together, so you see, these arranged marriages often worked out. I still have a picture of Lina that I managed to retrieve after the war and I cherish this photograph.

Eventually my troubled sister Helena also married, and she appeared to settle into the role of being a good wife. The husband of my middle sister was a lawyer, and he was a very good one. With my father's help he was able to obtain a beautiful apartment in a very nice neighborhood. It was just across a big park called *Park Stryski*. The neighborhood where they lived was completely Gentile except for my sister and her husband. Their home was quite luxurious, and even had a bidet! There were other luxury items in that apartment as well. Back then nobody had ever heard of an automatic dishwasher, but this place had something built in that did the dishes for you. This contraption was imported from Germany where people were very highly skilled in all sorts of inventions. We were all amazed by Helena's home because it already had all these modern conveniences in it. Unfortunately they only lived in it about a year, and then the second war started.

Until that time they were quite the modern couple. Half of the building belonged to my sister and her husband, and the other half officially belonged to my father. He used it as a sort of investment. If the war hadn't started my sister would have ended up owning it. My father was careful to take care of us in this way. He wanted to make certain we would be provided for in case something happened to him, or to our husbands.

Father arranged for my older sister, Lina, to live in a beautiful apartment home as well. It was given as part of her dowry. Father believed that real estate was a good investment, so there were maybe five or six buildings in all that he owned. He was proud of what we produced from the factory, but he didn't want to put any more into it or expand it at the time. He knew enough to diversify, and these buildings didn't take as much energy to manage. He had supervisors that helped to run things and the properties provided consistent income, but not so much investment of his time.

Although my father was an extremely good businessman and was even able to provide for his mother and siblings, he was the only one in his family to do so. His brothers were never as successful. As I said before, Daddy's mother put a lot of pressure on him to help out the other children. My mother would often shake her head and say, "Why do you work so hard to support your brothers? You are not obligated to give them money. You have already done so much for them, and after all you have three daughters who will all need dowries. We have to think about that."

My mother's family was more self-sufficient, and emotionally they were all very supportive of each other. They would never dream of asking for financial assistance from my mother. No matter how unfair it seemed to her, Mama tried to understand my father's efforts to continually help out his siblings. Still, even my father knew that he couldn't continue to do it all. In spite of his responsibilities in supporting so many people, he tried to slow down a little bit. At first he loved working in the factory. Ever since his childhood he was interested in that sort of work. But it meant traveling abroad to bring in raw material. As time went on he figured, "Well, by fifty or so I'll slow down." Today fifty is considered middle-aged, but back then people didn't live so long. He already had diabetes, and he was trying to take things a little easy because he wanted to retire and spend more time with my mother. He had worked very hard all his life and certainly made enough money to support all of us, so really he deserved a nice retirement.

BY THE END OF THE NINETEENTH CENTURY a large part of the food and beverage industry in Poland was dominated by the Jews.[1] It was not uncommon for these small concerns to grow into large family-run operations. Many Jews hired relatives to keep management of their businesses secure. Marcus wrote that: "...virtually all the Jewish enterprises had a family character. Mergers came about only between close relatives or through inter-marriage. Top managers were almost always recruited from members of the owner's family. The whole pattern worked smoothly until 1914."[2]

Sensing a local need for the service a larger mill could provide, Viktor Grütz set out to improve his operation in Soluki. With both capital and family assistance at his disposal, this new venture seemed to be a guaranteed way of providing his family with additional income.

The mill was doing very well, so in 1928 my father decided to expand it, and he engaged some engineers to assist in enlarging the operation. His brothers encouraged this idea because it would provide both of them with steady work. My mother, however, had misgivings. She said to Daddy, "The older girls are married, and with just one child to raise we need only one home. There's really no reason to maintain the estate as well as all of your businesses. It is time to prepare for your retirement, yet you continue to take on more and more responsibility that you simply do not need."

My father promised her that things would settle down eventually, and that he would sell off his various concerns. His brother agreed to help by bringing in some family to work the mill. Meanwhile, father purchased machinery from Berlin and Switzerland that cost thousands of dollars. By the time he finished expanding, it would be the biggest mill in the county.

The opening was planned for a couple weeks after they had installed the new machinery.

It was nearly finished, when suddenly, on a Saturday morning, we received a phone call. We were connected by telephone, which was a luxury not every family could afford, and in this way my parents discovered from the local officials that the mill was on fire. We later learned that it was most likely that our competition had committed arson! Our brand new mill was a threat to the other smaller businesses in the area, and it burned down completely because it was too far away for the city fire engines to reach it in time. There was a snowstorm slowing them down as well, so the few people who were able to help out were only using garden hoses on the flames. The cousin in charge of the mill was so upset about this catastrophe that he wanted to commit suicide.

My father was devastated. Here my mother had begged him not to expand and it seemed as if all her fears had come true. He had a hard time handling that. I don't remember my parents arguing very often, but I remember this particular discussion. Mama had never been as strong with my father as when she had tried to convince him not to expand the mill. She was so much against it but he just refused to listen. Sure, she was a businesswoman, but she was a woman after all, and what did she know about new ventures like the mill. He had been right, of course. A larger mill was very much needed in that area and it would have brought in a lot of money. But who knew that someone would hate us so much that they would set this mill on fire. I suppose it really brought the message home to us that Jews were not safe beyond the city limits.

Before the fire my parents had been under what you could say was a false sense of security. They had always been fair in their business dealings with others, and those living and working near the mill seemed to genuinely like my father and his family. Now it seemed as if the same old story was proving true. Jewish families could only do so well until people became jealous and resentful. My father learned this lesson the hard way.

In the meantime, all his expensive mill equipment was now nothing but smoke and ashes. He didn't have any insurance, and this meant that we were just about flat broke. The only thing my father had now was his good name, and he would have to rely on his reputation as a businessman to survive. He turned all his attention to the family factory in the hope of producing and selling enough products to turn things around. Compared to the venture of our big mill the factory was a tiny business. Luckily my family decided early on to sell some things in order to make it through the next several years, but they would never sell the factory and it was this little venture that saved us.

My father worked hard so that he wouldn't have to go bankrupt. He paid off every expense from that mill, which was really quite remarkable considering the debt. He was a tenacious man, and this is what brought him such success even in the face of failure. We managed to get back on our feet because people were still very much interested in buying our factory goods. We didn't have to deal with conditions brought on by a Depression like those poor people in America had. Poland was very different. If there was a Depression in Eastern Europe we certainly didn't feel anything. But we had our hard times, and this was definitely one of them.

I WAS SURPRISED to later learn through research that Poland did in fact experience a "Great Depression" during Nina's teenage years. Joseph Marcus wrote of Polish economic duress that exceeded America's Depression in both scope and tenure. There was financial progress during the years 1926 through 1927 due to a large U.S.-backed loan meant to stabilize the Polish economy. However, the program eventually failed, largely because of Poland's dependency on agriculture. Marcus stated: "At the peak of the depression, at least 40 per cent of the working-age population were idle, industrial production was down by 35 per cent, wholesale prices nearly halved, fiscal revenue was reduced by two-fifths, and foreign trade and currency reserves were down by two-thirds."[3]

Perhaps the depression in Poland had not yet taken hold in 1928 when Nina's father was struggling to recoup his losses from the mill. It is also possible that Nina was simply unaware of the monumental effort it took her father to save the family from financial ruin at a time of economic upheaval in his country. Either way, for Viktor Grütz to have emerged from the mill disaster with some assets intact says much about his skills as a businessman. The fact that Nina's childhood remained unblemished by poverty during this time illuminates how effective her parents were at shielding her from life's hardships.

The vandalism the Grütz family experienced at their mill might well have been the result of a growing jealousy among their Polish competitors. The smaller businessmen must have feared that Viktor's advanced machinery would phase out their own operations. There was also the possibility that the local peasantry were enlisted by outsiders to carry out the torching of the Grütz mill. Historian Edward D. Wynot wrote in his essay concerning the so-called "Polish Movement" taking place from 1918 to 1939: "The relationship between peasant and Jew in Poland has presented a complex picture of mutual dependency and ambivalent feeling for centuries. Each needed the other for economic survival, yet simultaneously each often regarded the other with suspicion, mistrust, and, occasionally, loathing and fear."[4]

It seemed that the fine line Viktor Grütz walked as both a Pole and a Jew had finally been pushed beyond acceptable limits. Nina's family began to sense the tension between themselves and their neighbors more distinctly. Many Polish Jews were coming to the slow realization that their situation was becoming worse. Along with the ominous rise in anti-Semitism, financial insecurity tested the Grütz marriage. It also began to bring to Nina a new awareness of what might lay ahead in the coming years.

My parents never built up the business again like before. They rebuilt the mill, but it was even smaller than the original one. After all it was the late 1920s, and the war broke out in 1939. There would never be quite enough time to get back on their feet the way they had during my father's most successful years. It was a terrible blow losing the mill and it put a strain on their marriage and a division between them that had never been there before. The feelings I had for my father began to change because of the mill disaster. I adored my mother, but before the mill fire I really thought the sun and the moon rose on my father's head.

Going against my mother's wishes and making such a big investment had cost them their time together. It seemed to me that his stubbornness had made my mother sad, and I couldn't stand for anyone to hurt Mama. I resented my father's family too because they encouraged the idea of expanding the mill to bring in more money. Through my mother and her family's business Daddy had a good start as a young man. Now they would have to work twice as hard to pay off debt. My father was a hard worker, and he deserved to take pride in how he had improved and expanded the family business. But I think that he should have listened more to Mama than his relatives.

Because father was always busy with work my mother traveled alone all the time. Now it seemed as if that routine would continue. They could still afford her gallstone treatment, so she went alone as usual to the famous spa, the Karlsbadd Marienbad, the following year. These visits could sometimes last up to six weeks, and there was no doubt that this spa improved her health. Besides being very elegant it was also very accommodating to the regular clients. There was a doctor on call and every imaginable amenity. Even today it would be considered luxurious, and few people could afford to go there, but somehow my father managed it even during the worst of times.

Meanwhile, my sisters spent their time enjoying the seaside. Copoty was the name of their favorite vacation spot. It was next to a town we called Gdanst but was also known by the German name of Danzig. We all looked forward to our little holidays and I know now that we were fortunate to have them. Now it is popular for families to go together on camping trips or to see some famous site. But for us it was not unusual to pursue separate interests during our summer break. It never seemed to bother anyone that we separated during the warmer months to visit our respective resorts. This was just how things were done among wealthy families, and we rarely went to the same vacation places together.

The days went normally along, and I personally did not notice any change in our lifestyle, other than the fact that my father seemed so defeated. All that mattered to me was that I was surrounded by the family I loved and was doing well in school. I saw less of my sisters once they were married, and Lina of course was concentrating on a family of her own. But Lina and Helena were never very far from me. I saw my sisters whenever I could, and I spent time with my friends from school. I felt loved by my parents and with great excitement I began to plan on one day attending a university. Everything was happening as I planned.

NINA'S LIFE APPEARED TO BE MOVING forward at a predictable pace. Like many European Jews during this pre-war period, the Grütz family attempted to go on as if there was little cause for alarm concerning Adolf Hitler's popularity. Occasional acts of violence motivated by the Nazi movement were regarded as simply another spate of pogroms destined to erupt from time to time, the prevailing hope being that this current anti-Semitic behavior would eventually taper off as it had in the past.

For the moment Nina's family would call upon a familiar strategy, that of maintaining a quiet life and a low profile. Like many of their Jewish neighbors, the Grütz family was confident that the nuisance of racial discrimination would subside and their lives in Poland would remain relatively unchanged.

My parents wanted me to get a good education. Both of my sisters attended Jewish schools when they were growing up. There they took some courses pertaining to the Jewish religion and I suppose that today you might look at them as parochial schools. These schools held very high credentials and my sisters did well there. But by the time I was ready to enroll, the school my parents planned for me to attend had lost its credentials. All of the Jewish schools at this time eventually closed for lack of students. After all, everybody wanted to acquire a higher education. If I wanted to continue on in a university I would have to go to a particular gymnasium. This sort of school would be similar to some of the private high schools they have in America, and the one I attended could supply the necessary credentials. My parents sent me to the best gymnasium available. Some schools were open to any kind of student, but in order to go to this kind of institution my parents had to pay seven hundred or more z_ote a month, which was quite expensive. The school they finally chose was named Zychovoeza.

There were twelve of us Jewish girls attending there, and we went to separate religious classes one day each week. Religious instruction for Jews was allowed at that time for one hour each day, even though it was a Polish school. I focused my studies on humanities. In Polish it was called *Humanis Tyczne*. I don't know how you would compare it to schools today. There the students study some math and physics, but mostly literature, geography, and history were the focus. By the name you could tell that we studied the humanities. We girls had only four schools to choose from while the boys had twelve different establishments to which they could apply. Some were private and of course there were the others you couldn't attend at all if you were Jewish. I managed to enroll in a very good gymnasium, though I didn't have many friends there. The friends I had in grammar school couldn't afford to go to my gymnasium. Still there were a few Jewish girls in my classes. Out of maybe thirty students there were still around ten who were Jewish.

My best girlfriend was Jewish, but I had both Jewish and Gentile acquaintances in my new school, and I remember feeling accepted by them for the most part. I was happy with my new friends and got along with just about everybody. However, I remember specific things about those school years that were not altogether pleasant. I recall, for instance, that I did not do well in math or chemistry. I absolutely died over those subjects. I used to dread going to mathematics class, and to make matters worse I hated my math teacher because she was so mean. I would do the homework well enough, but when she called on me I went completely numb! I loved my history teachers even though I was not the very best student in my class. I did all right in the languages, but I soon made the decision to switch from learning French to German which later proved helpful during the war.

ALTHOUGH PUBLIC SCHOOLING WAS AVAILABLE for their child, Nina's parents opted to send her to a private Polish school. According to at least two separate authors who researched this period, it was not unusual for Jewish children to attend Polish schools with their Gentile peers. In his study of Jewish culture, author Chone Shmeruk states: "It seems that after a certain crisis period in the early 1930s the number of Jewish pupils in Polish high schools was once more on the rise. In the school year 1936-1937 there were a total of 33,212 Jewish high school pupils; 15,301 studied in Polish government and communal schools, and the remainder attended Jewish private and publicly run gymnasiums."[5]

The private Polish school Nina attended required a rather high tuition be paid each month. She benefited greatly from such an education, and seemed to fit in well among her Polish peers. Her ability to seamlessly blend in with a group would later help her to masquerade as an ordinary Pole once the Nazis invaded her country. Jews who chose the strategy of hiding in plain sight coined the term "passing." Extreme measures of passing that Nina later used were unnecessary while Poland remained an independent country. As her years in gymnasium continued, however, she found it difficult to form any close alliances with her Polish peers. Soon she began to miss those friends who had transferred to other local institutions.

I know that many readers will expect me to write of the anti-Semitism I experienced as a child. There was always anti-Semitism in Poland, always hatred toward the Jews. I do not mean to imply that it didn't exist, but I have to say that I really didn't feel it as a young girl because I went to Polish schools and got along with the kids there. They didn't come to my house and I didn't go so much to theirs, but in school we got along. Perhaps it was unusual for a Jewish girl to have such an ordinary life in Poland at this time. I don't know. What I do remember is that we used to have school on Saturdays which was a bit difficult for the few of us who were Jewish because that's the Sabbath. The only day off was on Sundays because the majority of students, the Gentile kids, went to church that day. On Saturday a few of us Jewish girls went to school, but the rest abstained because Jews weren't supposed to do any work on the Sabbath, and this included writing. Back then a student had to be good at quickly writing notes, and the only real efficient way to capture words was to use a typewriter. Well, we certainly couldn't take one of those into class.

I took notes so well that I frequently ended up lending them out to my Jewish friends to copy. This helped quite a few girls because some of their parents absolutely insisted that no work be done on the Sabbath. They wouldn't even answer their phones on that day. These families were the more orthodox Jews. My parents were not such strict Jews, and I remember that we used the phone and conducted certain business without a care. We had our own telephone system at home and one at the factory as well. As I mentioned before, not everybody had phones in their private residences, but my parents found it a necessity in order to run the business. So I admit that I had a little bit more freedom than some of my Jewish friends. Because of this little advantage I didn't mind loaning them my notes.

Although we were not Orthodox, my family was very religious. My mother especially saw to it that we followed the traditions of our Jewish faith. She was a good Jew and a wonderful human being in many ways. She saw to it that we lived in a very traditional manner. For instance, when it came to having a kosher kitchen she made certain that things were in order. We had everything in double. No wonder we had so much silver because we had two of everything to keep certain foods separate. You almost got lost in all of the dishware! One set of dishes was for dairy and the other for meat. Everything was separated as well for holidays such as Passover. When it came to going to school, however, well I felt that I had to go on Saturday in order to prepare for university, and my parents agreed with me.

There was another girl from gymnasium that I recall quite clearly. I helped her to study for a time. As I said, there were not many Jewish girls at my school, but we all liked each other and got along well, and I never experienced racial hatred from a schoolmate until I began to help this one Gentile girl with her Polish. I was very good in the Polish language because I had always worked hard in this class. I met this particular girl because in our assigned seats this Gentile girl sat not too far from me. I knew that her situation was a little different in that she was from a family that normally could not afford to send their children to such a school. I think she was able to attend because her father had a government job or something like that, so tuition was waived for her. I have to say that she was not a very good student. Still I felt sorry for her because it was obvious that she was struggling to pass our Polish class.

I was quite good in our native language, and I actually enjoyed learning more about it. I spoke so well that my teacher would often ask me to read Polish in front of the class. I never considered myself a good speaker, and even today I don't like the way I sound when I speak in front of the high school students here in America. I don't mind telling them about the war, but I hate the way my Polish accent sounds when I speak English.

Speaking Polish is another matter entirely. My teacher used to tell me the way I spoke was quite melodious, and that made me feel so proud. Once we all had to do a reading, and I won a prize for being the best at doing so! So you see I would have made a good tutor to anyone who was having trouble in this subject. This girl I sat next to was running the risk of having to repeat her course if she didn't improve. That's how bad it became for her. I actually made the first move by offering to share my work, but eventually she asked me for help because she noticed that I was very good at taking notes. She was shy and quite frankly not a very like-able person, but I said to her, "Do you need some notes? I'll help you out and give mine to you for studying." Finally we started doing homework together. I corrected her grammar and spelling on various assignments.

This was right around the time people in Poland were becoming influenced by Hitler and his beliefs. So much was going on then, yet it was still just a whisper of change. No real anti-Semitism had troubled my family yet. One day while helping this girl at school she and I had an argu-ment. As I proceeded to correct her spelling she became defensive and angry. There were so many mistakes with her grammar that I suggested she write the whole assignment over with my help. She said to me, "Who do you think you are? I am Polish and you're telling me how to write my own language? Why should I let a Jewish girl tell me how to write? You Jews think you know everything. You think you're above everyone and the only reason you don't like my work is because it's not Jewish writing."

What the hell that meant I didn't know. What is "Jewish writing"? This was an assignment given by the teacher! I said, "This has nothing to do with being Jewish! What are you talking about?" Here I was helping her and she didn't even appreciate it.

With my help the grades on her papers went up to nearly "A" work. I never told the teacher I was helping this girl because I didn't want her to think I was doing another student's work. I had been helping and pro-tecting this student and here she was speaking in a rude manner with me! Well, I became furious. I have to admit that under the right circumstances I can have quite a temper. I wanted to tell her to go to hell, but of course ladies didn't use such language. Instead I asked her, "What do you want from me, an apology for being Jewish?" I was very straight with her, saying, "Because of me you got better notes and personal instruction. You could have eventually passed your Polish course, but I won't help someone who is unpleasant to me. You got plenty of help from a Jewish girl, but now you're telling me I think I'm too good? Forget it! Don't even think of coming to me again to correct your papers. I don't care if you pass or not. You're on your own. If my assistance is not good enough for you then go to a Polish girl for help." I was so angry I threw the paper back at her.

It was then that this girl suddenly tried to threaten me! She warned me that she could tell on me to the teacher, but this in no way bothered me. After all, what could she say? Only that I was trying to help a fellow student who no longer wanted my help for the mere fact that I was Jewish? I told her to go ahead and tell whomever she liked. What was I getting from helping her anyway? Here I was trying to be nice to her and she became an anti-Semite before my eyes.

I informed her that if I really wanted to be vicious I could go to the teacher and tell her myself that I had done all of her work. She said, "You wouldn't dare do that!"

"Don't push your luck!" I warned her. I later decided that she wasn't worth the effort.

This was the first open racial hatred I experienced. It didn't surprise me, but it did make me furious. I wasn't stupid. I had heard already about the influence of certain anti-Semitic groups. But somehow it hadn't touched me directly until this time. I was affected by this feeling against Jews indirectly, but it had never hit me in the face like this. Before arguing with this girl I didn't want to believe that people could hate me merely for being a Jew. I just pushed that feeling away. After all, I was young and carefree. I had everything I could possibly want to be happy.

Even after this girl's outburst I refused to dwell on it. I have one big philosophy in my life that has served me well, and that is not to let things bother me that I can do nothing about.

A ONCE SUBTLE ANTI-SEMITISM became more direct in Poland by the early 1930s. Many peasants began to resent the dependency they felt for their Jewish neighbors who offered popular goods and services. Suspicion and envy frequently caused the rural Pole to view Jewish suppliers as "parasitic middlemen." This type of jealousy toward Jews had existed for some time among the rural classes.[6] According to scholar Edward D. Wynot, specific events caused relations between Polish farmers and Jewish business owners to deteriorate by the 1930s: "Several factors combined to produce an environment hostile to the emergence of amicable peasant-Jewish relations. One was the increasing economic development underway throughout the Polish lands, which made the Jews appear to pose a major obstacle to the survival, let alone the prosperity, of a peasantry caught up in the changing agrarian structure."[7]

While the Polish peasant began to look upon Jews as a growing economic threat, an increase in nationalism caused other Poles to see the Jew as encroaching foreigner. Stoking the fire of this heightened anti-Semitism was the Catholic Church. To church leaders who preached to the Catholic majority, a unified Polish nation meant a Catholic nation. At this time, however, conversion remained the preferred tactic to force "Polonisation" upon minorities.[8]

Amidst an ever-increasing tide of anti-Jewish sentiment, Nina struggled to find her niche.

Even after the incident with my schoolmate I didn't feel any real discrimination from other young people. Still, I longed for more companionship. In order to be more social I became part of a club. It was a group of students who were planning on becoming lawyers. This group was called *Prawo* and they offered summer camping trips. It was sort of a specialized camp and they offered certain adventure-type excursions for interested students.

I was sixteen or seventeen, and still attending gymnasium. I heard about the arrangements one could make to visit this camp, and leave it to me...I said, "I'm going!" My mother didn't like the idea, but I insisted, "I'm going!" I told her, "I'd love to go. I have to go. I'm tired of Soluki, just so tired of it." I cried and cried over it, finally asking my older sister to help me convince Mama. "You have to do something, to plead my case," I begged her; "You have to back up this idea of mine to Mama. She will listen to you!" Lina's support helped my cause, but it didn't matter to me what my parents said. I had decided I was going and that was that.

Zacopane is in the Polish Tatra Mountains, and it is known for wonderful trails climbing up the hillsides. This was an excursion in which students could hike to the very top of the mountains. I registered for the trip, though I had to lie about my age. I know for certain that I was the youngest one there. They accepted me anyway, and I soon heard from the group of young people who arranged everything. They put us all into categories depending on our skills and interests. Certain campers would have activities by the lake, while others went hiking or engaged in other sports.

Well, when I heard that they were going to hike all the way up the mountain I had to go too! I didn't need any time at a lake. I had enough of that sort of fun at Soluki. I wanted to go to the mountains. But when I went to sign up for the hike they said, "No, you're too small for the climb, so we cannot take you."

"But this is the whole reason I wanted to come here," I cried, "if you're not taking me I'm going home and telling everybody how mean you were to me!"

I fought with them, until they didn't know what to do with me. Every day I went into the office where things were arranged and I asked, "Are you taking me on the climb today?" Each time they argued with me, insisting that I wasn't prepared physically or materially. I didn't have the proper shoes or other hiking equipment, but I told them that I would acquire it from another camper somehow. No matter how much I argued with the young man in charge the answer was always "no." Well, every time he said this I refused to listen, and I came back the next day with the same plea.

DURING OUR CONVERSATIONS Nina confessed to being a stubborn woman. She admitted that even as a girl her willful nature often got the better of her. While she appreciated her mother's desire for all of the Grütz daughters to maintain their ladylike composure, Nina's temper could easily erupt when she was denied the pleasure of pursuing a particular goal. It is my opinion that Nina's tenacity was more of a quality, for it was this character "flaw" that allowed her to survive the coming war. The mountains of Zacopane became a training ground for how Nina would deal with adversity during the war years. The teen's diligence and willful determination eventually paid off when she was finally granted the opportunity to participate along with her peers in the upcoming climb.

One day I became really angry and frustrated. "Look," I cried, "I know that others have gone on this difficult hike. Maybe I'm not trained to hike the way the others already are, but give me a chance! If you don't at least give me the opportunity I'll never know if I'm any good at it!" Anyway, to make a long story short, the boy in charge was so tired of hearing my arguments he decided to let me go. He even got me the special shoes I needed! When he presented those shoes to me I nearly kissed him. But, of course young ladies didn't do that. I was so thankful, however, and off I went! Getting to the top took almost three days while it only takes one day to go down. It's a well-known place in Europe, so they had places to sleep arranged along the way. Iron handles had been hammered into the more difficult passages to make the climbing easier. It was rather a reach for smaller people, and I suppose that was why they didn't want me to go in the first place.

I was a petite girl, but I just pushed my body a bit further because I was so pleased to participate in the climb. I had to use a little ingenuity, because, let's put it this way, I was close to reaching those handles, but not quite enough. I had to sort of jump to reach them. It was very scary because if a camper couldn't complete a portion of the hike he or she could easily be stuck somewhere on that mountain with other hikers behind them! There was another section that was so high we could only move upward by using chains. Here there were a lot of accidents, and if you dropped from the chain nobody could save you. A camper might fall from the cliffs and tumble all the way down into a ravine. Sometimes even to look beyond this trail was scary, so I tried to keep my eyes pointed up toward my goal. It took three or more hours to go up that way and I'll never forget it. That night we all fell into our sleeping bags exhausted. The next day we reached the top, and it was unbelievable! I remember today the glorious sensation of success, and I don't think any amount of money could buy such a feeling. It was priceless.

We all welcomed the trip down because it was so much easier! Going down the way we came might result in sliding out of control, so we took an alternative trail that seemed faster because it was all down-hill. We had guides to help us, and these young men who arranged the hike knew what to expect. They did it every summer and took very good care of us. By the end of the hike there was a little celebration. Nobody was hurt and the group had done it together. I walked up to the leader and smiled. "You see?" I teased him, "I told you I would make it! Did I give you any problems? No!" He had to admit that I had been right.

The leader of our group asked to date me after that. I don't think he knew that I was only sixteen. He was twenty-one or so and had already completed two years of law school. One afternoon he came to visit me in my cabin. I was tired and just lying on my cot. Our accommodations were quite simple with just a bed and a bureau for clothes. My door was open and he simply strolled in. He sat down on my bed to chat, but after we exchanged some words he tried to kiss me. Instinctively I slapped him across the face! This was not easy because he was tall, but his actions were so unexpected. I was unprepared for it and said, "How dare you!" The funny thing was, I knew him to be a good person, and I liked him very much. Maybe he thought I had been kissed at least once before, but he sure was surprised when I slapped him so hard! I was too embarrassed to tell him I had never been kissed. I simply panicked.

At the time I was too young to even understand what it meant for a boy to like me. The girls I knew had grown up very sheltered just as I had and we never spoke of what to do if a boy ever came for such a visit. After he recovered from my assault he asked, "What are you worried about? I'm not going to make you a baby!" I had no idea what that meant, and all I could think to do was to yell, "Get out! Get out!" Looking back the whole situation was pretty funny. I was so incredibly naïve that I couldn't even carry on a conversation with a young man, let alone handle a kiss! I didn't know how to treat a young man who might be calling on me with romantic intentions. Later on I realized I made too much of a big deal about it. Anyway he ended up leaving and I didn't see much of him after that. I went home from camp as innocent as ever.

NINA RETURNED HOME as a stronger and more confident teenager. That year she also became aware of her father's devotion to the Zionist cause led by Theodor Herzl. Shifting his focus from law, this prominent Viennese attorney instead directed all energy toward journalism and literature. His Jewish activism began after publishing "Juenstaat," or "The Jewish State," in 1860. Herzl believed that Jews had a right to live without fear of pogroms and he was convinced they could only flourish in a nation of their own. This became a popular view among European Jews, and by the early 1930s many Zionists had embraced the idea of a Jewish nation situated in the Holy Land of Palestine.[9] Once she was introduced to it, the idea of visiting the Holy Land appealed to Nina.

When I finished gymnasium I received my diploma and I began the application process to universities in other countries. I applied to a school in Italy because I heard from a girlfriend how wonderful it was there. Another application was for a school in what is now Israel. I wished to attend college in the Holy Land more than anything. I was brought up in a traditional Jewish home, but my father was also a Zionist. Like many other Jews he was tired of the hatred that was constantly aimed at Jews for no reason. He learned of Theodor Herzl's plan to form a Jewish state in Palestine, and not long before the war he purchased two lots there. They were located in a place called Bat Yam, and his intention was to have it developed by a group called Halu Zium. These young people formed a kibbutz wherever crops could be grown, and in this way settlements were created. Most Jews wished to live in what is now Israel because they believed it was the place where their ancestors originated. The belief was that the Jewish religion was established there where Moses received his Ten Commandments. I was very interested in going to school in Palestine for all of these reasons.

FOR JEWS PURSUING THE ZIONIST DREAM, forming a colony situated in the Holy Land of Jerusalem would be ideal. Polish Jews looked to Palestine as an appealing alternative in light of the anti-Semitic acts that continued to escalate in their own country. Young people were especially encouraged to volunteer for the hard work of forming settlements that came to be known as "kibbutz." Wealthy Jews such as Viktor Grütz were willing to purchase land in Palestine in the hope of later moving their own families to the safety of a Jewish homeland.[10] However, not every member of the Grütz family was keen to uproot hearth and home for a strange land.

My father was a big Zionist, but not so much my mother. My parents discussed moving to Palestine in 1938 but the plan ended there. Mama refused to leave the home she knew and loved in Poland. I can understand this now, but I had been excited about the idea, and so I was a little disappointed we never moved. When I was younger I really didn't consider myself a Zionist in the true sense of the word because I didn't know enough about it. I was serious about my religion and my family's traditions, but I had no set ideas about being a Jew to the exclusion of all else. For example, though I had few Gentile friends I never saw anything unusual about associating with non-Jewish companions. I was still too young to go out with anybody but my girlfriends, but I would never consciously think of trusting only my own Jewish people.

There were even some Christian traditions that appealed to me. Across the street from us there lived a Gentile family, and they seemed pleasant enough. I remember they had a beautiful balcony like ours, and when Christmas time came I saw through their windows their beautiful decorations. I was dying slowly but surely from jealousy every time I caught a glimpse! When I saw the Christmas tree I thought it was beautiful. Nobody knew it, but when I heard them playing Christmas music for their parties I used to dance to it in my room. On these occasions I became impossible to live with. I asked my mother, "Why don't we have something like Christmas?" I couldn't understand the difference, you see. I wasn't stupid; it's just that I didn't want to accept it. "That Gentile girl is just like me and I am like her," I often thought to myself, "so what's the difference between us?"

Around this time I missed an opportunity to go to the United States. My aunt and uncle Messing had moved from Poland to live there, but they traveled from America to visit us as much as they could. My aunt was very close to Mama, just as Lina and I were close sisters. Aunt Erna and her husband had done very well in New York City with their bakery business. They had 150 trucks a day coming and going every day to transport bread and cakes and pastries. My mother and aunt exchanged letters, but I think that it was hard on them to be separated by so many miles. I still have a postcard that my aunt received from Mama just before the war. It is interesting to look at because they wrote back and forth in German instead of Polish. They both spoke German perfectly so I suppose they were keeping in practice this way.

The last visit these relatives made to Poland was in 1937, and they stayed for almost a full year. One of Aunt Erna's daughters was named Miriam. This cousin of mine was very stylish with her American clothes and the way she carried herself. I admired the way she came across as so independent. I was just a young girl when they visited with Miriam, but I could see that my cousin was fully American. She did things my sisters and I would never dream of doing, like wearing makeup and styling her hair. When I was younger I had a habit of "stealing" ladies' shoes and parading around the room in them. I thought everything belonged to me and I was also quite the comedian. I used to hide under the dining room table and look at people's shoes. I did this when Miriam was having dinner, and I said to myself, "When I am older I am going to have high heels such as Miriam wears! I will be a fashion model!" Mama laughed at me, saying, "For goodness' sake, get out from under the table. There are better ways to admire a woman's shoes!" Little events like this from my childhood are more pleasant to remember than those of the war years.

I had heard a lot about America, and I so badly wanted to see it for myself. Aunt Erna invited me to go back with them that year, and I would have enjoyed living in the United States even for a little while. But my mother turned down her offer and actually became a little angry. "Erna," Mama said, "are you trying to take my baby away from me? Did you give her this idea to travel so far away?" My aunt tried to convince her that it might be a good experience for me. "I would take very good care of her, Rosa," Aunt Erna promised. "If she wants to go why not let her have a little freedom? It's not as if she'll never come back, and America is quite reachable now. See how we have come to visit you three or four times already?" But my mother would have none of it, and I often wonder how things might have turned out differently if I had been allowed to go. Most probably everyone I loved would still have been killed by the Nazis, and losing contact with them would have been unbearable to me. So I suppose it was better in the long run that I didn't go.

By 1938 it was time for me to decide upon which university I really wanted to attend. I had no desire to study something that I didn't take seriously, such as philosophy or art. I desperately wanted to go into the field of medicine. Unfortunately, Jews were barred from attending medical schools in Poland no matter how good our grades were. There was a government quota called *numerus clausus* that allowed only maybe one or two Jewish students out of a hundred to study medicine, and those few students who were accepted had to be absolute geniuses in their studies. Other fields allowed a larger quota, but they kept the number of Jewish applicants down in most professions in Poland because they were afraid we would take over all of the better jobs.

It was true that Jews often became good doctors and lawyers. When Jews first came to Poland these were the only professions open to us, so a strong work ethic was ingrained in Jewish children to do well in them. When a group of people have few choices over how to make a living, they tend to work very hard to achieve what they can. By the time I was looking into universities the Polish government had come to see this as a problem. After all, if Jews were allowed to succeed in these fields, how would Poles have any opportunities? I have to say, however, that when I was living in Poland the best doctors and lawyers were the Jewish ones, and the Polish people knew this. The funny thing was that, even though access to the schools teaching medicine or law was restricted, most Poles sought out a Jew for these kinds of services. Perhaps this was a strange relationship. To be honest I will never fully understand why there was such jealousy toward Jews.

BY THE EARLY 1920S, two-thirds of Jewish students graduating from secondary schools went on to attend university. Nina and her sister Lina followed the course favored by their peers, pursuing a degree in the few subjects that remained open to Jews. Historian Joseph Marcus found that: "As long as entry was not restricted, about one-third preferred to study law and political science; another third studied 'philosophy'…and nearly 10 percent studied medicine. Another characteristic was the relatively large number of female Jewish students. Their percentage of all the girls at university was about 70 percent higher than the corresponding percentage for male students."[11]

Like her sister's pursuit of philosophy, Nina's decision to study medicine was a common one among Jewish students. The problem of becoming one of the chosen few permitted to attend university still loomed. In addition to being one of the few females attempting to garner a degree in medicine, "numerus clausus," the official restriction of Jews attending Polish universities, had become officially instated after pressure was brought to bear by the Polish intelligentsia. A discriminatory quota already existed in many schools as early as 1919. It was an onslaught of rallies put on by young Polish nationalists in the early 1920s, however, that forced the Polish government to act with the more stringent "numerus." Polish president Pilsudski, beloved by the Jews for his tolerance and fair treatment of their class, was opposed to the measure. Yet the universities within his jurisdiction continued to enforce their own quota system. According to author Leo Cooper: "In September 1922 a memorandum was addressed to the senates of all universities demanding the introduction of a numerus clausus."[12] These restrictions limited the number of universities open to Nina, who decided instead to go abroad for her college education.

By the time I was ready for university I started to more seriously consider what it meant to be a Zionist, and it was then I made up my mind to attend school in Palestine. I put in my application to a medical school in Jerusalem. At that time they couldn't provide full credentials, but I figured by the time I studied for two or more years then the school would eventually be fully credited.

I immediately started to learn Hebrew from a private teacher. This seemed natural to me because my parents had sent me to private teachers to learn to play the piano and speak French. My parents provided for things like this because they believed it provided culture to us as well as a way of learning to concentrate. My grandmother had to be sneaky about allowing Mama to pursue an education, so my mother wanted her daughters to have every opportunity. In my situation both of my parents were educated and knew the value of it, so they encouraged us together and we never had to study something on the sly, as if it were forbidden.

I learned Hebrew from a tutor who was supposed to really know his stuff, but I have to admit I disliked him. He was a middle-aged man and was one of the most boring human beings I ever met! He presented Hebrew in such a way that induced a student to fall asleep. In my opinion a good teacher makes a good student. Desire and success go hand in hand. Nevertheless, I somehow had to overcome the boredom and absorb something from this man, because attending school in Palestine required learning Hebrew. It was very clearly a requirement and it wasn't easy. For one thing, the language is written from right-to-left.

I struggled with the entry exam concerning this language and was surprised when I passed it. I was accepted into the university in Palestine with the understanding that I would continue to study Hebrew once I arrived there. I even had to sign a paper promising that I would study the language even up to the time I planned to leave Poland. There were many different arrangements to make in order to travel to Palestine, and it made me furious at first. "Hey, the Italian schools don't insist that I learn Italian," I complained, "the Italians have already told me I could attend school there with no further requirements, so why do I have to learn Hebrew to study in Palestine?" I soon discovered, however, that being furious doesn't do a person any good when applying to schools. I had to accept certain things or I wouldn't be admitted.

I never told anybody this, but just as I was preparing to go to school I met a young man that I liked very much. He was bright and good-looking, and was also preparing to go to Palestine, though in a different manner. His parents were not well-off, and he could not afford to go to university on his own, so he was going to live and work on a kibbutz. We knew each other only for a short while, but we saw each other during classes, or on the way to them. I didn't really know if my parents would allow me to date at this time, so we socialized in this way. He told me the exact date when he planned to leave Poland, and where he would be staying. He said that when I reached Palestine I should try to find him.

I was only just eighteen and he was about twenty, I think. This young man was already very accomplished in Hebrew, which I thought was pretty impressive. He was kind enough to help me in my continuing studies and this allowed me to finally become more accomplished in Hebrew. Sometimes we got together to study and he would go over my reading and my pronunciation with me until I improved. He was very encouraging, and at the same time I liked his character. Spending time with him made that summer before the war quite pleasant. I never learned what happened to him. I believe his name was Johna Goldbein. Most probably he survived the war by going to Palestine.

We never even kissed, you know. Other than the boy who attempted kissing me at camp I still had no sexual experience, and besides the occasional rumor I knew nothing about it. Even up to the age of about sixteen, adults were still telling my friends and me that a stork brought babies! I don't mean to go on and on about this, but it just amazes me to know how different things were.

I once encountered a cousin if mine who was noticeably pregnant and I thought she had just had too much to eat lately. My mother said to me, "Well, maybe her stomach will go away when she stops eating so much." Can you imagine such a comment? When my sister became pregnant with her little girl I finally realized something wasn't kosher. I didn't know exactly what, but I sensed that something had been done to her physically. How else would she get that way? I recognized the fact that when the baby arrived a pregnant woman became slim again. In my mind I started to put two and two together. I learned only by observation and figured out the biology a little at a time. I suppose if I had been able to pursue an education in medicine I would have had many revelations about female biology!

Because there was no kissing or "going steady" with boys, my first social encounters with them involved hanging around with the brothers and cousins of my girlfriends. It began when we went to birthday parties and similar events, and this was considered acceptable. I specifically remember one party when a boy looked at me and smiled, so naturally I smiled back. I don't even remember what he said, but it felt a little different than when my girlfriends smiled at me. Only little moments between boys and girls occurred like this, but it was nice and in this way one could have friends among the local boys. Parties came in handy for other reasons as well. For instance, I used to love dancing, and every party allowed this kind of interaction with boys. They were always very polite so even though we were physically close nothing unexpected happened. There was usually a band playing and we would dance the cha-cha or polka. I eventually got very good at a number of dances.

Parties were well-supervised and elaborate affairs back then. Parents arranged for family and friends to come to the house, and the crystal and silver were put out. Maids served the very best food, and even a small party seemed elegant. In my day if a person invited you to a restaurant for a meal you assumed they were ashamed of where they lived or perhaps the lady of the house was ill. We felt sorry for those who had to entertain in restaurants. Back then people were very proud of their homes and their cooking. The parties at our apartment were, I must say, spectacular. We hired extra people to help and pushed all the furniture to the walls to make room for dancing. Three or four cooks helped with the cooking and my mother very carefully organized the menu. We never would have dreamed of ordering food from a caterer or, God forbid, calling for a pizza!

Before the war L'vov was a completely different world. My friends and I didn't know what was going on in other places like America or Africa. Even countries that were closer to us, such as Germany and Romania, seemed far away, and we had no idea what was occurring there. Life was quiet and very simple and my life revolved around family and friends and school. In those days a girl from a nice Jewish home usually married young and immediately tried to have children. I am certain this is what Mama expected of me. I never exactly felt pressured to do these things, but it was understood.

Things were slowly starting to change, however. We were traditional in our religion, but there were families such as ours that didn't keep such strict rules. My sisters were both married, so my mother didn't seem to be in any rush to have me, her "baby," marry any time soon. I had my own plans as well. I had always wanted to go away to study and my parents didn't try to talk me out of this dream. By the same token they did introduce me to nice Jewish boys, assuming that if nature took its course I would like one of them enough to marry at the proper time.

All of this preparation for womanhood was simmering away for me as I grew older. Girls didn't have bat mitzvahs like they do in America today, but I felt as if I had officially become a young woman when my mother purchased a new set of clothes for me. I received from her a pair of shoes with matching purse and gloves. This was the kind of outfit a lady wore, and it sort of expressed I had grown up and had become a young woman. I was seventeen or so and very excited to be wearing complete outfits that were so stylishly matching right down to the stockings. My mother wished for me to have the proper clothes before I went to university. She even arranged to have four additional outfits made to order for me so that I would be outfitted for the entire school year. One suit was a deep blue with a wine red silk blouse to go with it. My shoes and gloves were the same red and my hat was blue with red decoration. It all came together beautifully and I felt so mature. I still love hats and I have quite a few in my closet, but you know women don't wear them as much anymore, certainly not in California where I am currently living.

———

I suppose one could say I was a traditional Jewish girl. We were not Orthodox Jews, but we were serious about our traditions. We were in touch with modern times, but my sisters were married to men whom my parents chose, and I might have been too if not for the war. During this time people didn't live as long as they do now. My parents knew that I wanted to go to university, but they also knew that they might not be around to ensure my safety and well-being. They continued to believe that if they found an appropriate young man who appealed to me as well, then nature might take its course and I would marry. After all, this strategy had worked well for both of my sisters, and I was the last daughter to worry about.

So I was eventually introduced to a young doctor, a brilliant person named Doctor Been. He had studied in Poland, which was rare, but he received special permission to do so. He was admitted into school as a tutor for the son of an instructor teaching at one of the top institutions. This professor on the faculty wanted very much for his son to be a doctor too, but he needed help studying. By admitting the Jewish boy to the same university this professor could then ensure that the boy would serve as his son's tutor. The two young men attended classes together simply because his father approved it with the rest of the faculty. He went to all of this trouble just to make certain his son would have a tutor who felt indebted to him.

Anyway, Doctor Been received a very good education, and my parents wanted me to marry him. Dr. Been really was an ambitious man. He was one of the graduating physicians who applied to study neurology in France. His intention was to finish his general medical schooling, then travel to France and specialize in brain surgery. Doctor Been planned to eventually go into research, and I am certain that he would have accomplished a lot if not for the war. His parents lost everything during the First World War, but by marrying into a wealthy family such as mine Doctor Been could hope to make a better future for both of us. I had a dowry and a nice background, so naturally I was a reasonable choice for this young man and his family.

An introduction was arranged, and I had to agree to meet this young man. Do not misunderstand me. I obeyed my parents in this respect, but nobody was forced to marry back then. If I didn't like this man then the match would not be made between us. It wasn't like the stories you hear out of the Middle East, when a girl has to marry someone her parents choose no matter what.

I wasn't really angry with my parents for arranging time for me to meet with the young man they liked. I was only a little impatient with the whole process. I remember saying to them that I really didn't want to marry Dr. Been or anyone else for the time being.

"Go spend time with him," my mother suggested, "maybe you'll like him." Doctor Been certainly liked me very much, and right away he wanted to see me again. I, on the other hand, was bored to death! I was young, and maybe a little cruel in this respect. I actually had a different young man I was friendly with at the time, and I wanted to meet up with him more than spend time with Dr. Been. If I had to socialize with the man chosen by my parents on an official date at two o'clock…well that was fine. I would meet with him for about two hours over coffee. This usually took place in my parent's house and we would just talk. But by five o'clock I wanted to run off to a party where the young man I really liked was waiting. So I would say, "Well, this has been very pleasant, Doctor Been, but now I have to go." And off I went.

It was really a little gutsy on my part, but when I left his company that was when I felt that I could finally breathe. To be truthful I had much more fun when I was with my other young friend. I suppose I should have been flattered by Doctor Been's attention. He was already a full-fledged doctor who had obtained his degree, and any girl would have been honored to be his wife. But he was seven or so years older than I, and we really didn't have much in common.

Once he took me to a dance in an attempt to win me over. I had heard of a gathering that was to take place in my neighborhood that I desperately wished to attend. At first my parents wouldn't let me go. Well, when Doctor Been realized I liked dancing so much, he asked my parents if he could accompany me to this dance. It was only then that my parents decided that it would be all right. I am sorry to say that I was a little mean to the doctor, however. Once we arrived I recognized my usual dancing partner standing with a group of our friends. This boy walked over to me and asked me to dance, and that was that. I spent the entire evening dancing with this boy!

Poor Dr. Been. I suppose I should have made more of an effort to get to know the doctor since my parents approved of him. But I was only eighteen years old and I wanted to be with others my own age. At any rate I planned not on marrying, but on going to medical school myself. Not for a moment had I thought of getting married before I received an education. In spite of the fact that Doctor Been was a good man and a brilliant doctor I simply was not interested. What can I say?

I continued to prepare for entering university, and I looked forward to the summer break. It was sometime after 1937, and there was no real warning that a war was coming. Yet, somehow that year felt very different. Things were relatively normal in Poland until a very famous man, Joseph Pilsudski, died. He had been the ruler of Poland for some time. He had always been fair in dealing with Jewish affairs in Poland, and we truly mourned his passing.

UPON GAINING POWER IN 1926 Pilsudski worked toward eliminating dictates that previously limited Polish minorities. Almost immediately Pilsudski exercised his influence when Poland's Prime Minister, Professor Bartel, announced that: "…all restrictions applicable to Jews introduced by the former occupying powers are abolished and no longer applicable to the Jewish population."[13]

Understanding that Poland's faltering economy relied on the stabilizing force provided by Jewish businessmen, Pilsudski pursued more liberal policies that would greatly benefit the Jewish minority in his country. A momentary respite from anti-Semitic laws and restrictions allowed the Polish Jews not only to prosper, but to experience a moment of government protection never before offered to them as a group.

The security Jews felt knowing their president was at least somewhat sympathetic toward minorities would be fleeting, however. This brief period of peace was followed by an uncertainty all too familiar among Polish Jews, and the death of Pilsudski brought back a more repressive atmosphere. Author Leo Cooper wrote: "The death of Pilsudski, the 'protector' of the Jews, in May 1935 sent shock waves through the Jewish community. It was felt that with the passing of the liberator of Poland and the perceived defender of the rights of the Jews, the situation would worsen. For Jews it was not only the passing of a national hero but the death of a man who had been considered a proponent of equal rights for everyone, including Jews."[14]

Jews instinctively prepared for the racial backlash that was sure to come. Very soon anti-Semitic mandates were reinstated, and a wave of demonstrations against the Jews in Poland made life even more difficult. Nina Grütz, now a young woman with dreams of attending university in Palestine, faced the new reality that this inexplicable hatred toward Jews in her country might somehow alter her plans.

After President Pilsudski died we started to feel the effects of things going on in Germany. I wasn't a baby anymore. I knew what was going on because I read the papers and listened to the radio. A woman who was a terrible anti-Semite had an important role in the government in Poland after this man died. Things soon became very unsteady for Jews, and we all felt a bit more threatened. There were, for example, some boys from the architectural school *Polytechnicum* that began to harass us. Young men from this institution were known to be extremely anti-Semitic. The way they carried on was very much like how what we call "skinheads" act now. Even two or three years before the war I came to recognize how these boys thought. I remember one night hearing the sound of them marching through the streets of my neighborhood. I went to my balcony and saw these students marching with their arms linked singing, "We hate Jews!" They would sing this sort of slogan that implied how they would treat Jewish girls. They yelled out that, although they hated Jewish boys, they "loved" Jewish girls. This they meant in a very disrespectful way.

If we had any idea how bad things would get we might have taken action. We certainly would not have stayed and waited for the Nazis to come kill us. Even with all our possessions left behind we would have left had we known what to expect. We could maybe have liquidated everything from our businesses and left the country. But who really wanted to think of such a thing? Nothing like the Holocaust had ever happened in our lives, so how could we have understood the danger? However, we started to see that certain places we used to love to visit in the city were no longer open to us or safe.

One night not too long after Pilsudski died my friends and I were laughing and enjoying each other's company within the neighborhood park. We made up a group of about three couples, so we felt safe in spite of the recent racial attacks committed toward Jews. We were especially confident because our group included some older boys who were very tall and strong.

I suppose that since it was such a warm and beautiful evening we stayed a little longer than usual. I was with a good-looking boy whom I liked very much, and I never dreamed that we would experience any trouble. The stars were out and we were having a wonderful time. Unfortunately, my friend and I were strolling a little bit behind the others when we came upon some boys from Polytechnicum who decided to ambush us. You could tell who they were because they had insignias on their uniforms showing us where they studied. We didn't see them at first because dusk had fallen, leaving shadows around every bend.

I honestly don't know how these young men even knew we were Jewish. It was dark and we were all speaking Polish perfectly. My friend and I continued walking along, and for all purposes we could have been any young Polish couple. But somehow the boys from Polytechnicum sniffed us out as Jews. They soon cornered us and started to beat up my friend. When I began to scream more of these boys came up to me and tried to calm me down. I am not sure why, but they made a lot of effort to assure me that, even though they were beating my friend, nothing would happen to me. I didn't want or need their attempts at good manners, and I told them all to go to hell! If I'd had a rock or a brick I would have defended my friend, but I was only able to duck under their arms and grab my friend away from them. I yelled for my battered companion to run.

When we caught up with the rest of our group the other boys wanted to go back and take revenge, but we girls convinced them to come home with us. The boy who had been walking so peacefully beside me only moments ago was now bleeding and bruised from his encounter with the fine architectural students.

We went home as changed people, and we never again went to this park. It made me both furious and sad that things were changing so drastically in Poland. My friends and I wanted to rebel against all this anti-Semitism by continuing our normal routines. We were young and defiant, but we were outnumbered most of the time. It soon became obvious that we girls certainly couldn't go out at night. We could have very easily been molested, and we no longer went walking in the park or any other isolated place. There wasn't much we could do about the situation and it was very frustrating. Things went on in a strange quiet way, just as many pogroms had occurred in Poland's past. The police never did anything to investigate our reports of abuse, and no mention was made of it in the local papers or on the radio. But we all knew the tide was turning, and something was definitely in the air.

It was 1939, and perhaps because she felt it was too dangerous to travel to Germany my mother chose not to go abroad for her usual trip to the spa. Instead she decided to go to Krynica for a little vacation with me. As I mentioned, I rarely vacationed with my parents. This one time, however, just before the war, I went with Mama to a special resort. To this day it is a very famous and important spa. Krynica is located high in the Polish mountains, and many Jews visited this beautiful and luxurious place. I was very excited to be going with my mother to a resort, but it seemed a shame that my father was unable to join us. He was still trying to make up for the failed mill, and he was determined to work the summer away.

In the beginning I had a good time. My mother was a wonderful and relaxed companion, and as an outgoing girl I made friends easily. Mama and I were happy and having lots of fun until father showed up unexpectedly to bring us home. His sudden appearance seemed strange to me, because he had been adamant about working all summer on the family business.

Immediately Mama sensed something was up. "What's wrong?" she asked. Father told us it was no longer safe to be so far away from home. The situation in Poland had become so bad he felt that it was best for us to stay together. When I heard we were going home I was crushed. I loved Krynica, and it was confusing to feel any danger in the midst of these mountains and beauty. I didn't understand what all the fuss was about. Nevertheless, we packed up to leave. Once we arrived home to the city my mother and I knew things had changed. People were saying horrible things about Jews, and we could definitely tell trouble was brewing.

We tried to settle in as if things were normal, but there was an undercurrent of apprehension in the atmosphere. I was supposed to be preparing to go abroad for school, but I couldn't concentrate. It felt somewhat like America after 9/11, only worse. The terrorism was constant and right in our backyard. We never knew what the next day would bring. Hitler was already in power and had taken control of Austria. I was still just a girl, and at first I didn't realize what was happening.

I think the situation really sunk in when I attended a lecture shortly after returning home. A friend invited me to go with him, and I later came to understand that he never realized I was Jewish. I spoke perfect Polish and dressed in the same way the other Polish kids did, so how could he know that I was any different from him? Anyway, this friend of mine invited me to go to a lecture at a time when Jews had recently been restricted from certain activities. Although we were still permitted to attend university lectures, new laws stated that Jews were to be seated in a special section separate from the other students. These "ghetto benches" were the top seats which made it more difficult to hear and take notes. When my colleague asked me to accompany him I didn't even think about these "ghetto benches," because I had not yet encountered them. This boy was just a friend, so his invitation wasn't like a date or anything of the sort. But we were school buddies and had the same academic interests, so off we went.

I walked in with him and found that there were older students directing people where to sit. They yelled out, "Jews on the left side and Poles on the right!" I was proud to be a Jew, so I started to go to the left when my companion pulled me by the hand and asked, "Where are you going?"

"Well," I explained, "they said that Jews are supposed to sit on the left side."

His face suddenly went white, and he abruptly grabbed my arm and led me away to the right. "You're coming with me," he whispered. I tried to argue with him but he wouldn't have it. I really wanted to leave by this time, but he found a place for us to sit together and plopped me down very roughly next to him. We didn't say another word to each other until the lecture was about to begin. Then he hissed at me, "I didn't know you were Jewish!"

I looked at him with something of a challenge in my face, and I said, "But now you know!" What I saw in his face was a terrible look of disappointment. I thought then to myself, "Well, I'm not going to see him anymore after this." And I never did. The more time went on the more I felt this kind of thing happening.

THE "GHETTO BENCHES" which Nina described were part of the resurgence of anti-Semitic policy taking place in Poland just before World War II. Although there had been no official ordinance from the Polish government restricting Jewish students, many administrations took it upon themselves to enforce segregation within their universities. In his book *The Lesser of Two Evils*, author Don Levin wrote of the new conditions with which Jewish students were forced to comply: "Universities introduced separate seating for Jews in lecture halls and assemblies; the Polytechnicum of L'vov was the first institution where the administration and the academic institutions endorsed these 'ghetto benches.' Enforcement was left to Polish students, who were eager to discharge this duty with their fists."[15]

It would seem that the Polytechnic boys who had assaulted Nina's friend in the park would now be given carte blanche to further assail her and her fellow Jewish students. Nina, whose young life had once seemed so full of promise, was now experiencing the full impact of Hitler's ideology. His theories regarding racial purity were appealing to a large number of Poles, particularly young, impressionable university students aching to express nationalistic and Aryan views. Nina would not be the only Jew affected by new laws concerning her people and their access to higher education.

Leo Cooper wrote extensively on the phenomenon: "As a result of continued harassment, the number of Jews at the universities fell rapidly. Succumbing to the pressure from many student organizations, rectors and deans of Polish universities allowed the introduction of special benches (nicknamed 'ghetto benches') for Jewish students. By the spring of 1937, the rectors of virtually all higher education institutions ordered the introduction of the ghetto benches. In July 1937 the Universities Act was amended, allowing rectors to introduce segregated seating for Polish and Jewish students. Jewish students, unable to actively oppose this rule, refused to sit on separate benches and decided to stand during the lectures. To attend lectures and continue studies in an atmosphere of constant harassment called for a lot of courage and determination on the part of a Jewish student."[16]

Nina did her best to remain optimistic in the face of these new challenges and restrictions. Resorting to the strategy demonstrated by her parents, she carried on her normal routine, albeit with a cautious glance over her shoulder.

I still believed that my life would go on in a normal fashion. In spite of the anti-Semitism that seemed to be increasing in Poland, many Jewish families such as my own held out hope that it was a temporary situation as it had often been before. One learned to adjust and work around this racial hatred until eventually things settled down again.

In the meantime I decided to go ahead with my plans to attend university in Palestine, never once believing that I would not only lose this opportunity, but everyone I cared about as well. I was young, and I loved my life and my family. I didn't see any immediate danger. In my wildest dreams I couldn't imagine that in a matter of months my life would be turned upside down.

EVER HOPEFUL that the political climate in Poland would soon stabilize, Nina Grütz doggedly made her preparations for college life. She informed her parents of her decision to attend university in Palestine as opposed to Italy. While a murmur of trouble threatened to disrupt her plans for the future, the comfort and protection she had known throughout her young life was most assuredly slipping away as well. War was imminent for Nina's homeland. Borders soon would be closed and lives sent into turmoil. For the time being the Grütz family followed their daily routine and seasonal pursuits, closing their eyes to the disastrous changes to come.

CHAPTER III

The Good Times Are Over

(1939-1941)

NINA WAS ACCEPTED at the University of Pisa, Italy, but instead set her sights on attending school in Palestine. Sadly, a college education would elude the young woman, for the wave of German hatred toward Jews had already begun to ripple its way into Poland. This Nazi doctrine (seen in the Nuremburg Laws drawn up by Hitler's administration) was adopted by the new Polish government in ways that excluded Jews from society. Still, the idea of Nazi Germany posing any real threat to their existence was given little credence by the majority of Jews in Poland. Normal life went on in such a way that most were lulled into a false sense of security, eventually costing most of them their lives. Though change was in the wind, Nina could hardly have expected that the golden years of her youth were drawing to such a dramatic close.

Hitler had only just come to power in Germany by 1933, but it really was not long after that before we felt his presence in Poland. To begin with, there were fewer schools available to Jews, and Polish universities were now completely off limits to us. The Jewish gymnasium schools lost their credentials, and other restrictions gradually began to apply.

When we began to hear rumors of war by 1939 I was ready to go abroad to study. Although many Poles agreed with Hitler's anti-Semitic views, few wished to hand their country over to the Germans. After we returned from Krynica all I ever heard about was the possibility of a war. Because I was young and wished only to go on with my life, this was all very frustrating. I remember thinking, "People are always talking about war, war, war. If it has to be, let it come so we can get it over with!"

Of course, when you're young, your mind works differently. Now when I think back on things, there were so many indications that we would have a hard time. We should have seen this coming when Hitler came to power. Maybe some people, politicians and such, paid attention to Hitler, but many Polish Jews didn't take the Nazis seriously.

What should have tipped most of us off was the day Hitler expelled most of the non-German citizens who had stayed in Germany after the First World War. Many of them were Jewish and quite a few were children. We cared for a little Jewish girl at that time whose parents were placed elsewhere. There were also two students that came to stay from Germany because they had nowhere else to go. They were just told to leave and that was that. When you think about these things and how they became worse, well it should have been a sign to us that something wasn't right.

Sure enough, by September 1939 the war had broken out. I remember it happened during Friday morning around ten o'clock. We were preparing for the Sabbath, and my sister Lina was expected for dinner along with her husband. This was not unusual for them to join us, but still my mother went out with our servant, Hania, to purchase food at the market. I was home alone. It was the end of summer and I remember talking on the phone with a girlfriend about school preparations for the fall. There had been the usual rumors going around that a war would be happening very soon, so there was some uncertainty if anyone would be able to travel abroad. I refused to give it much thought at the time. I didn't really even know who was planning to fight whom or for what reason. We had no television to inform us, only the radio and I seldom listened to that.

Something was in the air but I chose to ignore it. When the bombing started that morning I was taken completely by surprise. Home alone and waiting for my mother to come home from the market, I was looking forward to seeing my sister Lina and her husband for the Sabbath. Talking away on the telephone with my girlfriend, I suddenly heard the first explosions.

I dropped the phone and ran to the window to see what had caused the noise. At first I couldn't imagine what it was. I had never heard bombs before. I never even heard the airplanes coming, but when the buildings around me were hit our whole apartment shook and I knew I was in trouble. L'vov was a large city with structures built up closely all around. When I saw old familiar structures crumbling and destroyed around our neighborhood I panicked. I ran around the apartment trying to find a place to hide until I became quite hysterical. I kept screaming like a five-year-old, "Mama, where are you?" I suppose I was in shock.

Finally my mother stepped into the apartment with Hania. I threw myself on her, weeping and trembling. It had taken them some time to get back to our apartment, and I was so relieved to see them both in one piece. After Mama settled me down a little we all made a run for the cellar. Poor Hania was so frightened! She was a Catholic Ukrainian girl and she kept saying, "Jesus!" and crossing herself. We didn't mind, because we were just as scared and saying our own prayers.

In a situation like that you pray to any and everything to ask for help. My father had not yet arrived home, and the telephone lines were down preventing us from calling him, so we simply waited. When he dragged in a few hours later he took us all to the cellar. Our beautiful Sabbath dinner sat there for the whole three weeks we hid down there. As the days passed it began to smell very unpleasant, but my father would not allow us to clear anything away. He had been wise enough to insist that we go immediately to the cellar, but sadly some people tried to retrieve their belongings first. The experience was so new to them that their first thought was to grab photographs and valuables in order to save them from being destroyed in the fires shooting up everywhere from the bombing.

I remember how shocking it was to me to see death after that very first assault. We saw a neighbor running outside to pick up some possessions, and instantly he was killed by shrapnel! It was stunning and horrible to me. Things we had talked about and heard about war, things that you knew about only from history books, were now right in front of us.

Once we got the idea that the situation was serious we took more care. As the bombing continued throughout the day and into the weeks we became more aware of each and every danger. If I wanted to go upstairs to get something the answer was always "No!" It was now a question of life and death.

IN SPITE OF THE CONSTANT RUMORS alluding to invasion on either side of their borders, Polish civilians were ill prepared for war. Those residing in cities were particularly vulnerable. Before long, the crippling disbelief most Poles felt was replaced with frantic efforts to survive the constant bombarding unleashed by German aircraft.

An eyewitness account echoes Nina's struggle to cope during the relentless bombing. In *Kiddush Hashem*, Rabbi Shimon Huberband's diary of Jewish life during the war, his experience echoed that of Nina's when recalling the gripping fear every Polish citizen felt as the first bombs disrupted their lives: "I rushed home; it was close to twelve noon. As I ascended the staircase from the ground floor, I heard the tick-tick-tick of artillery fire. Loud cries immediately went out from all the house residents. Mothers quickly grabbed their children and ran from their apartments to the cellar, which had been designated as the shelter. When we entered the corridor of the cellar, we heard the first boom of a bomb explosion. The entire building trembled. Soon there was a second explosion, and a third, and so on, continuing as it were without end. Women went through spasms, children cried, and several men fainted."[1]

Conditions inside the underground cellars were far from healthy. Meant as only a temporary solution to anticipated air raids, these structures were cramped and poorly ventilated. As the bombs crept closer to those huddled beneath their apartment buildings, the very real threat of being buried alive lurked with every explosion. Rabbi Huberband described the tense and claustrophobic atmosphere as he and his family waited out the bombing in their cellar: "The fear of death was so terrible. The cellar had a low ceiling and was damp. It was impossible to stand—one could either sit or walk hunched. The air was very congested, simply unbearable."[2]

While an ill-equipped and vastly outnumbered Polish army attempted to fight off the Germans, Nina and her family crouched in their basement praying that each bomb would fall anywhere but on their home. The Grütz family spent roughly three weeks in their cellar with few supplies to sustain them. Between bombing raids one brave family member would venture up to the apartment to collect water and food supplies. When the bombs finally fell silent the bewildered population of L'vov emerged from their cellars to find a world very different from the one they knew only weeks before.

The minute the war broke out I grew up. When the bombs began to fall we had to face reality. I was forced to make a transition almost overnight. I realized that whatever my plans had been, they would now have to change if I was going to survive.

I had a very strong feeling that there would be little in the way of security for my family and me. Even with all the rumors, nobody seemed at all prepared for the bombing, so no provisions had been set aside for such a calamity. To keep from starving, people had no choice but to take the risk and creep from their cellars to retrieve food and water from their homes.

I think even the Polish government was taken by surprise when the bombs began to fall. Certain people in the administration must have known trouble was coming. They were more informed than the general public, but I don't think war was expected quite so soon. We were all very upset to see the beautiful city we loved destroyed. People were frantically looking for relatives or crying hysterically by their burned-out homes where family members had died. As for us, we still had no idea if my sisters or any other relatives had been harmed or killed.

We stopped some retreating Polish soldiers and asked about the situation. Immediately after coming out of the cellar we discovered that our government no longer existed. Poland was defeated. Gradually we learned that we had completely lost this war, and that the Russians were actually coming to take control.

This was the first we heard about a "Pact" that had been agreed upon between our two enemies. We learned that part of Poland was taken by the Russians and the other part by the Germans. It appeared that we were on the eastern side with the Russians. We knew that the Germans hated Jews; however, we didn't know what to expect when the Russians came into our town.

The uncertainty was frightening and very unnerving. For me it was a moment of revelation because it was then I knew for certain that our lives were now forever changed. Our apartment building had been spared, and I hadn't even seen a Russian yet. But somehow I knew that nothing would ever be the same. As my family stood together taking in the sight of rubble all around us, I turned to my mother and said, "Mama, the good times are over." I was young, but already very realistic. My mother did not want to admit to this sad fact. She was very disturbed by my comment and she cried, "Why do you say this, darling? Your father and I went through the First World War and did all right. We had to travel to Vienna for safety, but we came back to our home and business. Everything worked out fine in the end. Lina and Helena were all right, and by the time you were born we had our lives in order. The same will be true for this little war."

I started to feel hurt that she couldn't be honest with me. Still, I didn't want to worry my mother, so I pretended to be optimistic for her sake. In my heart, however, I sensed that this war would be very different from the one Mama survived.

THE POST-BOMBING CHAOS spread throughout Poland and fed upon itself, leaving citizens confused and exhausted. Poles operated in survival mode without knowledge of who would be in control of their country and what the ramifications of that leadership might be.

Turning again to the writings of Rabbi Huberband, the mayhem that ensued directly after the September 1939 bombing becomes very clear: "During the entire day of the bombing, hundreds upon hundreds of people, [some] Jews but mainly Christians, abandoned the city. They ran wildly, without any destination or plan, wherever their eyes led them. As the evening grew dark, the bombings ceased and all was quiet for close to two hours. We left the shelter, first to the courtyard, and afterwards out onto the street. The streets were jammed with people. All were fleeing the city, carrying some linens and clothing in baby carriages. They were running in great confusion, wherever their eyes led them. Our courtyard became extremely alarmed. Many felt that we should leave the city, while others believed there was no need to run away."[3]

The Grütz family joined the throngs of frightened neighbors scrambling from cellars and crumbling homes. As their ancestors had done before them, Jewish families such as the Grützes made the best of things. As they were soon to discover, the Russians were now in control of eastern Poland.

When the Russians invaded we were completely in the dark about our new enemies. I realize now that before he started this war Hitler worried about the Russians causing him problems. To put them off guard Hitler led Stalin to believe that the Germans needed Russian support. In order to keep the Russians off guard Hitler reached an agreement with Stalin promising him the eastern part of Poland, just like that. It was as if he were handing us over like a toy to share with some playmate. Because of this we were quite suddenly under Russian control.

The other half of our country was to be taken over by the Germans, but of course Hitler meant to have the entire territory of Poland all along. In the beginning he and his SS went about gathering up and killing Jews on their own side of our country. The Warsaw ghetto was part of that German side, and we later learned of the atrocities committed there against our people.

I have to say that the Russian side of Poland was no picnic either. The Russian soldiers quickly kicked us out of our beautiful apartment and stuck us in a cramped attic on the top floor. They confiscated my father's businesses and took away all his wealth. The Soviet government proclaimed him a criminal because he had been a private businessman. Using this as their reasoning to take control they forced father to train their own Russian workers. It didn't take a genius to figure out that the Soviets would eventually take over the management of his factory entirely.

Even with all of this misfortune, however, from what we began to hear about the western side of Poland we were the lucky ones. In the end the Russian occupation was preferable to that of the Germans. At least the Soviets didn't target people simply because they were Jewish. They didn't like capitalists. That was very apparent. If we didn't find legitimate work they would certainly send us to slave away in Siberia. But we had a chance for survival that we never appreciated until the Germans took over completely. For the time being, however, we felt degraded and lost. Our home and most of our possessions were gone, and we were uncertain as to what they would do to my father, but at least we were together.

When you consider the difference between the Russian occupation of Poland and that of the Germans there was no comparison. The Russians could be brutal, but they weren't crazy enough to kill us for so-called reasons of race. It's true, we lost everything when the Russians came. Everything my father and my grandfather had worked for was taken away. It didn't matter that my father had been a good and fair employer and had worked hard for every penny. The Russians saw what they wanted and they used the excuse of communism to take it. For this we lost the factory, our apartment and all of the beautiful things in it.

For the first three months after the Russians arrived my father was permitted to continue working at the factory. But this was really only in order for him to train the Russians how to run everything. They wanted to keep the factory in operation because it provided vital materials. So for the time being he continued to work and we survived on what few supplies we had to get by. Soon, however, the Russians brought in more of their own people, until they no longer needed father's experience. We had no way of knowing that this would signal the time when Daddy was to be arrested.

With my father out of a job we quickly ran out of the money we had saved. In order to obtain any supplies they had to be purchased on the black market for triple their worth. We were in a better situation in the beginning because we had a lot of soap to bargain with. We put away quite a few bricks of that soap, and for a while it was as good as having diamonds! That and the candles we were able to save kept us alive. Nobody was supposed to use electricity, and at any time it could simply be turned off, so candles were essential. We soon realized both soap and candles had become luxury items. They were almost as valuable as bread. You could exchange soap for a sack of flour or sugar. This was the way things started to work.

Occasionally I would try to discuss our situation with Mama, but she refused to believe that this was a different kind of war. She would only remind me once again of how they managed during the first war. It was true that my parents survived that war with hardly any financial loss. We lost relatives and this was the tragedy that many other families felt. The problem was that my mother failed to see the difference between the First World War and the war we were presently dealing with. Now it appeared that we had two surrounding enemies that set out specifically to ruin us for what we represented to them. The Russians hated our capitalist lifestyle, and the Germans despised us because we were Jews.

Even the way people fought war now was quite different. During the first war technology had not been as advanced, and civilians had an opportunity to run away and find a safe place to wait things out. In this new war the bombing occurred in such a way that you couldn't escape it. Airplanes appeared out of nowhere and dropped very powerful bombs all around us. We were like mice scampering here and there, and it seemed to us there was no real safe place to hide.

THE SOVIET INVASION was as deliberate and brazen as that of the Germans who rapidly advanced into Poland from the west. This tenuous alliance between Stalin and Hitler would benefit both leaders in their quest for power. In Don Levin's *The Lesser of Two Evils*, Soviet intentions were made very clear from the moment the Communist army set foot on Polish ground: "... Red Army units rushed across the Polish border from the east, 'to liberate our Ukrainian and Belorussian brethren from their enslavement to the corrupt, degenerate government of Poland.'...After describing the lives of exploitation and humiliation that the Poles had led under the regime of the landowners, the Soviet press noted the establishment of 'provisional administrations' that would restore order in the cities and towns."[4]

The Grützes were soon identified as capitalists in need of "rehabilitation." Under the new Soviet rule Nina and her family were stripped of all wealth and personal property. The bias against people of wealth hit urban Jews especially hard. Levin wrote that: "The nationalization of houses and apartments, which usually took place in the second stage [of instilling Soviet rule], was marked by uncertainty and lack of explicit criteria. Local functionaries had broad discretion that they could exercise arbitrarily. The main victims were the Jews, who were the most urbanized population group. In principle, the property (including homes) of anyone who had ever employed wage labor was liable to nationalization."[5]

To Nina's family the confiscation of property included their beloved estate in Soluki along with the rebuilt mill. For the second time in his life Viktor Grütz watched helplessly as everything he had worked hard to provide for his family abruptly disappeared. The future looked dire for Viktor, and Nina began to see the writing on the wall.

It wasn't long before the Soviets began to rearrange Poland. The Russians had a very effective system and they implemented it right away. They were very smart about how they went about things. When they pushed us out of our nice apartment and crammed us into the top floor room we couldn't say a word about it. From what we had heard, the result of arguing with them was a one-way ticket to Siberia.

The Soviets gave our luxurious home to a major in the Russian army. Luckily for us this major was actually a very nice man, and he tried to help us in little ways. He really liked my mother because she treated him like a houseguest. Whenever she had coffee prepared she went downstairs to offer him some. It didn't matter to her that he was a Russian officer. He had been kind to us from the moment he moved in, so she in turn was also courteous. My mother could never be any other way. She knew very little about cooking, so she didn't make meals for him or do anything really domestic. But she was gracious in other ways, such as offering to get a few things for him at the market when she went shopping for us.

This was not an easy task because goods and supplies were tightly controlled. We began to avoid the black market. Instead, with our soap, we could trade with our neighbors for essentials, but our supply was running out. We didn't want to buy things from our occupiers, so mostly we traded with local people who had been allowed to keep their businesses open, at least temporarily. Even though we no longer officially owned our factory and retail store, we could still communicate with the locals as long as father helped to run things. In this way we managed to trade with each other, but we were very careful about it. Our home life changed drastically. We were allowed to keep our clothes and a few other household items, but the Russians took all the furniture, dishes and linens away and sent it east.

A FAMILY NEED NOT be particularly wealthy in order to feel the effects of the "reorganization" enforced throughout eastern Poland. The new system implemented by the Soviets was intended to strategically place top officials amongst the locals. In this way maximum surveillance was ensured.

That the Russian officers often benefited from placement in fine homes was certainly a plus. It appeared that many families of moderate income were also forced from their homes. Leon Wells, a teenage boy living in L'vov at the time of Soviet occupation, wrote of how he and his family suffered under the new Communist rule: "…under the Russians…everything had been taken away. Our accommodations had been restricted—nine people in two rooms. My father, as well as others, cleaned the streets 'voluntarily,' through fear of being penned with wife and children in livestock wagons and sent to Siberia…to be lost in that wilderness forever."[6]

Life in L'vov was to be enormously different from what Nina had known as a child, and she quickly recognized the need to change along with it. Surveying this new development with aplomb, the nineteen-year-old girl quickly decided that the best way to deal with her captors was to find employment, becoming in their eyes, if not one of them, then at the very least a worker of some value. It would not be the last time Nina saved herself by "blending in."

Life was depressing outside in the streets of L'vov. When I walked around the city it just didn't look the same. There were ruined buildings and ruined people all around. I started to wonder, "Well, what do I do with my life now?"

I wasn't a brilliant girl, but I knew enough to make the best of the situation and find a way to exist. I had to be resourceful. Now when I went out I began to take note of how other people were coping. Right away I noticed that most Poles were finding work in order to survive. Unfortunately, a Pole had to have the proper papers to do this, something like a passport or identification. What was especially difficult for me was that on the ID papers a Pole had to mark the name of their father and the father's occupation. I figured that I couldn't lie too much. The Russians

knew my father's name because he had been labeled a capitalist. Our occupiers weren't stupid and they kept track of people, particularly when it
came to those who had been wealthy. It wouldn't take long before they saw
the name of Grütz and, if I hadn't been working, they'd see to it that I
found a job in Siberia.

It was one of those situations in which I could lose either way. By
now there was no reason for me to believe I would be attending university anytime soon, so I began to seek out work right away even though
I didn't have the proper papers. Almost immediately I found work in a
hospital! The Catholic nuns that ran the hospital were willing to give
me cleaning work along with the odd task, and I jumped at this opportunity.

My mother didn't even know that I had applied for the job. I knew
that if she learned I was working she would be disappointed and maybe a
little angry. She wanted to continue believing my life would be that of an
educated young lady.

ALTHOUGH THE RUSSIANS had many logistical challenges in establishing
a new Soviet government in Poland, the reorganization of Polish society
took place at a rapid and determined pace. Russian officials made certain
that the local populace recognized the new order that deemed any individ-
ually-owned business as a "capitalist" venture to be confiscated. Those who
dared oppose Communist ideals were swiftly spirited away, many of them
never to be heard from again.

The invading Russians expected this new way of life to be embraced
wholeheartedly and without complaint. Levin explained that: "After
describing the lives of exploitation and humiliation that the Poles had led
under the regime of the landowners, the soviet press noted the establishment of 'provisional administrations' that would restore order in the cities
and towns."[7]

Having skirted the challenge of obtaining the proper work papers,
Nina attempted to earn a living that could in some way aid her once prosperous family.

We had no clue at all as to what would happen to my father once he finished showing the Russians how to run the factory. We simply lived day to day. When I wasn't sneaking off to work I stayed home with my mother and Hania, who was still living with us. This girl had no other family and she liked Mama very much. When she begged to stay my mother said yes, even though we weren't supposed to have servants living with us anymore. She became more like a housemate, and really it would have been difficult for her to find another job. We shared food and other essentials as best we could. We weren't going hungry yet, but there wasn't any fancy stuff around anymore and our stomachs were never really full.

As I said, my mother didn't even know at first that I was working at the hospital. I kept it from her because I knew that she would argue with me about going out working every day to help our family. She still had it in her mind that everything would eventually settle down just as it had during the First War. I, on the other hand, had nothing to compare my current experience to. I didn't have the same expectations that my mother did, so it was easier for me to adapt and change as needed. I had a strong feeling that the Communists would make things difficult for those who didn't work. I always understood this for some reason and perhaps it was because I was young with my ear to the ground.

I suppose it might even have been instinct that caused me to search desperately for any job available to me. When I came to ask the nurses if they were hiring I told them about my former plans of becoming a doctor. I suppose I didn't want to give up the idea of working in some way with the medical profession. There were regular doctors at the hospital but the nurses were all nuns. Maybe they gave me work because they knew that I had wanted to study medicine, or maybe they just felt sorry for me. I'll never know for certain. At that point I didn't care. I soon settled into the position at the hospital and began to work with great enthusiasm.

The Catholic nuns ran our hospital very well, and I didn't mind the job involving cleaning up and caring for patients. I told them I was happy to do it. In the beginning I was put to work with other women just scrubbing the floors and cleaning up the mess left by those who had evacuated when the Russians were coming.

It was hard work and not altogether pleasant, but I didn't care. I simply did whatever was asked of me because I was so happy to have a job. The nuns gave me my daily responsibilities and I worked as hard as I could for them. Many times I had no idea how to do some of the simplest of domestic tasks. I had never been asked to do this sort of work before. When I was growing up we had maids to do every little chore.

For example, the nuns once asked me to collect coal from the cellar and start a fire in one of the ovens. It was beginning to get cold even though it was only September, and they used little ovens to keep the rooms warm. Not only was I ignorant in the art of starting a fire, I was also afraid of going into the cellar. That was where they put the bodies that had accumulated from the bombings. This temporary morgue was jammed with corpses until they could be buried. In the winter there could be even more dead people down there, waiting for the spring when the ground thawed and they could be properly interred.

The war was just beginning and everything was so mixed up. Nothing was as it used to be, and the services we once took for granted no longer existed. The days were gone when a funeral parlor took care of such things. People did the best they could back then and so it was up to the hospital staff to care for the dead.

Now the nuns wanted me to collect coal from this horrible place. I was appalled that on the way down they warned me to be careful of the fresh bodies they had only recently put there. I suppose they didn't want me to trip on them! The idea made me shudder and with all my heart I didn't want to go down there myself! To me a cellar was a place to hide during the shelling. Now I had to imagine that a cellar could also be a morgue.

Other than our neighbor who had died in the bombing I had never been around a dead body, and I certainly had never seen one close up. Now it looked as if my opportunity to see a dead body close up was inevitable, so off I went to the cellar for the coal, but I was shivering in fear. I was only about eighteen years old, and a little slender from a reduced diet. This made the cellar seem even colder, and I did my best to avert my eyes away from the covered mounds of what were once my fellow Poles. I quickly collected the coal and got out of there as quickly as possible.

I brought the coal up to the kitchen, even though I had no idea what to do after that. At the hospital we had two gas burners as well as two or three ovens that burned coal. I finally gathered my nerve and asked one of the other workers about how to start a fire. "Look," I explained quietly, "I don't want the sister to know that I'm ignorant of certain things, because they might not keep me here. I'll help you out with food or anything extra that comes my way if you'll occasionally show me how certain chores are done." So we struck this bargain and I learned how to do domestic things in this way.

THE ABILITY TO THINK on her feet and negotiate with others would become a valuable skill that Nina enlisted throughout the war years. For the time being she became acquainted with hard, manual work for the first time in her life. Pleased to have found employment, however, Nina happily plunged into her work at the hospital with a feeling of purpose. The situation for her and her family was far from ideal, but at least with her work at the hospital Nina had some sense of control over her life.

I didn't make much working at the hospital in the way of wages, but for me it was a blessing just to have a job. I had my family with me, I had a little something to give my mother, and the nuns were so good to me. I was willing to do anything they asked me, and I was elated to be working with the patients in a way that allowed me to use my brain. This was my first job ever, so I was very obedient, and the sisters seemed to approve of my work. The head nun, called Mother Superior, really was a wonderful woman. She told me that I could work on the children's ward as long as I liked, because, as another young person, I would be good with them.

I was thrilled when they put me on this ward, and I felt honored to help care for sick children. When I had been on the children's ward for a little while I revealed to one of the nuns exactly how much education I had acquired, and that before the war I planned on attending university abroad to study medicine. I was too afraid to tell them anything very personal about my past or my family. I still feared that they might not accept me as a Jew. Maybe they would think that as a girl who had grown up wealthy I might not be a good worker after all. Or maybe they would be afraid to hire me because of my father's crime of being a capitalist. I said very little about myself just in case, and it made me feel more secure in my job.

NINA WAS WISE to have kept her background secret from her new employers. Had they known of her father's situation she might have been dismissed from her work at the hospital. Those with any capitalist affiliations were hard-pressed to find any sort of job and were often denied the most basic rights. Finding work outside L'vov would also have been impossible. The social and economic upheaval of Soviet rule sent Polish citizens clamoring for any advantage and led to the hoarding of resources. Levin wrote of a system fraught with difficulties for the newly outcast businessmen and minorities: "People whose political and social past made them suspect of disloyalty found restrictive provisions written into their new ID cards. Notable among them was Article 11, which proscribed permanent residence in district capitals or any location within 100 kilometers (approximately 60 miles) of the international frontier."[8]

As a new employee with no real experience Nina's job security was, at best, precarious. She continued to show the sisters her willingness to work long hours and quickly absorbed any new skill that could improve her position.

I worked on the children's ward for about three months. I had many opportunities to learn about nursing because the number of patients increased every day. It was a very bad winter that year, and it felt as if the Russians had brought the Siberian weather with them. We had many cases of exposure and frostbite. Children were brought in with fingers completely black from the cold.

I felt such compassion for these children. The Russians were confiscating everything, so many of the poorer families didn't have shoes or adequate clothing. Farmers would find children in the forest half-frozen. These pathetic little things were then brought to our hospital where the doctors would often have to amputate their fingers or toes. It was very sad. The nuns felt that I was catching on to things very quickly, so they put me in the position of receiving patients and directing them to the proper care.

They told me that I would be a very good pre-op nurse and that maybe I could even work in the operating room. Sure enough by the next week the sisters allowed me to assist a little during surgeries. I tried to be of help when the doctors had to perform amputations, but it was hard to watch.

During one of these operations I became totally overwhelmed, and I fainted. I am embarrassed to reveal this, but I couldn't help it. The smell of ether and blood, and seeing such a small child receiving such intense surgery, well I couldn't stand it. I had never seen anything like it in all my life.

After living such a protected existence these images were quite a shock to me. I was still desperate to prove myself, and very willing to help, but this was a particularly difficult experience. On that first occasion my fainting was not treated as a big deal, and the nurses took me someplace to rest, suggesting that I wait before I tried to assist again. They told me that I only needed to become accustomed to viewing surgeries. But seeing human beings get cut up continued to affect me. I fainted several times in the operating room after that, until eventually the nuns decided that I should take a break from that sort of work.

My mother saw less of me at home once I got a job at the hospital. I had to leave in the early morning in order to make it to the hospital in time for my shift. I quietly washed up and dressed at four every morning and slipped out of the house so as not to disturb her. All this time she was still in the dark about my job. I would eat a little toast and then head out for my two-hour walk to work.

The hospital was quite far away and none of the trams were working. The recent bombing had destroyed most of the city's transportation and so everybody was walking. In the beginning I managed to arrive home at a decent hour every day, and in this way my mother didn't suspect much. I really had a lot of nerve to keep my work from her, and I wondered how much longer I could avoid telling Mama what I was doing. She finally became suspicious and asked me directly where I was going every day. When I told her that I had found a job she just cried and cried. My mother said that it was unnecessary for me to work so hard, and that I certainly didn't need such a horrible job. I tried to settle her down, but I told her that I was determined to keep working.

"Mama," I asked, "do you want the Russians to send me to Siberia for being a useless capitalist? I need to work and we all need the documents that prove we are working. We are not the same Grütz family that we once were! The sooner we all realize that things are different the better it will be for us!"

What could she do but let me leave every morning? Now, however, she made certain I had a little more to eat in the morning. It felt good to have a job to go to every day, and I enjoyed working on the children's ward. One day I met a little girl who was scheduled for an appendectomy. She was quite young, only about eleven or twelve years old. The nuns warned me that after her operation she must not have anything to drink, even though she would be very thirsty.

Well, after her surgery the poor thing was calling to me over and over for something to relieve her very dry mouth. "No," I told her, "you're not allowed to have anything because you've just had an operation." She was sedated and really didn't understand what I was saying to her. I couldn't bear to hear her crying, so finally I thought perhaps it would be all right to just wet a little piece of cotton and put it on her tongue. That way her throat wouldn't feel so dry and it would ease her suffering a little bit. Unfortunately the little bit of moisture I gave her only made her cry for more. I begged the girl to try and sleep. "I'm sorry," I told her, "but I'm not allowed to give you any water at all." It was horrible. I was too afraid to go to the nuns about the situation because I didn't want them to think that I was questioning their very specific instructions.

Eventually it was time for me to go home, and I hoped that the girl would fall asleep from exhaustion. I told myself that she would be okay. I was working the evening shift for a change and had been there since six o'clock, so I left for home at four a.m. The next day I came to work and went to her bed first thing. I wanted to know how she was doing, but her bed was empty! The mattress was turned down and she was gone. In a panic I and ran out to look for her in the other rooms. My heart beat in my chest like a drum as I wondered what might have happened to her. I finally found one of the nuns who knew what had happened. She told me that the girl died during the night!

I blamed myself for giving her the little napkin of water to suck on. I thought that this was what killed her and her death was entirely my fault.

I decided to confess to the Mother Superior about what I had done. I went to her with shaky legs. This was the first time I had ever had to deal directly with death. I had never personally known someone who had died, and I didn't know how to take it.

The Reverend Mother listened to my confession, and then patiently told me that the girl had died of complications and that it had nothing to do with me or my work. This made me feel a little bit better, and I began to wonder if maybe I had done a good thing after all. At least that bit of water I gave her meant that she was able to have some comfort before she died.

Still, so much had happened to me that year and I was emotionally ragged. I felt confused and shaken when I went home, and I cried in secret. This experience really affected me because for the first time in my life I felt so close to the circumstances of death. How could I know that, as the war continued, I would become much more acquainted with tragedies far worse than this?

———

I soon began to realize that, to the Russians, my position at the hospital was a temporary one. After I fainted in surgery the Russian doctor in charge told the nuns he didn't want me in the operating room at all anymore. I had only been working at the hospital a few months, but I sensed that I may have to look for another job very soon. The Russian doctors had a lot of influence in the hospital, and they were replacing everybody one by one with their own people. It was just a matter of time before I was asked to leave. Besides this my mother was constantly after me to give up work entirely, or at least to find work closer to home, so it was just as well that I re-evaluated my situation.

Mama was right about one thing. Working at the hospital was taking its toll on me.

IT WAS NOW BECOMING quite clear to Nina that not only were her days under Soviet employment numbered, but her father's were as well. Viktor Grütz was only useful to the new regime as a temporary worker. Once the staff of the Russian army was installed and sufficiently trained, Nina's father became nothing but a reminder of Poland's "decadent" past. His situation was not unique. A growing number of government and factory workers were dismissed as the Soviets gained control of Polish infrastructure.[9]

Nina faced one of her darkest days of the war in February of 1940.

The number of Russian workers at our hospital was beginning to grow, so I started to diligently investigate other job opportunities. By this time my father was no longer managing his factory. He worked for a time as one of the workers, but he soon lost this position as well. One night a number of Russian officers came to visit him at home. This group acted as the Gestapo later would, but they were called by the Russian name of Ennkawuda.

Most Poles knew them as secret military police. One could tell who they were by the uniforms they wore. These officers decided to arrest my father, though on what basis I will never really know. Most people were afraid to even ask such questions. When they came to our home that night, however, I certainly wanted to know why they were taking my father from me. I suppose I put up quite a fuss. I cried and screamed at them, yelling, "No, no, don't take my father! What has he done that you would take him? He's done nothing but help you!"

My mother was petrified as the man in charge told me, "If you aren't quiet we'll take you too!" Upon hearing this Mama tried to silence me, but I pulled away, telling her, "I'm not going to be quiet while they take my father away! He didn't do anything wrong!" I was screaming so loudly that finally Mama had to put her hands over my mouth. I think now that if she had not done this I would have been taken away to prison along with my father.

We stood in the cold in only our bathrobes while they took my father away. As the Ennkawuda threw him into a car they yelled some ridiculous charge about how he had not treated his workers well. They claimed that as a capitalist he automatically took advantage of these workers, and they called my father a dishonest businessman. We later learned of the jail where father was held. It was a very difficult place in which to live. If a prisoner didn't answer "Yes" to the Soviets' accusations they would put him away without food or other necessities until he got it right. Each department of the Russian police had their own little methods of doing this.

NINA AND HER FAMILY were living under a police state in which they were considered not only minorities but social outcasts as well. The brutal "Russification" of eastern Poland would be complete only with the removal of those considered offensive to the Communist system. Reliable Soviets replaced the bourgeoisie in both business and home. This transfer of power included "widespread systematic arrests" beginning February 8, 1940.[10]

Nina's father had, for the time being, escaped deportation to the Soviet interior. The chances of his survival in prison were another matter.

For us there was no warning, no charges, and no information about what they would ultimately do to my father. I had a hard time just standing around while he starved in prison, so I decided to make up a petition that stated he had been a fair employer and had treated his workers well. My father's employees liked him very much, and they all signed this petition without question, though the whole idea frightened my mother out of her wits.

I brought this petition to the prison, but the Russian officer in charge just glanced at it, and then threw it in the trash. When I saw how futile telling the truth was I wanted to cry and ask to stay with my father in his cell. I asked the Russian major who was staying in our apartment what I should do. He felt sorry for my mother and I, and he tried to help, but there was little he could do. He did manage to find a way into the prison where they kept my poor father, and through his connections we were able to send occasional packages of provisions. In this manner we were able to help him to survive and lift his spirits. I even had the nerve to ask the major if he could bring a little proof that my father was well. I said to him, "Please, if it's possible, could you just have my father sign his name on a little piece of paper so that I know he's okay? Then I would also know that he got his package."

The major was a little put out when he heard this and said, "I told you that I would see to it he received these things. Don't you trust me?"

"We trust you, wholeheartedly," I explained to him, "but these things go from your hands to another's hands, and we don't trust the people in the prison. We also have no real contact with my father, and it would mean so much to us if we could just see a note from him." In a way, I suppose this would be like having a small connection between us. Seeing my father's handwriting became proof to me that he was alive. Surprisingly enough, the major managed even this for a while.

We sent Daddy any little thing we could; a piece of soap, or some scrap we could find for him to eat. We dreamed that our small measures were allowing him to stay healthy and provided some small comfort. Every now and then the major returned with notes from my father for me, but soon he couldn't even obtain these. We lost contact with him entirely, and we learned only that he had been moved from the prison in L'vov to God knows where.

We knew that what they said about communism being fair to everybody wasn't true. It never made sense to us that a person who worked very little could have the same things as a person who worked very hard. Hard work and ingenuity were what paid off in the real world. We believed that anyone who worked harder deserved the advantages and responsibilities that went along with their efforts. It was only logical that everyone should work to his own capability. With enough perseverance most anybody could achieve a decent life and pursue whatever they dreamed. What the Communists told us about everyone being equal certainly didn't mean equality to us; it just seemed unfair.

Anyway, the Russians were calling the shots now and we had to follow their rules. We had no choice other than protesting, and as I said, this could easily get a person shipped off to Siberia. I now believe that my father was sent away simply because he was a wealthy businessman. It didn't really matter that he treated his workers well and that they loved him. The Russians ignored the voices of my father's workers, and they sent a good man away to what we assumed would be hard labor.

It was very hard not to hate all Russians after this. But soon we had our own survival issues. A lot of other people were going hungry at this time, so we all just tried to adjust. Even before the Germans came I instinctively became aware that I should become invisible to the enemy. The Russians didn't care that we were Jews, but they certainly did mind that we were capitalists. I did everything possible to blend in once the war started. The last thing I wanted was to be ostentatious. My father had been put in jail for his wealth, so why would I want to complain about all we had lost? They were just material things, after all.

I learned to adapt to these changes, and this new way of dealing with things really stuck. I learned not to stand out, doing my best to keep to myself and to remain very guarded. I carried on with this attitude for the remainder of the war. Even afterwards when I came to America I remained something of a loner. This was simply the manner in which I protected myself, and I must admit that the habit has never entirely gone away. Holding back is one way of dealing with trauma.

But what I would like readers, especially young readers, to come away with, is that even though I had lived a privileged childhood, I was able to persevere and survive poverty as a teenager. I really want young people to understand that a person can do anything if they have a strong character. I would never want someone to end up as frightened and careful as I was, of course. This was what the war did to me. But I am proud of the fact that I ultimately survived such an experience.

MASS ARRESTS of those deemed undesirable by the Russians often included entire families. Detainees were rarely granted even the illusion of a trial, and ultimately faced deportation. It was not unusual for the condemned's family to be arrested during the night in order to accompany him on the long journey to Siberia.[11]

The survival tactic of "becoming invisible" would benefit Nina later during the German occupation. Under Soviet control, however, this strategy could only last so long. Nina would have to devise an alternative plan if she and her family were to survive.

It wasn't long after they took my father that I decided I would stop going to the hospital for work. I could see the writing on the wall, and by the middle of winter there were more Russian doctors and nurses arriving to take over.

The whole city was full of workers from the Soviet Union. At first I thought I might be able to keep my job if I spoke Russian. I was still young, so I could pick up a little of the language even though I had not yet taken a course in it. I learned a little bit from the Russian officer who was living in our apartment. As ever he was helpful to my mother and me. But I couldn't really have a full conversation in Russian, and I certainly didn't know any medical terms in that language. I began to feel very strongly that there wasn't a place for me in the hospital anymore. The Russian nurses were more strict and demanding than the nuns, and the Russian doctors had no tolerance for us Poles at all. I left before they could kick me out.

For some reason I got it into my head that I would take a statistics course. I don't know what made me decide this, because I never liked mathematics. I still hate dealing with numbers. I vaguely recall finding a brochure about this kind of work after hearing people in town talking about it. They mentioned how the Russians needed people with mathematical skills, so I figured why not? I knew that I would have a real problem with the math, but I signed up for the course anyway thinking that I had nothing to lose. I had no choice but to find the best job possible so that I would be considered somewhat valuable to the Russians. I took the statistics course and hoped for the best.

The instructors told everyone in class that while we were taking this course we would already be receiving assignments and information that could lead to future work. They encouraged us to learn their new system. It was called *Piacilatka*, and it was used to evaluate local business. The plan was to prepare for running these businesses based on their numbers. Apparently this was why the statistical training was so important. The Soviets wanted to know exactly what to expect, and how to plan economically five years ahead of time.

It was all very intense, but I finished the course. To this day I don't know how I made it through the examination. Along with the statistics I also took a course in the Russian language. This language was very difficult for me. For one thing the alphabet was completely different! Still, I was pretty motivated, and I managed to study enough to pass this course as well. I honestly believe that I was only able to succeed in these subjects because I knew it would be important for me to find a more permanent and secure job. Whatever the reason, I was successful and was soon accepted into a job using statistics.

The firm that hired me was run by the Soviet government and was responsible for evaluating the worth of all local eating establishments. They would then reorganize them according to Soviet standards. We had to count, for instance, how many restaurants were in our town and put them into categories from the level of little cafés all the way up to the fancy places where people went for a luxurious meal.

It wasn't like today where one has access to a million fast-food places. In Poland we had only very specific establishments where people dined. The job of my firm was not to run these places, but to determine how many people it would take to manage a particular business. In this way the Russians could adjust things to the Communist system. Organizing work into fair portions was very important to the Soviet government. We had to keep books that listed every piece of information, and we gathered this information by going "into the field."

One of my duties was to go from one place to another and ask how many people were employed there and for what purpose. Slowly but surely all of these places that were privately owned were then placed into the hands of the Russian government. The Russians then decided for themselves how many workers were truly needed, and the business was run by Soviet standards. If it was determined that only a small number of people were needed, then people lost their jobs and that was that.

Even our own team of workers was stretched thin. I remember that I was the only woman working there at the time. The rest of the workers were male bookkeepers and attorneys. Most of them were old enough to be my father, and as I recall there was only one unmarried man there. Quite a few of the men were Jewish, so I was treated like a daughter by all of them. They were all successful in their fields and very bright. Of course, I didn't understand much of what they were asking me to do. Every day I would come in, say "good morning" in Russian, and then ask, "Who is going to help me today? If there isn't anyone available I cannot keep my job!" You see I didn't waste any time asking for help. I was pretty desperate.

FINDING WORK meant finding salvation to Poles like Nina. With her father languishing in some unknown prison, and two other family members either unwilling or unable to work, the pressure was on her to provide both a living as well as a sort of alibi for the family's continued residence in L'vov. Author Don Levin noted: "The most desperate job-hunters were persons who had reason to fear because of their previous political or social positions. For them, a job would both confirm their rehabilitation and provide an 'insurance policy.'"[12]

Though clearly in over her head, Nina had improved her chances of keeping her position. By learning the Russian language well enough to communicate statistical information she proved herself capable. Her talent for quickly learning foreign languages proved to be an asset, and her strong work ethic endeared her to her co-workers. Through sheer will and determination, the daughter of a capitalist factory owner had found employment directly within the new Communist government.

Intent on establishing a society based on Communist ideals, the Soviets occupying eastern Poland set about the task of collecting information regarding Polish resources. The imminent need to gather such information created temporary positions for locals like Nina who were desperate for employment. Still, the possibility of being discovered as the daughter of a capitalist made Nina's employment tentative.

According to author Ben-Cion Pinchuk, who studied Shtetl Jews under Soviet rule during World War II, the Soviet economic system in Poland was quickly put in place: "Nationalization, at the beginning of Soviet rule, meant the confiscation of banks, larger factories, larger estates and houses… The owners of the larger fortunes were not yet deported, or arrested, or transferred to other places in the annexed territories. In many enterprises the former owners were asked to remain in a managing or advisory capacity... The massive arrival of technical and administrative personnel from the East and the removal from managerial positions of former owners indicated that an effort was being made towards economic Sovietizaton. To find a job was not that easy in the former Polish provinces, particularly for the large numbers of middle and lower-middle-class Jews. Finding a job and earning a living, which were not necessarily identical, meant adjusting to the emerging Soviet regime. What made the situation worse was the inability to escape one's class origin. It stuck to one by being included in the passport and was also transferred automatically to the children… It was a vicious circle of being punished for your past and being prevented from changing it."[13]

Determined to keep her job, Nina did all she could to present herself as the model citizen of a now Soviet-ruled Poland.

I eventually learned to speak Russian well enough to get by. It never became an easy language for me, but I knew it was necessary to at least try and understand the way my Russian bosses wanted things done. I learned that *Piacilatka* meant "gathering information five years in advance." It was a program that involved a huge amount of detailed figuring, and we followed the same procedures for any café or restaurant and even for hotels.

Everything was done with numbers, and there were many days that I had no idea of what I was supposed to be accomplishing. But at least I was useful in the eyes of the Russians. I think that a lot of my co-workers felt sorry for me, because when I asked for help they never seemed to mind. Some mornings I didn't even know how to start a particular project, and these men would have to patiently explain what I probably should have known already. Well, how could they say no to me when I begged them for help?

What I really preferred to the office work was going into the field to collect information. Whenever somebody had to do this sort of assignment I asked to come along and assist. I knew that I was good at taking notes, and I soon proved this after going out a few times with one of the men. The fieldwork allowed me to get out into the fresh air and avoid the endless figures back at the office.

Maybe this was what got me through each day without getting myself fired. As time went on I became more comfortable in my position. I stayed there for many months, until the Germans came.

The winter was upon us and the war continued, with the Russians still in control. We began to hear less word of my father and eventually even the major couldn't help us any longer.

The Russians were very unyielding about many things. They were trying to establish themselves as occupiers, I suppose, and they imposed a tremendous amount of rules on us. I am of the opinion that the Soviets did this because so many Poles were against communism. A lot of Poles claimed that every one of us Jews were pro-Communist, but of course this was not entirely true. We were also doing our best to do exactly as we were told. Nothing we did seemed to help, however. Eventually, we began to wonder if my father was still alive. There was no way of knowing, of course. It wasn't as if you could hire a lawyer to plead your case to the Russians. As far as they were concerned my father was an enemy prisoner of war, a political prisoner.

My sisters were broken up over the situation as well. They tried hard not to show it to me, but I knew that my sisters and their husbands worried about Daddy day and night. We heard that the Germans were pushing into Russian territory, and that whenever they took over an area they immediately shot everybody in the prisons. These were the kind of dreaded rumors we had to live with throughout the Soviet occupation.

Lina and Helena tried to adapt just as I had, but their whole lifestyle had changed practically overnight. Both of my sisters' husbands had been very successful before the war. They had set up beautiful homes and had enjoyed a wonderful life of plenty. My sisters had always employed steady domestic help, and they were both living as society ladies before the Russians came. Suddenly everything changed and life became nothing but hardship. Things were different for everybody. With the Russians came a different set of rules and an entirely different philosophy about how one should live. We could never have imagined that there would be still more pain and hardship to come. We were only aware of our daily struggle to find food.

One thing we were thankful for was that, except for the loss of my father, we had at least managed to stay together. Some families had not been as fortunate. For the time being it seemed that all the Russians really wanted from us was to work and accept their government.

Now I should explain a little bit about my two sisters. My middle sister had hair that was lighter than Lina's and mine, but that wasn't the only difference between us. She really didn't have the same personality that we did. What I'm trying to say is that she handled things differently and not always in a better way. When the Second World War broke out I felt right away that everything was changing, and I tried to accept it as did Lina.

But Helena could never completely understand that her life had changed. She was lost in many ways. I constantly told her, "Helena, you need to find work. Even if you're married, the Russians expect you to contribute to their system. Women in Russia work just like men in all different positions. Go to school and learn the Russian language." I was always telling her, "Get something steady! You have to prove that you can be useful." My sister eventually did obtain a little job here and there, but ultimately these positions were never really considered steady work.

Helena didn't know how to work at anything consistently. She had always been that way even when we were young. I kept begging her to try and be productive, and I knew it would be good for her to take her mind off things. I tried to explain to her that it was dangerous to look unproductive in front of our Soviet occupiers. Though I was much younger than she, I knew finding work was crucial if she were to escape deportation to Siberia. We were, after all, the family of a well-known capitalist, and certainly the Russians could arrest us all if they liked.

My older sister had a better grasp of things. She let go her staff because she and her husband could no longer afford help. The Russians would not have permitted her to keep any of her servants anyway. Because my brother-in-law was one of the most respected doctors in the city he had also been one of the highest paid. He was even known to doctors in Warsaw, and as a heart specialist he was often sought out for consultation. He was even the first physician who privately offered diagnosis with an electrocardiogram! This new machine was already in some hospitals and in one or two clinics, but privately he was the first doctor who would operate this machine.

The EKG didn't work like it does today. Now when it is used in a doctor's office the results are available right away. This was not the case in the 1930s. A physician who was well-trained to operate and read the results of this machine had to go into a darkroom and develop the images like one would a photograph in those days.

The reason I know this is because I often helped my brother-in-law to do it. I only handed him things he needed, but I used to love helping in the darkroom. A doctor really had to know his stuff to read the EKG results properly, and at this my brother-in-law was one of the best. I'm sure that he didn't really need me to assist him, but he was always very good about letting me help.

I loved and respected Lina's husband. Just about everybody who knew Bernard felt the same way. As his wife, Lina was given the same kind of respect, so she felt a responsibility to help others in our community.

All of this prestige and privilege changed the minute the Russians came, however. Suddenly my brother-in-law's education didn't seem to mean as much. The Poles who knew him still held him in high esteem, but the Russians wanted to bring in their own doctors, and they wanted to do things their own way. Besides this, the Russians seemed a little jealous of his knowledge of the EKG machine. They intentionally made life difficult for Bernard and my sister, but they managed to avoid arrest.

Unlike Helena, my older sister knew things were different under Soviet rule and that she would have to be flexible. She once told Mama, "I have to be realistic. Since I am no longer able to keep a maid or nanny I'll simply do things myself." One must understand that it wasn't so much the money that we felt was a loss to us. It was more the freedom to pursue a life that was the least bit familiar to us. My brother-in-law, Buzio, would still receive visits from the local Poles seeking medical help, but he had to care for them quietly. Everyone by then was desperately poor but my brother-in-law would still provide help for anyone who asked.

Besides being an excellent doctor, Buzio had a very big heart. He would say to these people who could not pay, "I am a doctor, not a businessman. The first thing I must do is to cure you." Naturally he had to make a living in some way. He had a family to feed, and when food could be found it was always expensive. But to Buzio that wasn't the point. Working out some kind of payment or trade could come later.

Trade was really the only way to pay for things anyway. This was how things worked during the war, and whenever Buzio's patients could they would pass along things they either grew or traded for themselves. This worked out well, and my brother-in-law appreciated the eggs, flour or potatoes patients gave him. Once he even got a chicken! Another time we received two big cans of milk. All of this meant more to us than money. Meanwhile, my sister Helena and her husband were really struggling. My middle sister couldn't keep a job and this meant that her husband had to take on most of the responsibility for their survival. Helena never quite grasped the new rules imposed on us by the Soviet government. This caused her a lot of anguish and her husband a lot of concern.

UNDER SOVIET RULE, pre-war Poles who had enjoyed a professional status now found the worth of higher education depleted, while those having practical skills were in greater demand. This meant that, although Helena's husband, Leopold, who was a lawyer, could count on much less of an income, Lina's Buzio could at the very least be assured of some economic stability. He continued to see patients in private, collecting fees in the way of food and other now-precious materials. For her part, Nina focused on her work in the statistical agency, and hoped for the best.

During this time we knew very little about the progress of the war. We didn't have contact with the outside world, so the only way to keep up with the news was to try receiving something on the radio. We assumed that the Russians were going to stay for some time. I personally didn't have a moment to worry about it because I was working so much. Whenever I had some spare time I shared it with Lina and Buzio and their little five-year-old girl Alma.

My niece was a beautiful little bundle of joy with big, blue eyes. She was always happy and smiling, and I played with her whenever possible. I tried not to listen to the frightening rumors circulating around L'vov, but we began to hear more and more of arrests. Anybody taken away for being a capitalist had their entire family threatened as well. My mother never knew when they might come for her or even for me. My sisters had different last names, so they were relatively safe for the time being.

Because the situation was getting worse, my mother and I debated over what we should do to avoid arrest. We finally acted when our friend the Russian major suggested it would be better to move somewhere the Soviet secret police couldn't immediately find us. It was decided we would move our few things out entirely and separate. Everything was so mixed up and out of control, and by this time we were all becoming a little paranoid. We simply decided to fly by the seat of our pants. We would make a decision and think, "Well, maybe we will find some relief this way or that way." So we left our tiny room in the building that had been home since before the war. At least this way if the Russians decided to come for my mother and me we would be harder to find.

We didn't wish to endanger Lina or Helena by staying with them, so that idea was out. There were other relatives who were not as easily linked to us, so my mother frantically asked around this group to see who we could stay with. To be honest, I was so busy working that I barely had time to pay attention to what was going on around me. I didn't really care where I stayed, but one day I came home to my mother and the decision had been made.

Mama would stay with relatives in a completely different town. In the meantime I would stay at my aunt Mialcia's home that was not too far away. Lina asked that I occasionally stay a night or two with her just to stay in touch. My mother had recently experienced trouble with her gall bladder, so she would need some care wherever she went. Because of this she would be staying with my cousin, Doctor Roth, who was married to a nice woman named Lucia. Lucia's mother was also living with them but they assured my mother they could make room for one more.

The whole idea was to spread out so that the Russians couldn't find us. I thought that perhaps the Russian secret police were not yet interested in arresting me, and I had my job gathering and processing information for the government, so I was able to convince my mother I could safely stay in L'vov.

I didn't want to be separated from Mama, but it seemed to make sense to move apart for the time being. It was certainly pointless to stay in our apartment building without any hope of hearing from my father. By now we doubted we would ever see him again. I presumed the worst, and I had to come to terms with it. Siberia was a very difficult place to live, and they worked people quite hard there, so it was almost impossible to get by for very long. He was middle-aged, and before the war broke out he was under a doctor's care for diabetes. If he had not been arrested by the Russians he might have fooled the Nazis into thinking he was a regular Pole. He didn't look Jewish at all. Maybe he could have acquired a different identity and hidden as I did. Polish people and especially Ukrainians could somehow tell if someone was Jewish, but I think my father might have been able to fool them. He spoke very good Polish and German, so who knows. It seemed that everything in our lives was unknown, a huge question mark. It was a terrible feeling, but there was nothing we could do about it.

The pay was not bad at my new job, but I couldn't buy much because most of the things we really needed had already been rationed with the Russian military given priority. I worked at my statistical job while moving between my aunt's and my sister's place. I would also occasionally stay at a friend's house, so I felt as if I had enough safe places in which to sleep at night.

Even so, it was the first time that I didn't have an actual address, and I walked around town not really knowing where I belonged. I tried to look at the positive things I had. I was young, and I had a good job at a place where I was treated like everyone's daughter. I felt relatively secure in my position, and in addition to having a steady job I really liked my aunt. I stayed at her apartment most of the time and she made me feel very welcome. She was such a lady, and a respected elder in our family. My aunt was the one whose family had a store selling perfumes and ladies' gloves. Things such as these usually sold at high prices and my aunt lived well until the Russians came. By the time I moved in with her she was struggling like the rest of us. I often thought that my aunt resembled the Queen Mother of England. The way she looked and carried herself was so refined.

Auntie took great care of me and treated me very well. During this time there were other things to be thankful for as well. It was difficult to find food, but we weren't starving. To pay for things that were obtainable we could rely on my brother-in-law. Somehow Buzio was eventually able to find work in the local hospital. The Russians began to respect his work as a doctor, so there was less worry of arrest for my sister.

Our lives were nothing like before, of course. One could never compare the way we used to live to how we lived with the Russians in control. But we heard things were far worse on the western side of Poland. It was rumored that the Germans were arresting or killing Jews left and right. At least in L'vov people weren't trying to shoot us. By the summer of 1941, however, more changes were coming.

RESOURCES WERE indeed becoming increasingly scarce under the Soviet regime. Economic hardship was felt by many Poles as early as December of 1939, when the Polish currency or "zloty" was replaced with the Russian ruble at a reduced exchange rate. This event, coupled with a reduced access to supplies, goods, and raw materials, caused a rush on the few resources still available.[14]

While struggling with her aunt to make ends meet, Nina looked forward to the day of a promised company picnic.

I'll never forget that Sunday. I was supposed to join my co-workers for a picnic. I learned about the picnic from one of my bosses. Every year he was supposed to make up an evaluation of everybody's work hours, and the Thursday before our company picnic I was instructed to count up all the people and their hours. Unfortunately by the end of the day I was missing, of all things, half a person! How I managed to come up with only half a person I don't know, but I was very worried about it.

Some of the other workers were trying to help me find the missing hours, and the report had to be done for the next day. I was concerned that my error would keep me from the picnic, and I became so frustrated that I started to cry. This young attorney came over to help me, and he very nicely gave me a lot of his time that day to do so. He was one of the men who took me out in the field to work. Even with this nice attorney helping me I was getting nowhere, and it seemed I would lose my job over the statistics I so hated. It was driving me crazy, and I was so afraid that I would lose my position over my mistake. To make matters worse it was getting late, and I still didn't exactly know where I would be sleeping that night.

This young man seemed determined to help me figure out where the half-person was. He was very soft-spoken, but he was also a confident lawyer. So when he said to me, "The missing hours have to be here somewhere," I knew that he must be right. He suggested, "When the office closes at five o'clock, make believe that you're leaving, then come back and I'll let you in with my key. We'll work on the numbers until they're right so that you don't get fired."

I did as he told me and we pored over the figures for the longest time. Oh, how I grew tired of looking at endless columns of numbers. We were there for practically the whole night! There were so many figures that I almost went blind from searching them over. By one o'clock in the morning I was ready to give up. I cried, "Forget it! I don't care anymore if they fire me." But this young man just told me to go get some cold water and rest my eyes, then come back to work some more.

Sure enough, by early morning we found the mistake. It had been entered incorrectly in one of the yearly books. Because we found the problem I was able to go home and get a little sleep. When the department picnic came around that weekend this nice young man who had helped me said, "I want you to go with me to the picnic. You deserve a break." I remember that his name was Shimon Kerner, and even though I considered Shimon just a friend I was very pleased to be going with him. He was a great boss and a good human being. Much later I thought that I would have liked to run into him after the war.

I was excited about the picnic and that night I tried to decide what I would wear to the event. I was still a young girl and I looked forward to finally having a social outing. I was still full of life, and I thought it would feel good to smile at a young man who might joke around with me and perhaps even ask me to dance. I suppose with my mother away I felt a little more independent and free. I was also able to behave more like a young girl and think less of the bad things in my life. In spite of all the hardships we suffered, it seemed to me as if the world was going ahead at full speed.

I knew that I had to work hard and keep an open mind if I was to survive. I was thankful that the people I worked for had not discovered my father was a capitalist, because in spite of what seemed like a secure position I think they would have fired me if they knew about him. I was determined to act like everyone else, and I felt that if I didn't at least attempt to put a smile on my face they might have wondered what was wrong with me.

This marked the beginning of my pretending to be someone I was not, and I continued this strategy throughout the war. For the time being I really appreciated my job and I would have done anything to stay there. All of this was going through my mind on Saturday night. As I fell asleep I thought of how nice it would be to relax with the people I worked with, but the day of the picnic never came.

THE MOLOTOV-RIBBENTROP PACT signed between Russia and Germany in August of 1939 officially disintegrated early in the morning of June 22, 1941. Begun by Hitler as a way of buying time until his armies gained a foothold in the West, the Führer was now eager to push eastward with an eye on Soviet resources.

In spite of intelligence warning of Hitler's ambitions, this aggressive move took Stalin by surprise. What had been an attempt to secure his own borders and obtain land in the East, including the Baltic States, now became a disastrous alliance with the devil himself.[15] While the Russian armies scurried toward Romania, the citizens of eastern Poland awaited their next fate.

At four o'clock Sunday morning, June 22nd, 1941 the bombing started. I was staying with my aunt, and when I woke up I didn't know what was going on. Then I remembered that only about a year and a half ago we had heard the same kind of commotion. I suppose that we all wanted to pretend that this first bombing had never happened, and now here it was coming back.

And who was it coming? Well, by now we knew very well the Germans were certainly making their way toward us. During the entire Soviet occupation we had only rumors to go by concerning the outside world. We managed only a sketchy idea about what was going on with the Germans and the rest of Europe. It was a sudden and crushing blow to hear the Germans were taking over the rest of Poland. It was a surprise not only for us Poles, but also for the Russians. They began to scurry away almost immediately, and I saw this occur the very first day of German bombing.

Usually my aunt made sure that I had a little coffee and bread for breakfast the days I went to work. But that morning when we heard the bombs we fled from our beds without a thought of food or anything else. All we had time to do was to run. We didn't even bother going to the cellar as we had when the Russians came. After experiencing that hell for three straight weeks I was in no mood to head down below a crumbling apartment building again. My family was so scattered that we wouldn't have known which cellar to dive into anyway. My aunt and I didn't want to be in her cellar alone, and my sisters' homes were too far away. Who knew where Mama was during the bombing? We could only hope she was all right with Lucia and her family.

The noise was terrifying, just as it had been when the Russians came. I remember praying, "Dear God, if I'm going to die then take me quickly." I didn't want to be like the people who became wounded by shrapnel. Some of them were in such shock that they simply wandered around in a daze even in the midst of this bombing. Those who were badly injured just lay on the ground dying. They cried for help, but nobody would assist them or even comfort them as they died. People were very busy hiding and trying to save their own families.

As I explained, up to this point we had only learned in bits and pieces about the war going on in the west. Now it appeared the Germans would ignore their pact with the Soviets and would begin to turn on Russia as well.

The transition from Soviet to German takeover was what you would call surreal. There was such chaos with Russian soldiers and workers running here and there like crazy. It was unbelievable to me that it took little more than a week for the Russians to become entrenched in our city, and now they were leaving Poland in a matter of days. Even some Poles were trying to find a way out. The Russian Jews were in a particular hurry to leave because they knew what would happen if they stuck around.

As for us, we still couldn't quite believe the rumors about what the

Nazis were doing to Jews. Anyway, we had little time to think of anything because there was terrible panic all around. Some people escaping the city were even stealing horses from the outlying countryside just to reach the east as fast as possible. It seemed like the whole world was running.

A CONTEMPORARY OF NINA'S by the name of Leon Wells wrote of his own experience with the Soviet exodus. A young resident of L'vov, Wells recalled the chaos during transference of power from Russian to German control: "At two o'clock in the morning, the hours of uncertainty have come to an end. Radio Moscow brings the numbing announcement that, during the night, the Germans have crossed the border and invaded Russia. At two o'clock in the afternoon, L'vov was bombed. When evening came no one dared set foot outside his own house. We lay on the sofa, still fully dressed. Then the air-raid sirens sound again. All dash to the air-raid shelter: the earth is already trembling. The light goes out. The windowpanes burst asunder. The doorframes are blown out. A bomb has fallen on the street directly outside our house. So passes the first night of war." [16]

The Russian major living in our apartment tracked me down and offered to take me east. He told me it was very important for my family to escape the Nazis. He was a high-ranking officer and had his own responsibilities and concerns, yet his first thought was to help us! I was so grateful that he wanted to take us with him. He had a wife and children of his own to think about back in Russia, for goodness' sake, but he wished to help, and he assured me that I would be welcome in his home. He was very convincing, advising me very strongly to get out of Poland.

"Come with me," he said, "and I promise you that with my family you will be safe!" I wanted to go, but my mother was in the next town. There would not be enough time to find her and accompany us to the border. If she could have come along I would have gone with that officer that very minute.

When I look back on it I always think of how kind a gesture this was. Here he was a high-ranking Soviet and not even Jewish, yet he cared for us. But as I said, my mother would have been left behind, so I would not go. The officer waited for as long as he could. He knew that the Germans were coming in a matter of days, and he was cutting it close. He told me that he was concerned about my mother, but if she could not come he wanted to at least save me. "Look," he explained, "the Germans hate Jews. Save yourself now and perhaps we can send for the rest of your family later." I appreciated his efforts, but I knew once I was in Russia it would be impossible to send for my family. I told him no, and that I couldn't leave my mother. We had already been separated once, and I didn't want to be apart from her now when she would be enduring such a difficult time. I thanked the officer and never saw him again.

THE TRANSFERENCE FROM RUSSIAN to German power meant more to Nina than merely adjusting to different rules dictated by yet another ravenous occupying army. Advancing German forces ushered in a fresh and terrible way of life for the eastern Polish Jew. Jewish contemporary Shalom Hamiel reflected on the fear spreading throughout his community as the Germans advanced. As many Jews were aware, the Soviets truly had been the "lesser of two evils." Hamiel recalled hearing a neighbor lament as the Russian armies fled his village, "I know who the Bolsheviks are. I know they'll take my property, but they will leave me with my life."[17] Staying alive would indeed become increasingly difficult for Nina, and preserving the lives of her family impossible.

(Above) FAMILY BUSINESS
The factory building that once housed the Grütz family business (manufacturing soap and candles). This factory remains in operation, now producing mustard. Along with a number of other present-day images, this photo was obtained when Nina returned to L'vov, Poland, with daughter Carol and Dr. Harold Marcuse in 1999.

(Left) ROSA
Nina's mother, Rosa Roth-Grütz, early 1900s.

(Above) KOPERNIKA
Ten Kopernika Street, Nina's home in L'vov. The Grütz family occupied the entire second floor.

(Left) ROSA AND LINA
Rosa Grütz with eldest daughter Lina. L'vov, Poland, around 1915. Photos reproduced courtesy of Jewish Federation of Greater Santa Barbara, California, "Portraits of Survival" exhibit, August, 2006.

(ABOVE) THE MESSING FAMILY
Nina's relatives, including (upper far right to left) Aunt Erna and Uncle Leon Messing with daughter Gladys. Seated right to left are Nina's parents, Viktor Grütz and wife Rosa.

(Above) L'VOV TRAIN STATION
The train station in L'vov, Poland, where many have passed through on their way to visit the "Vienna of the East." This building, constructed in classic turn-of-the-century style, served as a gateway to the eastern metropolis that retained an aesthetic and cultural western influence.

(Above) KOPERNIKA COURTYARD
The inner courtyard within the family residence. Though badly neglected over the years of Soviet rule, the private enclave once boasted a garden and shade trees.

(Right) SOLUKI ENTRANCE
Road sign marking the entrance to Soluki, Poland, where Viktor Grütz established a productive farm and comfortable family home.

(Above) RELATIVES AND VIKTOR IN SOLUKI
Left to right, Nina's uncle Leon Messing (seated); her sister Helena's husband, Leopold Frostig (legs crossed); and her father, Viktor Grütz, on the Soluki estate, mid-1930s.

(Above) SOLUKI
The Grütz country estate where Nina played as a child. At the height of its operation the farm boasted a dairy and a mill.

(Above) PEASANTS
Nina reminisces with current residents of Soluki. The elderly lady wearing a babushka remembered Nina's father.

(Left) MILL SITE
Site of the mill owned and operated by
Viktor Grütz. This business provided timber
for the local community from the early
1920s until the start of World War II.

(Right) ALMA
Two-year-old Alma Tanne, Nina's niece (daughter of sister Lina and
brother-in-law Bernard). This photo was taken around 1938,
roughly four years before Alma and her mother disappear
and are presumed murdered by the Nazis.

(Below) LINA AND BERNARD
Wedding portrait of Nina's oldest sister, Lina, with husband
Dr. Bernard Tanne, 1931.

(Left) VOTING REGISTER
While touring L'vov in 1999, Nina searched for any existing records of the family she lost during the war. While searching the city archives with Dr. Harold Marcuse she discovered this voting register listing the names of her father, mother, and sister, Helena, (inaccurately spelled as "Hela"), when they cast their ballots in a 1929 election.

(Right) BRIDGE
This bridge in L'vov, Poland, is most likely the site of Rosa Grütz's execution in November of 1941. While en route to a Jewish cemetery to pray, Nina's mother was the victim of a Nazi round-up of Jewish children and the elderly considered unfit for labor. During these round-ups (or "Aktions"), unsuspecting Jews were simply plucked from the street, arranged into tight groups, and shot.

(Left) MEMORIAL
Memorial commemorating the souls of those Janowska prisoners who perished under the Nazi killing machine. It was here that Nina escaped execution and fled to the nearby woods.

(Right) JANOWSKA
Janowska Labor Camp, the holding area where many Jews worked and lived under horrific conditions until they were ultimately executed or transported to larger death camps. The building now serves as the L'vov prison.

MAPS — Following Pages

L'VOV ENVIRONS (page 124)

The city of L'vov in southeastern Poland. Highlighted are points of violent actions against Jewish residents from 1941-1942, and the rail system that enabled the Nazis to transport large numbers of Jews to death camps elsewhere in Poland.

LABOR CAMP MAP (page 125)

Detail of Janowska Labor Camp as it existed in the Fall of 1942. The ravine shown at the far right of the map is believed to be the site where SS and Ukrainian soldiers carried out executions, one of which Nina was able to escape.

(Maps from the book, *Historical Atlas of the Holocaust,* MacMilllan Publishing USA, is used with the permission of the U.S. Holocaust Memorial Museum, Washington, D.C.)

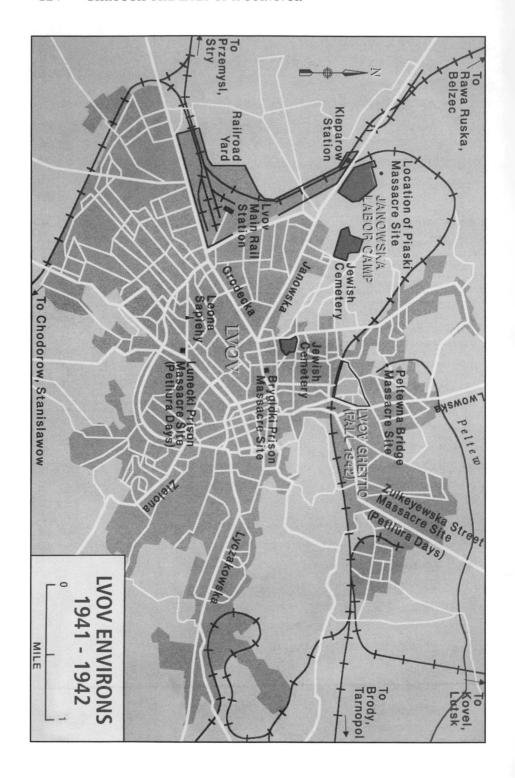

LVOV ENVIRONS
1941 - 1942

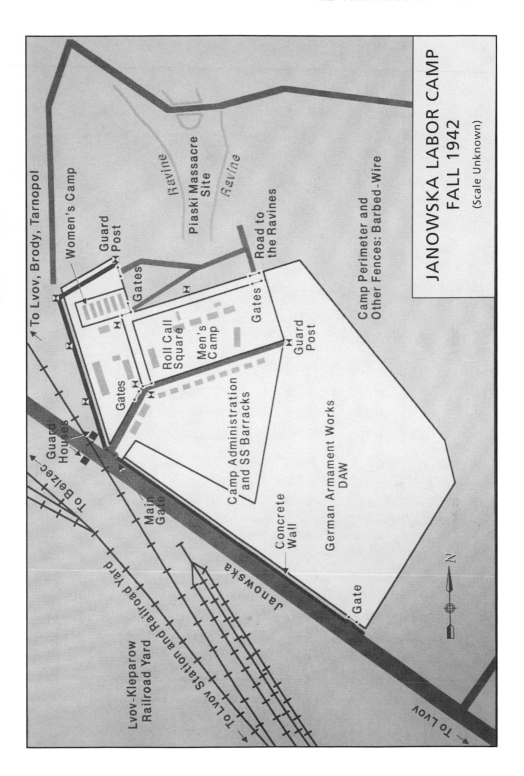

JANOWSKA LABOR CAMP
FALL 1942
(Scale Unknown)

To Lvov, Brody, Tarnopol

Women's Camp

Guard Post

Gates

Piaski Massacre Site

Ravine

Ravine

Road to the Ravines

Gates

Roll Call Square

Men's Camp

Gates

Guard Post

Camp Perimeter and Other Fences: Barbed-Wire

Gates

Guard Houses

To Belzec

Camp Administration and SS Barracks

Main Gate

Concrete Wall

German Armament Works DAW

Janowska

Gate

N

Lvov-Kleparow Railroad Yard

To Lvov Station and Railroad Yard

To Lvov

PART 2

A New Enemy

As the Russian army fled east, German aircraft continued a relentless barrage on the once Soviet-occupied Poland. This eerie changing of the guard replaced communism with fascism in the space of a mere week. Living under German rule would prove devastating for the Grütz family. Survival became a daily concern, forcing Nina to hone her skills of eluding, hiding from, and often out-smarting the Nazis.

$\mathcal{L}ife\ \mathcal{I}mpermanent$
(1941)

WITH THE BELIEF that they made too easy a target as a unit, each Grütz family member relocated to a separate location. Alone and in pairs they crept off to stay with other relatives in the country, or in discreet apartments within L'vov. As one appointed to stay within city limits, Nina slept at an auntie's place, and during the day checked in with her sister Lina who also remained in the city. By Monday, June 30, 1941, German troops were steadily marching past the astonished inhabitants of L'vov, every goosestep marking a painful change in the young Nina's life.

I was staying with Aunt Mialcia, my oldest aunt from the first marriage of my grandfather. My mother was now staying in a different city with cousin Lusia. Right after the Germans arrived, my aunt moved from her apartment to a friend's place outside the city. I understood her fear of staying in L'vov, but I didn't know where I should go, so I also decided to stay with friends.

Eventually, the bombing stopped. We went back and forth to hide in cellars for about a week's time. When it was all over we came out to see what was left of our town. This was the second time L'vov had been bombed, and in my young mind the destruction seemed even more devastating than when the Russians invaded. I was completely overwhelmed by how sad it now appeared. Everyone was looking around to see who had survived.

That was when we saw the Germans coming. I can remember as if it were yesterday. I went down to the street and watched their big tanks roll up. I can still see the soldiers in front of me, with their flashy uniforms and shiny boots. Some of them were on horses, but mostly they came in tanks. I had no definite thought of what was in store for us as I saw the Nazi army approaching, but I knew it could not be good.

For the time being the general public welcomed these Germans with open arms. Only the Jews were really frightened of them. Most of the Poles didn't want Communists to take over their country, and they would have accepted any alternative at that point. As for the Jews, to be honest, most of the Poles really didn't care what happened to us because most of them never liked us anyway.

The persistent rumor that most Jews were Communists was not true at all. We even knew some Poles who were Communists, and everyone we knew who was Jewish had been involved in business before the war. I suppose some of the Communists' ideas were good. Equality is important. But the way the Soviets tried to implement their rules for sharing was in fact corrupt. Perhaps this was why the Poles were so pleased to see the Germans.

What they didn't understand was that the Germans were only out for themselves and had no intentions of letting regular Poles live a normal life either. We later learned that Hitler was planning to force Poles into slave labor once he was done with the Jews. As more Germans were sent to fight in the war a shortage of labor would occur. Since we were to be exterminated in concentration camps, of course the Poles were to be the next work force. If you told a Pole on the street in 1941 that this was the plan, however, well they never would have believed it.

As Jews, we were the first to be affected by the German presence. We sensed trouble starting almost as soon as the Nazis showed up. Soldiers began to catch us on the street and force us to work. First they made us clean up the mess of rubble and dead bodies left over from the bombing. I have to admit I was a little tricky about getting out of those jobs. When we were ordered to clean up the bodies the smell of it got to me. This caused me to faint, and that made me pretty useless to them. Because of this I was able to avoid the work of hauling away bodies.

Under certain stressful conditions I was inclined to faint, and this came in handy on quite a few occasions during the war. It was not long before the Germans simply pulled people onto trucks and sent them away to perform hard labor. I decided on a temporarily effective technique of avoiding these trucks. When I heard the Nazi soldiers go through the streets yelling, "Raus, raus!" I just stayed in my apartment. I simply refused to rush out like everyone else. I had to be quiet about it, however, because if the Germans knew a person was avoiding work they gave double the punishment.

The Soviet soldiers had not been quite this bad. With the Russians, as bad as things got, at least I had a chance to prove myself by working. During the Russian occupation I usually had a job, and even though I had to move around a lot, I never did get arrested nor did the rest of my family. Living with the Soviets had in no way been easy. Because of them I had to give up my dream of going to university or of even having a normal life. I felt that my future had certainly been destroyed. But I came to accept that I would never enjoy the life my mother or my sisters had. In spite of these limits put on my life, things never seemed hopeless. This wasn't so with the Nazis in charge. When the Germans came to L'vov things got worse from minute to minute.

And as I said we knew right away that things would be especially bad for us Jews. Even before the war the Nazi ideology had affected us. Gentile children were told not to play with Jewish kids, and then came the ghetto benches, a very clear act of discrimination. Still we never thought the Nazis would establish something like the concentration camps. Who would have ever expected that? We only knew enough to be apprehensive about the German occupation.

From the very beginning there was a lot of bloodshed. They gave the Poles and Ukrainians the right to do with us whatever they wished. They could come to our homes and pull everyone out to beat and murder, and then move into where we had lived. The Germans did not exactly know who was Jewish and who was not, so they depended on the locals to figure it out for them. Many Jews were left dead or dying on the street those first few weeks. Nobody bothered to either save them or bury them. When the Nazis finally gave orders for the Jews themselves to carry away bodies it was clear that they only did this to prevent disease.

Since the Gentile population was temporarily in charge they had a free hand in dealing with us in any manner they chose. The hatred most of them felt toward the Jews became quite apparent. I could never really understand why the Poles and Ukrainians hated us so. It was clear that over many years Poland had become very anti-Semitic. Now there was nothing to stop our fellow countrymen from robbing, killing, or molesting us in any way. Because these crimes were committed against Jews no Pole would go to jail for assaulting us. The Germans actually put up signs stating that nobody was to assist a Jew in any way, and things became so bad we were afraid to go out for food or essentials.

Jews had experienced pogroms before, but nothing like this. It was a massacre! This went on for a week or two. We were afraid to even breathe let alone go out looking for food, so we made do with what we had in the house, which was very little by then. I suppose it didn't matter much if we had to stay home, because even if we made it safely through the streets there was not much in town to buy. Everything decent had been snatched up or ruined by the Russians, and the Germans took whatever was left after that. The stores were completely empty and everyone was slowly starving.

MANY JEWS ALTERED their strategy for survival at this time. It now seemed best to do the exact opposite of what seemed to have worked during the Soviet occupation. Desperate to maintain contact with each other, families now banded together in whatever dwelling proved the least open to attack. Crowded into small apartments to share what little food supplies were available, Jews sought to look after each other. This was by no means a guarantee of protection against those who were intent on robbing and killing Jews. Yet the tactic of staying together, come what may, provided some solace in that families were temporarily united. Conditions became worse throughout L'vov as Jewish residents crouched in anticipation of the Nazis' next move.

Leon Wells describes a situation in those first days of German control that is strikingly similar to Nina's experience: "We Jews know that hard times were in store but no one guesses what horror is ahead. Hardly anyone will venture into the streets. Now and again a solitary individual appears, his head bent, edging his way along in the shadows of the houses…Unless it's absolutely unavoidable, we too will not leave the house in the next few days. The other occupants of our house join us in our apartment. The time is passed in discussing politics and in making conjectures as to our immediate future. But not one among us can indicate with the slightest authority what our fate is to be."[1]

The Wells family also suffered under local Ukrainian forces empowered by the Nazis to round up Jews for work and the occasional beating.[2] In spite of the steady progression of violence and hardship, the Jewish population could not have imagined things would become much worse. Nina did her best to avoid the melee and recalculated her hopes of survival.

I stayed at my sister's place where things were somewhat safer. My brother-in-law still had the privilege of living in this neighborhood. I suppose the Nazis felt they needed him until he could be replaced with a German physician. As for the people staying in the Jewish neighborhoods, well they all began to sense that something terrible was going to happen. The Orthodox Jews really stood out and were very easy targets, but those who were not so obviously Jewish tried to hide who they were.

As Polish Jews we had no idea what the Germans had in store for us. Our ancestors had managed to survive by cooperating and respecting civil authority whenever possible. By obeying the law my people had, throughout time, avoided trouble. For the most part the Polish government had allowed us to live in peace. Like everyone else, we believed that if we simply complied with the authority that was temporarily in charge, then things might get better later on. We hoped to start rebuilding our lives once the war ended. This was why when the Germans called out on loudspeakers that all Jews should surrender their valuables, their diamonds, money, everything, well we just handed it all over! They collected all of our gold, silver, and jewelry, everything of worth.

CONFISCATING ALL JEWISH VALUABLES was one way in which the Nazis were able to gain a practical and psychological advantage over the Jews. By humiliating the "enemy of the German state," German troops successfully commandeered Jewish valuables with virtually no resistance from Gentile Poles. Many personal accounts corroborate Nina's painful tale of relinquishing every meaningful possession to the Nazis. In the personal narrative of Liza Chapnik, herself only a schoolgirl living in Grodno, Poland, at the time of Nazi invasion, one method of retaining a few precious items was made known: "After the Nazis occupied the cities, they issued an order directing Jews to turn over all their radios, and all gold and silver objects, to the Germans. We buried our radio, but a friend of mine, Lovka Lubich, hid his family's radio in the cellar. There we usually listened to the latest news from Moscow, sometimes from London, and we wrote down the news to distribute to others—mainly to the youth."[3] The disappearance of all material reminders of her family and their heritage riled Nina long after the war ended.

Though it was painful to give up family items that were precious to us, it is not the loss of valuables that bothers me so much now. What really angers me is that we were all stupid enough to have obeyed the Germans without putting up more of a fight. To this day, I cannot forgive myself for blindly doing as I was told in the beginning. I was the one in our family who brought all of our things to the German authorities, and I kick myself every time that I think of it! But we were hoping that, with our cooperation, the Nazis would somehow be appeased and then might leave us alone. How were we to know that the Nazis would eventually try to wipe us out completely?

Once the Nazis finished collecting our valuables they began rounding everybody up for the camps. We were completely oblivious to the fact that they had developed a system of extermination. The amount of manpower and money that went into the concentration camps with their gas chambers and crematoriums was incredible, considering they were trying to fight a war at the same time. Resources were low, but still they focused on this ridiculous project of eliminating a people because of their religion! It was an evil idea, and quite a few Poles and Ukrainians in my country seemed willing to do the labor it required.

The only thing we could do was try to hide anything of value that was left to us. We thought maybe we could bargain for our lives with the Poles who were assisting the Nazis. Some Jews managed to hide family silver, jewelry, and cash. Although family photographs did not represent any material wealth, they were emotionally valuable and so were hidden away as well.

Unfortunately, we had no plans whatsoever for escaping. It was too late for that. We felt that we had no control of our lives at all. I suppose even the non-Jewish population had their problems with the Germans at this time as well. There was even some talk about the Nazis closing down some of the schools, but really they couldn't do much in the beginning.

THE ARRIVAL OF NAZI TROOPS brought with it a sense of apathy that crept through the Jewish community of L'vov. Feeling the net of German control closing in, there was among the Jews a kind of resignation that escape would now be impossible and control over their lives was a thing of the past. In Ronnie S. Landau's *The Nazi Holocaust*, this malady could be defined as a collective melancholy brought about by the Germans' continuing assaults: "[One] factor explaining the comparative lack of resistance belongs to the realm of psychology. In the grotesque world which the Nazis created for them, Jews had to contend with the unrelenting fear, degradation, the constant loss of loved ones, and, above all, what has been termed the 'normality of death' around them. Consequently, they all too easily lapsed into a state of helplessness and paralysis, which, for most of them, made effective armed resistance a psychological impossibility."[4]

Although Nina had experienced her share of degradation at the hands of the Nazis, she maintained a defiant attitude toward her German enemies. Her resolve to fight against the constant acts of racism, however, was soon to be tested. Following this humiliating episode would be the loss of a dear friend. The war began to wear on Nina, and she found herself gradually slipping into the seductive apathy so common among her fellow Jews during this time.

As I have said, my experience with boys had been quite limited up to this point. Once the war started there was very little opportunity for a social life anyway, and my circle of friends had become very small. There was one friend from this time who I recall vividly, however, because he was the first boy I let kiss me. We considered ourselves in love, but of course we never went, as they say, "all the way" physically.

His name was Ziun Bodmer *(pronounced "zhawn")*, and this was my first real relationship with a young man. We got to know each other at my cousin's party. Before the war started she had a little gathering and Ziun asked if he could see me again. I was so stupid I said, "What do you mean? You're seeing me now." "No," he went on to explain, "I mean without so many people around." I was confused by the whole idea and asked, "Why would you want to see me without our friends around?" I was really very naïve even though I was almost nineteen.

We did eventually find time to be alone, and our first kiss was in the park. Of course I slapped him as I had the boy at camp, even though I liked him. Ziun was very surprised at my reaction, and I never explained that I was simply afraid of my own feelings. I think he ultimately forgave me for that slap, because he still came to see me afterwards. I remember he had the most wonderful voice. He could really sing and he wanted to do this professionally. Sadly, his father would never allow such a career for his son. For most Jewish parents a job in the arts would not have been acceptable, so instead Ziun prepared to study law.

Ultimately my friend was killed. He disappeared six weeks after the Nazis came. Just before he disappeared some German soldiers recruited Ziun to collect books in the Jewish neighborhoods. He was on his way to his apartment when they cornered him and gave him this job. He truly was the best man for this job because he knew the neighborhood well. Even the Russians had enlisted him to go around and record who lived in what building and how much rent they paid. No one was to have any private property, so he was forced to do this distasteful job.

Now he was stuck with another unpleasant task, and poor Ziun again came to be the bearer of bad news. We had previously been ordered to burn all of our books, but the Nazis were well aware that few of us could bear to destroy all of them. I suppose they thought that if they put a Jewish boy in charge and threatened him, well we would give up the rest of our books to avoid trouble.

I don't know why it was so important to the Nazis to destroy our personal libraries; maybe they felt this would help to destroy our culture. Our family owned a lot of very big books, some of them quite old, and I loved them all. The Russians had already taken away a good portion of our family collection. Yet they didn't clean us out entirely because they couldn't read Polish. We also had books written in German and Hebrew, but the Soviets only took the books they believed were worth some money. The Germans didn't want any part of our fine library because they considered our culture decadent. Instead it was decided that all of our wonderful books of literature, science, religion, and history should be burned into oblivion.

Ziun was very sad we he came to our place and said, "You have to take out your books and give them to me. We have to set them all on fire, and it is my unfortunate job to help you to do it." He was heartbroken, but what choice did he have? If he failed to report back to these Nazis they would have hunted him down.

It was a painful task, but I was all by myself at the apartment and really didn't know what else to do. Ziun had to help me carry all of the books out. Then he built the fire. I felt so humiliated doing this while the people from the neighborhood watched. We were instructed to carry out these orders on the street. Whatever they demanded of Jews was to be a message or example to others. This was why the first insults against us were done in public or full view.

The Nazis wanted more than to simply kill us. Our humiliation was also important to them. They wanted our own neighbors to know that we were Jewish and therefore less than human. In order for things to go smoothly for the Germans they knew they would need to ostracize us. This method worked very well. Some Gentiles would point us out and yell, "He's a Jew! Hey, and that one's a Jew, and this one is a Jew as well!"

THE SPITEFUL ACTION of pointing out Jews to German authorities was not unknown in other parts of Poland. It became a common game for anti-Semitic Poles bent on assisting the Nazis in their relentless. An old grudge or a desire to get the better of wealthier neighbors need not be the only excuse for betraying a known Jew to the Germans. Other than the desire to ingratiate themselves to the Nazis, the only real reason for notifying the Gestapo and prompting an arrest was their sheer hatred of Jews. Leo Cooper wrote of Jews that were "…constantly under threat of being identified by any Pole who was not well disposed toward them. This could be a landlord, gas employee, or electricity meter reader, house janitor, neighbor, or even a passer-by, often on the lookout for a Jew appearing on the street—a practice unknown anywhere in occupied Europe."[5] For Nina, the betrayal at the hands of those she once counted as neighbors and friends was a great disappointment.

*Z*iun and I watched all of the beautiful books go up in flames until we couldn't stand it anymore. He said he had to go home, but he offered to first walk me back to my place. I had been invited to Ziun's house quite often in the past. I knew his parents, and was also friendly with his brother. I asked him to take me with him so we went together to his parent's apartment. I couldn't say why, but I was afraid to be alone.

THE PRACTICE OF CONFISCATING and destroying books belonging to Jews had begun not long after Hitler took control of Germany. As they advanced into a conquered area one of the Nazis' primary goals was to eradicate any existing Jewish culture. This meant the immediate collection of Jewish goods and destruction of Jewish literature and religious artifacts.

In his recordings of Jewish life under Nazi rule, Rabbi Shimon noted in *Kiddush Hashem* that whenever "Hebrew books, or above all, Torah scrolls were found during a search, terrible things took place…They took the Hebrew books, tefilin, and mezuazahs, ripped them apart, and burned them. They confiscated talis kotons in order that they be used by Jews to clean toilets."[6] Sharing the humiliation of collecting and destroying their people's books created an even stronger bond between Nina and Ziun. Just as every relationship that mattered to her would be destroyed throughout the war, Nina's bond with Ziun was soon severed by the Nazis.

I often wondered if he had survived, would Ziun and I have eventually gotten married. Unfortunately, no plans for the future could be made once the Nazis took over and Ziun's plans, like mine, were based on day-to-day decisions.

Before things became worse he went to another town to study leather-working, since law school was out of the question. Then he found work in an office for a short time. But one awful day he just disappeared! When a couple of days passed and I hadn't seen him, I said to myself, "What has happened to my friend? Something is not right!"

I went straight to his place, but his mother informed me that she had not seen her son and was also worried. He had been enlisted once more by the Nazis to collect more books in a different neighborhood, but he had not returned. A neighbor informed her that her son was going down the street with books he'd collected when a Ukrainian pointed to Ziun and said to some soldiers, "In case you'd like to know…see that boy there? Well, he's a Jew." At that point the Germans grabbed Ziun and disappeared. His mother had no idea where they took him. This was what happened all the time, but it always came as a shock when it happened to people close to you.

THE ROUNDING UP OF JEWS, or performing an "Aktion," as the Germans labeled such an act, was generally done every two weeks. Once the Gestapo commandeered local officials for assistance, the typical procedure involved picking from the streets those Jews (or other undesirables including Gypsies and suspected homosexuals) who were incapable of labor. While the idyllic Fatherland would eventually be devoid of every individual considered impure by Arian standards, the sizeable workforce they represented was a valuable resource to the Nazi regime. It was imperative that this source of labor be exploited while the majority of able-bodied Germans fought the war abroad. To this end every Jew considered of the age and physical condition to bear hard work was, at the Nazis' will, plucked from the street and made a virtual slave until worked to death.

Leon Wells described a typical "Aktion" and the presumed outcome of each violent act: "The numbers were made up by hauling people arbitrarily out of their houses. People who were engaged in work for the armed forces, and the women who looked after them, were spared. It was mainly old people, girls, and young children who were taken away. Relatively few young men were called. In the first week the Aktion was carried out only at night. In the second week it was carried out during the daytime as well. The roundup was carried out by the 'Jewish militia,' assisted by the Gestapo. As the militia entered each house, a car, occupied by Gestapo agents, was drawn up before the door, and into it were bundled those who were being detained. Once the car was full, it was driven to a school in the vicinity of the Jewish quarter and its contingent dropped off. A commission had been set up at this collecting point for those to be 'transplanted,' and it saw to the registering of the victims handed over to it, and made arrangements as to provisions for the 'journey.' Then, when night had fallen, the émigrés were brought to the railway station, loaded aboard a train, and the journey began. To what destination no one knew; no one ever saw them again."[7]

Losing a dear friend she had known since childhood was a terrible shock to Nina. Unwilling to accept his disappearance, she sought out those who might know where he was sent to work with the idea of pleading for his life. Nina immediately felt the effects of Nazi occupation when, in her efforts to save Ziun, she became a pawn in the game of one unsavory Gestapo officer.

I never told anyone this before, but I was so desperate to find out what happened to my friend that I actually approached a man working for the Gestapo for help finding him. Can you even imagine the nerve that I had? I just said to myself, "If there's one thing I can do, I will find out what happened to Ziun."

I asked around about who was in charge, and then sought out the man heading up our local Gestapo office. I knew he was Gestapo by his uniform which was very distinctive and of a grey color. Whenever they walked into a place they gave a very strong "Heil Hitler!" All of the officers were sharp dressers, and the higher their rank the better they looked. Their boots shone like mirrors, even those who ran the labor camps. Their boots were very heavy, so that when they stepped on or kicked a person they did a lot of damage. I usually tried to avoid any figure that looked this way because I knew they had the power to kill me. Even after liberation I was afraid of the American soldiers. For the longest time uniforms of any sort represented someone who might beat or kill me. Just as the Ukrainians could spot a Jew, we could spot a Gestapo man a mile away.

It came as no surprise that he was a Ukrainian and already had a reputation of being a real bastard, excuse my expression. Whenever such a man had a little prestige and power they became quite dangerous. He was middle-aged, somewhere in his fifties I think, and old enough to be my father. His intentions were not good ones, and I would discover that he actually wanted me in the worst way.

I suppose in the back of my mind I sensed this danger. Even so, I said to this man, "I don't care what you want from me, only tell me where my friend is." I was ready for anything, and I didn't care at the time if this meant I would have to sacrifice my own body. By then I had come to the realization that women could get used in this way. I had a vague idea that trusting such a horrible man was dangerous, but I felt that my dear friend was worth it. I told this officer that I wanted to find out anything I could about Ziun, even if all I could learn was where he had been taken and what they planned to do with him. He listened to my plea, and then assured me that he would get the information for me. He also informed me that I would have to return the favor in some way.

When I was supposed to go see him, he sent his attaché to pick me up. The attaché was about my age, maybe a little older, and he actually seemed rather kind. He was very polite and appeared to be a decent man. He picked me up in a nice car, and we chatted a little on the way. "Look," he said to me, "be careful with this man you are going to see. If you don't understand what he wants from you I can tell you, but whatever you do don't give him what he wants." I pretended not to know what the attaché meant.

I actually met with the Gestapo officer a few times. Each time the attaché drove me to a little restaurant and I had dinner with him. I was so scared that I couldn't eat a bite of the meal offered to me. I cannot describe the feeling I had. I was really hungry, but somehow just looking at the officer eating made me want to choke. I couldn't swallow a thing.

He eventually told me that Ziun had indeed been caught on the street, but he was having difficulty finding out where my friend ended up. Each time I asked about my friend the officer said, "Give me time. What's your rush? I'm still working on it." The last night the attaché drove me to see the officer he asked me, "What are you doing with this man you're going to see? Do you know what he wants from you?" "I only know what I want from him," I said, "I have no idea what he wants from me, and I don't care." By this time I had sunk pretty low in my desperation to learn about Ziun.

Something was different about this night, because my driver was looking at me with a worried expression. He asked me, "What has this officer been doing with you?" "Nothing," I answered, "he just offers me dinner, but I'm always too nervous to eat anything." The attaché didn't say anything else, but I was driven to a different place for dinner that night. It was like a little suite, and I could see through an open door a room with a bed in it.

The young man said to me, "Do you see? This is what the officer wants from you. If you want nothing to do with this, I will help you get away." I realized then that the officer wasn't ever going to help me find Ziun, and I told the attaché I wanted to go home. Just then the officer walked in. When he saw us talking he became very angry.

"What are you doing here?" he asked the attaché. My savior made up a story about a message to deliver in the building. The officer gave him a stern look, and then excused himself for a moment, telling me to wait there in the room until he returned.

After the officer left the young man motioned with his eyes that I should run. He pointed to a door that would take me out a different way, and whispered, "Leave as fast as you can! I'll find a way to cover for you, only go now!"

I didn't need to hear any more, and I ran out of there, through the streets and all the way to my aunt's apartment. I managed to escape because once again I was able to find a decent person to help me. I saw the attaché very soon after, and we spoke for only a moment. He told me the Ukrainian officer never had any power to find my Ziun. He had lied about everything just to get me to go to bed with him!

The officer had to have been angry when I wasn't there in that room. I don't know how the attaché explained it, but he could have easily been blamed for getting me out of there. I thanked that young man for all he had done. I never told anyone this story because I was ashamed of the lengths I was willing to go in order to save Ziun. I couldn't look at myself in the mirror for some time after that night, and I assumed my friend was shot or died in a camp.

———

Personally, I think that the Germans were stupid about how they went about getting rid of us. If they had been smart they would have allowed us to fight in the war. They wished us dead after all, and what better way than to put us at the front lines? I think quite a few Jews would have preferred this, because at least they would have a chance of survival. I know that sounds crazy, and of course I wouldn't have wanted my loved ones to die fighting in the war. But in order to comprehend why I would even suggest such an idea one has to understand the lunacy of the Nazis' plan. They spent so much money and devoted so many resources to eliminating us. Why didn't Hitler direct those resources toward his troops? What did they think they were accomplishing? I will never understand it.

I think that we Jews were stupid as well. Here Adolf Hitler had written a book declaring his plans for getting rid of us, yet we were caught completely by surprise by the Nazis' attack. In *Mein Kampf* he wrote about his desire to dominate the entire world, but nobody believed him. His "Final Solution" was to eliminate every Jew from Europe and destroy every Jewish community. There is one town in Poland where there was not one survivor after the war. All I am saying is that we should have seen it coming.

Very soon after taking our possessions the Nazis started to collect Jews for "work detail." All Jews were to identify themselves by wearing an armband with the Star of David on it. This made it easier for them to pick us out. Most people don't know this, but we had to make our own stars. It was up to us to create something out of cloth. I don't know why they are always depicted as yellow stars in Holocaust films, because ours were white. The Germans even dictated the exact measurements the star should be, which was six inches. It had to be done perfectly according to the SS soldiers' instructions, and if it was done improperly you were pulled aside and beaten. It had to always be clean in order to be highly visible. God forbid it had so much as a spot on it.

The star had to be worn right in front. Make no mistake, the Nazis wanted to see who was who. When I walked around with that star it gave me a feeling of constantly being under the Germans' eye. They announced the law of making this star over the radio as well as over a loudspeaker throughout town. They told us quite plainly that we were to obey this new rule or we would be shot instantly. We knew now that the Germans would do this without a thought. We also began to notice that a lot of Jews were not coming back after being rounded up for labor. People just started disappearing. Then I said to myself, "I'm going to do my utmost, damn it, to make sure that they shouldn't get me!"

When they began to issue orders for us to wear our stars, well I went out without mine. I justified this by saying, "It is ugly and besides, everybody knows that I am Jewish so why bother?" This was silly of course, but I was determined to go without the star on my arm.

I used to get so angry at the idea that they were making us wear this thing, so I hid it instead in my pocket. I thought to myself, "The hell with them, I'm not wearing this thing! I'm going to have to learn how to get around things sooner or later, so I'll practice by going out without my star whenever I can. If this results in my getting shot, well at least I will be killed with some dignity, not like some animal that is worked to death!" The Germans were going to harass us anyway, so as far as I was concerned what difference did it make?

I thought of what to say if I got caught without my star. I would just tell the soldiers that I forgot to put it on, and then show them that it was in my pocket. I once went right up to a German without it! I was on my way to register for something, I don't remember what. I think it was for a real job, and I had the star in my pocket. It was always just a spur of the moment thing not to wear my star, and believe it or not I never did get caught.

I suppose you could say that I rebelled, but I was young, and people do things such as this when they are young. I knew that I risked my life by not wearing my star, but I didn't care. I never once regretted going without it. Later on, most who wore the star did die. I later learned that in Denmark the king himself stood up for the Jews in his country. I heard that, after learning of the Germans' law about wearing armbands, the Danish King said, "If my people have to wear an armband as a way of identifying them, then I will wear one too. I will be the first one to wear it in my family, and I'll insist that every single citizen wear an armband as well."

This one incident proved to me that if people had stood up to the Nazis there would have been a lot less killing. The Germans needed collaborators in order to run large operations such as the death camps. By refusing to bend to the Nazis' orders the Danes became a wonderful example of what one leader and his people could do during the war. Unfortunately, this was a rare occurrence. The rest of Europe took advantage of our plight. There were individuals who risked their lives to help, but the majority wanted nothing to do with us.

NINA WAS NOT the only defiant Jew refusing to wear the armband that branded them as outcasts. One Jewish shop owner, bolstered by her middle-class status and business sense, risked going without the Star of David in order to keep her Gentile customers. According to author Dalia Ofer, this subterfuge was accomplished "because she looked Aryan." The savvy businesswoman managed to run a thriving business due to her "good relations with Polish customers and neighbors [who] helped her carry off the impersonation; many patrons never suspected that she was Jewish. Unfortunately she was later forced into a transport bound for the ghetto."[8] Accounts also exist that actually describe in detail the white star of David armband that Polish Jews wore according to Nazi command.

After a day of forced labor Leon Wells found the latest Nazi directive posted "…by placards which proclaimed that, as of the middle of the month, all Jews must wear a white armlet with the Star of David on the right arm, above the elbow. This provision extended also to half-castes as far as the third degree; that is, one was a Jew if he had one Jewish grandparent. It was stated in addition that failure to comply with these provisions would result in the imposition of severe penalties."[9]

Amidst the constant demands and assaults of the new ruling government, Nina did her best to remain hopeful that things would eventually improve. She soon realized, however, that so far as the rest of the world was concerned, Jews in her situation were very much on their own. This abandonment by humanity was particularly disheartening for a young woman raised to believe that, with perseverance, one could accomplish anything they desired. Now it was all she and her family could do to live from one day to the next, and it wore on all of them to the point of madness.

Things were getting worse, and we were running out of ways to outsmart the Nazis in order to live to see another day. Most people were denied access to news of what was going on in the rest of Europe. All we knew was that the Germans were in charge, and so far they were winning the war. Apparently the Allies either didn't know or didn't care about what was happening to us Jews. With such a big war nobody wanted to hear about our suffering.

I cannot explain or describe the pressure and uncertainty we experienced. We were in total disbelief that one person could treat another so horribly only because of their religion. Let's face it, not all Jews were terribly religious, just as many people today don't go to temple or church. It didn't matter to them whether we were practicing Jews or not, we were the enemy. My family was getting by all right and still living in the Polish section of town. The Germans knew where to find us and could have easily rounded us up, but for now they still needed good doctors. My brother-in-law was one of the best, and some of the officers continued to seek out Buzio for medical treatment.

The apartment where my sister Lina lived was very close to a neighboring family that tried to help us a little. Buzio saved the husband of this family I think, and so they were close friends. Buzio and this man's family were still able to communicate because they lived downstairs from us. Because he was Polish this man had been able to keep a radio for the time being. Whenever it was safe to do so he allowed Buzio to listen to what-ever news he could find on their radio.

This was immensely helpful to us during a time of uncertainty. My brother-in-law would go downstairs at night and listen to any news he could find. It was a big secret and he had to make sure that nobody would see him slip into his neighbor's place. But he was always able to go unde-tected, and because of this man's kindness we were able to learn that the Germans were winning and that we were on our own.

The Nazis could be very destructive, and they were from the very beginning. We didn't know what was coming for us personally, but we soon found out. My brother-in-law was forced to give up his EKG machine to the Germans, though he was permitted to carry on as a doctor for some time because he was so skilled. I wasn't officially supposed to be living there with him, but my sister made certain I stayed at their apart-ment whenever possible. This little bend in the rules went by unnoticed for a time because the Germans couldn't establish a ghetto right away. It took time to rearrange everyone and build barricades, but when I went to work I heard what was going on. It was easier to hear about things that were happening to Jews when I went through the Polish neighborhood, so I kept my ears open.

Unfortunately, even in the Polish neighborhood we were starving. We had no money at all and there was nothing left to trade. We were down to a few bars of soap and definitely using up our last reserves. My mother was still staying with my cousin's family in Drohobycz. I had a feeling that she was all right, but our aim was to get her back to us in L'vov. We felt so insecure by this time, however, that all we wanted was to be together as a family as much as possible. In this respect Lina's place would be a safe home for all of us.

Buzio had his office below the apartment because the Russians never got around to taking that from him. After two months of occupation, however, the Germans helped themselves to this dwelling, and they moved all of us into a neglected little room on the top floor. It was awful compared to our old place. Fortunately, my sister had been very good to the people who were taking care of the building when the Russians were in control. This couple was in charge of maintaining the building, and they had small children. Lina always gave those clothes that Alma had outgrown to this family as well as any other extra supplies Buzio collected from practicing medicine. The janitor and his family never forgot Buzio and Lina's kindness. When my sister and her husband were relocated to the worst apartment in the building, well then these people helped out with beds and essentials.

———

Two or three weeks after the Germans showed up my mother returned. She came with news about my cousin, the young doctor. As it turned out he had been enlisted by the Russian army to serve as a doctor. The news was difficult to take for my mother who had helped to raise my cousin practically as her own. The last word we had was that he had been transferred to a mobile unit. When the Russians pulled out he was made to evacuate with the troops, but this in a way was good news. Although he had to leave his family behind, at least he was not taken by the Germans, who most certainly would have killed him. At least, as a Major, he had a good place in the Russian army.

My cousin survived the war, but the rest of his story is quite tragic. His wife, brother, and his wife's mother were all eventually killed during the war. Before any of this chaos hit them they were wise and kind enough to put my mother on a train and send her back to us. She had stayed with these relatives for maybe three or four months before they all decided it would be best for Mama to come home.

I had been begging my sister all along to bring my mother back. By the time everyone decided she should come home I was becoming hysterical. Poor Lina was doing all she could to keep us all together, but she had her own family to care for and all of the responsibility of making a decent home for us. When the Russians were in control they allowed Buzio to have an assistant in his office. Now with the Nazis in power the assistant disappeared along with many of the supplies needed to run his practice. The Germans had use for a Jewish doctor's skill as well, but in a different way. Their plan was to use Buzio for his knowledge as long as a doctor was needed amongst the Jews.

The Nazis also took advantage of free medical care whenever they needed Buzio, but his life was as uncertain as any other Jew's. I am sure Buzio realized he would be killed once the number of Jews used for labor diminished and they no longer needed his skills to keep prisoners alive. For the time being, however, my brother-in-law still had a little influence, so he was able to arrange my mother's safe journey back to us. I cannot express how anxious I was to see her! Luckily the requirement to wear a star for identifying Jews had yet to be fully implemented. Not long after my mother arrived the Nazis became very strict. A woman wearing a star could never have traveled, certainly not by train. None of this mattered to me once I saw Mama. I was so happy when she stepped back into my life that I cried and cried.

So here we all were, together again. We had lost many friends and had no idea where many of our family members had disappeared to, but we had each other. We no longer had to fear the possibility of being shipped off to Siberia. How could we have known that soon we would have far greater worries?

TRY AS I MIGHT I could never adequately put into written words the deep feelings Nina had for her mother. Though she adequately relayed her happiness upon seeing her mother home again, I still felt that Nina was holding back while recalling this important moment in her life. One moment during our interviews stands out to me above all others. Upon completing each chapter I dutifully sent my friend a copy for review. One week after sending her the first three chapters I received a call from Nina. She seemed to be in great distress over a particular portion of the story. The writing was fine, she assured me, but I had put a thing or two in the wrong way. "You make my father into something of a hero," Nina lamented, "he was a good father to me when I was younger, but I want to make very clear that it was my mother whom I admired most. She loved and understood me more than anyone, and she was kind to everybody…even to strangers. Everyone who met my mother saw her as a saint!"

The relationship between Nina and Rosa Grütz was noteworthy not only for its closeness, but for the very fact that a daughter and mother could remain so connected throughout the very stressful experience of adolescence. At a time in life when young women traditionally find fault with their mothers as a way of gaining independence, this was instead an intense season of closeness between the two Grütz women.

Perhaps it was the stress of war and the reality of imminent death that softened a period of time that would normally create dissension between the two female generations. Who could explain the bond between these two very different individuals? Rosa Grütz had done her best to reflect the epitome of a good Jewish wife. Her daughter Nina, on the other hand, had grown into an independent and ambitious young woman. At the very moment when she should have been pursuing a career in the medical profession Nina was forced to cope with very unique and brutal circumstances. Only by trusting her instincts, or "flying by the seat of her pants" as Nina put it, did Rosa's youngest daughter take on the horrors of Nazi degradation.

Their differences notwithstanding, this mother and daughter team managed, for a short time, to support one another. During our interviews I attempted to unearth my friend's innermost feelings upon reuniting with her beloved mother. With what I hoped was the proper amount of diplomacy and patience I tried to discover what Nina felt during a homecoming that must have been both welcome and complex. Did Nina not resent her mother for her absence, and at the same time rejoice in her return? This would have been the normal reaction for a young daughter in a similar situation. How did Nina feel about her dear Mama's return? What sort of reunion transpired?

I received no details or explanation. There were moments when my friend revealed what had to have been very painful memories without hesitation. Other times she held things very close to the vest. Perhaps by keeping some details private, Nina found a way of preserving the memory of those people in her life she held most dear. Respecting this, I tried to anticipate the moment my questions were becoming too invasive. When necessary, I let well enough alone and allowed my friend to take the story where she liked.

Not long after my mother's return I had a very disturbing encounter. It was the first time that I really understood what being a Jew in Poland would mean now that the Nazis were in control.

I was walking down the street one day, and I was wearing my star armband for once, when a group of Ukrainian boys began to approach me. By now it was winter in Poland, and there was a bit of snow on the ground. These Ukrainian boys began to throw snowballs at me and call me dirty names. They were about thirteen or so, and though they were younger than I was, some of them were pretty big! They called me a "dirty Jew" and told me that I wasn't allowed to be in that neighborhood. When this sort of treatment came from a German soldier it was terrible, but at least he represented some sort of authority. Here these insults were coming from kids younger than me!

I don't know what got into me, but I decided I'd had enough. The words they said to me were simply unacceptable, so I let them have it. I actually swore at them. I said, "Get away from me. Go to hell!" I could not understand how I deserved such treatment. I gave all of their insults back to them until they left me alone. It was only after they left that I started to cry. I cried all the way home to Lina's place. She saw by my face something was wrong, and she asked me what had happened, but I refused to talk about it. I didn't want to worry my sister, and by this time I was getting better at keeping all of my feelings inside of me. Lina was suffering enough with worry for little four-year-old Alma.

The hatred I encountered made me so upset and unhappy. I began to doubt everything I had known before about God and justice and our duty to help others. I became so angry that sometimes I would find a place to be alone and to yell, "Well who is it that can help the innocent people in Poland now? Where is the justice?" I had so much frustration inside of me that I eventually had to force myself to put everything out of my mind just to get through the day. I walked around with a blank expression on my face, and I think that if I hadn't resorted to this I would have gone a little crazy.

For many of us Jews the idea of ending it all was very attractive. On some days I thought that if a German asked the slightest thing of me, I really would have tried to kill him. If I had a knife or a gun there were times when I would have done it! We were so close to not caring at that time. If things had been normal one could never imagine doing such things. But when you watch enough of your loved ones disappear or get killed before your very eyes, well you want to fight back no matter what the consequences. Fortunately, I never had a weapon during those moments…or unfortunately, however you want to look at it.

THE CONSTANT FEAR and humiliation had pronounced psychological effects on the Jews living under Nazi rule. Typically, the younger victims expressed their frustration with their new living conditions through angry outbursts of defiance, while older Jews chose to hold out hope that the war would end quickly and in their favor.

For those who found no other way to cope with the demeaning rules and brutal killings, suicide was the only answer. In her memoirs, survivor Judith Magyar Isaacson recalled witnessing each of these responses to stress brought on by the Germans' demands: "Grandmother and I were doing the dishes, when mother entered. 'You forgot to sweep the hall this morning,' grandmother reminded her. 'Who cares?' mother retorted. 'And why do you wipe those plates Mama? Smash them to the floor, instead!' Grandmother's worn hand trembled in mid-air, her eyes begging for pity. 'Sorry, Mama,' mother whispered, 'I'll sweep the hall right away.'…It was a humiliating day. At the synagogue, male officials examined our packs, ruthlessly grabbing anything that took their fancy." Ms. Isaacson later learned that a close neighbor had committed suicide rather than be subjected to further assaults at the hands of the Nazis.[10]

Nina sensed the Nazis' dragnet closing in around her, and like many young Jews caught in the Germans' web of destruction, she rebelled. While she realized the futility of publicly objecting to the new regime ruling her homeland, the obstinate Miss Grütz performed small acts of defiance as a quiet protest and proclamation of dignity. Going out in public without the hated brand of Jewish armband was one way in which Nina accomplished this.

L ife continued to be unpredictable and the Germans became more controlling. Every single day somebody went missing. Whenever I went out without my star I had to walk right by Nazis as if I were a regular Pole. The Germans could tell if you were a Jew by how afraid you were around them, so I tried to be very casual. I walked by and showed nothing on my face, but it was scary.

We all tried hard to be invisible. As things got progressively worse my older sister and I tried to be strong, but Helena was lost right away. Unlike Lina and me, I think that in her heart Helena gave up on herself. I spent more time explaining to her, "Helena, your husband is working and you should too! You have no children at home to care for so there's no reason for you to sit around all day. If you don't show that you can work you'll be seen as a Jew unable to do labor and they'll kill you!" My sister just ignored me, saying, "No, I don't wish to work. What's the point if the Nazis plan on catching me on my way to work anyway? Besides I have never worked before, so what could I possibly do?" She was just giving up from the very beginning.

One day she couldn't stand to sit in the apartment anymore, so she finally found some little job. On the day she finally acquired a job, she left the house with hardly a "good-bye." I suppose she wasn't thinking of how dangerous just walking to work might be, and she had such an ambivalent attitude at the time she probably didn't care.

She left that morning, but Helena never came back from that job. She might have not been paying attention and run into some Germans rounding people up, but we never found out for sure what happened. We waited for days but never heard any word from her. We had to eventually accept the idea that she might be dead.

The only thing I learned about Helena caused me even greater frustration than if I had remained ignorant, and that was something I found out in, of all places, Washington, D.C. I went there with my family long after the war, to visit a museum in which they had preserved Nazi documents from the war. There I found my sister's name, Helena Grütz! It was her maiden name, not her married name of Frostig, but it would not have been unusual for her to give this name. The name was spelled correctly as we always put it, but that was the only information there was. It was on a sort of list, and I asked the people of that museum what it meant, but they had no answer for me. I never knew if it was a list of camp prisoners or people shot right away. She was very clearly registered, and I personally think she was taken to a camp and eliminated somehow.

I felt such sorrow for poor Helena. My sister was a complicated young woman, but she did not deserve to die in such a way.

———

Sometimes when we were gathered up to work we were permitted to return home after the job was done. If a Jew was smart he did as he was told and worked very hard to show how valuable his labor was. Some of the tasks they gave us were extremely unpleasant. They had us working the strange job of moving tombstones in the cemetery, for instance, but that was better then digging a ditch. I always tried to find ways to become involved in the task, providing a better chance of survival.

We were never supposed to ask questions. I learned this the hard way when I once asked the German soldier collecting us, "Where are we going? What job will you have us do?" When I asked the SS man this he struck me right across the head! He used a rubber baton, and he hit me with such force I fell to the ground. I didn't even see it coming. He screamed at me, "How dare you ask where you are going! You go where we tell you without question." It makes me laugh now at how I had such nerve to speak this way to an SS soldier! They left me lying there on the street because after he hit me so hard I was no good for any work. I passed out for a little while, and when I finally got up off the street I discovered that I had even lost a tooth. After the soldiers drove off, a few people helped me up, which I thought was surprising because they must have known I was a Jew. Maybe they felt sorry for me. I don't know, but as I said I did meet the occasional kind person during the war.

When I returned to my sister's I lied and told her my injuries were caused by falling down. I'm not sure that she believed me, but she let it go and helped me to get cleaned up. I just didn't want to worry her and Buzio. Besides, I knew that if I told Lina the whole story she would have prevented me from going out altogether.

After that day I truly realized that we were the Germans' possessions. Whatever they wanted to do with us they were going to do. To instantly become slaves was an unexpected situation, and we didn't think about how to protect ourselves. Later on those of us who managed to survive caught on to things very quickly. It helped to remain one step ahead of the Nazis, so we tried to be on our guard.

———

One day all but Buzio received orders to officially move into the ghetto. When I first heard this order I had to ask, "What do they mean? What is a ghetto?" I had never even heard the word before. Jewish neighborhoods in the old days were segregated and not very nice, but by the time I was a girl in Poland many of us had assimilated so successfully into the Polish culture this living separately did not exist, at least not in L'vov. Now the nicer Jewish homes that had not been taken by the Russians were to be occupied by German officers or Poles. The very best of what any Jew had left was shipped off to Germany.

The place they were sending us to was the most neglected neighborhood in L'vov. There were checkpoints erected at the entrances of this neighborhood, but at first they were not that secure, so we could go back and forth to Lina and Buzio's place on the Polish side. Anyway it looked as if we would have to spend at least some time in this "ghetto," and so we packed our remaining possessions. I don't know how these Germans expected us to survive with less than nothing, but maybe that was the point. I still had three dresses of my own, so I decided to put them on one over the other. I was thin enough to do this without looking too strange, and I had no intentions of living in the ghetto with only one dress to wear every day.

This was when my luck ran out and the soldiers at the ghetto checkpoint caught me transferring these possessions. I was being searched with a group of people and they noticed the three different hems of my dresses. The SS men took me to a building nearby, and in one big room I was brought up to a long table where others people's possessions had been confiscated. There were soldiers and German officials sitting there drinking and laughing. They had collected a lot of money and jewelry, so I suppose they were celebrating a little.

The one soldier who brought me in told me to undress. I was very frightened because it wasn't unusual for them to strip a person completely naked in plain view. Maybe he thought he would have some fun with me, but I was not interested in giving him a thrill. I decided that I wasn't about to get naked in front of these men. I didn't move and he began to yell at me to begin stripping. I yelled back at him every time, "No, no, no!" I held up my hands to protect myself, and he didn't like that. He brought up his hand to whip me with his baton, but just then a higher-ranking official grabbed his hand and shouted, "Let her go!" He pulled me from that place and threw me into a different room that had a door leading outside. "Run!" he yelled at me.

For a moment I stood there like a statue. I was so stunned that he was giving me a chance to escape that I stood there like an idiot. The officer was losing patience, so he pushed me and yelled again, "Run! What's wrong with you?"

I ran for my life. I had no idea where I was going, and I had no clue as to why this man had helped me. As I said, these bits of good fortune occurred on quite a few occasions during the war, and I don't know how I got so lucky. It is almost as if God had sent an angel for me and said, "Protect this one."

———

It hurt so badly to think back on the life we had before the war. We Jews had such a beautiful temple in L'vov, but the Nazis destroyed it along with the others. By this time it was immensely difficult to find a city or town in Poland that had been able to keep their places of worship intact.

It must be understood that women like my mother as well as young girls didn't really go to temple in Poland. Jewish culture was a little bit different back then, at least it was in Eastern Europe. For one thing, girls did not have Bats Mitzvahs as they do in America. Even a boy's Bar Mitzvah was not an elaborate affair. A Bar Mitzvah boy's parents would just arrange for the family to get together and have a little refreshment. The ceremony would take place in the temple and the celebration would be modest even in the wealthiest families. The biggest celebrations were focused on the High Holidays, and most of these took place in the home. It was always nicely done, with the nicest linens and dishes put out. But the actual ceremonies took place in temple, and it really was a terrible shame that the Nazis burned up the most beautiful synagogues. Some people were still in the buildings praying when the Germans came to set them on fire. The SS men simply didn't care about the fact that they were burning people alive, because that meant less Jews to deal with later. The worst part was that I saw my fellow Poles helping them to do it!

This intense hatred was brought home to me when I once saw an old man beaten on the street. It happened right before my eyes. I could only assume he received this beating because he was old and wearing a star. This elderly person lying in the street was most probably somebody's husband, father, or grandfather. He had a long beard and the men were trying to cut it off. He was screaming at them not to do this, so they began to beat him. It made me very angry, and I suppose at the time I had a lot of *chutzpa*, because I walked up and began to yell at them. "What are you doing? Leave him alone!" If I had taken the time to think about the consequences to my outburst I might not have been so brave, but I was too angry to think about anything but challenging them. Well, one of the soldiers yelled back at me, "Who are you to tell me what to do? Go away or we'll do the same to you!"

THE COLLECTIVE HATRED many Polish people felt for Jews was given free reign when the Nazis took power. Humiliation, intimidation, and assault were behaviors encouraged by the Germans and every Jew became a moving target. William Woods' interviews revealed the oppressive fear Jews were forced to tolerate on a daily basis: "People woke in the morning with the quite conscious thought that there was nowhere on earth to hide. One was surrounded by enemies and might not be alive by nightfall. The safety we take for granted, the protection of the police for example, the money, the work, the influential acquaintances, the very reasonableness of normal existence and intercourse no longer held true. If a man was shot down in the street (and this happened often and unexpectedly) his very friends walked by and pretended not to notice."[11]

In his text about Jewish life in wartime Poland Rabbi Shimon recorded the lengths to which Jews would go to protect themselves: "…neighbors stopped gathering together. Everyone hid in his own private corner. In addition, everyone shaved off his beard, either entirely or partially, and put on European clothes. The sense of terror, panic, and fear was unbelievable. When the day finally passed, and the night drew near, people sighed with relief."[12]

———

Young people often see themselves as indestructible. Anger over the restrictions forced upon Nina made eluding the Nazis her own obstinate game against them.

B ecause I was a young person I felt confident that I could elude danger by using my wits. I saw violence in front of me all the time, yet I always managed to escape it somehow. Even if I ran off to a different town I was taking my chances regardless, so I stayed in L'vov, and avoiding Germans became second nature to me.

There were times that I wasn't as careful as I should have been. I remember one particular day when a Polish man stopped me on the street. I didn't know him well; he was only an acquaintance from before the war. But he certainly remembered me, and he knew I was a Jewish girl. He warned me by saying, "If I were you, I wouldn't be on the street right now." I wasn't wearing my star, and he must have realized the danger in this when he recognized me. I actually had the nerve to ask him why I shouldn't be on the street, and he said, "Look, I'm not going to explain it to you now. You know why." It made an impression me, and I was shivering like a leaf as he walked away without another word. He was one of those few Polish people who helped me in some small way. But as I said, this was a rarity.

I knew that in order to avoid the roundups for labor I would need to find more secure work, but the only real job I could find was in a Jewish café as a sort of waitress. I wasn't paid a thing, and only received meager rations approved by the Jews in charge of things, but it was better than forced labor.

The Germans had established the Jewish Council, or *Judenrat*, and I was working through them. Some of the most important Jewish citizens were delegated to head it up, and a good number of them knew my father. Some of the elected Judenrat members were quite prominent people in our community. These men were happy to take on these positions because in the beginning they believed they could help their fellow Jews by providing a line of communication to the Nazis. They were in charge of organizing Jews to work in the ghettos as well, and in this way I was able to get my little job.

To be honest, most of us were working there just so that we could have a paper stating we were doing something productive. At that time the Germans had constructed a labor camp in our area, and though we only heard rumors about it, we did know that Jews were disappearing from the streets all the time and being taken somewhere. We thought that perhaps having a place of legitimate work might keep us from disappearing, but this was most probably an illusion.

Twelve members of our Judenrat were killed just for asking about the disappearances. These members of the Jewish Council were in charge of collecting people for work details. When so many people went off to work for the Germans and never came back the Judenrat members became suspicious. Finally they asked some Nazi officials what happened to these people. They threatened to stop collecting laborers until they got some answers. For having the nerve to question them, the Nazis executed these men. They brought everybody out to the marketplace, so we knew something terrible was going to happen.

They hung those twelve men like they were nothing but criminals. It was a horrible shame because these were good men, and some of them were still quite young.

WHEN I ASKED NINA about how she felt about the hangings she avoided the subject. "We were all hoping that something good would come of the Judenrat members asking about the disappearances, but it ended in disaster." "Were you there?" I asked Nina. "I was there but I wasn't there," she explained. "I didn't want to see it," she went on, "if you started to protest any killings the Nazis would beat you senseless. I would rather not remember that I witnessed the hangings. It was terrible to see these people, some of them young and quite innocent, not at all collaborators, being treated in such a way."

Nina went on to explain how some members of the Judenrat helped her.

These were the men who helped me to obtain my job and I will always be grateful to them for doing so. Now calling this place where I worked a "café" was laughable. It was only a shabby room in a building the Germans had no immediate interest in, and there was very little food to serve. But at least we had coffee, and I was grateful to receive the occasional ration for my trouble. There were many days that we didn't even have water to make coffee.

The Nazis allowed this place to exist for some reason, though to this day I do not know why. Little did they know, but some of us hid there during a few Aktions. Once they came looking for us at the café, but we hid under the little bandstand where musicians sometimes performed. Luckily the light was so dim the Germans couldn't find us. They kept yelling, "There must be a switch somewhere. Find it and turn it on!" Because the lights weren't working we were well obscured. They walked right by us as we lay under that little stage.

If the light had been on I'm certain we would have been discovered. We didn't move an inch and had lots of time to hear other people crying and pleading not to be taken away. For those of us hiding the thought was, "To heck with them! We're not going to help them fill their quota of Jews this time!" We stayed there all night, and in the morning we crept out from under the tables stiff and barely able to move. I think each Jew who survived at this time was evidence of a little miracle like this one.

———

My mother was not as lucky, however, and I'll explain about that. As I said, my mother had a special feeling for her homeland. Even though my father was a Zionist and wanted us to someday move to Palestine, she never liked the idea. My mother would always say, "How could I go to

Palestine? All of my family was born here in Poland and my beloved ancestors have been buried here. L'vov has always been our home and all of our memories are here. I will never leave!" And she never did. Mama couldn't imagine leaving the place where her history was so deeply rooted. Her family went back five hundred years, and she took great pride in that.

By the time the Nazis invaded Poland it was too late for Mama or any of us to even think of moving to the Holy Land. My mother was by then a very different person. She had changed after my father's arrest, and her stay at Lusia's did not seem to have done her much good. When she returned from my cousin's home I could really see the suffering in her face. She began to look like a very old woman. She had always been careful with her looks and had dressed with such style. After they took my father away, however, she stopped bothering to even attempt fixing up her hair. I suppose one could say that without father, she simply lost interest in herself. She was deteriorating from day to day, night to night. It was so strange, because Mama had always looked young for her age, but after she returned from Lusia's I recognized my mother was slipping away. Slowly but surely she went from even looking her age of fifty-two to looking like someone much older.

Life was a hardship. Every single day you were fighting to exist. We were all consumed with finding ways to evade the Germans. We didn't think about tomorrow and lived in uncertainty. Young people today may understand a little of what this is like. Now they have to consider the sad possibility that a terrorist might take over the airplane they're traveling in and crash it, or a terrorist could walk into their school and just start shooting.

Although it saddens me to know our world is now like this, these things do not touch our children every single day. With the Nazis in our country we expected tragedy every moment. Ours was a day-to-day, minute-by-minute existence. This was true primarily for Jews, and I think I should be clear about this. Other Poles were experiencing hardships to be sure, but nothing like the constant threat of death that the Jews were feeling. We lived constantly encircled by our enemies. The Germans, Poles, and Ukrainians surrounding us determined our fate. Eventually they determined my mother's fate as well.

NOVEMBER OF 1941 marked one of the most difficult episodes of the war for Nina. The one person Nina could always rely upon for love and understanding would disappear from her life forever. Although their roles had become somewhat reversed, with youngest daughter providing emotional and financial support to her mother, Rosa Grütz continued to represent all that was family and security to Nina.

Aged by the constant struggle to survive wartime conditions and the effort to endure Nazi humiliations, Nina's mother was in great danger of becoming caught up in the next "Aktion." Nina pleaded with her mother to take care and stay off the streets of L'vov. Rosa did not share her daughter's concern, however. Life for the once elegant and vivacious woman had come to have little meaning. Numb to the danger around her, Rosa spent her time visiting the cemetery where she could pray and dream of better days.

I will never forget the day my mother died. It was two or three weeks after she had returned from Lusia's and just before the Germans had sealed up the ghetto. The SS soldiers were still busily trying to establish this area, and they were becoming more aggressive every day. My mother did not see the increase in danger of being out on the streets, and every Thursday since she had returned she went to the Jewish cemetery for prayer and time alone. Many traditional Jewish families felt that it was more appropriate to pray in the cemetery as opposed to the synagogue. This was especially true for women who customarily sat in back of the synagogue anyway. In any case my mother had no choice because all of the temples had been destroyed.

The last day we saw her was a particularly nasty one: gray and chilly. I believe it was in November, and in Poland that month can be quite cold. Since it was a weekday I went out to earn a little money at the café as usual.

On this particular Thursday my mind was not on hiding or on my work. I had a sense of foreboding, and I suppose this instinct served me well throughout the war. I had only a feeling in my stomach of course, yet all day as I prepared coffee and washed dishes I worried about my mother. I cleaned up quite awhile that day because all the recent bombing had left a thin layer of dust everywhere. There were few supplies available to do this, so things were generally quite a mess.

It took me all day, but finally I finished work and was heading home through the Jewish section. I remember telling my sister that morning, "Lina, please don't let Mama go to the cemetery today. It's raining and she might catch cold. Remind her not to go because I'm going to work and won't be able to stay with her." Now here I was heading home with my hands buried in my pockets and carrying a bad feeling that would not go away.

I turned the corner heading to our apartments and suddenly saw small groups of Jews, mostly elderly women and some children, who were being rounded up by the German soldiers. I knew that they were Jews because they were wearing the white star armband that I always refused to put on. I also saw men who looked like Gestapo. They had that special insignia on their lapels, and looked very angry as usual. Something was going on that I couldn't understand, but I was too afraid to go toward the commotion of screaming and crying. Instead I took the side streets and avoided any confrontation with these soldiers. I hurried home to check on the rest of my family.

When I reached my sister's apartment I knew something was wrong. The minute I opened the door I had that feeling. I asked my sister, "Where's Mama?"

"Mama went to pray," she told me, "I am sure that she will be home soon." I froze for a moment, then immediately ran from our apartment and headed for the cemetery. It had taken me almost a half-hour to reach that area on the way home from work. This time I covered the distance in fifteen minutes, my heart pounding out of my chest the whole way. As I drew closer I heard more screaming, only now it sounded louder and more desperate. There was a bridge that one needed to cross in order to reach the cemetery. As I came upon the cemetery I saw people gathered under this bridge, every one of them crying and screaming.

By this time I knew in my heart that the Germans found my mother coming home from the cemetery, and had somehow included her with these people during the roundup. The Gestapo men were throwing people one way or the other, but most of them were getting pushed toward some stairs leading to a doorway underground. I was in a complete panic and grabbed a man hurriedly passing by. I asked him if he knew where that door led, but this stranger shrugged me off and kept walking. Then I began to hear over the screaming and crying some shooting. Well, I wasn't stupid. I knew then what was happening. They were using that place to collect Jews and kill them.

This experience was different from the previous occasions that I had seen Jews being rounded up. Watching these Aktions one always knew that something wasn't right. Still you told yourself they were being sent to work somewhere. We were lying to ourselves that they were being held somewhere in some sort of prison. Nobody wanted to admit the truth.

Finally I understood with real clarity that I was actually going to lose someone very dear to me. It was also the first time I saw people killed right in front of my eyes. At least before it had not been so obvious; now I could see that if my mother was indeed in that group she was going to die, if she wasn't dead already. There were so many thrown into that cellar. Some of them were grabbing at the soldiers' coats and screaming that they didn't want to go. The SS men simply clutched them by the throat or the hair and tossed them in that hole as if they were rags.

In all this chaos I thought that I heard my mother's voice amidst the screaming. I was sure that I heard her crying in that cellar. Don't ask me how I could hear one voice among all the others, but even now I swear that I did. I knew she was in there, and I wanted to go to her. I couldn't bear the idea that she was in there all alone without me to hold her. I heard a final scream, then many gunshots.

I couldn't take it anymore. I had to be with Mama, so I ran toward that cellar. It was as if I was running toward hell, but at least I would be with her in the end. Unfortunately a soldier stopped me. "My mother is down there," I screamed at him, "let me go to her!" But he refused to let me go. Instead he threw me down, saying, "We have our orders and they don't include young people. This is not for you yet."

I later thought back on that word "yet." That certainly meant that eventually I would meet the same end as my mother. For the moment it didn't register, however, and I fought hard with this man. I didn't want to live a day without the one person who meant the world to me. I begged with him, "Please, just let me join my mother. If I get killed then that's what I want!" Certainly he would understand that I should be by her side.

But the soldier only became angrier with me, and he tried to kick me away. Soon he became fed up with me and threw me to the ground. I got up and attempted passing him from the other side. I tried to sneak around him several times, but he threw me back every time. It was the same story when I encountered other soldiers. They knew how to follow directions, and they kept me from joining those getting shot.

Maybe if they didn't have to follow orders so strictly they would have just thrown me in with the rest of the Jews. I will never know. But it was very clear that keeping me from that cellar was not an act of compassion on their part. One Nazi finally pointed his gun straight at my forehead and yelled at me, "If you don't leave now I'm going to shoot you." "I wish you would!" I screamed back, "go ahead and do it so I can join my mother." By this time I was hysterical and could not care less what happened to me. The soldier didn't like my answer, so he grabbed me by the hair and threw me down the street, yelling at me, "Get out of here now! Run!"

I couldn't fight with him anymore. Still I could not control my anger and agony over leaving my mother alone as she died. At that moment I hated that German more than I had hated anyone or anything in my life. For once I was wearing my armband, and I ripped it off and threw it at him screaming, "The hell with you!" He looked at me as if I were a bug and simply walked away. All I could do was stand in the street crying. I had to go home empty-handed, knowing that I would never see my mother again, and I never did.

THE GERMANS were working feverishly to draw Jews into an ever-tightening circle, beginning with the ghettos and ending in transports to concentration camps throughout Poland. It was becoming clear to many Jews that the Nazis meant to systematically dispose of those who were in no way a resource of workers for the Third Reich. Author William Woods wrote: "…Jews were brought in as to a collecting point from other towns, (and) month after month the old, the weak, the useless, the mothers with children were sent out in the transports, mostly to Treblinka…"[13]

That Nina witnessed such an overt act of Nazi execution may have been due to the fact that more clandestine methods of killing Jews had not yet been developed. Certainly camps such as Treblinka existed at the time of Mrs. Grütz's murder, but arranging transports took time and logistical precision.

Nina's mother had clearly been in the wrong place at the wrong time. Facing the loss of her mother was too much for Nina to bear. Having virtually witnessed the execution of the person dearest to her heart, she became inconsolable. Like her mother, the reality of her loss plunged Nina into such despair that she lost all desire to live.

After seeing that there was nothing more I could do to convince the Nazis to kill me along with my mother, I stumbled home completely defeated. I don't know how long it took me to get there because I was lost in so many ways. When I returned from the cemetery that day I was sobbing and hysterical, and I must have been a sight to Lina and Buzio. I couldn't even speak to my sister. I was very angry with her for letting my mother go to the cemetery in the first place. Here I had acted on instinct and asked Lina to ensure that our mother stayed home, and it amounted to nothing. If Lina had only listened to me maybe Mama would still be alive. Who knows if she would have survived the war, but I've often thought about the possibility.

In the beginning, just after returning home, I couldn't even tell my sister and brother-in-law what had happened. They figured it out in bits and pieces, and Lina was as miserable with the news as I was, but I didn't notice. I went to my tiny room to lie down and cry. I think that I cried consistently for nearly a month. After a while I became very sick because I didn't want to eat. It seemed as if my entire system was shutting down from grief.

I was like a dead person, and to tell the truth I really did want to die. This would not be the first time I felt this way. I was so very close to my mother, and her death left me emotionally destroyed. I didn't know what else to do, so I just lay in bed waiting to die. At first my brother-in-law had to put me on some medication just to settle me down, and then he tried to convince me to keep my strength up. He made me take medicine for this even though I was not interested in life.

I realized later that I was being selfish and not thinking about what I put Lina and Buzio through. At the time I felt no compassion for anybody. The Germans could have marched into our apartment, lined us all up and shot us. I wouldn't have cared and I think I would have welcomed it.

Finally, after some time had passed, Buzio came to me about my sister. He was concerned because she had been continually crying as well. I loved Lina with all my heart, and he reminded me of this, saying, "Enough is enough, Nina. You're not the only one who lost a mother. Your sister is suffering too. Do you want her sorrow on your conscience? You're destroying her with the way you're acting." For a moment it didn't dawn on me what he was saying. But soon after his remarks I began to come back to life. I had lost a mother, but I still had some family left and here I was punishing them! I respected Buzio very much and by this time he was like a father figure to me. I began to talk to Lina again and show her some affection, but I never discussed Mama's death with my sister. I knew that if I had that conversation, I would end up accusing her, and I felt that I didn't have the right to do that. She had pain in her heart too, so why increase it?

My brother-in-law later tried to find information about what had happened to my mother. Somehow it would have made her death more bearable if we knew for certain what had happened. But there was no paperwork and certainly no remains available. The Nazis didn't want these kinds of events made too public. Perhaps they thought it would create a panic among the Jews, or it might make us more willing to fight them. Whatever the reason for the secrecy, we had to accept the fact that Mama was gone and had been killed in the most horrible way.

I was only twenty-one when we lost Mama. I had failed her, and I knew this deep in my heart.

ACCORDING TO RONNIE S. LANDAU'S research in *The Nazi Holocaust*, the elimination of Jews, Gypsies, and other undesirables was done in two ways: first through mobile killing operations, then later by the organized deportation to labor camps where death was inevitable.

Once the German armed forces successfully took over a city or village, the SS set about identifying, rounding up, deporting or immediately shooting Jews.[14] The tactics employed by the Nazi SS were well documented. Editors Ofer and Weitzman stated in *Women in the Holocaust* that: "As the German army swept through the Soviet areas with large Jewish populations—such as Vilna, Lovno, Minsk, L'vov, and Kiev—they murdered hundreds of thousands of people. It was during these mass executions that the 'surviving' Jewish population was rounded up and put into ghettos. Thus the Jews in these newer ghettos had already experienced the loss of their family and friends and the destruction of their communities. They hoped that the worst was over and that the Nazis had an interest in keeping a small minority of Jews alive."[15]

By now the young Miss Grütz had few illusions as to what lay in store for her and her remaining family. Witnessing the execution of her mother had been more than traumatic—it forever changed the way Nina viewed the world around her and her place in it. As a way of protecting herself she pushed all emotion and pain deep inside, merely functioning on a moment-to-moment basis. Yet Nina resolved to somehow stay alive, if only as an act of revenge against the Nazis who had taken her mother from her.

CHAPTER V

Ducking and Hiding

(1942)

AS FOR MANY EUROPEAN JEWS, 1942 was a year of turmoil for Nina Grütz. Never one to sit and wait, she continued to believe that no matter how risky her spontaneous actions might be, better to be a moving target than to wait and fret over the next Nazi roundup. Nina's brother-in-law devised a plan that he hoped would keep his sister-in-law out of harm's way.

Once I began to finally recuperate, I became restless. I had to concentrate every single day on how to find food and avoid the Nazis. We were all trying desperately to survive, so we really had no time to dwell on things from the past. Each day we needed to find a way to feed ourselves, so I decided to try to reach my cousin Lusia's home where there was less trouble brewing with the Germans. I hoped I could find work and get a little money to send home. Besides, I was not the same after my mother died and the atmosphere at Lina's place was tense and depressing.

My brother-in-law encouraged me to go and promised to let me know when things were safe again. Just as she had welcomed my mother's visit, Lusia got word to us that she would love to have me stay with her. She promised to find room for me at her little place but I had to figure out how to get there. The walk from our place to the Grand Station was quite a distance and it was risky for a Jew to be walking anywhere, but we were not permitted on the tram.

As soon as I was ready to go my sister Lina began to change her mind. She cried, "Maybe Nina should remain with us. I think that we could protect her better if she's here." I felt differently and was starting to think that my presence was causing confusion in Lina's family. I loved my sister and her family and I would have liked to stay but they had plenty of other problems to think about without worrying about one extra person, and I knew that I could take care of myself. I made up my mind and told them it was time for me to go away and find work.

I walked out with my star armband and a little satchel, but without any of the required identification or travel papers. I was taking a very big risk. I thought I would be better off pretending not to be Jewish, so before I got on the train I took off my star. I had decided right away that when I traveled to Lusia's house on the train I would convince myself that I was not a Jew in order to pull it off. I managed to purchase a two-way ticket for myself and boarded the train without any incident! It was amazing to me that once again I got away with it. I kept my mouth shut, fearing that no matter how well I spoke Polish someone might discover I was Jewish if I couldn't pronounce a very distinct "R" sound. We Jews tended to say them differently. Eventually I became a real pro at saying the "R" sound correctly.

When I think about it now I don't know how I had the nerve to do some of the things I did during the war. I sometimes don't understand who I was back then. I was constantly thinking on my feet. Once I got on that train I pretended to be very tired and that I only wanted to sleep. That way I wouldn't have to converse with anyone, and hopefully nobody would discover that I was Jewish. I was surrounded by Poles, Ukrainians, and German soldiers! I think that I held my breath the whole way. We only had two more stations to go, and suddenly the train just stopped!

We weren't even in a station, and I saw some commotion outside my window. I thought to myself, "Oh God! They know that a Jew is on the train. What do I do now?" Instructions were given, and everybody started to get up and make their way down from the train. I hesitated and wondered if I shouldn't try to hide in the bathroom. This seemed like a good idea, because if I was discovered I could just say that I felt sick and had not heard the announcement to de-board. I followed everybody down the aisle until I found a bathroom I could slip into and held my breath waiting until I heard the Germans yelling up at the train, asking if everybody had gotten off. Other than my shaking knees I was absolutely frozen.

Well, after nearly having a heart attack from waiting I heard all the passengers begin to board again. I learned that the entire incident was based on a simple repair issue! Everything was in ruins from the war and apparently some maintenance man hadn't properly fixed a pipe or something. Once I heard that everything had been fixed and that people were re-boarding I felt a sense of relief, and began to make my way back to my seat. That's when I walked out and bumped right into a German soldier! When I looked up at him I was sure he would see me as a Jew and have me shot. I had become an accomplished actress, however, and he only reached out to steady me and then he actually apologized for bumping into me!

All during the war I always tried my best to be invisible, but when you make such an effort to do so then you also become afraid that fear reflects on your face and in your eyes.

Finally we reached the town where Lusia lived. Again, I had an unbelievable experience. Just as I was stepping off the train a German soldier who was in front of me extended his hand to help me down! Naturally it was because I was a young girl and he was trying to be polite, but my heart was in my mouth as I sweetly said, "*Danke schön.*" I tried hard to regain my composure as the soldier walked away. I would need my strength to make the long walk to Lusia's home. It took some hours, but I followed her directions, and when I finally arrived they hugged me and told me how happy they were I had made it there safe and sound.

I stayed with Lusia for a little over a week. She was very dear to us, not only because my mother had raised her husband, but also because she was such a lovely addition to our family. Lusia was a very intelligent lady and a wonderful daughter to her mother, who quite frankly could be a little demanding. It was so good to see her because it reminded me of the old times. In a way, she kept my spirits up which had been quite low.

AN ORDINARY CITIZEN moving throughout German-occupied Poland faced severe punishment if traveling without permission. For a Jew, it could mean immediate execution. Nina made her way to Lusia's town at a time when Poles were required to obtain travel permits "for any journey of more than fifty kilometers." Making things even more difficult were the impromptu searches done by Nazis periodically stepping onto trains in search of smuggled goods. False traveling papers, as well as forged ration cards, became increasingly popular among Poles, though discovery could result in swift deportation to one of the many labor camps now popping up in the eastern countryside.[1]

In spite of the very real threat to her safety, Nina had successfully traveled to her cousin's home. As ever, she began to focus on finding any sort of work that would provide for her family and distract her from bad memories.

Before the war Lusia had a very good job at the local bank in her town. Because she had been so well liked there she had very good Polish friends that she felt she could trust, and they informed her that things were going to get bad in the Jewish neighborhood where she lived. These friends felt some trouble was coming from the Germans pretty soon, so Lusia and her mother suggested that I go somewhere else to find work, perhaps just outside of town. They knew some people there who ran a little market, and they decided to send me to them with a reference saying that I was a good worker. Lusia was beside herself worrying that something might happen to me if I stayed at her place. She didn't want me to take the chance.

I didn't know who these people with the grocery store were, but I found the people and their little market somehow. The storekeepers were very nice and willing to give me a job, though they could not afford to pay me much. Just to be on the safe side I never told them that I was a Jew, so they simply assumed I was a Polish girl. I said that all of my family had been killed in the bombing and that our home had burned to the ground, destroying all of my papers. This did not bother them and I think they even felt a little sorry for me. As usual, I was so happy to find a job that I think I would have worked for whatever amount they wanted to pay. This family also allowed me to occasionally stay for a meal or two in their home, as long as during the day I could help out with customers in the market.

I liked the work and everything was going just fine. Then, after two or three days of working a young man came in the market and decided that he liked me. He was very good-looking, and any other girl would have been pleased by the attention. But I wanted nothing more than to blend into the scenery. I became very worried when this man started coming to the market every single day for cigarettes and other little purchases I think he could have done without. He was always trying to make conversation with me, and it could be that he was only trying to be nice. Finally he asked me to go to a movie. I pretended to be pleased by his offer, but inside I was hoping that he would just go away so I could keep to myself and be safe. I put him off, saying, "Oh yes, I would like to go to the cinema. I don't know if I can get free from work, however." He was very respectful and he didn't loiter around, but every time he came in my heart would beat like a drum. I didn't want him to know how much I was afraid of him and why. Back then I was afraid of my own shadow.

I sensed that I would have to run away again as quickly as possible. I was certain that he would check on me and find out I was Jewish. By then I was staying in a little apartment that was behind the store. Just to be safe I had asked the family if I could sleep in the little shed out behind the market where milk was delivered. I told them that this would be handy for the nights I worked late, but the truth was that I was afraid to go back to Lusia's. She told me that there were rumors of roundups occurring in her neighborhood and suggested I try to stay at the storekeepers' if it were possible. So I was fortunate enough to have access to this little apartment and I slept there almost every night for a week.

There was no reason for anybody to come calling there, so I was terrified to answer the knock that came one early morning on my door, and they kept knocking until I thought they would soon break the door down. I finally gathered the courage to answer it. And do you know who it was? The family had sent a message telling me that they would need the room tomorrow, and could I stay at the store all that day. When the messenger left I broke down and cried from the pressure of it!

The day soon came when I knew that I would really have to leave my nice job at the market. Neighbors were starting to ask who I was and where I had come from. It would not be long before they learned that Lusia was my cousin and that we were a Jewish family. The day before I left I finally promised to go to the movies with my suitor. I was not trying to be unkind. It was just that he had become so curious as to why I wouldn't go out, and I felt that if I agreed to go out with him it would put him off long enough for me to escape. It never entered my mind that he simply wanted to take me out to the movies. Now I can see how paranoid I was being, but that suspicion was what kept me alive throughout the war, so I cannot say I am sorry for it.

I informed the storekeepers that I had to leave in order to attend to "family matters," but they didn't want me to go. I kept the place clean and was nice to the customers. They were very good to me but I made it clear to them that I had to go, so off I went back to L'vov. I was worried about taking the train but Lusia had already supplied the ticket, so I went with my heart in my mouth once again.

———

To be honest, it was good to be home again. I did not like wondering how everyone was doing and if they were all right. I told my family why I left Lusia's town, and they agreed it was probably a good idea. There were times when we tortured ourselves unnecessarily because the Germans didn't have a clue what we were up to. But how could we know? We all became overly cautious, but as it turned out it was for good reason. The Germans proved over and over again that they wanted to destroy us. It was so exhausting, and there were times I just wanted them to get it over with. I thought more than once that I should just let them catch me and finish me off. That way I wouldn't have to think about hiding anymore.

ONCE MORE Nina evaded possible detection and deportation; however, time was running out for the young Miss Grütz and her family. Jews were disappearing from the streets of L'vov at an alarming rate, and virtually every family could claim a member of their clan as either shot or taken away to some unknown destination. Whether it was under the guise of fulfilling a work detail, or as a blatant execution, the Nazis were quickly and efficiently decreasing the Jewish population in L'vov just as they had in the cities and villages further west.

William Woods described how the SS operations were carried out: "At the most unexpected times, without apparent rhyme or reason, there would come the order for a lapanka, a roundup. Twenty or thirty SS men would swarm into a café, demanding papers. If your Ausweis showed that you worked for the Germans or—strangely enough—in the Lazienki Gardens, you were allowed to slip through the net. If not, you were marched out into the street and in many cases never heard of again. Or a tram would be stopped, all the passengers ordered off and herded perhaps to the nearest wall where they might be lined up and shot. Or in the middle of the night the occupants of some huge block of flats, men, women, and children, would be ordered down into the courtyards. An announcement would be read, according to which the building was needed for Germans, and by morning the Poles would find themselves in cattle trucks on the way to Auschwitz."[2]

Nina soon began to realize that she could not evade the Nazi roundups forever. Since her mother's death she began to lose the desire to play cat and mouse with the Germans, and often managed to save herself only by making a last minute decision to do so. Wavering between this apathy and desperation, she ultimately chose to cease making any more plans, large or small. Nina's approach to life now consisted of dealing with each moment as it arrived. It was only when she surprisingly found that she had survived one day that she would she even begin to consider what to do for the next. Strangely enough this strategy proved effective for Nina's survival throughout the war.

As time went on more and more people just disappeared. We wondered where they were going. At that time no one knew anything about the concentration camps. But we knew something very wrong was going on. My brother-in-law was distraught when he soon learned that his sister, Gina, just vanished. Gina was a physician like her brother, and had actually just gotten her credentials before the war and Buzio was planning on helping her to set up a practice in town. She had studied in Prague and was going to study for her specialty of pediatric care in L'vov. Back then it was required that a doctor study in Poland for at least two years in order to qualify to practice there.

The war changed all of Gina's plans, and for the time being she was staying with Buzio and my sister. How very sad that, like many of our friends and family, one day Gina walked out to do an errand and never came back. Buzio actually saw her from the window, and she was picked up right by the door. There was nothing he could do, but he never got over that.

Not long after that we lost track of Lusia and her mother as well. It was horrible to learn that the family I had only recently been staying with had now disappeared. I later found out how Lusia and her mother were taken. My cousin, Dr. Roth, survived the war by working for the Russians. We were able to track each other down some time after the war, and he told me that a friend from his town saw Lusia going with a group of older Jews to what must have been their execution. The Aktion had taken place in the marketplace which was where the Nazis could always find Jews from the smaller towns.

Lusia had actually been separated out with some other young people to do hard labor, while her mother was put into a group of the elderly and children. Lusia's mother had cried out to her, asking, "How can you leave me? Why are you leaving me like this?" Apparently Lusia could not bear to see someone she loved so much suffering alone, because she broke away from her own group and joined her mother. This must have sealed her fate with immediate death, but I could certainly sympathize with Lusia.

So you see the Germans were much, much worse than the Russians as an occupying people. The Russians would, in many cases, send people to Siberia as a disciplinary action. Yes, a person could die from the conditions because Siberia had such a brutal climate. But at least there was the prospect of living through the experience.

The Russians' motives were quite different from the Germans'. The Soviets sent many people I knew away, but I think that the official purpose was to "educate them about the value of labor." They believed that all employers were capitalists exploiting their workers and therefore must learn what it meant that everyone should be equal. A lot of people who went to Siberia died, but it was rare to hear of somebody getting killed outright by the Russians. This was the difference between their tactics and the way the Germans handled things. By the second or third month of German occupation we began to long for the days when the Russians were in control.

As time went on everyone noticed that Aktions were happening more frequently. By this time the Germans had already come up with the Final Solution, as it came to be known. They wanted to kill as many of us as possible in a quick fashion. We had no idea where they were going, but trains were delivering thousands of Jews to the camps every day. We knew that some of the people loaded onto trucks were still being used for labor, but now even less of them ever returned.

I experienced how it was done because once I almost got on one of those trucks. I was out on the streets trying to find food when I saw a truck, and I knew what it meant that it was there. In those days each house or building had a little entryway so that the front door stood a little apart from the street. When I saw the truck I ducked into a doorway. Before long I heard screaming and yelling, but I stood there and didn't move. It was total chaos whenever they rounded people up, so that was a little bit in my favor. Between the Germans yelling, "*Schnell, schnell!* Quick, quick! Get on the truck," and the people screaming, I went unnoticed. I just stood there in the doorway like a statue. I thought to myself, "Either the Gestapo will find me or they won't. If they find me they'll shoot me right away because I'm hiding. Or they'll put me on a truck. Either way I am probably never going to get back home."

I knew that I could not hide there long without being discovered by a Nazi, and looking behind me I noticed a cellar door. It was open, so I snuck in and was able to hide down in that dark little place for the remainder of the Aktion. Finally, I heard their motorcycles start up, and soon it began to quiet down a little bit. I stood there for maybe a half-hour or so, afraid to move. Eventually I had to get out of there and attempt going home again. I didn't want my sister to worry about me. If she went in search of me she might get rounded up as well. I could not bear the idea, so I came up from the cellar, poked my head out from the doorway and saw that the street was empty. Then I ran as fast as I could back to Lina's place.

One came to conclusions over time. At first I saw things that I couldn't believe. I would ask myself, "Am I in a dream? Do horrible things like this really exist?" It's difficult to trust yourself in situations like this, because things happen so unexpectedly and you never know how you'll react. It was…how could I say it? It was surreal. It was so frightening that I began to wonder where I was and what I was doing even trying to exist in such a way.

There is no way to explain the feelings I had at this time to a person who never experienced it. For most people the heart went dead and they operated like robots. If we were lucky enough we survived another day, if not, we were dead. We lived by the day and even by the minute. The pressure to stay one step ahead of the Germans got so bad that eventually I stopped caring. I thought that if they caught me and killed me they would be doing me a favor. There came a time when you wanted death. Then the torture of living would be over.

SUICIDE WAS A COMMON CONSIDERATION among Jews struggling under conditions that were less than human. The idea of taking control of one's own life and death was vastly appealing to a people who had been living according to the whims of the Nazi regime. For many Jews the only question regarding suicide was how to go about it. Marion Kaplan examined this phenomenon in her studies of *The Jewish Response to the Third Reich*. She noted that: "Whereas in the early 1930s many suicides [by Jews] were impulsive, by the time of the deportations, as reports and rumors of suicides raced…the vast majority of them seem to have resulted from careful consideration. Women and men planned these later suicides well in advance, paying an exorbitant price for the drugs with which to kill themselves, and carefully choosing the time in which to do the deed."[3]

For Nina the thought of suicide was not a fleeting one. Meeting with one calamity after another, she considered taking her life time and again throughout the war. At one point her plans were thwarted only by the chance appearance of a passerby.

There was a moment when I was standing at a window and I thought, "Why not just end it now? It would be so easy and then I wouldn't have to feel so scared and alone." This was right after I had lost my mother and I didn't know how I would survive or even if I wanted to.

I had decided to take off my star again, and I went walking down to the Polish marketplace. After looking around at the food I couldn't afford to buy, I saw a woman who I thought had to be Polish, not a Jew. She had left her purse sitting not too far from me, and it was a little bit open. I will never forget that moment. I thought, "God in heaven! Look what is in front of me!" I could plainly see her documentation papers and they were like gold to me.

I wanted so badly to steal her purse and use her documentation for myself. I didn't want to steal anything else from her purse. I would never take someone's money or valuables, but those papers of hers looked very good. I thought that if I could just get some documents that claimed I wasn't Jewish then everything would be all right somehow. I could be a whole different person, and let me tell you I was dying to do it. I can see her standing in front of me right now. She looked to be about my age and coloring, so why not? I was just reaching for her handbag when she walked back and almost caught me in the act! She turned around right when I was getting ready to take her bag, and I was so disappointed. How can I accurately explain how much I didn't want to be "Nina Grütz, the Jew" anymore? I began to believe that even the life of a Polish prostitute must be better than being a Jew at that time.

These were the days I began to contemplate suicide as a solution to my horrible life. I didn't know then that I would withstand much worse, and I wanted to end it all. I had heard of people taking poison, but I didn't have any, and I couldn't ask my brother-in-law to get it for me because he would know what I planned to do with it. I was more than willing to kill myself, but I didn't want it to hurt too badly. Isn't that strange?

One day I was in the ghetto looking for food and wandered into a building with four or five stories. I reached the top floor and slowly walked to the nearest window and opened it wide. I thought that if I jumped it would be like flying and hitting the pavement would be a fast way to go.

Then I could be with my mother and I wouldn't have to watch people leave me one by one. I had my hand on the window ledge and started to go out, but a man walked by just at that moment and shouted, "Who are you and what are you doing here?"

I certainly didn't want to explain that I was going to kill myself, so I said, "I don't know. I was just looking for somebody." He just stared at me and wouldn't leave. I was actually angry at him for interrupting my plan. These kinds of things happened to me all throughout the war. Just as I was ready to die, something would happen that allowed me to live. Some chance thing or person who didn't even realize they were helping me would come along. It seemed like luck, but there are times now that I wonder if I was allowed to live for some reason.

We were constantly looking over our shoulders. The closest I can come to describing how we felt is to compare it to what America had in the 1960s with racism in the South against blacks. Of course there were no black people in Poland, so instead there was hatred of people who were Jewish. I suppose every society needs a scapegoat, and in Poland it was most convenient to blame the Jews for everything. Our situation seemed worse to us because the killing was encouraged by the ruling government and even carried out in a systematic way. It must be understood that many Gentiles were taught from a very young age to hate us Jews for one reason or the other. The Germans knew this and took advantage of it. With the Nazis in control, every anti-Semitic Pole and Ukrainian had free rein to steal from and assault any Jew they liked.

It would, however, be inaccurate to say that every single Pole hated us. One of my father's friends remained loyal to us throughout the war. As the Germans started to kill us off, this old friend offered me assistance. This was the man whose family came to our defense when some people in town wanted to destroy our store. He was the director of our local bank and his nephew had guarded our store from vandalism years back. This director's name was Ravitsky. I went to see him not too long after Mama was shot by the Nazis. Even though it would be difficult to tell him the story behind her killing, Mr. Ravitsky would want to know what had happened to her. When he learned that she had been killed he told me, "If your mother were still alive there is nothing I wouldn't do for her. If she had been a Gentile and not Jewish she would have been considered a holy person for her kindness to people." Mr. Ravitsky made himself very clear to me, saying, "If you need anything please come to me. I will assist you in any way I can." So I tucked Mr. Ravitsky's name into my mind as a possible escape plan. Sure enough he ended up helping me during the war.

NINA NOW SPENT HER TIME skulking back and forth from the ghetto to her sister's apartment situated in one of the better Polish neighborhoods. Access in and out of the ghetto became more difficult. Because conditions were so poor there, Nina took her chances traveling through the non-Jewish parts of the city in order to reach her sister's family. On any one of these excursions Nina could be apprehended by the Nazis, but she had no choice. The payment given to her brother-in-law for his medical services was often in the form of food, and this was the only daily nourishment Nina could possibly obtain.

Dalia Ofer and Lenore J. Weitzman illustrated ghetto life in their collective studies of Jewish women living under German rule: "The goal of the German policy in 1939 was to facilitate the forced mass emigration and expulsion of Jews from all territories under German rule. This was a general directive; a specific law creating ghettos was never announced. Thus, the establishment of ghettos in Poland did not proceed in a uniform manner…Usually the ghettos were created after other punitive measures had stripped Jews of their jobs and businesses, confiscated their valuable possessions, barred their access to their savings in bank accounts, and deprived them of food. (Food-rationing regulations…allotted each Jew a mere 184 calories per day.) As a result, by the time they were forced into ghettos, many Jews were already suffering from impoverishment and starvation. Jews from villages and towns were deported to the ghettos in the cities, which led to overcrowding. Sanitary facilities were overtaxed, and with few medicines available, disease was rampant. Contacts with the city and surrounding villages were crucial for obtaining food supplies and for lessening the psychological impact of isolation and exclusion."[4] Nina was able to visit Buzio and Lina while her ghetto remained open. However, this precious conduit to food and her only remaining family was threatened daily.

Things were exceptionally bad and my brother-in-law heard once more from his Polish neighbors that a very thorough Aktion was going to take place to catch every last Jew in town. As it turned out, the Gestapo had quotas to meet. They had not been moving Jews out of the cities and towns fast enough. Because they relied on the element of surprise to catch us off guard, one never knew where they would strike next.

Buzio figured I was clever enough to stay out of the Germans' way, so I remained in town to work where I could and hide out with friends. But he decided to send my sister and their little daughter Alma to a different city. Even though he was nervous about letting them go, he thought that they would be safer apart from him. Buzio had arranged some kind of connection with Poles in this other town and they promised to keep an eye on his wife and daughter. So he sent them away and waited to hear back from his friends that his family had arrived. It was torture for him to wait day after day and hear nothing. It wasn't long before Buzio began to regret his decision. He didn't hear a word, and finally we had to assume the worst. Mother and child must have been intercepted by the Germans somewhere along the way and simply vanished.

For weeks we waited and hoped, but we never heard from them again. My brother-in-law then fell into a deep depression, so I had to keep finding ways to find food for us. There was no time for me to think about my loss. I did the best I could, but I felt very alone now that most of my family was gone. Occasionally, I checked in on Buzio and many times he was not home. The day finally came when my brother-in-law met up with me at his apartment. He had a funny expression on his face when I came into the apartment. He was sad and tired from losing his family and he said, "There's going to be another very big Aktion tonight. I cannot bear the idea of losing anybody else, and I don't think that you're safe here anyway. Perhaps this would be a good time for you to make your own way." He told me quite plainly, "I don't want you here anymore. Quite a few people in the neighborhood know that you are a Jew, and it's only a matter of time that you're caught and taken away. I think that they'll leave me as one of the last to go because I'm a physician, but I cannot sit here and watch you get put on a truck. You'd better do something about getting away." We had seen so many of our loved ones go out and never come back. His bitterness was so intense that he could no longer bear having people he cared about to remain with him. He blamed himself for losing his family.

I didn't understand at the time what he was trying to say. "You don't want me to be here?" I asked him. He said, "No. I don't want you here. Go and try things on your own. I believe you are strong enough to survive." Back then I could not know what was actually on his mind. I was confused and hurt because the last of my family was sending me away. I tried hard not to cry and said to Buzio, "If you really want me to leave you I will, but where should I go?"

He just looked at me awhile and said, "Any place is better. I have this feeling that if you go away then somehow you will end up safe. I cannot explain it any more to you, so please leave."

The last time I saw Buzio he was sitting alone with a vacant look. I know now that he only wanted me to save myself. True, he was so overwhelmed with the tragedies that had been going on, that he couldn't really take care of me and he certainly no longer cared about what happened to him. Can you imagine the sacrifice on his part to send away his wife and only child to what he could only hope was a safe place? He must have thought that he had failed his family, and for all his efforts he ended up alone. He had absolutely no other family except for me at this time. His sister Gina had gone missing just as my sister Helena had disappeared one day on an errand. I was his last responsibility, and I suppose he did not want to see me go. He sent me away as a way of allowing for my survival.

BUZIO'S ACTIONS toward his beloved sister-in-law may be seen by today's standards as a rejection. Nina later came to see that his insistence that she leave was a way of saving her life. By distancing her from him she would avoid a deportation that was sure to come. It was also clear that Lina's husband was no longer as determined as Nina to struggle for his life. With his wife and child gone without a trace, life had lost all meaning to Buzio.

Those who had survived the relentless Nazi roundups were all too often pushed beyond their limits. As fellow L'vov Jew Leon Wells confirmed, this sort of despair could be crippling. Following one last and terrible Aktion he described an excruciating emptiness: "I was petrified, unable to feel shock or grief, quite numb. First Mother, and now Father too (were gone). All my trouble, all my hardships had been in vain. I sank into an indescribable melancholy. I sat down on a chair, unable to speak."[5]

Nina realized that any attempt to convince her brother-in-law to allow her to stay, or even to flee in search of a hiding place, would be in vain.

I think that if Buzio had not been a physician he might have been able to hide somewhere, but by then he didn't have the spirit to escape. He had been offered a way to hide out by a leading official of the Catholic Church in L'vov. He told my brother-in-law that he could get him to Italy if he went disguised as a monk, but Buzio wanted to stay put long enough to find my sister and their little girl Alma. Anyway, there was no place where he could run because the Nazis kept a close eye on Jewish doctors. They had no idea who I was, however, and Buzio must have thought that he might try to save one last person.

As for me, I didn't know what else to do, so I left Buzio sitting there. My brother-in-law never moved as I collected my few things to leave. I slowly walked by him and closed the door on a broken man. I stood outside his apartment door for a moment, and then as I took the stairs down to the street I began to cry. I said to myself, "See, nobody needs me. So why even try anymore?" At that time I mistakenly thought that Buzio didn't want me with him anymore because my sister was gone. Deep in my heart I sensed the real reason for Buzio's asking me to leave, but I couldn't think clearly of that as I left his apartment. I only felt completely rejected, and leaving my last relative was a devastating experience.

I went to see a friend of Buzio's, the janitor who had been so generous in giving him and Lina food in exchange for medical services. The janitor's family put me up overnight but I knew that I shouldn't stay there for long. That night I slept under one of their children's beds. There were three or more people living in that little apartment, so I thanked them the next day for hiding me and left. I asked God, "Why are you keeping me here on earth? There's no point to it anymore!" I know that if I had access to any kind of poison I would have taken it that night. I looked for the easy way out because I didn't see any tomorrow. All I saw was suffering and I didn't know how much longer I could take it.

DESTITUTE AND DEFEATED, Nina wandered the streets of L'vov with no real destination in mind. Her situation seemed hopeless, yet she felt that returning to the ghetto would certainly mean starvation. Somewhere in her memory Nina recalled the words of Mr. Ravitsky, the family friend who so revered her mother. If she was in need of assistance had he not promised to take her in?

The occasional offer of Poles to assist Jews in hiding was rare, yet it did occur throughout the war. In Lenore Weitzman's study of Jews who attempted to live among the Poles during the war, she wrote of a young man who, upon escaping from the ghetto, was hidden by a Polish family. According to the account the Poles were "overjoyed" to see their former neighbor alive, and were quick to offer him a hiding place within their home.[6] More often than not, however, the Polish population was not keen on having anything to do with their Jewish countrymen. Acting as bystanders, they witnessed the beatings and killings of Jews without offering aid. As William Woods wrote in his studies of the Polish reaction to the numerous Aktions taking place around them, "...far too few were even willing (to help the Jews)... To be sure, German anti-Semitic propaganda fell on stony ground, for the Poles were only too clearly aware that they and the Jews were in the same terrible predicament. But the plain fact is that Poland stood by—in the main—and watched the murder of its Jews, if not with complacency, than at least in silence."[7]

Nina was fortunate to have a Gentile friend on whom she could rely for sanctuary. Even if it were only a temporary hiding place, staying at the Ravitsky's home would allow her the opportunity to clear her muddled head and perhaps conjure up a better plan of survival.

As I walked through the Polish neighborhoods of L'vov, crying my eyes out, all I could think was that I was tired of being Jewish. I wanted to be as far away from other Jews at that moment as I could. I know that sounds crazy because I love the Jewish people and I still consider my faith to be Jewish.

After walking around a while I realized that I didn't have a clue where I would sleep that night. Up to that point I never would have believed I could be more alone with everyone I loved erased from my life. Now, without even Buzio to call family anymore, I felt completely and totally alone. Through my tears came the realization that I was on my own and would have to think on my feet once again. It was very difficult to think in a rational way while feeling so lost, but I finally remembered our friend Mr. Ravitsky. In my sorrow his words came back to me, "If your mother wasn't Jewish, but was instead Catholic, then after her death she would be considered a saint among the Poles because of all the good she did for them." I thought of the High Holidays when my mother would make a special matzo fried in eggs that Mr. Ravitsky loved. Now maybe he would agree to hide me as he had implied earlier in the war. Perhaps he would do this as a way to honor her.

The last time I had seen Mr. Ravitsky was when I came to tell him about my mother's death. I heard his words, "I will be here for you if you ever need me. If ever you are in a position where you have nowhere to go, come to me. Whatever you need do not be shy to ask me." By this time I was certain that he and his family knew what was going on throughout L'vov. They had to have known that I had no other options when I showed up at their door.

AT THIS MEMORY Nina began to cry. Never one to feel sorry for herself, my friend usually put on the same brave face she undoubtedly displayed on countless occasions during the war. Nevertheless, the more poignant moments of her life had not faded over the years, and there were times during our conversations when Nina fought back tears. I felt badly about asking her to relive her father's imprisonment, her mother's death, her sense of abandonment, and all the other painful memories I asked her to dredge up. Yet we had to tell her entire story and this was the process.

Initially, I tried to convince myself that re-evaluating her past would be cathartic for Nina, but it simply was not true. Nina had moved on and accepted what had happened during the war, but she could never release the anguish and sorrow that had been part of her wartime experience. She had lost every person that had meaning in her young life and this changed her forever. Nina could never deny this, and I eventually had to accept that the pain I witnessed as she retold her story was the very same pain she felt years ago. The hurt was just as raw, the wounds in her heart just as fresh, and I was asking her to deal with these emotions over and over again.

I have to admit it, when my brother-in-law told me that he would no longer allow me to stay with him I absolutely panicked. Luckily, our apartment was still on the Polish side and the Ravitskys only lived two or three streets away from Buzio's place, so I had a chance to avoid these Nazis so intent on killing me.

Understand, Mr. Ravitsky's wife was a very strict Catholic. Almost every single day she went to church. I knew that she was very devoted because my mother told me Mrs. Ravitsky attended Mass at six every morning. I admired the fact that this woman was always praying, but I have to say that, like many Polish Catholics, she did not like Jews.

When I showed up at her house Mrs. Ravitsky answered the door. I reminded her who I was and very directly asked for help. I was not going to take up her time explaining too much about my situation, and as I stood in the entryway she didn't say a word. She listened to my story and then allowed me in. I stood there thanking God that at least I had not been turned away, and Mrs. Ravitsky asked me to wait while she went for her husband. She left me to go find him, and sure enough he soon joined me in the foyer. I told Mr. Ravitsky my predicament, and he immediately told me, "Well, I want you to stay here. There is no question about it, you may hide here in our home as long as you like."

I actually ended up staying there for just a short while. The Ravitskys had a little attic above their kitchen with a ladder that led up to it which was hidden by a curtain. This was around early spring so the attic wasn't unbearably warm. I was small, so I was able to stand up and move around and this was where I hid during the daytime. I was afraid to even come down to use the bathroom. Don't ask me how I held it that long, but I did. A person is capable of doing unusual things when it's a matter of life and death.

In the evenings the family brought down the ladder and let me out. That was when we had time to talk a little bit. They were very, very nice to me, and I began to feel badly about endangering them. During the day I heard the German soldiers' dogs barking, and the occasional shooting and screaming reminded me that they were still rounding people up. Those roundups were complete chaos, with beatings and raping and who knows what else. Once the Germans had things organized they could take large groups of Jews at a time without so many disturbances. I suppose this made things easier for them. I didn't really know what was going on as I hid up in the Ravitskys' attic, but I could hear the Nazis running around like crazy day and night, twenty-four hours a day, to finish the work of gathering people up and throwing them into trucks. I was afraid, but I knew enough to guess things would eventually become quiet again.

The ghetto still existed at this time and I began to wonder if I shouldn't just go there and try my luck. In that way I wouldn't be endangering the Ravitskys. After some time I sensed that the real danger of getting shot or transported had passed, and this was when I began to think about leaving. I had been considering my options the whole time I was in that attic, and I said to myself, "For heaven's sake, what am I doing? I cannot stay up here forever!" I could not stand the idea that other people were in peril all because of me! The Germans were fully aware of the fact that some Jews had Polish friends who wished to help them out. Everywhere there were signs posted, as well as Germans with loudspeakers telling people, "Whoever assists Jews will be prosecuted in the worst way." Every Pole had seen the SS marching from one home to another looking for Jews. They came with big dogs that were trained to smell people hidden anywhere at all.

I was uncomfortable with the idea of staying with the Ravitskys any longer, so I planned to come down when the house was empty and leave quietly. I wanted to slip away without their knowing. I didn't want to say goodbye, because I was afraid that Mr. Ravitsky would try to convince me to stay. But as I started through the stairwell I ran right into Mr. Ravitsky's servant! It seemed as if I couldn't even do this simple thing right. Their maid's name was Kasha and she had been with them a long time. She was very old but really a very nice lady. She had been coming up the stairs as I was sneaking down, and I think that she was very surprised to see me heading outside. She addressed me in the way Poles do when they are being respectful.

"*Panenka*," she asked me, "what on earth are you doing?"

I tried to explain my plan to her. "I think I'd better go," I whispered, "I don't think I should even say goodbye. My conscience is starting to bother me and I don't think I should put this family in danger anymore." Well, Kasha would have none of this! She grabbed me by the hand and started taking me back upstairs.

"There is still gunfire heard outside! You cannot go; it would be as if I were handing you over to the Germans myself. I am a Christian and could never allow that." You see Kasha was as religious as Mrs. Ravitsky was. I tried to pull away from Kasha but she was very determined to have me stay. Here was this old woman telling me not to go and I was fighting with her! I suppose I got a little hysterical. But Kasha wouldn't let me go. She yelled at me, "You will go upstairs right now!" She actually ordered me. I finally agreed to go back into the attic only after she agreed to inform me when the Aktion was truly over.

I have often wondered whether it was my bad luck or my good luck that I ran into this servant. I cannot say for sure. I often would look at situations like this both ways. If something I didn't expect happened then maybe it would work out in such a way that I could survive longer. But if it led to my getting caught and shot, well then that was fine too. I had lost everybody I ever cared about, so what difference did it make, after all? I came to look at things this way all throughout the war.

Ultimately Kasha helped me survive, as did the entire Ravitsky family. These people were the first to save me from the Germans, and in a way they saved me from myself, because I would have walked out that door into who knows what.

Eventually the family came home and we talked things over. Mr. Ravitsky very reluctantly allowed me to leave. Before I walked out of their home his wife pulled me aside. As I explained before, she was not fond of Jews in a general way, but she had been kind enough to hide me. I imagine she did not hate Jews in the same way the Germans did. I was a little surprised when she put a bunch of beads in my hand that I knew Christians believed aided in their prayers. I know now that they are called "rosary beads." Mrs. Ravitsky put these in my hand and held it closed very tightly. Then she said to me, "I cannot give you anything more. I do not regret giving you shelter, but now I understand why you believe you must go. Still we are all worried about you, so please take these. They will help you to pray to God and perhaps protect you."

AGAIN NINA BROKE DOWN and wept. She frequently marveled over the unexpected kindness she received from strangers during the war. She felt overwhelming gratitude to these "angels," and she never forgot that without them she would most certainly have died just as the rest of her family had. After collecting herself Nina quietly continued, saying, "It's okay. I'll come back to myself now."

I was very surprised by this gift of rosary beads, but I thanked Mrs. Ravitsky and told her I appreciated all that she had done to hide me. I left the last of my possessions with them. I think I had a dress and some mementos of my family. I put them in a box and just asked them to keep them for me so I would have some small memories when I returned. I said my thanks again and shook Mr. Ravitsky's hand. Then I left.

I kept those beads with me during the entire war, can you imagine? This was not always easy, particularly when I was later sent to work in a labor camp. I don't know that I ever held them in my hands and prayed with them. I cannot tell you for sure, and then if I said that then maybe it would be a lie. I just don't remember if I prayed to those beads. But I will say this, that little necklace with the cross got me through some difficult moments. Every time I had to move on and avoid capture I grabbed onto those beads as if they made me invisible. I would hide them close to my heart when I could, or I would put them around my leg. I don't know how I did it, but those beads survived the war right along with me. I never told anybody about them until now. I must say that I owe my life to the Ravitskys.

I left with only the clothes on my back. I still had no idea where any of my family had ended up. I didn't know where else to go, so I returned to the apartment where my brother-in-law lived, but he was gone and then I ended up in the ghetto. With my family completely gone, however, I had nowhere else to live. Eventually the Nazis caught me and I was forced to stay there because the order was that all Jews who were still living in the Polish sector must report to the ghetto.

So I followed orders…for once. I avoided going to the ghetto for some time but eventually I went in because I felt it was safer there for me. I did not know if I was walking away from my death or straight to it, but at least I would be with my own people. In all honesty the ghetto was not safe either. People would do what they had to in order to keep their little job or get a little food. Soon after I re-entered the ghetto it was closed off for good. I couldn't have left through the check points and barbed wire even if I wanted to, but I was at the point of not caring.

BY THE TIME NINA DECIDED to take up residence there the ghetto had become little more than a way station for Jews on their way to labor camps or execution. Children, the elderly, and those sick from the many diseases now raging within the ghetto walls could not be cared for, and were often left on the streets to die. Overcrowded conditions only spread disease and made life unpleasant for those still strong enough to seek out provisions.[8]

In his study of ghetto life, author Michal Unger described a situation in which: "The ghetto houses were dilapidated and poorly maintained. Most lacked such basic sanitary facilities as toilets and running water. Any cleaning or washing operation required tremendous effort."[9] Unger went on to define the importance of maintaining some semblance of health in order to survive Nazi selections for deportation: "From 1942 on, [Jews] had no choice, because the Germans regarded anyone not working as unproductive and consequently superfluous. Therefore, labor became a prerequisite for survival."[10]

Although she might have attempted to survive outside the ghetto, Nina entered the L'vov ghetto just before its complete closure. Living among other Jews seemed preferable to life on the run. Her family having disappeared, Nina deemed it senseless to continue her efforts to hide. Apathy now took hold of her entire being. For Nina, there was nothing left but to accept her fate and hope for an easy death.

192 — T<small>HROUGH THE</small> E<small>YES OF A</small> S<small>URVIVOR</small>

It was not unusual for Jews to leave their hiding places in one final act of apathy. The young man described by author Lenore Weitzman as having been welcomed into hiding by his Polish friends eventually joined the ghetto Jews. No longer able to stand the tension of living among his non-Jewish countrymen, he decided: "I'm going back to the Jews…. back to the ghetto, … to die with the rest of the Jews. In the ghetto it was a relief, I felt like I belong to the same people, and whatever is going to happen with everyone else will happen to me… On the Aryan side you are fighting for your life all the time. Even with all the dangers in the ghetto it is better than the Aryan side."[11]

Nina now cared little for her own life, and she kept to herself as a way of protecting her heart from suffering further loss. Although her stay in the ghetto would be a short one, the daily struggle took its toll on morale amongst the Jews. Separated from those living outside the ghetto walls, news of the war's progression was rare and unreliable, and many Jews found it hard to conceive of the war's end.

Most of the Jews that were left were young and strong enough to work or had certain skills, but we didn't know what was going to happen after the Germans were done with us. Only the Nazis knew what the ultimate plan would be. Not all of the soldiers knew the details, but the higher officials were informed.

As it turned out, the Germans had suffered a terrible winter in Russia. They got close to Stalingrad, but the war was turning, and the Germans were not always the winners now. They had every intention of going beyond Stalingrad, but they were stopped. When the Americans got involved in the war the allies had more resources and things were different for the Germans. We knew nothing of this, but it was interesting to find out later.

When I was living on my own, in the ghetto, I started to learn about what was going on in the outside world. There was an illegal paper that went around telling us we were on our own. It made me furious and I wanted to live just to tell these politicians off who decided not to help us. I liked Roosevelt at first, but then I realized he did nothing about bombing concentration camps for whatever reason. I feel the same way about the man who became Pope during my old age. He finally visited the camp museum like it was a big deal. He knew what the Nazis were doing, and he could have protested something. Can people honestly say that Mussolini didn't tell the Pope what was going on with the Jews?

Finally, the countries that were attacked by the Germans were beginning to stand up for themselves. Even in Poland there was an active underground, as I would later discover. I think that people began to see what the Germans' intentions were. The Poles thought at first that when the Germans came it would be paradise. The Nazis were accepted as an authority that would bring order and prosperity. It wasn't long, however, until even ordinary Poles realized that the Germans were doing exactly what the Russians had done. They were friendly while getting acquainted with how things worked. Then, once they knew the situation, they ran the show. This left all Poles to do the dirty work.

The mentality of the occupied people began to change after this realization. Many people who at first collaborated began to resent being treated as slaves, and this was how the Germans ultimately saw them. There were some that continued to assist the Nazis, because they were still benefiting from their association with them. Others would pretend to be pro-Nazi. Meanwhile they would work against the Germans in secret. It is sad to say, but in truth it was usually the Ukrainians who seemed to enjoy tormenting and killing us. This had been their history, and most of them hated Jews with all their heart.

IN MANY WAYS the Ukrainian bias against Jews stemmed from the same misconceptions and ignorance that permeated the entire Polish population. Certainly the majority of Ukrainians could be economically classified as peasants, most of whom held a strong belief in the Catholic faith. William Woods writes that, "Among a nineteenth-century peasantry that belonged to the Middle Ages, fear and distrust of the Jew were always there. To the largely illiterate Polish serf the Jew was an enemy of his church."[12] The average Pole also practiced a strict Catholicism; however, the overriding attitude toward their Jewish countrymen appeared to be one of indifference if not outright hatred. Although the majority of Poles was at least guilty of becoming "passive accomplices"[13] to the annihilation of Jews in their country, most records point to the Ukrainians as embracing the role of tormentor to their Jewish victims. That Ukrainians held a fierce and special contempt for the Jew is a concept that may never be fully explained.

The Final Solution was underway full-force by the time I ended up in the ghetto. I don't even remember the exact date they closed off the L'vov ghetto, but it must have been around 1942. It is difficult to say because they walled some places up while leaving some open. For a while we could come and go to work but eventually even this was restricted and we were very closely monitored.

Before long those of us who were very young and looked strong enough for work were collected. I was taken with a group of people to work at a nearby camp. It had been running for some time, but I was there just before the ghetto was completely liquidated. I went back and forth between the ghetto and the labor camp until one day I was simply told to remain in the camp. I know that I lived in the ghetto for some months, but I lost track of time, so I really cannot say for certain. I think it was spring when I left the ghetto for the last time. It had to have been about four o'clock in the morning because this was always the time they ordered us to get up to work. If I had to guess I would say that I lived in the ghetto for nine months, maybe less.

NINA NOW FOLLOWED the final leg of the journey experienced by so many Jews. She would be worked close to her death and eventually executed. In a sense, the exhausted and emaciated young woman welcomed the change, even if it was for the worse. Conditions in the L'vov ghetto of Janowska were by now quite grim. When sleeping accommodations could be found they were typically filthy and cramped, the average living space being thirteen to a single room.[14] To Nina it hardly mattered where the Nazis shuttled her, so long as her death would be quick and painless. Whether in the ghetto or in the labor camp, Nina lived by her wits and her own rules.

Ionce read of a Jewish man who had been placed in seven different camps! Can you imagine? And every single camp had guards who became more and more brutal. I believe I was working in the labor camp in the winter and spring of 1942. Perhaps it is difficult to recall details of this time because there seemed to be not much difference between working at the camp and living in the ghetto.

I lived with nameless people. There were very seldom families because the elderly and most of the children had been taken away by then. Mothers and fathers were separated or shot, so the little kids who looked strong enough to work were left to roam the ghetto. They could not last long like that, without someone to provide food and shelter, so eventually most of them disappeared as well. I lived with groups of young people for the most part. I wanted to be alone by this time, because I didn't wish to feel any emotion, good or bad. This was what worked for me, and for many of us it was the only acceptable way to survive. If there wasn't room for me or I wasn't immediately accepted in a place, no questions asked, I would go elsewhere. I just wandered from one dwelling to the next. I was a nameless Jew, and this somehow made me feel safe, at least for the time being.

UNTIL ITS LIQUIDATION on June 21st, 1943, able-bodied Jews concentrated within the L'vov ghetto were shuttled to and from the nearby labor camp of Janowska to work long hours under difficult conditions. The desire to avoid new relationships was overwhelming to many survivors. As they struggled to maintain their sanity in the ghetto, keeping to oneself seemed not only logical but preferable. With every loved one killed or having disappeared, remaining Jews believed that forging any friendship that would surely result in eventual separation invited only more pain.

In the ghetto there was very little food. Before they sealed it off it was easy to find vegetables, but even then it was nearly impossible to find bread. To this day I love bread. I can get full on one piece of bread. Some people were smart about bringing a little rice or flour into the ghetto with them, and a few of them were nice enough to share with me. Once they closed off the ghetto it was harder, and I was always hungry.

We were supposed to get rations, but even when these came you had to save a little for your next meal because you never knew if more was coming. There were little unofficial markets where you could trade a piece of clothing or something for food. These people at the marketplace would find a way to smuggle food in. They had a Gentile friend who left a package or two when a Jew instead of a German was guarding the fence. I saw packages people obtained that had bread, a little Kasha, or rice in them. I even saw a piece of meat once! That was a luxury.

Most of the time finding food was simply a struggle by the minute. Maybe you could get a hold of a little coffee and a rotten potato or carrot. So many Jews who had once been wealthy died from starvation and disease. It was often the luxurious life a person led that killed them because they had no survival skills and became so weak. It seemed that by working we might have a better chance of survival and I was more than willing to work. If we worked we sometimes received two pieces of bread and some coffee. Whatever the Nazis were planning on throwing away they gave to us.

I was not a stupid girl. When good fortune came in the way of a dirty, old blanket or a bitter cup of coffee, I looked at it as enough to keep me living one more day. I was curious, in a cold removed way, as to how long I would survive and what would finally kill me.

THE TRAUMA of going hungry for long periods of time left an impression on many survivors. One Tomasz Sobanski, a former inmate at Auschwitz, recalled how the fear of hunger remains with him still. "'One cannot be logical about these things,' he explained, 'I have a wife who's an excellent housekeeper, but every night on my way home I buy a loaf of bread. I know perfectly well there's bread in the kitchen... But I can't help it. I still buy bread.'"[15]

The Nazis took as many people from the ghetto as they needed to do a particular task but eventually they transported us to Janowska for good. I didn't know what was waiting for me there, but I considered it the end of me and the whole exhausting business of staying alive would be finished. After all, what difference did it make? I was completely and totally alone. I never saw anybody that I once knew, and L'vov was no longer my city. It was a good plan that I had to never have a relationship with anyone, because that would have been too painful. I didn't want any connection with someone who might disappear the next day or die before my eyes.

I ASKED NINA if she could have tolerated her stay in the camp any better if she had known that things were going badly for her captors. Later learning of the Allied success must have seemed to Nina like reading a book from the back to the front. Nina never really answered my question. She became focused on correcting my image of the Janowska Labor Camp.

When I hear that word I want to think of the places where I went in the summertime when I was just a girl. I don't like putting such a pretty name on Janowska. It was not a labor "camp," it was a place of torture and killing. They looked at us from the watchtowers and would shoot at us for practically nothing. I was like a stone when I was in that camp, moving my body but never really aware of what I was doing. Although they were clearly our enemy, it seemed as if even some Germans were uncomfortable with what was going on regarding the Jews. Some of the soldiers looked confused and almost tormented while carrying out orders. As the war went on and they suffered such a horrible defeat in Stalingrad many Germans must have started to ask themselves, "What am I doing here? Am I dying for the Fatherland? Am I sacrificing for Hitler?"

Now, do not misunderstand me. Everywhere we went it was clear that the Jews were despised, to speak in a general way. But when the killing got out of hand I believe that many Gentiles began to despise themselves. Their Christian faith must have been in question when killing and brutality were happening under their very noses. But there were very few who said a word or stood up for us.

THE JANOWSKA LABOR CAMP was known to be in operation as early as September 1941, closing in November 1943, earlier than the more expansive concentration camps. As with all concentration camps, their function was meant to be a temporary one. Those Jews who did not die of disease and hunger in the ghettos would be forced to labor in one of the many camps hastily erected in eastern Poland. Jews who could not physically work were to be killed outright by various means ranging from chaotic shooting sprees to well-organized gassing, the Nazis' eventual method of choice.

Adolf Eichmann stated very clearly the purpose of labor camps within the minutes taken at the Wannsee Conference, where the "final solution to the Jewish problem" was formulated in January of 1942. Eichmann dictated that: "The Jews are to be utilized for work in the East in an expedient manner in the course of the final solution. In large (labour) columns, with the sexes separated, Jews capable of work will be moved into those areas as they build roads, during which a large proportion will no doubt drop out through natural reduction. The remnant that eventually remains will require suitable treatment; because it will without doubt represent the most (physically) resistant part…"[16]

By the time Nina was made a permanent resident of Janowska she had few illusions as to her ultimate fate. She expected long days of hard labor until the Nazis decided to end her life, hopefully with a fast and painless execution.

It has been written that the Nazis planned on making the Polish people their slaves after they did away with us Jews. You never, however, saw a Pole in my labor camp. Maybe you would see some Gypsies, but no Poles. It bothers me to read about Polish people complaining about their conditions during the war. Compared to what was happening to us their complaints are ridiculous. We never had any official warning that we were to be sent to work at the labor camp. Sometimes you were just in the area where something dangerous was going on and you would get caught up in it. We didn't ask questions. After all, who were we to ask what was to become of us? We were the possessions of the Nazis. Just like a piece of garbage, they could throw us any place they wanted. There were plenty of Poles and Ukrainians working for the Nazis, and I think that maybe not all of them were bad people. They wanted to get by I suppose.

I have my own theory about why the Ukrainians were especially vicious toward Jews. These guards and workers in camp were mostly people from small towns and quite a few of them were illiterate. I remember that many of our servants who came from these small towns could not read or write. It wasn't their fault. The little towns simply couldn't afford to build a school. Most all of them had a little church, however, and consequently they tended to believe whatever their priest said. Few peasants ever bothered to verify if something was right or wrong. If a priest told them that Jews were no good then they believed it. I personally didn't encounter this kind of prejudice until shortly before the war, but I knew that it went on. It had been going on since before the First War. We heard again and again from the Ukrainians that the portion of Poland where we lived was originally theirs. I believe that this anger came from this feeling because before the First War part of Poland was divided up into Prussia. Later on it was established as a Polish territory. This was why in school we all spoke Polish. When the Ukrainian students tried to speak their own language they got into trouble.

When you punish a people for their culture there is bound to be some resentment. Unfortunately, this resentment was directed toward Jews because after all, we were an easy target.

I came to feel as if I had done something terribly wrong to deserve this kind of treatment. I would pray to God to help me, but they were empty words. I had no feeling behind them. I didn't have much in the way of faith at this time. I felt that He didn't see me or hear me. I didn't feel His presence around me.

———

Because of the recent interest in the Holocaust, many concentration camps have been described in detail. But there is very little information available about Janowska. There were very few survivors from there. It was small and very temporary, so there's less written about it than Auschwitz and Dachau. This is a shame. The atrocities committed there should be recognized. My information is also limited because I have blocked out many unpleasant things that happened to me there. I never wanted to remember these experiences in the first place. It was only after I was asked to speak as a survivor that I forced myself to recall those years.

It was truly horrible. The soldiers woke us up at four in the morning to work. Sometimes they were not ready for us to march off to whatever task they had planned for us, so we might stand at attention for hours at a time. This senseless waiting was called *appells (Zahlappelss, or "roll calls."*[17]*)*. There were many times I simply wanted to sit down but then I would be considered weak, and the weak were taken away to be shot. If somebody fell during the course of work, they would be immediately helped up by other Jews. Hopefully, the Germans wouldn't see their fall. A person would be better off leaning against something so that they looked as if they were strong. I saw a few cases like that, but I didn't want to remember it, so I turned away and tried to think of other things. I closed my eyes to a lot of things.

The food they gave us was just enough to keep us alive. We received some coffee and maybe a little soup with one piece of potato or carrot in it. When we first arrived we used to get a little ration of bread, and I would drive myself crazy wondering if I should eat it all at once or save some for the next day when they might not give us any. I constantly went back and forth in my mind while looking at the bread. I fought with myself, saying, "Shall I, or shall I not?" Sometimes if someone saw you standing there with your bread they would take it from you! And you couldn't really blame them because we were all dying from hunger.

Anyway, they eventually stopped giving us bread altogether. Of course the Germans didn't suffer. They ate very well and the Poles who helped to run things also ate well. There were other people working in managerial positions. The Poles had some less significant work; however, if a Pole was considered a good patriot to the Germans' cause, they might get a better position.

The Ukrainians were mostly assigned to guarding and disciplining us. As time went on the Germans had to rely more on the local people to help out. I believe this was because more Germans were being sent to fight at the fronts. Anyway, you never knew whom to trust. If you were lucky you could find a German soldier who had a little more compassion than the others, but you never really knew. The same was true with the Poles and Ukrainians; they could be real bastards sometimes. We were surrounded by people intent on beating and killing us, and this was the reality. After a while I became immune to the hardships. I couldn't think, and I didn't want to. I only prayed the Germans would finally finish me off. I was always ready to die, and yet I survived somehow.

I did see quite a lot of killing, but I cannot bring myself to speak of it, I just can't. The brutality was unbelievable. Usually the Nazis simply tried to beat a prisoner to death. People would lay there bleeding and none of us were permitted to help them to their feet or show any kind of care. This included killing children. I am still afraid of German shepherd dogs because they would release these who were specially trained to attack small children. You should have seen how well the Nazis took care of these dogs. We even had to help to keep them clean, and God forbid anything happen to them. Can you imagine?

THE USE OF DOGS as both guard dogs and means of torture was only one of the sickeningly effective methods Nazis employed to keep their Jewish charges under control. To the sadistic SS guards, children were known to be a favored target. One account told of how "…younger Jews" were chosen for a game of life and death inflicted by the Nazis in which "A huge dog was set on a Jew, who was required all the while to stand straight without batting an eyelash. If, God forbid, the Jew gives the slightest bend or turn as the dog jumped on top of him, he was beaten incessantly."[18]

The Germans demonstrated a cold and efficient manner of disposing of infants as well. Survivor Maria Bankowska described the horror women experienced upon entering a camp with their babies, where children were treated as instruments of torture to their mothers: "'I saw and heard it myself,' she insisted, 'It would be the turn of some woman with a baby in her arms (for execution). "Shoot me first," she would beg. But almost invariably they would shoot the child first. The only possible explanation is that it gave (the guards) pleasure.'"[19]

As soon as we arrived to stay at the camp for good they divided us up into male and female groups. They were taking care of our reputations maybe. The Germans guarding us would have been happy to see us all dead, and here they were showing this ridiculous morality. It was all so strange. They never even bothered to give us a number tattoo like they did in other camps. I imagine this was because they planned to kill us as soon as we finished whatever work they had for us.

When we were transported to the camp for good we were also made to give up the last of our possessions. We received a uniform, but they were dirty and often too large for us. This uniform had stripes up and down from one end to the other. After we were liberated and I moved to America I had a scare because of those stripes. We had purchased a sofa bed, and when it first arrived I opened it up to make the bed. The mattress had the same stripes as my uniform from the labor camp, and I fainted! The memories of that place stayed with me that long.

They had us dig holes in the ground where we were supposed to go to the bathroom, and just thinking of this makes me sick to my stomach now. Here the German people were supposed to be so clean. They wouldn't tolerate so much as a smudge on their boots, yet they kept us living like animals. Under such unsanitary conditions it's no wonder diseases were spreading like they did in camp. We were all so thin that we women ceased to have any menstruation to speak of, so luckily we did not have to deal with that problem. My cycle did not even begin to resume until after the war. In the barracks we slept in bunk beds. There wasn't much of a mattress really, just straw covered with cheap fabric. It was just a thin and dirty thing. Before long we were all full of lice and dirt.

Shoes were nonexistent for most Jews at this time, but we had to wear something on our feet in order to work. I suppose I could have taken a pair from somebody who was dead or in the process of dying, but I could never bring myself to do this. Eventually I was able to obtain some, but these were uncomfortable and useless too. All I could ever find were wooden clogs. Distribution of these shoes wasn't very organized, and I ended up with two left shoes. This made it very difficult for me to walk, let alone to work, because my right foot was cramped and in pain.

And let me tell you, the days were very long for us. Sometimes we would get up early to work and in the end all we accomplished was picking up debris around the camp. The Nazis were not organized well enough to give us a full day's work. Not that we were complaining of course, but why have us stand at attention in the early morning if there was no work? One day they took us on what we referred to as a "death walk." We believed that we were being marched to a place where they planned to shoot us, but something happened and there was a change in plans. Orders were changed for some reason. They ended up taking us back to camp! We never knew what was going on. We had to try and figure things out on our own.

AFTER HEARING NINA speak of her wooden shoes I was reminded of a similar story told by camp survivor Leon Wells. He had worn the same kind of wooden clogs, and like Nina working in the same camp, he would eventually stare death in the face at the edge of a pit.[20] For the time being, however, the Jewish prisoners were needed for labor, and many met death in this way through sheer exhaustion.

You had to be careful not only for yourself, but also for other Jewish prisoners. Sometimes they wouldn't punish only you, but they would punish or shoot the entire group of people you were standing with. One had to be cautious about what was said or done, because there was the constant threat of endangering others by carelessness. Automatically something comes out of your mouth and then everybody paid for it. I saw people beat up all of the time.

One day I was hit for the slightest thing. I don't remember what the beating was for. I think that I wasn't standing in line properly or something. The injuries I received from that beating gave me an infection that came back even after the war. We were directed to keep ourselves clean, but it was impossible. In the winter it was terribly cold but we actually welcomed this change because it meant that you didn't sweat and this allowed you to stay cleaner.

Anything we took for granted before the war became precious in that camp. We stood in line to take the occasional shower they allowed us. We stood in line for getting food, and we stood in line to find out what we needed to stand in line for. We shivered, naked every time we were permitted a shower, and they often made us stand there for an hour or so, just because they were angry about something. I lost my entire dignity as a woman, and all of us felt so morally low.

As for the labor, it was continuous. We worked mostly at cleaning up rubble in the city, at least in the beginning. We put bricks in wagons because apparently they were to be used for building other things. After working with the rubble we were assigned to factory work and that wasn't as bad. We sorted things and assembled pieces of machinery. It seemed strange to me that one day they would put us on an assembly line, but before we could completely understand the work they would switch us around to a different task the next day. I could only assume that they didn't want us to grasp too much about what they were doing. They didn't want us to get acquainted with the area or the people around it. This may have been a wise move because we would often try to find things out. Let's say there was a Polish man standing around who looked like he had a decent face. Well, we would take the chance and say, "Where are we exactly? What are the Germans planning for us? How is the war going?" We knew that we weren't supposed to be talking to anybody, but we were desperate for information.

We didn't know exactly what was going on, but there was definitely something in the air. The Germans were feeling others working against them. I learned later that the partisans in our country were starting to give them trouble. Apparently there were problems at the front as well. My observation was that in the beginning the Germans went full-strength to war because they were very confident. By 1942, however, you could sense morale among the German troops was down. They still carried out orders to the letter, of course, but you could tell things were not the same. I suppose Hitler realized that he might not win the war, so he was desperate to win the war he had against the Jews.

I worked as hard as I could at the camp in order to appear useful to the Nazis. I remember there was a day when we were sorting something in the factory. I was struggling to pull apart some piece of machinery that had been improperly assembled. We were required to work quickly but this piece was giving me so much trouble. I got to the point where I was actually trying to knock it loose. A Nazi soldier passed by and saw what I was doing. When I noticed him watching me I simply froze.

"Well, this is it," I thought, "he's going to shoot me for doing the job poorly." My heart was pounding out of my chest, but instead of beating me or shooting me he took this piece out of my hands and examined it. I suppose he found the right spot to loosen it, because he gave it a knock and it came apart. When he handed it back to me I looked at him with what must have been complete shock. I didn't know if he was truly helping me, or if he would now beat me for making him fix the piece himself. I didn't even know if I was permitted to say "thank you."

The whole thing had happened so quickly. Perhaps the soldier didn't want others to see him assisting me, because he immediately walked away. The other workers around me saw what had happened, however, and I knew that they were disturbed by it. Maybe it was a sort of jealousy because a German had shown me kindness. I knew that they were thinking, "Why would this Nazi help her but not me? Is it because she doesn't look like a Jew?" This was the mentality of survival that existed in the camp, and it was very…how could I put it? It was a little competitive. If one person survived that might mean that another would not. It is difficult to explain unless a person has been in that situation. I knew of course that that soldier had merely acted on an impulse. I don't believe that he helped me out of any special feeling. I was just grateful that I hadn't gotten a beating or worse. Any time nothing happened to you in the camp was always very satisfying. An uneventful day was quite welcome.

ALTHOUGH THE GUARD'S ASSISTANCE with her factory work could hardly be defined as an act of kindness, the recognition between one human being and another did much to lift Nina's spirits. She would witness only one other display of mercy while in the camp, that of a female guard who offered food to the camp Jews.

I feel it is necessary tell about the one person in a position of authority within the camp who showed us some care. There was once a woman who worked there for the Nazis, and as it turned out she was a relatively decent person. Maybe she just needed the money and was working for the Germans so that she could to put food on the table, I don't know. But this was the woman who one day, to our great surprise, brought us food! Now this was quite an event because we only received very small amounts of food from the Germans. Because this was immediately devoured we never had any extra, and we certainly were not supposed to ever have food in our barracks. Perhaps this was because the Germans didn't want us to dirty up our beautiful bedrooms. I never understood how this woman managed to smuggle food to our barracks, but she did it somehow. She entered at a time when we were supposed to be ready for lights out, and she told us all to be quiet. We were very nervous to see her, because you never knew when the Germans would barge in to check on us.

We stopped thinking about getting caught when we saw what this woman had brought us. It was only some bread and cheese, and a little meat, but we looked at this food like it was from heaven. It was the wintertime so it must have been around the holidays. Perhaps this woman was thinking about Christmas and felt sorry for us. I thought her actions were incredibly brave, because really she could have been shot for helping us like that.

The Nazis were manipulative in making certain we were kept isolated. They made sure that everyone knew that a little humanity could cost your life. So, even if a person wanted to help us in some small way they had to be so cautious. At any rate, this lady decided we were worth the risk, I suppose, and we were grateful for her kindness. She had to leave quickly, but she never got caught to my knowledge. She left her food with us and we quietly took our shares and began eating. It was hard not to cry, it tasted so good to have real food in our mouths.

The work at camp began to vary a bit. Sometimes we worked in the fields, and other times we would be assigned something completely new in the factory or elsewhere. There were many times when I was given work with machinery and I had no idea what I was doing. I had to pretend to understand until I caught on; otherwise they might kill me for not being useful. The trick was to glance to the left and right of you, and then mimic what the others were doing. If one or two people caught on right away we begged them to slow down because they made the rest of us look unproductive. They didn't always listen and would go on showing off about how well they knew a procedure.

I believe I was at this camp for a little under a year. It must have been around that time, because I don't think I would have lasted longer than that.

We all lost complete track of time other than taking note of the seasons, so it is very hard to say exactly how many months I worked in Janowska. What I later realized was that they were planning on killing all of us before the year was up. We sensed it too. After a while there was a general feeling that they were going to eliminate us. One had a feeling of death all around, and our instinct screamed at us that it would not be long before we were too weak to work anymore. Even the way the Germans began to look at us was different. I cannot explain it, but we all felt that our time was nearly up. All this time we remained ignorant of what was going on outside our little world. We didn't even know what was going on at the other side of the camp.

When they first took us to the camp we were placed in a large hall, where we slept on the floor. After that we had a sort of mat, but no blanket unless you brought one from the ghetto or stole somebody else's. We were later put in something like a barracks and beds were sort of stacked up for us. But we didn't dare ask for anything because questions only resulted in a beating.

The latrines were filthy and we had to stand in line to use them. This could be a miserable experience because already people were starting to have diarrhea, and it was difficult for them to hold on. The smell was horrible. The guards always ordered you to clean it up, although I don't know what they expected us to use. Sometimes they caught the right person who had done it, and sometimes they blamed whoever was standing nearby. If they accused you of doing it you had to clean up somebody else's mess. It was more degrading than the ghetto. We were not human beings at this point, just instruments in their hands.

I began to think that the quicker they kill me the better. With all the horrible things happening around me I didn't feel as if I should connect with anybody. Maybe it was just my way of coping with things, but I especially didn't circulate around very much.

There were two reasons I stayed isolated while in the camp. One was because I somehow felt it was a better way to survive, and the other was because I still mourned in my heart for the family I had lost. I lived for the day or even for the moment. It felt incredibly lonely to know that there would be nobody to cry for me if I died. Knowing all of this made me walk around as if I was dead already, and in a way my heart really wasn't beating.

AT THIS POINT Nina was merely functioning from day to day with very little regard as to what might lie ahead. Increasingly numb to the squalid camp conditions, she felt only a gnawing hunger and an intense loneliness. Vaguely aware that her time of death was drawing near, Nina told herself that death would come as a relief.

A final act of fate would occur, however, and this accidental event gave Nina yet another chance to survive.

It must have been 1942, around early spring, when the Germans marched us into the forest. They took us in a little deeper than they normally would have if we were to be set to work chopping wood. On this particular day they ordered us to dig a big pit. It wasn't our usual work and at first we had no idea what the purpose of this work might be. A rumor went around that this pit was for a well of some sort. I was losing strength and had to concentrate on looking healthy, so I didn't think about why we were digging such a deep ditch. The guards simply threw me a shovel and I started digging.

At the end of the day this ditch was very wide and very deep. We were filthy and tired and went back to camp too exhausted to give it another thought. A week or so later they ordered us into a truck and drove us to the same place again. As we made our way back it started to dawn on us what was happening. I cannot speak for the other people in that truck, but when they took us there something connected in my mind that told me this was going to be our final destruction. There were other clues that told me something was different. First of all, we were going by truck to a place where we had walked before, and in my mind I came up with the idea that the soldiers did not want to march back alone with no prisoners. Maybe they didn't want to draw attention to the local people as to what was going on. Also there were quite a few Ukrainians there who usually assisted with the dirty work of killing us outright.

They ordered us out of the trucks with *"Schnell. Schnell!"* I moved as quickly as I could, but my legs were like two pieces of dead wood. I could tell something was going to happen when the Germans lined us up into rows in that empty field. The first groups of women were lined up in front of the pit we had prepared just a week before. The soldiers started to load their guns. I suppose we all knew that our deaths were inevitable, and we were all so tired of working and starving that maybe it just didn't matter.

I was in a group of women from the very last truck, so I waited a long time to die. Further away they were already shooting the men. I suppose they were from the other side of camp, but we had never seen them. For some reason, the Nazis still had us separated by gender. My group was marched to some trees apart from where the shooting took place. I think they did this so that we could not see clearly what was going on. Maybe the soldiers didn't want a lot of panic because this would have made their job more difficult. It was dark now, but we could still hear things.

Finally, the soldiers came to my group and we were called up and ordered to the pit. I remember that I was standing in the middle of this group of women. I have read accounts like mine that tell of Jews getting shot while facing the pit where they would fall. This was not the case for us, however. We were facing the soldiers who were to shoot us. As I stood there with the others waiting to die my mind went numb. Some women began to scream because they could not hold themselves together any longer. Others were crying and begging to the soldiers saying, "No, no, no."

It is so strange, but I wasn't thinking about my own death at that moment. What came to my mind was a feeling of sorrow for those who had not been killed completely. I could hear them behind me moaning and weeping. It was as if they wanted to make us suffer to the very end. I almost called out to the soldiers to please make sure that they killed me right away and avoid any mistakes. I was ready to die, but I didn't want to suffer. I never said a word, however, because I had by then been conditioned not to speak.

How funny that I remembered at a time I was going to die that speaking to a soldier could get me beaten up.

I know that in some camps prisoners were asked to disrobe, but I don't remember taking my clothes off. This part of the experience I have blocked out for obvious reasons. All I remember is that I stood there as if I were frozen. I think that it must have been springtime, because a warm breeze was blowing the smell of people dying in front of me, and it started to make me sick. We were told to remain facing front, and seeing the soldiers point their guns at us made me feel dizzy. I have no other memory beyond that. I am sure there were gunshots, but I felt nothing and everything went black. It was 1942, and I was sure that I had met my death.

NAZI METHODS OF EXECUTION in Janowska were, at least at the time of Nina's ordeal, still quite rudimentary. Fellow camp prisoner Leon Wells' testimony of camp conditions corroborated Nina's accounts down to the wooden shoes they were issued. Finally, Mr. Wells faces his own death and, like Nina, experiences a mysterious detachment from the macabre scene around him: "…the morbid sight of five hundred fellow internees awaiting death swims unreal before my eyes. I am dumped in among them, but this scarcely makes an impression on me…We are led out onto the 'sands,' an open space outside the bounds of the camp. We obey the order to remove all our clothes, and then shovels are distributed to us. We must undergo the last extreme of mental torture that can be inflicted on us—digging our own graves… Since the first shots were fired, I stand there with eyes closed, feeling my life slip away from me piece by piece, as if I am stripping myself of my apparel a second time. And with each piece goes some of my pain, and it is replaced by a yearning, a desperate yearning for that moment when I will have been stripped of everything."[21]

Like Nina, Wells narrowly escaped death. For most of those assembled for execution, however, death was a certainty. An account of one such chaotic scene was given at the Nuremberg trials of 1945, by a German worker who witnessed the slayings of countless Jews in one day: "The militia provided the guards on the lorries and drove them to and from the ditch… During the quarter of an hour in which I stood near the ditch I did not hear a single complaint or plea for mercy… I walked round the mound and stood in front of the huge grave. The bodies were lying so tightly packed together that only their heads showed, from almost all of which blood ran down over their shoulders. Some were still moving. Others raised their hands and turned their heads to show they were still alive. The ditch was already three quarters full. I estimate that it already held about a thousand bodies…The people, completely naked, climbed down steps which had been cut into the clay wall of the ditch, stumbled over the heads of those lying there and stopped at the spot indicated by the SS man…Then I heard a series of rifle shots."[22]

Nina told all she could recall of her own attempted execution.

When they began to shoot us I suppose I fainted. This is the only reason I can come up with to explain how I survived. I don't recall actually fainting, but I do remember waking up. I think that it was the moaning all around me that finally brought me around, that and the smell. When I opened my eyes it was dark, and I really thought that I was dead. I said to myself, "Oh, this is what death is like. What a surprise!"

Then I noticed the smell around me. The air was thick with the smell of blood. It must have been around dusk. I might have been there for three or four hours, maybe less. The constant sound of shooting was gone and now it was very quiet. The soldiers had done their job and they were gone! It felt strange to be by myself with no soldiers around.

THERE IS NO DEFINITE WAY to explain Nina's unexpected survival. Perhaps it was the fact that the Nazis' killing tactics were disorganized and inefficient at the time her group of prisoners assembled. In addition to the guards' clumsy efforts to kill Nina and her fellow inmates, there were other exceptions to the procedure. The women were, at first, only directed to dig a ditch, and then upon completion of their task were allowed to return to camp. There were no orders to descend into the ditch before the shooting, and the guards made no attempt to ensure all the victims had effectively perished. It could be that none of these facts had a thing to do with Nina's ability to escape. Once again my friend could only point to a lucky streak that seemed to follow her throughout the war.

Lying there with all the other dead and dying prisoners I was not convinced that I was not also dead. Then I asked myself, "How can I be dead if I can smell blood? Yet how can I be alive with all of the shooting that went on?" I was very confused. I didn't know what my condition was or even where I was.

I pinched myself, and determined that I was alive. I remembered then that the soldiers might come back to bury us, and I got a very strong feeling that I had to get away.

I tried to stand up but my feet wouldn't hold me. I decided to try and crawl, but I had to go over bodies. This in itself was horrible because many of them were still warm and some of them were not quite dead and were moaning in pain. I expected to feel pain as I crawled away, but other than being very weak I had none. I could not believe that I wasn't injured! Once I realized this I made more of an effort to move quickly out of the area. It was a very bizarre experience. I once heard of another Jewish woman who fainted during a shooting such as mine. It was very unusual, but it happened more than once and this helped me to later understand the situation a little better. Sometimes fate allows you to beat the odds.

I didn't know why I had survived. All I knew for certain was that I couldn't make myself walk for some silly reason. Maybe the fear had left me paralyzed in a way, but I worked hard at pushing myself away from the bodies and the smell of blood. Finally I was able to stand up. I looked around to see if there were any soldiers around and found that I was completely alone in that field. Stumbling toward the woods I began to run. I no longer had on any shoes because they took our wooden ones away before the shooting. I had on only the worn remains of my uniform. Now and then I had been able to find a little *shmata* to put on. You know what that word means? It is really nothing more than a little rag. This was all I had for protection, but I didn't feel the cold. Let me tell you I ran like crazy.

I don't know how I got the strength, but I made it into the woods and eventually collapsed under some trees. I was just too tired to go on. It had gotten darker and I couldn't see very well at all. I didn't know where I was or even if I was heading back to the Germans! The forest was very quiet, so I lay there gathering my strength and decided to just go deeper into the trees where I could hide. I don't know how long I was in those woods, but it was long enough to become very hungry. I ate some leaves and even the bark from some trees because I was absolutely starving. I heard water from a stream nearby, so I was able to get a drink and clean up a little bit. I slept in the woods for a long time. To this day I couldn't say if my time there lasted a few weeks or a few months. I was so confused by what had happened to me, and I was very weak.

I grew so tired of running that I was ready to give up again. What was the point of living through the shooting if I were to starve to death in those woods? I prayed, "God, be good to me and just take me. I don't want to run anymore." I started to walk as much as I could during the day so that I could see where I was going, and then I slept at night. I thought, "Well, if I meet somebody who wants to kill me then that's that. At least I won't have to run anymore. What will be, will be."

I think after witnessing the killing at Janowska, I was sorry for myself for not having been killed too. I could not help feeling this way because I was so miserable. Everyone else had finally found peace in death, and here I was struggling as hard as ever. It seemed so unfair. What made me continue, I will never know. Was it my destiny to survive? There are feelings I had during the war that are impossible to describe, especially after so many years.

Finally one evening I saw a light! At first I believed I had imagined it. I felt almost unconscious most of the time. Really I was walking around only half-coherent, so that light could very well have been a hallucination. It was strange to see something besides trees, because all this time I hadn't seen a soul. So I gathered up the rest of my strength and slowly walked closer to it. As it would be many times during the war, I didn't know if I was going to my death or away from it, and most of the time I simply didn't care either way.

Was I going to find in that light more Germans? Would I find a bear or some other animal that could hurt me? For a moment or two I was certain that I was imagining that light because I was so tired and hungry. But as I got closer I saw that it was the light of someone's home! Now it would be risky to just walk up to a stranger's home, especially considering how I looked, but something inside pushed me toward it. I came closer and saw that it was really just a hut. I held my breath and knocked. A peasant man came out and looked at me with complete surprise. I was already thin and dirty at the camp and all that time in the woods must have made me look as if I were not even human. I stood there trying not to fall, and all I could manage to do was to say my name. After that I fainted right on their doorstep.

I COULD NEVER BE CERTAIN if Nina had given me every detail of this horrific event in her young life. Was she truly not forced to undress before her executioners, or had she somehow blocked out the humiliation of it as a way of preserving her sanity? I did not have the heart to press my friend for these details as it seemed excruciating for her to bring up any memory of this brush with death.

The next phase of survival had begun for Nina. With the help of strangers she would soon be transformed from despised Jew to ordinary Polish girl. No more wretched than her neighbors who struggled to make ends meet during the German occupation, Nina now possessed the same chance as her countrymen to survive. It would take all of her acting skills to keep from betraying herself as an imposter.

CHAPTER VI

The Whole World Is Running

(1942-1943)

BY 1942 THE NAZI REGIME had begun to implement the "Final Solution to the Jewish question." The systematic annihilation of every Jewish man, woman, and child was discussed and organized during the Wannsee Conference in January of that year. Headed by Heydrich Reinhard operating under the orders of Adolf Hitler, Nazi officials devised a cohesive plan that involved transporting Jews and other political prisoners to collection areas located primarily within Poland.

Upon arriving at these concentration camps, the young and infirm were immediately separated from family members deemed strong enough to work. This heart-wrenching selection process was followed by the horrific cramming of the undesirables into large gas chambers disguised as showers. Those selected for labor did so until death due to exposure, disease, or starvation. In typical Nazi fashion, the number of Jews destined for execution was carefully calculated in order of those countries the Germans wanted to conquer, yet they also included neutral states such as Switzerland and any sworn allied nation such as Italy. The final number of victims came to eleven million.[1] What the Nazis did not calculate were those slated for death who, like Nina, actually managed to escape under the rarest of circumstances.

It did not matter how many times Nina and I went over that dreadful night when the Nazis attempted to execute her along with her fellow prisoners; she could never recall the event in much detail. I always managed to glean enough information from my friend about any number of wartime experiences. This was accomplished by simply returning in our interviews to a particular subject, and over time Nina would reveal some tidbit that had previously eluded her. My friend wanted to present as complete a picture of her life as did I. Although it was painful for her, she gave up the details concerning her mother's murder without hesitation. Why, then, did Nina find it so difficult to recall the circumstances of her own close call with death?

It could be that she subconsciously erased the nightmare of the mass shooting as a way of protection. By the age of nineteen Nina had, after all, witnessed the death or disappearance of every significant person in her young life. Perhaps, after enduring so much emotional stress, she was no longer able to cope with another Nazi assault. To deny the reality of her near-death experience, and allow her mind to black out nearly every detail revolving around it, would be a very wise tactic for Nina's emotionally battered psyche. I had to accept the fact that no further information about this event would be forthcoming, whatever the reasons for her lack of recollection.

With this in mind, Nina and I focused on what happened to her after crawling from the pile of dead and dying prisoners. Since she could not exactly say how long she hid in the surrounding woods, I could only assume that she lived there long enough to grow very cold and hungry.

Happening upon the peasant's cottage could have been a blessing or a curse for Nina. Poles did not collectively accept Nazi anti-Semitic propaganda but they were acutely aware of the penalties administered for hiding Jews. Among the rural class there also existed a residual distrust of Jews, which had carried over from the Polish peasant movement of the late nineteenth century.[2] There was considerable risk involved whenever a Jew sought sanctuary among the rural population in Poland because of the anti-Semitism that continued to percolate within these communities. It would not have been uncommon for a Polish farmer to turn in the rare Jewish escapee, either for profit, or from fear of German retribution. As would occur so often during Nina's escapades, luck was on her side, and she was fortunate enough to drop upon the threshold of a sympathetic peasant couple who nursed her back to health.

I cannot recall certain things about the war no matter how hard I try. I should remember, for example, more details about the camp and how the Nazis tried to execute me, but I have blocked them out. I think I would have gone crazy if I had done otherwise. While I was standing at the edge of that pit waiting to be shot I felt as if I were standing among faceless people. Why would I want to remember how sad and lost these people looked? I was one of them and I barely knew myself anymore.

One thing I will never forget, though, are the people who helped me during the war such as this husband and wife who took me in with no questions asked. I was lucky because most people at that time would most probably have turned me in. There are many people in Poland even now who hate Jews. I went back there in 1999 to visit my hometown and see what was left of what I thought of as home. I wanted to see if it was the same L'vov that I remembered. I also wanted to find out if anything remained of the bad memories, such as the ghetto and the labor camp.

I went to the site of the Janowska labor camp, but they had turned it into a jail of some sort. Some of the towers were still standing, but it seemed different, cleaned up from what I recall. Still, it was very strange how standing there gave me a familiar reaction. My skin felt as if it were stretched very thin when I looked at the towers, and I felt my body go numb as it had the day they tried to execute me. These feelings came as a surprise to me, but I wanted to scream at that moment just to get away from it all.

It seems to me that nothing has changed in my heart and my mind about what happened to me. Even today when I think about these places, and how they played a part in my life, I feel the same way. If I could find a place to scream about it in secret I would do this. Now that this part of my story has been told, my life as a Jew running from the Nazis, I would like to not think about it any longer.

It is easier for me to remember the details of my life after escaping execution. That is because I was more of a whole person once I got away. I was still scared and running and I was still a Jew. But I was not as dirty and hungry, and so I was thinking more clearly. I suppose I didn't feel the need to shut myself completely down as I had in the ghetto and the camp.

I will say quite plainly that I would not be alive if not for the man who opened his door and allowed me to faint into his little house. This peasant man and his wife took me in and cared for me, and for this I will always be grateful. I never forgot what they did for me, and like so many other moments in my life, I was fortunate to have stumbled into the right people in a time of need. I am certain that this couple was aware of the risk they took in helping me. Even the poorest of peasants knew that if you helped Jews, who were considered by the Nazis to be an enemy of the German people, then you were no better than a Jew. Certainly many Polish peasants hated Jews, but I didn't feel that from this man and woman. Lucky for me this couple was also brave enough to hide a Jew.

This was still risky business for me. Some people who had been paid by Jews to provide a hiding place would later turn their Jews in. They did this for money or food as the war became worse. Other Poles initially agreed to hide their Jewish friends, but as time went on they were afraid that their own families would be killed if the Jews were discovered. In a way I don't blame these people, but I cannot help but have a bad opinion of them. We Jews had no choice but to march off to wherever the Germans chose to take us with their guns aimed at our backs. Those who watched it all happen could have made the decision to help us in some way. There were a few Poles willing to help, even if it was for a little while, and they were angels as far as I am concerned. As for the peasants who helped me, I think they must have seen the posters tacked up everywhere that shouted: "He who helps a Jew is worse than a Jew." Naturally this meant they would be killed right away for assisting me.

NINA WAS CORRECT in assuming that the Germans strictly forbade any assistance to Jews. Radio announcements and ubiquitous posters made it quite clear to the Polish masses that aiding a Jew in hiding would result in swift and harsh punishment. In his research of World War II Poland, author William Woods noted that, "[By] the summer of 1941…huge placards began appearing in the streets, and they read: 'Jews mean lice.' Or there would be the drawing of a Jew, and across his face the word: Typhus."[3]

Yet historical record clearly points to instances in which local Poles assisted Jews in spite of these warnings. Eighteen-year-old Liza Chapnik managed to survive an execution similar to that attempted on Nina with the help of a peasant woman: "I suddenly heard the sounds of women and children crying. I was frightened and hid in the hollow of a tall tree. The shouts and crying were awful, absolutely unbearable. I don't know how long I stayed, trembling, in the tree. Finally a Belorussian woman walked by. She saw me and said, 'My little flower, what are you doing here?' She took me in her arms [and] on the way to her house, she told me to tell everyone that I was her niece, Danusia…She risked her life for me. (Notices had been posted everywhere warning that those who hid Jews would be immediately shot or hung.)…Later I learned that the Nazis had gathered [Jewish] children, women, and old people. They took them into the fields, forced them to dig large pits, placed the women and children on the edge of the pits, and shot them. The victims fell down into the pits, even though a great number of them were still alive."[4]

Nina's protectors were among those who made the often spontaneous decision to protect a Jew in need. Woods' research indicated that: "…there were hundreds, indeed probably thousands of very brave people…In fact, between September 1942 and May 1944, some two hundred peasants were executed by the Germans for harboring Jews. In at least two instances, the inhabitants of an entire village were burned alive…For in some places, in a hamlet called Osiny, for example, the peasants deliberately assumed collective responsibility and arranged that each should hide a Jewish girl for a certain period so that everyone would be guilty and no one could inform. All in all, there was probably more done to help Jews than will ever be known, for of course we are less likely to hear about the helpers who were caught and murdered."[5]

Nina's appearance and manner of speech would later allow her to infiltrate the ranks of those bent on eliminating her race. While recuperating from months of hard labor and starvation, however, it was imperative that she stay hidden from view. As they nursed her back to health, Nina's saviors must have realized that their unexpected guest had once been a prisoner of the Nazis.

I later learned that this couple's name was Niekolawitz. But it took a little time to become acquainted at first, as all of us were careful of what was said. I didn't even know that I was alive when I first woke up from fainting. The first thing I saw was the woman who had taken care of me. I will never forget the new feelings I had and I thought maybe I was in heaven. I opened my eyes to discover that for the first time in ages I was clean. I had a dress on that certainly wasn't mine. Oh, it felt so good to be a human being again! I was afraid to even ask for a mirror, because I thought it would all go away if I saw my reflection.

My new protectors were kind to me. They filled me in a little about where I was, and who they were. That first night we didn't talk very much because they wanted me to rest. They spoke Polish fairly well, but they were obviously simple farmers and working very hard to survive. They didn't have any children that I could see, so I was alone with them all day.

I lay in their attic recuperating for maybe as long as a month. I was very sick and thin, and it took some time for me to get better. Even after I began to feel somewhat normal, it was decided I should keep to my hiding place during the daytime. We had an unspoken agreement that it was best for me to stay out of sight. In the evening, however, I could come down and join them for a meal. It felt very much like the arrangement I had with the Ravitskys, and I felt that I could trust these people.

Although I had a million questions about how the war was going, I felt it would be better to keep quiet and say as little as possible. Instead of talking so much I listened to what they were saying to each other about the state of things. This helped me to understand what was going on in Poland. The husband and wife didn't seem to mind my listening to their conversations, and although I was a stranger to them, I knew they were not afraid of me. They must have known that I was in need of a plan, because in their conversations they began mentioning various groups who were working against the Nazis, and I suppose they were collectively considered the Polish Underground.

This was the first time I had ever heard of such a thing, and it sounded very promising. Trying to find these partisans and working with them seemed like a good idea to me. I needed to come up with some kind of plan for myself, and the thought of doing anything to stop the Nazis was very appealing. Besides that I felt as if I was depending too much on the nice couple who took me in, and it made me very uncomfortable. Again I was in a situation that placed others in danger. As soon as I regained my strength I thought of leaving to find the partisans they spoke of. The days soon became warmer, so it must have been the end of spring when I left the peasant couple. I remember that the trees were getting very green, and it was easy to find soft branches to sleep on. I had lived in the woods before when it was cold, so I felt that I would be all right if I tried to do so again in the spring. I didn't want to hear the Niekolawitz' arguments about why I should stay, so I left very early in the morning without saying a word to them. I felt badly about disappearing without so much as a "thank you" to them. But I knew that, in this way, they could honestly say they had no idea where I was if questioned. Sneaking away in the dark I felt a little relief and a little sadness. The little house represented a kind of comfort to me, but in the woods I felt less responsibility for the lives of those innocent people. Anyway, it was life in the woods for me yet again.

I cannot remember how long I lived outdoors, but I immediately began looking for people from the Polish Underground. I do recall that it was scary living there for so long. If the wind whispered in the trees I would become startled thinking someone was coming. The days and nights stretched out and I lost track of time again. I went without speaking for so long I could not remember what my own voice sounded like. I was jealous of the birds I saw in the woods. I said to myself, "Why can I not be a bird and go wherever I like without being afraid?" I don't know if people can understand this now, but I hated the fact that my life was nothing but hardship simply because I was a Jew. I didn't hate Jews. That would be ridiculous. I loved my faith and the culture in which I had been raised. But I hated my situation.

Maybe I was being selfish, but all I could think of was, "Why me? Why do I have to be a Jew in this place at this time? Why could I not have enjoyed the pleasure of it as my grandmother and mother had known?" When I think about it now I can look at the way I felt as making perfect sense. I had been surrounded by a loving family, and then suddenly I was completely alone, and dealing with so much tragedy without a soul to speak to of it. Anyone would feel desperate and sorry for themselves, but at the time I battled with my feelings.

The loneliness became so unbearable it took up every thought I had in my head. It was worse than my hunger, or how filthy I had become again. Eventually I got used to the idea that I might be alone for some time. I settled into it in a way. This characteristic stays with me even today. I am still a loner. I suppose some habits are hard to break when you learn them at a young age. I see it in myself now, that unless someone approaches me I keep to myself. The war left a strong imprint on me.

SURVIVOR JUDITH MAGYAR ISAACSON described a similar personality trait acquired during the war, explaining how experiencing the Nazi transports developed later into anxieties over normal tasks. She found that she would, "...get frantic in crowds, hate standing in line, and dread packing for a trip." Like Nina, Mrs. Isaacson's aversion to wasting food was a byproduct of suffering near starvation while a prisoner of the Nazi regime.[6]

Once again on the run, Nina had little hope of surviving in the woods for long. According to author Nechama Tec, there was great risk involved in seeking out partisan groups for assistance. Ms. Tec's investigation of Jewish women's lives during the Holocaust showed that, "life in the woods posed serious challenges and threats," and that Jews were "easy targets for unruly partisan groups. Some of these fugitives were robbed and murdered; others were stripped of their meager belongings and chased away." The odds were against Nina in joining, let alone surviving, any Poles operating as underground soldiers. As a half-starved and clearly vulnerable young woman it would be difficult to convince the rough gangs to take her in, since, as Ms. Tec's studies indicated, "usually only young Jewish men with guns stood a chance of being accepted in a non-Jewish partisan group."[7] With no other chance of survival, however, Nina continued to search out these groups, eventually gaining their trust and ultimately being given her very own mission.

Finally I stumbled upon some partisans. I heard them quietly talking in the woods. I didn't even know if they were the actual "Polish Underground" the Niekolawitzes had spoken of, they might have been a different group trying to work against the Nazis at this time. When they realized a strange young woman was approaching them they surrounded me and began to ask questions. "Who are you?"

How I looked, I can only imagine what they thought of me. After living in the woods I was even worse than before: very dirty and thin. I don't recall how I carried out the simplest of physical demands during this time. I believe that I forgot some things I did to survive because they were just too disgusting to remember. Things like soap and water and food were luxuries I couldn't even think of! From what I remember, I told these people my name, but I was too weak to say much more. I collapsed in front of them just as I had with the Niekolawitzes.

These people were not like my peasant friends, however. They gave me some water, but kept asking me questions. There were only about five or six of them, some of them women. One of the ladies asked if I was alone, and I said, "Yes, but I would like to stay and work for you. Some people I know told me about your work against the Germans. I want to do something like that." Well, they weren't about to confirm they were this underground group. They acted as if they weren't sure what I was talking about at first. Then they told me they would have to check with someone else, their leader who wasn't there, and find out if they could use me. I never told them I was Jewish, because I really didn't know what kind of people I was dealing with. They never asked me, so luckily the question never came up.

My first impression was that they wanted to get rid of me as soon as possible, but they allowed me to spend the night with them. I was so disoriented, and I'm certain that I came across as a little crazy. They gave me a little bread so I wouldn't be hungry, and this helped me to sleep in a way that I hadn't enjoyed for some time. The next day they left me there in the woods, and told me to wait. One of the women leaving looked at me with some compassion, so I had a tiny bit of hope they would come back. I lay down to rest and just prayed that these people would return. I had to consider the possibility that they would only come back to hurt me. For all they knew I was lying just to turn them in somehow. I thought of running away, but where would I go?

It became dark and I fell asleep. The next morning I woke up wondering if I should move on to find people that truly were from the

Underground. Just then one of the men came back and spoke with me. My heart sank when he said they had spoken to their leader, but decided that they couldn't use me.

I don't know if these people were anti-Semitic, or if they even figured out I was a Jew. They did not ask me and I never offered them the information. They did make it clear they didn't trust me, however. Ironically enough, they might have thought that I could be a spy for the Nazis! Somehow they had determined that I was no good for them. The man's words woke me up. I sort of came out of my stupor and I yelled at him. I was so tired of being alone. I shouted, "Go ahead and shoot me if you doubt who I am. I would rather die than to live one more second on my own!" I became very impatient and angry. I had gone so long without human touch that I really think that even getting beaten up or shot would have made me feel more alive.

When you lose contact with other human beings for such a long time, you lose your own sense of self. I know it sounds crazy, but people really do need other humans in order to survive. I looked at that man deciding my fate, and I said to him, "Well, I was supposed to be shot along with all the other prisoners in my camp, so why don't you just finish the job and be done with it." I could easily say this because I simply didn't care anymore about what would happen to me.

THE PARTISANS that Nina had encountered could have been affiliated with any number of groups existing at the time. The "Home Army," "People's Guard," and "National Armed Forces" were only a few of the titles given to various underground operations. Though they all were steadfast in their anti-German sentiments, many were also anti-Semitic.[8] In order to place operatives in positions most likely to thwart the Nazi war machine, however, these groups needed volunteers who looked convincingly innocuous and were adept at thinking on their feet. If the occasional Jew fit these prerequisites then some partisan groups were more than willing to enlist the services of those eager to prove themselves.

For Nina, the choice was clear. She was determined to either become part of the Underground, or die in the process. Luck would remain kind, and the man who had no doubt been sent to kill Nina decided instead to take advantage of her innocent appearance. As a new recruit she had much to learn and very little time in which to prepare for the deception.

I am pretty certain that if I had been no use to these partisans that man would have shot me as nothing more than an inconvenience. I suppose he came to realize that I would be the perfect sort of person to work for them. I was clearly a desperate young woman, and I had no attachments that would stop me from doing dangerous work. It was obvious that I had become sort of fearless even if it was in a stupid way. I was, in many ways, perfect for their work. I was young, and knew how to speak different languages. It would be very helpful to have someone working for them who knew both German and Russian as I did.

On top of all this, they may have recognized that I looked like an innocent girl, not at all like a shady character who might be a spy. After hearing me rant, the man said to me, "Okay, we will see." It was as simple as that. He left me alone in the woods again, and went back to speak with his group. This time it wasn't long before they returned and began to tell me what they had in mind. The man said, "Maybe we do have a job for you. It is extremely dangerous, but if you are willing to do it then we'll give you a try."

Since I spoke both Polish and German, they decided to put me in a position working for the Nazis. They said, "We will get you very convincing papers that state that you are the kind of person who could work for the Germans." The one man I had yelled at gave me my instructions about where to go and what I should try to do. They never did tell me what group they were from. I suppose that it was better to know as little as possible about each other. That way if one of us were captured and tortured there would be less to reveal. It was just as I had operated with the Niekolawitz couple. This made sense to me, so I asked very few questions.

I couldn't believe that these partisans wanted me to work undercover posing as a regular Polish girl! This was when it really sunk in that I didn't "look Jewish," whatever that truly means. The game had worked for me before, but I'd always thought it was pure luck that I got away with so many things as a Jew without an armband. Now these people, in what I assumed was the Underground, had arranged for me to obtain a new identity completely different from my Jewish one. And wasn't this what I had hoped for?

Still, it felt very strange to become a different person who was not a Jew, or even someone's daughter or sister. They gave me papers that stated I was a Catholic Pole named Marysia *(pronounced "Maria")* Kvasigroich, and without any living family. The best part was that one of the women gave me a fresh dress, and I was able to clean up a little in a stream. That in itself was heaven! I then received a little suitcase with a few more changes of clothing. Why would a Polish girl show up for work with the Germans with absolutely nothing but the clothes on her back? That would have been very suspicious. The people in this group were smart about what they were doing. There were a lot of Polish girls looking for work, and the Germans were providing minor positions in all sorts of things to keep up with the war. As the war went on the Germans got tougher about rations, and young Poles were hungry for work. I was supposed to come across in this way and be very natural about my desire to find a job.

It all seemed like a big risk to me, but what else had my life been for the last two years? The partisans, or whoever they were, had the power to make me into someone the Germans would actually hire instead of shoot! They changed my name and told me, "You are Polish now." And that was it! I had false papers, and all that was needed now was to register somewhere to work. They told me that I would have to walk quite a distance to take the train. Then I would travel by train to a town where they thought I would do the most good.

The way they worked was really very smart. Most every time I spoke with someone in the group it would be a person I had seen only once or twice. In this way I wouldn't be able to pick them out or describe them to the Germans. They told me, "If you are ever detained by the Germans, remember, you don't know us or who gave you your false papers." In a way this would not be a lie, because I really had no idea who these partisans were, or with what group they were associated. They were organized and careful, and they worked very quickly. Everything took place in the privacy of the woods. To me, they were brilliant, and they were giving me a chance to do something important. With a new dress and a new identity I was being sent to Dnepropetrovsk, which had been part of Russia before the war. It was a very big city even then, and still exists under this name. I was supposed to present my documents to the registrar there, and I went off thinking I could pull it off.

By the time I got to the station, however, I began to lose my nerve a little. After living with a star on my sleeve for so long I felt as if people could still see it on me. I thought for certain someone would realize I was a Jew. With my false papers everything was hotsy-totsy getting on the train, but when I looked for a seat I realized I was almost completely surrounded by German soldiers! I was absolutely dying on the train out, because it was full of military personnel. Still, I loved being able to travel at last, and to be surrounded by other people. For the first time in a long while, I felt like a regular person and not one of the walking dead. Just by doing ordinary things in a crowd I felt as if I were being treated like a queen!

The soldiers on the train were actually very polite, and a few of them tried to strike up a conversation with me. One of them even asked if I wanted something to eat or drink! I suppose this was because they believed that I was a Polish girl who was going to work for them in occupied Russia. It felt very peculiar to be treated so kindly by a people who only recently were concentrating on killing me.

Because of the constant stress, the train trip seemed to take forever. I passed the time pretending to be asleep so that I wouldn't have to speak to anyone. I was so afraid that by opening my mouth I would somehow give myself away. Each time the train made a stop I contemplated getting off and finding someplace to hide. But where would I go? I had to face facts that the best chance for survival was to go through with the plan given to me by the partisans.

It ended up taking two whole days just to travel what would have normally taken perhaps only half a day. Our progress and speed dragged because the condition of the tracks was so poor. Bombs had destroyed a lot of the rails, so the train moved very slowly through so much wreckage. Though I didn't know it at the time, the trains going west to the concentration camps were moving efficiently; possibly they were carrying the last of my family to their deaths. I couldn't think about my family, however. Not if I was to be helpful to the Underground. So I held my breath and tried to act as if I was as normal as everyone else on that train.

I arrived at my destination without any problem. This surprised me and gave me courage to keep going. I didn't really know who I was supposed to seek out, or what I would say once I actually stood face to face with a Nazi. I didn't even know anything about the organization where the partisans were sending me. Just to have a name to give them I call this group "the Underground," but I never had a clue who they really were. I suppose I was taking a big risk even trusting them, but what choice did I have? Everything seemed so unclear. What sort of qualifications was I supposed to pretend to have, and who exactly was I to seek out for employment? For the first time I was irritated that these partisans didn't want me to know too much, even if it was better for everyone that I remain in the dark. I would have at least liked to know more about the job I was applying for. As far as I was concerned this small detail could not have been some dark secret or too much information for me to have.

I finally found the building where I was supposed to report, and I had been told that I had to register in an office upstairs. As I made my way up I saw a good-looking officer coming down the stairs toward me. The German soldiers could be very handsome, but I was still so afraid of them. I had no idea where to go or what to do, but I had to do something daring to snap out of my fear, so I took a chance and stopped this man. I was so scared that my hands were shaking. I had to hold one hand with the other to keep from shaking as I handed him my papers. I don't know where I got the nerve, but I just thrust my papers at him and I said, "I have been hired!" Well, he just took my papers and told me to follow him. He didn't even look at the documents! The Underground had done a very good job with them, and I think that was why I was so convincing. Still, there was no picture of me to go with these papers, so I was a little surprised they worked so well.

The documents said that I was Polish woman and suitable for office work. It was a very good recommendation for the job they had for me. I was led to another man who looked over my information, then he said to me, "Okay, okay. Everything is in order. Just go ahead and register and that's it."

It was like a dream. He didn't look at me or pay me any attention. I went to another office to register. They were very organized and in full operation. Here they typed my name onto the list of workers. There was a Polish man in charge of hiring; I suppose you would say he ran the personnel office. He looked over at me for no more than a second. I never actually spoke with him, but he was consulted for a few minutes, and then I was given a position. Nobody ever double-checked my information, or said anything to me about my papers. Once I registered I never saw those forged papers again. No one ever questioned the legitimacy of my identity until just after the war. I never did learn how the Underground made arrangements for these kinds of jobs. They had some kind of connection with the Germans to find workers. I still have no idea how they did it, and if you asked me all day I couldn't tell you.

POLISH RESISTANCE GROUPS became exceptionally skilled in the art of forgery during the war, going so far as to create stamps identical to the Germans' to authenticate Polish dollars.[9]

With her papers in place and, at long last, a purpose to her life, Nina re-entered Polish life. Having been brought up to embrace Polish as well as Jewish culture, Nina was at an advantage. Jewish women who had grown up in the cities were particularly good at "passing" for regular Poles. Ms. Weitzman noted that this was because, "Jewish girls were more likely than Jewish boys to attend regular Polish schools, learn the Polish language, become involved in secular activities, and grow up enjoying Polish literature and culture…" According to Weitzman: "Jewish women's prewar involvement in economic and secular activities in Poland provided them with important networks for securing false papers, with resources for locating jobs, and with friends to help them find a place to hide or live (illegally) outside the ghetto. Their ability to speak Polish and their knowledge of Polish customs were tremendous assets in helping them escape from the ghettos and pass on the 'Aryan' side."[10]

Although Nina had the appropriate look and bearing to pass as a Pole, identity papers were crucial not only for her to obtain work, but to safely walk the streets. According to Weitzman, "Perfect Polish and Aryan looks were no protection from an immediate arrest if one did not have a valid

'Kennkarte', or Polish identity card. A bad forgery might be even more dangerous than no card at all, because it might make the police suspect that a Jew was trying to pass."[11] The constant fear of being discovered required Nina to walk a fine line between putting on a confident air while remaining vigilantly cautious. This farce proved especially difficult when the young Miss "Kvasigroich" came under the employ of the German military.

It felt good to be around people again, but every time somebody looked at me I shivered inside, wondering if they knew I was Jewish and basically a spy! Outside I was smiling and behaving like a nice Polish girl, saying *"Goodendach,"* but in my heart I was struggling with my new image. When I lay in my bunk at night I thought every little noise was a German coming to arrest me!

The first job I got with my new identity was in a company mailroom run for German soldiers. I didn't like that there were other Poles working in the same building. I no longer trusted Poles, and I was afraid I might run into someone I knew who would give me away. I tried to avoid them as much as possible. I was given a room to sleep in next to our office. We were told that later on we would have to find our own apartments somewhere in town. I was happy to do this because I wanted to be as separate from the group as possible. The Poles who worked for this organization were a separate group, but at first there weren't many of us so I ate lunch with the German officers. They asked me to join them in the dining room. These people had no trouble acquiring supplies, and for the first time in years there appeared to be mounds of food in front of me. The Germans had their own chefs and plenty of everything. Later on I put my Russian to use when I was sent to purchase food from the local Russian shopkeepers. Generally, however, the Germans had everything they needed shipped in.

I was so hungry when I saw all of that food on my plate. But I was in a new place and surrounded by German officers, so I was too nervous to eat. As the only woman at the table I was more than a little nervous. This remained the case for some time. The Germans were always short of staff, and they constantly had to rotate people around to do administrative work. Anyway, the first time I walked to the lunch table all the officers stood up and we greeted each other with "Heil Hitler." Let me tell you that felt a little strange. They must have thought that I was very shy because I didn't talk very much. They asked me why I wasn't eating and I said, "Oh, I've just always eaten my meals very slowly." I wanted to pick every piece of meat off the bones on my plate, but I was simply too nervous to finish my meal.

There was not much time to eat as we were still on a very tight schedule. This organization was a military arrangement in every way. They were military men and used to a different kind of life, but I think I represented to them a member of the family they had left behind in their homeland, maybe a sister or a daughter. I was a very young person at this time, and I looked even younger than I truly was. I think they wondered where I came from and what I was doing out there. They must have felt a need to take care of me. They also seemed to appreciate my manners. I didn't come across as someone too forward, a woman who might be thought of as cheap. I behaved well and so they were protective of me. After all, there was a war going on and they were very far away from home. If something or someone reminded them of that home then it became very dear to them.

NINA'S BRAVADO and quick thinking saved her on countless occasions. Many times during our discussions I wondered how I would have reacted under the same circumstances. I tried to imagine what it might be like to convincingly present myself as a woman raised in the Jewish culture. Even in today's homogenous society I know that I would most certainly give myself away to other Jews. Nina found herself in a far worse situation, for the line segregating Jew from Gentile was much more defined in wartime Poland. To properly execute the illusion required a certain frame of mind that would force her to completely discard "Nina Grütz" for "Maria Kvasigroich."

As a tool safeguarding this persona, Nina told herself that she was "a regular Polish girl," and not a Jew. To reinvent oneself under duress might do substantial harm to a young woman's identity over time. The degradation suffered under both the Soviets and the Nazis had already chipped away at Nina's sense of self. The act of discarding her Jewish self, along with losing her family, finally created a schism in Nina's personality. All that saved her from a potentially crippling depression was the demanding position she held working under the Germans. Losing herself in work, Nina had little time to mourn her family, or to question her ability to keep up appearances.

In the beginning of my career working for the Germans I was under the supervision of a rather difficult woman. She was a little cold and demanding. I think she was in her thirties, and she very clearly presented herself as my boss. As a German she considered Polish people to be inferior; maybe not as inferior as the Jews and Gypsies, but definitely not an Aryan. Many Germans knew then that the ultimate plan of Hitler was to turn all Poles into slave labor once the Jews were gone. I think my new boss resented that she needed me to translate Polish into German for her, and could also speak a little Russian.

It was a good thing that I spoke Polish so well without any trace of the glottal "R" that many Jewish people had. I passed as a Pole many times in this way. I was raised to speak Polish and even a little French, and I suppose I was a little proud of it. The Germans, on the other hand, were often unable to communicate with the locals in an effective way. They spoke what was considered the more refined languages, such as English, but the people working for them were often simple peasants. The Germans tolerated these peasants because they were needed for skilled labor, but it was not a friendly relationship.

I soon learned that the woman I worked for simply didn't like me. We had an argument over a stamped package that was short two cents. She became angry with me over it, but I said, "Look, I didn't put the stamp on this package, and I don't like your accusations. If you have a problem with my work I don't have to stay here!" She was nasty to me so I was nasty right back. I suppose I was a little nervy, and when I think about it now I realize I was risking my life. Without a job I would lose my usefulness to the Underground and the benefit of posing as a Pole. But in the end I was pleased that I answered back to her. Nobody liked her anyway. Later on she found the misplaced stamp, but she never apologized to me.

We didn't speak about it again, and soon after I was transferred to another position in a similar department. I never learned if it was because of what I said, but it was the best thing that ever happened to me. I still worked with the mail, but in this new department we were directly involved in its transport. Because of the war it was difficult to send and receive mail, and we had to constantly adapt.

I was put in charge of walking to the main post office to collect the military mail. I didn't mind this because I enjoyed being outside, especially on pretty days. We received the mail for soldiers stationed at the front, and held it until notified of the soldiers' locations. Everything had to be marked in a certain order so that when the soldiers came back they were certain to receive it. In this way, I always knew where the front was, and a little bit of how things were going in the war. I also had occasional access to the stamps used to validate certain documents, and these were papers that could be useful to the Polish Underground.

Once I almost got caught because I didn't get the stamps put away in time. I was using them to create illegal papers when I heard the other workers coming back from lunch. Some days I would start to go to lunch along with everybody else, then say, "Oh, I forgot to arrange some papers properly, I'd better go back and correct it." Sometimes people offered to help me, and I would have to convince them it was somehow better I do the work myself.

I was constantly trying to figure out ways to get alone with those stamps. As the others were leaving work I would have to dream up some reason to stay. "I'll leave in a little while," I would sigh, "but it won't take long so you all go ahead." The whole time I copied these stamps my heart was beating out of my chest! As quickly as I could I stamped blank papers I thought would be important to the Underground. At times I could do up to fifty of them. Even now I don't really like to reveal too much about what I did for the Underground. You never know if someone is still alive who might want to retaliate for what I had done. I've kept certain secrets for a long time, and I try not to say too much to the students I speak to because what I did was so dishonest. How could I justify living a lie for so long? Some young people might not understand why I did it.

OBTAINING THE PROPER DOCUMENTS and stamps was risky business, but to the Polish Underground it was essential to their work. Forgeries were much more convincing with these tools at hand, and Nina was not the only partisan providing valuable articles needed for travel, reconnaissance, and creating a general nuisance to the Nazi war machine. In Weitzman's research it was determined: "If one could not get real documents with the name of a real person, it was best to have real papers with false names…Blank forms and stamps might be stolen (or supplied by friendly clerks), and the bearer could fill in a false name and biographical data. Finally, the most common and the least valuable documents were total fabrications—which about 51 percent of them (those 'passing') had."[12]

Nina literally risked her life with every effort she made to use the precious stamps available at her workplace. Out of necessity she became skilled at creating excuses for staying behind while her co-workers left the office, and then finding still more reasons to leave work and spirit the illegal documents away.

I worked for the Germans first in Dnie Propetrosk, and then in a nearby city called Vinnica. All the time I was smuggling stamped papers to the Underground I tried not to think about the penalties if I were caught. Prison wouldn't be the outcome. The real problem would be when they cut me to pieces for this forging of documents! I would be considered a spy against the Germans, and so the Gestapo would certainly have tortured me to find out whatever I knew. Still, I continued and was able to communicate with the Underground through some unknown person at the post office. Once I had the papers I needed I would make an excuse to leave work and walk there. I left because of so many "headaches" my co-workers must have thought I had a brain tumor! There was a tiny little outlet, a small compartment where I could leave things for the person at the post office.

Nobody saw me doing this, thank God. I became friendly with the postman at the window, and found ways to distract him so I could place the papers there without him seeing it. I would say to him, "Oh, you have the prettiest postage stamps," or sometimes I would bring him part of my lunch and say, "Why don't you eat this. I am so full, and you've been so nice to me." This worked like a charm because everybody was hungry at this time. Nobody had enough food. Sometimes this postal worker would go to answer the phone, and I wouldn't have to do anything to distract him. But most of the time I had to manipulate things to work in my favor. I don't think this man was ever aware of the little slot where I put the documents. For all I knew it was where they put garbage! It was just a little opening and not very noticeable. I left the documents there, and from there I don't know what happened.

I also had to be careful not to move from one apartment to a better one, because it would have drawn attention. My papers would have been more closely scrutinized if I went to another town. I was particularly careful around Ukrainians. I don't know how the Ukrainians could tell if you were Jewish, but it was as if they had a nose for it. Though I must say, I saw that sometimes they suspected people of being Jewish who were not Jewish at all. Thank goodness I spoke Polish perfectly. I haven't used that language for almost sixty years. It feels a little rusty, but I can still read, speak, and write in this language.

I RECALL THE FIRST TIME I actually heard Nina communicate in her native language. It was at Carpinteria High School where my own stepdaughters attended Casey Robert's social studies class. Nina was present to tell the students of her wartime experiences. By this time Nina was a dear family friend, and my daughters approached her beforehand with hugs and warm conversation. Always by their side was Jennifer Kosvo, a young friend who had met Nina once or twice at our home.

Nina and Jenny immediately hit it off. Not only were they both of Polish background, but they also shared a wry sense of humor that could both delight and surprise. The girls shared a brief conversation with Nina as the classroom filled up with other students. Soon it became time for her to speak, and the room was silent except for Nina's voice, small but strong, speaking of her family, the Nazis, and all that had happened to her as young woman. Nina finished her story, and as ever a hush fell over the group of young people. The time had come for questions, and many hands eagerly shot up to ask Nina things I had heard before as well as things that surprised me. Finally Nina recognized Jenny's hand, patiently extended and accompanied by an impish grin. "Yes, honey?" Nina asked. Jenny proceeded to ask her question in the Polish language her parents forced her to study all throughout her sixteen years.

Nina's face reflected so many things at the sound of her native tongue: recognition and delight mingled with a touch of confusion. There had not been many opportunities for her to converse in Polish, and as a young immigrant to America, Nina had all but discarded her native language in order to more rapidly learn English. Even so, she seemed pleased to try out the almost forgotten language. The words seemed to hang on her lips like an old, forgotten friend. She answered Jenny's question in her native Polish, then explained to the rest of us who were, by now, intensely curious over the exchange. "She wants to know if I still speak Polish, and if I miss the country where I was born." She then addressed Jenny herself, saying, "You know, honey, it is a little difficult to understand you, because you speak Polish with a Californian accent!" At this Jenny blushed, but I was proud of her for having the courage to stand out among her peers at a time in her life when fitting in was the most important thing. I admired her parents for instilling a respect in their daughter for their native land.

At the same time it seemed sad that Nina had been forced to abandon her own culture at an age not much older than Jenny's. Above all I felt an odd sense of nostalgia at hearing Nina speak Polish in such a natural way. It suddenly occurred to me that this was how my friend spoke during her years of "passing" as a Pole. The perfection of grammar and pronunciation had lent a certain amount of prestige to the Grütz family before the war. As a Jew hiding in the open, this skill became an armor that, along with the careful camouflage of any Jewish inflections, saved her life.

While listening to Nina speak Polish I felt as if I were transported to those places of loneliness and desperation when she worked for the Nazis. It brought home the reality of my friend's solitude as she lived in uncertainty and fear. In the midst of her own inner chaos, she did her utmost to reflect a hard-working, efficient Pole employed at a German military outpost.

I worked in a unit that was part of a larger company in charge of rebuilding the bridges and railroads. They repaired whatever had been destroyed by the fighting so that German troops could travel back and forth more easily. I hesitate telling you the name of this company because I don't want to endanger the man I worked for. I know that sounds silly and a little paranoid, but I was so young and he was so good to me. I will say that his name was Mr. Zgoda. It actually wasn't a German name, but more of a Polish one. In Polish it roughly translates as "one who keeps the peace." Isn't that funny? I always wondered if he was of Polish ancestry, but who knows where Mr. Zgoda came from. He held a high position in the Nazi army, and this helped me later when I was once interrogated by the Gestapo. Mr. Zgoda had been a lawyer before the war, and since most professional people were given a high rank when drafted, they made him a major.

Anyway, I wouldn't want him to know that I lied about who I was. I worked closely with this man who was considered the director of our department. When I met him I had a bit of a scare that turned into good fortune. My good luck came out of a dangerous situation once again.

The first day I began working at my new job I walked into the director's office and said good morning. Herr Zgoda stared and stared at me until I became uncomfortable. I immediately thought, "Well, he knows that I am Jewish!" I looked straight into his eyes and in my heart I said, "The heck with it. Whatever happens is destiny and if he turns me in, so what?" He showed me to my desk and the moment of fear was gone. I later learned that the reason he couldn't stop looking at me was because I looked so much like his daughter! She and I were about the same age, and he lost custody of her when he and his wife divorced. I felt so sorry for him that he had to be without his daughter.

Perhaps because of this Herr Zgoda and I became somewhat close. Sometimes we talked about our families, but I couldn't tell him much about mine, so mostly I listened while he talked. I told him that I lost all my relations in one of the earlier bombings. I lied about not having other siblings and claimed to be completely alone. I excused this lie because it kept me safe and working at a job I liked. I made it seem as if I didn't like to talk about this bombing incident, and that made it an easier subject to avoid. Mr. Zgoda probably felt a little guilty that his government had caused the death of my whole family. Although he never knew I lost my family because they were Jews, I felt that he sincerely cared about me. He protected me the entire time we worked together.

I did well in my position in spite of the fact I wasn't quite sure of what to do in the beginning. I have always been inquisitive, and this curiosity saved me many times during the war. I was never afraid to admit when I didn't know something and constantly asked questions. If an answer wasn't clear, I would ask even more questions until I got something right. Most probably I drove some people crazy with this method, but it always worked for me. In this way I brought my level of learning up a little higher each time. I still believe that if someone is kind enough to explain something, everyone gains in the end. If you don't ask questions, you never learn. I learned how to do my job just as I had at the hospital and in my statistical position with the Russians. I asked questions and remained flexible. The only difference was that I was basically working for the enemy, so I had to be more careful about keeping to myself.

While I was working at the post office with Mr. Zgoda I became terribly ill. I couldn't come in to work for days. Soon he became worried that I didn't have everything I needed, so he sent someone over with medication and a vaporizer. I eventually got better, and when I returned he asked how I was. I have to admit, I was actually angry at him! I thought he hadn't come to see me personally because he was too much of a big shot and didn't have time for me, a lowly worker. Anyway, when I returned to work he noticed that I wasn't acting as I normally would, and he asked me if something was wrong. At first I didn't want to tell him what was bothering me. But when he insisted, I said to him, "It just seems to me that because I am only a Polish girl it wasn't fitting for you to even come and visit me. I suppose it goes against your prestige to associate with an employee just because she's sick." I considered Mr. Zgoda a good friend and father figure, so I was very hurt when he didn't come to see me even once. I had been very sick, and when he didn't come for even a short visit to check on me, I thought that perhaps I was wrong about our friendship Maybe he was just being nice to me because I worked for him. But then why had he told me that I reminded him of his daughter, and why did he treat me practically like family?

When he heard what I said his face grew very serious. "What a child you are," he said to me, shaking his head. "What do you think people would say if they saw a man like me coming into your place while you're in bed? Don't you know that such a visit could really damage your reputation?" This had not occurred to me, but he was right! One little rumor could get me thrown out of my apartment, and it would have been extremely difficult to find another place to live. He said to me, "You are so young that you don't even think about these things. You have no idea about what life is all about." I argued with him, saying that I was very grown up. I was working and had managed to survive the war up to this point. "Yes," he said, "you have done pretty well and can take care of yourself I suppose. But if somebody saw an older man like me come into your apartment with food and drink, the talk would start. It was not my reputation I was worried about, it was yours!" He was right. I had been smart enough to find work and a place to live, but I wasn't sophisticated about situations between men and women. He gave me a whole lecture and I think I deserved it.

I suppose that I was in the dark because I lost my family right at a time when I should have learned about men and women. My mother and sisters weren't around to tell me how to deal with men in certain situations, though I must say that people did not speak freely of these things. My sisters probably learned a lot of things on their wedding night. Well, Mr. Zgoda set me straight about how appearances matter. I learned that day that even though I was still an innocent girl, I might not remain that way if I trusted men to automatically respect me. I would have to be careful and remember that I was vulnerable as a girl on my own. In this way Mr. Zgoda treated me like a daughter. He kept an eye out for me and protected me. He also helped me not to starve on more than a few occasions. He often received packages from home, and would only open them when I was in the office. He shared the food and nice things that were sent to him.

I could never reveal to Mr. Zgoda my true identity, but there were many times I wanted to. Instead, I had to act as if I believed in many of the principles he seemed to take very seriously. I had to pretend, for example, that I was pro-Nazi. One day we were having a little chat in his office, and knowing that I never received news of what was going on in the world he told me what he had heard from certain authorities. "The war will be over soon, Maria," he said to me.

"Oh, why is that, Herr Zgoda?" I asked.

"The Italian leader Mussolini has joined the Axis and is fully supporting the Führer," he replied. "This will increase our strength and perhaps send our troops home early."

My heart was in my mouth, but I was a good actress. "Oh, that sounds wonderful," I smiled and said, "so Hitler is winning!"

When I got home that day I felt the need to do something physical to release the rage within me. "For heaven's sake," I screamed into my pillow, "why does God allow these things?" The Pope and the Vatican were in Italy, after all. Did this mean that God was on Mussolini's and Hitler's side? I thought, "Where is the end? Where is the salvation?"

I never really knew for sure how much of a Nazi Mr. Zgoda was. He was a wonderful person in every other way. And though a lot of people acted as if they were behind Hitler, they were only afraid of the Nazis, and were doing whatever they had to in order to survive.

I had no real friends at this time because I was afraid of giving myself away. After I received my new identity I knew that there were a few Poles who were against the Nazis. I was too careful to ever investigate who these people were. I was a loner back then because I had to be. I met a couple of Russian people who I sometimes went with to market, but we weren't very close. I didn't want to risk knowing anybody because it could be dangerous. I even avoided the few little office parties we had because they often included drinking of some sort. At the time I just could not handle my liquor very well. Once I became older and knew to avoid the strong stuff, then I was all right. But when I was young I couldn't drink.

I came to this conclusion after joining in on a little party with friends from work. It was a spontaneous party that none of us expected. The Germans had captured a part of France, and I cannot tell you how many big loads of trucks came with all sorts of alcohol. They didn't want the soldiers to get too drunk, so they just started giving the champagne and wine to people in our office. We had a Polish kitchen at this time where we could gather with some of the workers from Russia, and let me tell you Poles and Russians love to drink. Perhaps we all got tipsy a little sooner because we were a bit on the thin side. We were surprised at this lucky break and over-celebrated.

There were two people there at our little gathering that helped me out of what could have been a lot of trouble. There was a manager at work by the name of Henryk Klaczkowski. It's so funny that I remember like it was yesterday the names of some people I met during the war. He was very intelligent, and an important figure in this organization. I never really liked or trusted him, but on this particular night he did me a real favor. He had a girlfriend that was working in our office as well, and her name was Danucia. She was a little mysterious and was my roommate for a very short while. I will tell you about my problem with this couple later. For now I have to give them credit; it was Henryk and Danucia who saved me from myself that night.

Once I started to drink I felt dizzy and found it difficult to stand up. I was very young, and I didn't realize what a little bit of alcohol would do to me. Henryk noticed that I was having trouble, so he told Danucia to help put me somewhere I could sleep it off. They locked me in a closet where I lay down, and for this I was grateful. There were quite a few young men who wouldn't have thought twice about taking me for a little walk, if you know what I'm saying. Henryk and Danucia locked the door from the outside so that nobody would take advantage of me, and they checked in on me from time to time to see if I was okay. Who knows what I was drinking, I certainly don't remember. The Germans allowed some of the men to have that batch of liquor, and I know I could have easily been raped by a drunken soldier if I'd left that party.

I later found out how precarious my life was when my job was threatened by the manager, Henryk. He and his girlfriend Danucia kept trying to befriend me. Knowing that it was better to be a loner I tried to stay away from them, but Henryk kept including me in their conversations, and acting as if we should all do things together as Poles. He actually asked if Danucia could move in with me temporarily, since she was new in town. I sensed that this girlfriend of his was Jewish, and thought this probably meant he was Jewish too. My feeling was that they were pretending to be Polish and hiding like me. I thought that Henryk must have smuggled Danucia out of her ghetto somehow. Anyway, he didn't leave me much choice but to have her move in for a week or so. After all, he was my superior and I really could not say no to him.

My new roommate was a bit of a talker with me, and from what Danucia told me she and Henryk had become close after his wife died. I listened as she talked and talked in my apartment, but I really didn't want to know anything about her or Henryk. I sensed that it could be dangerous. There was one very clear indication to me that my new roommate was a Jew like me. The first day I met her was in the winter. She walked into the room and I saw that she was shivering from the cold. What I noticed most, however, was that her winter coat had markings at the collar and wrists from thread that had been ripped out. I remembered our own coats at the beginning of the war had these marks, because Jews weren't allowed to have fur. We had to take it from our coats, or else we would be arrested. It made me very sad at the time, because my father gave me a beautiful coat just before the war. It had fur lining on the inside. It was blue and I don't even think I got to wear it much even though you couldn't see the fur. When I saw Danucia's coat this memory registered in my mind, and I thought, "Oh, this girl must be Jewish!" I didn't say anything to her, but I really wanted her out of my apartment as soon as possible.

DANUCIA COULD COUNT HERSELF quite lucky that her identity became evident to one as sympathetic as the young Nina Grütz. Something as simple as a winter coat could easily give a fugitive away. It was true that Jews were not permitted to own fur, and were forced to relinquish such goods to the Nazis almost as soon as the Germans took control of a territory.[13] Jews who were successful in passing as Aryans did so by maintaining a healthy paranoia. By continually imagining what sort of behavior might give them away to the Gentiles surrounding them, these imposters managed to refine their "other" selves to such an extent that the most suspicious acquaintance would not question their ancestry.

Sandra Brand, a Jewess in hiding, kept her hands still while speaking so as not to give away this Jewish "habit." Survivor Nechama Tec claimed that Jews could be recognized by "the sadness in their eyes." She recalled her parents telling her to "pretend to be happy. Think about happy things. You must have happy eyes." In her research Lenore Weitzman came to understand that: "Although the perceived importance of blond-haired, blue-eyed Aryan looks (were essential for passing during the war) many testimonies suggest that manner and bearing were just as important as physical appearance. Most of those who were passing went to great lengths to try to conform to what they saw as the appropriate bearing and manner."[14]

Nina wisely gave no indication that she was on to her roommate's secret. Not only would it have drawn attention to herself, it might also have forced her to one day betray her own sham. Aside from the feelings of empathy Nina had for her Jewish sister, there was also the inescapable sense of distrust toward Danucia and Henryk. Who could say what calamity could occur should the Gestapo take any one of the trio in for questioning? By revealing her own Jewish identity to these co-workers, Nina would have placed herself in a vulnerable position. Instead, Nina followed the tried and true pattern of keeping to herself, and she breathed a sigh of relief when her temporary roommate found alternative lodgings.

D anucia eventually moved into a little place that Henryk found for her, and for the time being I had no trouble with them. I even joined them socially in a town called Zmerinka. As the war went on we were all getting a little thinner and somewhat desperate. It was hard to find certain kinds of food and materials because everything was going toward the war effort. We began to crave things that we used to take for granted like butter and sugar or even a decent winter coat.

One day I heard some people talking about a place where you could obtain certain things that were, by now, luxuries to us. I don't remember exactly who was talking about it. I think maybe it was something I heard in the marketplace. By now I had enough courage to go up and ask these people about it. They told me about the town called Zmerenke *(presently spelled as Zhmerinka)*, that had a restaurant, a coffee shop, wonderful pastries, all the things we no longer had in our town. The only problem was you had to cross the border into Romania. The idea of it really appealed to me. The next time I went to Sunday market with my neighbor, Maria, I told her of this place. She told me that it was possible such things existed in Romania, and in fact she had a very good friend in that country. She used to visit this acquaintance quite often before the war, and had often wondered how this friend was doing. I told Maria I was going there, and she expressed some concern about my safety traveling over there, but I was determined to go.

No one was supposed to travel from one country to the other without permission from the Germans. By now only German troops were on the trains, and travel was strictly limited. I don't know if I could find any of the towns that existed in Romania on a map today. Even during the war borders were changing, and little parts of some countries became part of Russia. That sort of thing makes it difficult to point places out I knew during the war. But I believe Zmerinka is still there, and a group of people from my workplace was planning to go to this town that might provide the luxuries we craved. I believe it was Henryk and Danucia who were always asking if I wanted to join them on this excursion, and I thought of declining their invitation. I was convinced that they were Jewish, and I was afraid to accompany them anywhere for fear of getting found out myself.

The day they said they were going to this town, however, well I really wanted to go. Besides, this would be a large group of people who really were Polish. They always socialized together as Catholics. One of the men was actually from my town of L'vov, and I always thought he suspected me of being a Jew. I didn't worry too much about him, because he wasn't very bright. Every time he received pay for his work he drank it away. I think he was a little crazy too. This man had a wife back home, but I remember one day he said to me, "I'm going to marry you!" He said, "If you're ever in trouble and need some kind of security I will do this. I will make you my wife." I wondered if he knew that I am Jewish! Otherwise why would he suggest such a thing?

This man accompanied us to Zmerinka along with me, Henryk, Danucia, and some other people from work. It was a brave adventure because we didn't have any passports or documents of any kind! We decided to go on a Sunday morning, and then return in the late afternoon. One of the young men was able to get a truck for us to drive over there. If we hadn't found that truck it would have taken us two days to walk to the border, and that would have been impossible because we had to be back in time for work.

We made it over without any problem at all! It was amazing, and the town was everything we had hoped. There were pastries there that we hadn't tasted since before the war. Oh, they so were good, and I purchased some for my friend Maria. I think the people in Zmerenke thought that we were Germans, so we were treated with a lot of respect. An official finally confronted us and asked for our papers. He was *Zandaremarmenia,* which is like a Gestapo official. On the Romanian side this was what they were called. He saw that we didn't speak Romanian, and he wanted to know what we were doing there. Well, to make a long story short, we all got arrested!

NINA LAUGHED wholeheartedly over this. It was as if she and her group of friends had merely been caught in a prank. This was basically how Nina saw the event, and it didn't appear to have frightened her much, though certainly she must have been in some danger of being found out as a Jew.

The whole group of us got hauled in! They were afraid to keep us too long because they found out we actually worked for the Germans. After an hour or so they let us go. We went straight back home. We were a little afraid, but mostly we had to laugh over why they arrested us. We couldn't figure out if we had been detained because we didn't have our papers with us, or because we didn't speak Romanian. It all seemed so funny at the time. It wasn't as if we had stolen anything, or committed a crime really. When we got back home we decided no more Zmerinka for us! This was too bad, because at this point in my life it was my favorite place. I found out later that it had an open ghetto where many Jews survived the war. This was where my future husband actually lived. It was run by the Russian regime, and many of them knew the Jews from before the war. They took care of that ghetto their own way, and they refused any Nazi interference. How they were successful in doing this I don't know. But those Jews survived the entire war. Can you believe it?

Things settled down again after our little adventure, but before long I found out that my friendship with Henryk and Danucia had been based only on what they could get from me. Henryk learned that his girlfriend's position was going to be taken away. The war was not going well for the Germans, and they were planning on pulling out of Dnie Propetrosk. I suppose the Nazis were beginning to get rid of some of us before moving west. They were losing the war, and planning on pulling back toward Germany. I found out about this later in a conversation with Mr. Zgoda.

Anyway, Henryk soon decided that he wanted to get rid of me so that he could give my job to his girlfriend Danucia. I learned this one day as he walked into my office and said, "I think that you'd better start looking for work somewhere else, because someone is coming to take your place." I believed that Henryk could do this to me quite easily, because he was in a pretty good position to order people around. Everybody had to show him respect because he was in a high position. He was in charge of hiring people, and he spoke perfect German. But when he came for my job, that's when it really dawned on me that he was Jewish just like me, and he had survived in the same manner I did.

When Henryk told me I no longer had a job everything made sense to me. He wanted his girlfriend to stay close and have a job in his department. I kept my mouth closed as tight as could be. I just knew that they were Jews like me, and therefore dangerous people. He wouldn't be hiding a Jewish girl unless he was Jewish as well. He wouldn't dare. Henryk was in charge of hiring people, so what could I do? When he told me I would be replaced, it hit me like a pile of rocks. I said to myself, "What am I going to do now?" It was very gallant that he was trying to save his girl-friend, but I would soon be paying for it. Danucia's fate was suddenly all on my shoulders.

Usually at work I was friendly and said *"guten tag"* with a smile to my supervisor, but with my new concerns this soon ended. After a couple days of my sad face Mr. Zgoda said to me, "Maria, what's wrong?" I tried to make less of it and said, "Oh, nothing is wrong. Everything's fine." He said, "No, something is bothering you. You haven't come in lately with your usual smile, and it looks like you have some problems." Anyway, he pressed me on the subject, so I finally said, "Well, I think that I'm leaving this place."

"What!" he yelled. He looked as if somebody had slapped him. I didn't want to say that Henryk told me I had to leave. I was afraid that if confronted with the truth Henryk would turn me in as a suspected Jew. His behavior implied that he knew I was a Jew in hiding just like him. Why else would he ask if Danucia could stay with me? So instead, I said that I had simply heard a rumor about someone else taking over my position. With this Mr. Zgoda became furious. He said, "How dare anyone tell you something like that. You're working in my office, and what I say goes!" This came as something of a relief. I have to admit that I was very frightened about being out of a job. I could very well end up on the streets, and I didn't know who had my forged papers, or how to retrieve them.

This uncertainty must have shown on my face, and I said, "Herr Zgoda, you know how I feel about working for you. I'm going to miss you very much."

He said, "You are not going to miss me because you're staying here, and that's the end of it. Don't you still want to work for me?"

"You know that I do, Herr Zgoda," I answered, "I have no family and nowhere else to go. You have been very good to me and I would like very much to stay here."

"Well," he assured me, "I think I have something to say in the matter." He told me not to worry and that he would look into the matter, but I was still afraid. I never once told Herr Zgoda who was trying to get my job from me. I just agreed to wait, and walked out. I could only hope for the best.

Soon afterwards Henryk, who worked in personnel, took me aside and let me know he was very angry with me. "You have some nerve saying something to the director about my giving your position to Danucia! How dare you?" He looked like he wanted to kill me in that moment. I glared right back at him and said, "I never mentioned your name at all! All I told the director was that I was losing my position to somebody else!" He must have thought that I would just go quietly, but I had nowhere to go. "You're lying," he hissed, "I'm going to get you back. You know what I mean."

I was very calm, and I looked in his face and said, "If you get back at me I'll do the same to you! I'm fighting for my life and I have the right to do it!" He still looked like he wanted to strangle me, but after my comments he just walked away.

IT MIGHT SEEM PECULIAR that Jews striving so diligently to blend in with the general population would also possess an uncanny ability to recognize one of their own. We might also wonder why they would fight the urge to rush to each other's aid, and bind together as a means of survival. It is important, however, to discern between those Jews in hiding, who had to depend on other non-Jews for providing food and shelter, and Jews who attempted to pass as Gentiles while living among other non-Jews. This was most successfully done in cities where, by taking advantage of the sheer numbers of a community, one might maintain anonymity.

Weitzman concedes that Jews who "passed" "had to rely on their own wits and initiative to take care of all the practical details of life. In addition, they were always 'out in the open' and had to engage in continual social interaction with their Polish neighbors, co-workers, and landlords."[15] Even the most iron-willed individuals might crack under such stress. The anxiety of living day to day with the knowledge that the faintest slip might send one to the death camps took its toll. A survivor by the name of Niusia described how the constant fear of discovery ruled the "passing" Jew's every moment: "I was always afraid I had said something that could have made somebody understand that I am a Jew. That somebody will tell and that I will have to go to the Gestapo…Every step and every word, everything, was under control. What to say and how to look and how to speak and how to move…Every night I tried to remember what I have done and what I have said—from the morning, the beginning of the day. It was like seeing a movie picture. I saw the whole day and I heard everything, every word I said, who I met and what they said… and maybe I said something wrong or did something wrong and maybe I have to change my dwelling. Maybe it is impossible for me to live anymore in this place. It was just terrible to live like that. And of course, I was always afraid."[16]

I often wondered how Nina, whose survival depended on her ability to remain guarded under the most extreme conditions, was able to open up to me in every way for our interviews. "People say that I am a closed book," she often remarked during our conversations, and this was true even at the age of eighty-five when we completed our work. Although she was exceptionally candid when discussing her wartime experiences, I was under no illusions that Nina kept many of her life stories, and parts of stories, forever buried in some safe place within her heart. Living with the enemy had taught my friend some hard lessons, and she found it impossible to shake off old habits that had kept her alive as a young woman.

Her skill at maintaining her composure in the most dire of circumstances would be tested when Henryk no longer reported for work.

I never saw Henryk after that day. I learned that soon after our conversation he lost his job and disappeared. It might have been discovered that he was helping someone without going through the proper channels. I know that he used his authority to get a position for Danucia, but he did this illegally without even a hint of paperwork. I have no idea whether he gave himself away, or if he was involved with something that got him into trouble. But Danucia was frantic! Even though neither of us ever admitted that we were Jewish, she pleaded with me to help her. She had eventually secured some other little job with Henryk's help, but she didn't know how long it would last. A few days later she called me at work on the telephone. She whispered to me that she found out that Henryk had been arrested. At this time the office staff had not heard this rumor. "I don't know what to do," Danucia gasped, "but you have to help me. I have to run away!" She was placing her call to me right there in the office, and I thought, "Oh my God, if somebody hears this conversation somehow we're both dead!"

It was a terrible risk. Anybody could have walked by and heard this woman revealing everything. On the phone she was practically yelling at me! She could not understand how an important employee like her boyfriend could be arrested, and she was probably correct in thinking it was serious. I was worried that she would go to just anyone and, in her desperation to find help, bring the situation up.

"Be quiet," I told her, "I'm going to the post office to pick up the mail. Make up some excuse to leave so that you can meet me there." At least at the post office no one would overhear us and make the connection we were associated with someone who had been arrested. On my way to the post office I tried to think of what we could do. One thing I knew, we were very close to the Romanian side, and this was a lucky thing. When Danucia came up to me at the post office I told her, "You can't just run anywhere. You have to get to the Romanian side by train somehow." I thought that the best thing I could do for this silly girl would be to put her on a train going east.

Danucia was desperate as we made our way to the train depot. It was a small station, so the train wouldn't stay there for too long. I told her to run and catch it. I thought that maybe if Henryk got away he could find her in Romania. All I really wanted to do was send her on her way, because if someone saw me with her I might be arrested too.

I put her on the train, but as it began to pull out she threw something to me from the train window. She yelled, "Here is the key to my apartment." Why she threw it to me I will never know. Why would I want to go anywhere near her place after she left so suddenly? It landed on the ground in front of me and I thought, "What do I do with this bit of incriminating evidence?" At first I simply used my shoe to cover the key with a bit of grass. I stood there with my heart pounding until the train was completely gone. Once I was certain there was nobody looking I scraped my shoe on the ground and scooped up the key. Then I went to the outhouse and threw the key in the toilet. I couldn't think of anything else to do. I certainly had no plans to visit her apartment! The Germans might be waiting there, and they would then know that I had seen her.

Hurrying back to the post office I picked up the mail, then headed back to work as if nothing happened. I arrived back around noon, and I heard people in the office already start to ask where Danucia was. As I sat at my desk I could not decide what kind of a heart I had inside me regarding Danucia's escape. I had very mixed feelings and wondered if I shouldn't have gone with her. I figured that if I did not return to work, things could be much worse and we were more likely to be caught. I kept to myself for the rest of the day and assumed that that was the end of my involvement with Danucia. Well, the very next day people were wondering out loud again about where she had disappeared to. I heard my co-workers asking around if she had gone home sick. The management was trying to figure out how to act on the situation, and they asked each of us if we had seen her. I pretended to be completely ignorant of her whereabouts.

When Danucia's boss asked if I knew what happened to her I shrugged and said, "Maybe she's sick. You might want to check where she lives, but I have no idea where that is." I could say this quite honestly because I really did not know where she had ended up. Thank goodness nobody had seen me talking with her at the post office the day before. I wasn't too worried until the next day I was called into the main office, which was where the Gestapo-type security people worked. My heart was beating a million miles a minute, and I was sure they had found out about my work for the partisans.

When they led me to a little office and sat me down they started asking about Danucia and about her relationship with Henryk! Apparently he had managed to escape, and they were very suspicious of any person who had known him. I didn't get all the details, but they assumed that because I had worked in the same company, and because I was a fellow Pole, then I must know something. At first I could not look my interrogator in the eyes. Inside I was shaking and very nervous, but I tried hard not to show it. I hoped that they would simply think I was intimidated by them, but not really guilty of anything. They said to me, "You are Polish just as our two missing workers were Polish. Surely they told you what they were doing with themselves." They kept on asking me questions, particularly about Danucia, until I became angry over the whole thing.

I decided to gather a little of my nerve and talk back to them. I had to say over and over to myself that I was, in fact, a Pole and not a Jew. I don't know where I got the guts to say it, but I looked straight into the interrogator's eyes and said, "I have no idea where this man Henryk is or what he is doing." I could say this with conviction because I never got close enough to him or Danucia.

The interrogator said, "But you're Polish!"

"Yes," I answered with exasperation, "but that doesn't automatically mean we spoke about our lives to each other, just because we're both Polish! He had a girlfriend. I didn't bother with their life and they didn't bother with me. I don't even know how close they were. We are from the same country, but other people at my office are from Poland too. Why not ask them where these people are?" A lot of us Poles were working in these areas that had been part of Russia because Germans civilians didn't want to work so close to the front, but we didn't socialize together as a group. I don't know why they singled me out for questioning, and for all I know they did this with other people from work as well. I never heard of it, though, and it certainly seemed as if they found me particularly suspicious. I went back and forth with this man for some time until it became late. They allowed me to go home, but I was sure they were watching me. The very next morning I was ordered in again for more questioning.

I never told them anything, because of course I had nothing to tell. I kept to my story, always saying, "I never really had any real friendship with Henryk and Danucia. They spent all their free time together, and I only saw them at work. I never would even think of interfering with their lives, because I have enough to do surviving on my own." Still they were never satisfied with my answers. They kept me overnight in a little room that was not entirely comfortable. I think they were trying to wear me down. I slept in a chair, and the next day I gave them the same story.

I really wasn't lying about Henryk. I had no idea who he really was, and so I really was innocent of what they were accusing me. I had always felt something wasn't kosher with him and Danucia. It was like a cloud that hung over them that you couldn't quite touch. But I wasn't about to tell my interrogators this.

Finally the director saved me from further questioning. He had become concerned when I didn't report in for work, and when he learned where I was he came right away to defend me. Mr. Zgoda came in very angry and said, "I will take responsibility for this girl! She is a good and trusted employee, and I am taking her back to work! The mail is piling up, and I need her at the office!" It was true that everybody had his or her own job, and I was particularly good at mine. Even if I hadn't done it well, somehow I have the feeling that Mr. Zgoda would have said this in order to get me out of there. He was very convincing, and he could also honestly say that he was not well acquainted with Henryk. Ours was a very big operation, and the different department heads were very busy overseeing their own employees. Thank goodness the Gestapo let me go because of Mr. Zgoda.

To this day I do not know why they arrested Henryk. Not much later after I went back to work I heard a rumor that he and Danucia met up in Romania, but somebody then spotted them who knew they were running away. From what I understand they were then reported to the Romanian police and were shot while trying to flee. When I heard this I felt very sorry for them. I never wished them any hardship.

NINA WAS FORTUNATE to have avoided torture at the hands of her interrogators. Without Mr. Zgoda's intervention, some manner of harsh coercion would most likely be the Gestapo's next step with her. Clearly they were bent on extracting information that might lead to apprehending the young Polish couple. As for Henryk and Danucia's ultimate fate, Nina could never be certain whether either of her former co-workers escaped execution. Murmuring continued to swirl around her office that Henryk, at least, had been captured, interrogated, and shot.

There were other rumors circulating throughout the occupied area where Nina continued to work. Word of Allied bombers flying over German cities and factories seeped into Polish conversation. Whispers of a failed campaign just short of the Soviet capital trickled through the tight net of Nazi propaganda, and reached the ears of those waiting for an opportunity to flee.[17]

It would not be long before Nina sensed the tide was turning against the German army. She could finally dare to imagine a plan in which she might escape east toward the liberating Soviet army.

By 1943 the Germans were losing the war. We had no idea about this because it was all kept very secret. I wouldn't have dared to ask about the war's progress. I did know that not every Polish citizen was pro-Hitler. Let's face it; by then the Poles were having a hard time too, and everyone complained about the hardships of this war. However, quite a few Poles did collaborate with the Germans, and a lot of them were real bastards about it. Excuse me for using this word, but when I think about how they treated their Jewish neighbors…well I have to be frank in stating this. As far as taking advantage of the Jews' predicament, they were disgusting in every way. With us Jews out of the way many Poles thought that they could move into our homes and take our property. Instead, the Germans moved in and took over everything, including our possessions. I know this because when I worked in the mailroom I helped to produce papers that directed valuables back to Germany.

After going through that horrible interrogation process I had the feeling I should try to leave soon. Life was becoming more unpredictable, and I felt as if the ground was on fire under my feet. I knew that if I was going to leave my job I should try to escape closer to the Russian front. As the Germans were losing the war it became more dangerous to work for the partisans anyway. People were becoming more desperate and, therefore, unreliable. You couldn't trust anyone anymore. For me it was a joy that the war was being lost. But I had to be practical and eventually stop sending things to them. It was just as well, because by this time I was really worn out from the stress of my clandestine work.

As I began to seriously consider how I would leave I briefly thought of asking Mr. Zgoda for help. He had been like a protective angel to me, and in my heart I knew he was not a Nazi. At the same time he was working for them, and all that time I had been working against them. I wondered what would happen if Mr. Zgoda came to know this. Perhaps if I asked him to help me to travel east he would discover that I was working for the Underground or worse yet he would find out that I was a Jew. I wasn't sure how he felt about Jews. I used to think that if life someday brought us together I would have liked to open his eyes with my story. I would have told him, "I would never have done anything against you. I always appreciated what you did for me, but you were working for the Nazis. I had to lie to you because I was Jewish."

ALTHOUGH NINA could not be certain when the Nazis would be defeated, that liberation would eventually come in some form seemed certain. Still she forced herself to wait. If she left for the eastern border too early Nina faced arrest and eventual execution. Leaving too late might result in getting swept along with other evacuees to the west. Without any idea how she would go about it, Nina decided to wait for the right moment to slip away. Until then she struggled along with her co-workers to survive. Resources were now funneled to the German troops at such a rate that civilians found it difficult to find food on a daily basis. A once reliable infra-structure now crumbled within city limits, making it nearly impossible for inhabitants to maintain some sort of hygiene.

Conditions became worse and worse as the war went on, and even a clean place to sleep became a luxury. One time in particular I almost went out of my mind over a new and unpleasant experience. I got lice from a straw mattress that was given to me! There was just a wooden frame to my bed, with no box spring or mattress until I received an old one from a neighbor. Well, I got up in the middle of the night scratching my head and body. When I turned on the light I could see that I was covered with little red blisters from some kind of insect bite. I knew it was from the mattress, so right then and there I threw it outside in the yard. I shook out the blanket and pillowcase as well. I didn't really know what was going on because I had never encountered such a thing. I didn't even know what lice were!

When I was a kid we had nice linens and a bathroom with running water. I had no idea how to solve my itching problem, and the only thing that came to mind was to use vinegar, maybe because that's what we used to clean with when I was a child. I remembered it was very acidic and killed germs. It's funny how so many things are connected to one's child-hood. When I was little and staying in Soluki I ate so much there that I gained three or four pounds! I had heard that water helps you to lose weight. So I drank a lot of water with vinegar in it. I'm not even sure why I did this, because it made me sick. Anyway, after I threw out the mattress I remembered that vinegar kills germs, and I thought it might kill what-ever was making me itch as well.

I went to my neighbor's apartment to see if she had any vinegar, or could help in some other way. Maria was an elderly Russian lady and a very kind person. She liked me, and had once asked if I could move in with her. Unfortunately, I couldn't do this because I had been instructed to remain in the apartment assigned to me by the Germans. I was wary of doing the slightest thing wrong, and I was afraid that if I went to live in the home of a Russian, the company I worked for might report me as some kind of troublemaker. They would wonder if we were planning to overthrow the local government or something.

I was going crazy with the lice, and Maria was fresh out of vinegar. She said she had a better idea, and took me to the market the next morning to buy some crude kind of alcohol. The Russians liked to drink vodka, but it wasn't always available during tough times. Instead they drank something called *Somangonka*. This stuff was made from beets and it was very strong. I tried it once and nearly died. They were selling this at the bazaar right by the beets, but it was hard to get. Maria was convinced that this liquid would do the trick, however, so we pooled our money and purchased a bottle of Samangonka. Maria instructed me to wash my blankets and pillow in this. At first my landlady was angry about the mattress thrown outside, but when she learned of my problem she helped me to burn it. I burned the bed as well, just for good measure. Unfortunately I never got another mattress, and from then on had to sleep on the floor.

We were able to purchase a little vinegar at the market as well, so I poured that on my head to kill the lice. I was afraid to use the Somangonka because I thought I might lose my hair! I was grateful to Maria for her companionship and advice. I felt I could trust her, and we were both terribly lonely. In my sad little apartment all I had was a little lamp, a bed and a table with chair, and I possessed very little clothing. But because Maria knew how to sew she made me an outfit, complete with a little jacket. It was one of only two outfits that I had. She was kind to me in this way. Her son was in the military, and she wanted me to stay in town after the war so that when he came back I could marry him! Oh, she was such a sweet woman.

Every Sunday I took the little money I made and purchased whatever food was available at the market, then went to Maria's to enjoy a meal together. She would always be so grateful and say, "You would be the best daughter-in-law I could imagine." She didn't know that I was Jewish, but I'm not sure it would have mattered to her. She once mentioned having a very good friend living in Romania, and I started to think about heading that way to escape. I would be closer to the invading allies if I went east, so I kept Maria's friend in mind hoping I could look her up if I made it to Romania.

———

Common sense told me that the Russians would invade from the east, so I was always trying to make little connections with Russian people. When we were all liberated they might help me to find my family. I even went to the Russian churches some Sundays with my friend. Those who were real Communists wouldn't go, but some of them still wished to attend church. My elderly friend went as often as she could. She went to the Greek Orthodox Church, and always invited me to join her. I only went a few times because it was too far away. I was always worried that Maria would be too tired from the long walk, but it seemed worth it for her because she loved church. People at work didn't know I was associating with a Russian woman, but I really enjoyed her company.

Maria and I did all right, but really by this time everybody was struggling to survive. The pay I received for working with the German company was just enough to get by. We Poles were allowed free use of the company kitchen, and that helped a lot with meals. A group of us would often have our meals there, and if we had extra money we could buy things at the bazaar, which was a kind of "Farmer's Market" like they have in many cities now. I used to like to buy *Siemiczki*. They have these in America too. You put them in your mouth and the little seed comes out. How do you call them here, "Sunflower seeds"? In Poland there were two kinds. One was dark and had a blunt cover, and it was so much fun eating them! Once I started I couldn't stop. I would munch on those things every Sunday, and it was good to be with Maria at that time.

I had to be very careful around my co-workers because the smallest thing could have given me away. One day I had to excuse myself from a little office party because I didn't know the Christmas songs they were all singing! When I was a girl I had wanted so badly to attend one of these parties, but at that moment I had to tell everyone I felt ill and had to leave. It made me feel so sad and alone. Most of the people I met at work were pretty decent and hardworking, and I liked them, but I preferred to spend my evenings with Maria. We had meals together in order to make the food stretch out. Sometimes I had leftovers from my little dinners at work, and because I didn't have a refrigerator I couldn't keep food too long. In the wintertime it wasn't as bad, but in the summer you had to be careful of things spoiling. Whenever I had leftover potatoes or rice I would cover it up, and the next day I would bring it to Maria. She always insisted that we eat it together. I just loved her.

As time went on I could tell things were going badly for the Germans. My suspicions were confirmed when the director had a private discussion with me in his office about the progress of the war. This was the one moment I almost confessed to him my real identity. I'll never forget it. Nobody was supposed to speak of defeat. The Nazis would kill anybody who spoke of even the possibility or how we would survive it. So when things were getting really bad the director took me into his office and brought out a bottle of sherry and poured us both a little glass. He said, "Maria, let's have a little wine." He never called me by the Polish surname of Kwasigroch that the Underground had given me. He was never so formal as to call me Fraulin Kwasigroch, but I still have papers with this name.

I never could handle my liquor, so if I became a little tipsy I could have told him I was Jewish or anything else he might want to hear! So I just pretended to sip the wine as Mr. Zgoda took me over to this big map on the wall that showed all of Eastern and Western Europe. As we stood there having our little drink he pointed to Romania and said, "This is where our forces are, and this is where the Russians are." He was trying to show how the German army was moving away from the East and going more westward. He was trying to tell me that the Germans were losing the war without coming out and saying it. I was certain that he was afraid to talk too much. He must have known that it could be dangerous. He tried to say things in a more…how can I explain it now…more in a "politically correct," or approved way. He quietly suggested to me, "I think it would be more convenient if we moved a little bit this way," showing me the West. I asked him, "Oh, would that be better for us?" He didn't answer, but he knew that I was not stupid and that I wasn't really asking.

He said to me, "Maria, many of us here are soon going to be traveling west. Would you like to come with us?"

My ears really opened up when I heard this, and I thought, "What's going on? Something is not kosher...If the Germans are going west, something is changing in this war."

To Mr. Zgoda I said, "Oh, well, if everybody is going west, then naturally, Herr Zgoda, I would like to go with you. I wouldn't think of doing anything else. I have nowhere else to go, and I'm all alone."

"Oh, it will be so good to have you with us!" he exclaimed. I wished then that I could have told him I was afraid to get closer to Germany because I was a Jew. I had no intention of going west. I wanted to go the complete opposite direction, closer to the front where ultimately I might be safe. I wanted so badly to tell him the truth about myself, and maybe if I had another minute or second to talk with him I would have. I was so weak by this point that I could have just blurted it out. I was tired of lying and not being myself. I had managed very well by pretending to be someone else, but the uncertainty of life was getting to me. The situation was so stressful, and I wondered if I dared reveal my secret. "Oh well, why not tell him?" I wondered, "I'm no longer attached to this life, and I don't care anymore what happens to me anyway."

I couldn't be sure how Mr. Zgoda would react. He might be disappointed that I hadn't trusted him enough in the first place to tell him I was a Jew. After all, he had always treated me like a daughter. But he was a German, and Germans had killed everyone I cared about. It is hard to trust someone who could possibly put a rope around your neck! I thought, "I am not afraid to die, but what if I am tortured for information about the Underground?" I knew that I couldn't handle that. In that last moment I decided that I would never tell Mr. Zgoda the truth. Instead I began to work out plans in my mind about how I could escape east.

He asked me if I would like another glass of wine, but I said to him, "No, it would probably give me a headache." Mr. Zgoda probably thought that I declined his offer of a drink on moral grounds, but I simply knew that I couldn't trust myself with alcohol. I stood there for a while just looking at the map with Mr. Zgoda, talking about how nice things were before the war, but I wasn't really listening. The wheels were turning in my head. I knew very well that I could never go west ith Mr. Zgoda. No matter how much he liked me, I could not be sure that he would remain a loyal friend if he knew I was Jewish. I didn't know who we might run into as we made our way west, and I didn't want to see a Pole from my old neighborhood who could point me out as an imposter.

As soon as I could I excused myself from Mr. Zgoda's office and went back to work. But most of my time I spent thinking about how I could break away. Before this, I couldn't begin to even visualize what would happen to me. I had been beaten down to such an extent that I couldn't imagine such a thing as real freedom. Only by learning of the Germans' retreat west could I put two and two together.

All during my time with this operation the Nazis had been winning the war. Now finally things were moving in the other direction! I cannot say that I actually started to have hope. I was still far away from that. Soon the bombing would increase and life would become even more terrifying. When you're in the middle of something like that it is hard to think of the next day. But when the time came I knew I would be ready to run.

HERR ZGODA took considerable risk in discussing the possible movement of German troops with Nina. Ordinary citizens were subject to immediate execution for making any disparaging remarks regarding the outcome of Hitler's war. In his account of life as a young leader in the Jungvolk, or "Hitler Youth," Alfons Heck recalled the atmosphere of distrust that permeated the more seasoned troops. Boys of the Hitler Youth such as Heck were, by the mid 1940s, frantically thrown together with men who had witnessed first-hand the increased destruction brought on by the Allies. Hardened by their combat experiences, the older soldiers ridiculed Heck for his optimistic behavior. As young as Heck was, however, he was still a leader, or "Bannführer," of his unit. These veterans knew the penalty for even hinting at defeat, and were very careful not to pronounce the war a failed effort. Nazi fanaticism continued to dictate law, and Heck claimed that "altogether 40,000 soldiers were sentenced to death for 'treasonous' behavior, which could be as minor as advocating that it was 'stupid' to continue fighting."[18]

As a Nazi official, Nina's employer placed himself in a very dangerous position by even hinting that they might escape the advancing Soviet army. Anyone passing by Herr Zgoda's office could have turned him in for making the suggestion to move westward out of harm's way. The fact that he chose to warn his Polish employee of this development says quite a bit about his affection for Nina. Although she appreciated Herr Zgoda's offer of safe passage west, Nina had her own ideas about escape. With this confirmation of the shift in the Nazi armies' fortunes, she felt more secure in carrying out her plan to move east. Nina now had only to wait for the right opportunity, and quietly slip away.

PART THREE

Escape and Evasion

Knowing her days working for the Germans were numbered, Nina wondered how she would make her way toward the eastern border and her ultimate freedom. "I always made my decisions at the last moment, without any thought at all," she once explained to me, "and this is how I came up with the idea to leave everything and try to get into Romania. It was at the spur of the moment." The time soon came when Nina felt she must "make a run for it." With little more than a fragile plan, and anticipating disaster, she took the chance late one New Year's Eve.

CHAPTER VII

"Passing"

(1943)

BY 1943, the unit that employed Nina had operated from Dnepropetrovsk, Zaporozje, and Vinnica. The people from whom she had received her false papers remained nameless and elusive throughout Nina's covert operations with them. Without a way to inform these partisans of her movements she could no longer pass off the stamps so vital in forging documents. As she continued to work for the Germans in Vinnica (for, as she recalled, "around four or six months") she worried that the Underground would see her lack of contribution as disloyalty to their cause, and out of spite somehow betray her true identity to the Nazis. She had no choice but to stay with her unit until an opportunity presented itself to flee.

Although far more transient, Nina's company still managed to provide some sort of mail service to German soldiers, even after another move took place to Ghivan, a town close to the Romanian border. In total Nina had been under the employ of the German military mail service for a year and a half, most of the work taking place on Ukrainian soil. Things continued to go badly for the German army, however, and by the Anglo-American Invasion of June 6, 1944, the writing was very clearly on the wall to many a Nazi soldier.

By June 20th the Russians launched an offensive on the central front. Unfortunately for Hitler, this is where he had concentrated his strongest forces. The German Army Group Center was completely overwhelmed, and the front to Poland opened wide for advancing Russian troops. Hitler's highest officers could not convince their Führer to pull back and condense his remaining men and resources. An attempted assassination on the

Führer's life caused the once arrogant and seemingly unshakable leader of the Third Reich to retreat to his mountain estate in Berchtesgaden. Increasingly paranoid and far less lucid, Hitler began to throw everything he had at the Allied forces, with little concern for military or civilian loss.[1]

Not long after my conversation with Herr Zgoda I spent one restless night thinking about what I should do with myself. I sensed that we were getting closer to the end of the war, but I couldn't be certain. I felt as if things were changing very quickly around me, and because I had not yet formulated a new plan for myself, I found it impossible to sleep. It was winter, and the snow fell outside while I just lay there thinking. Inside my head I kept saying, "I have to leave. I have to leave. I have to leave!" Every moment I felt as if I had a fire underneath my feet. I was afraid Mr. Zgoda would notice that I was acting strangely at work because I was so preoccupied with getting away to the east. Surely it was only a matter of time before they discovered I was not who I claimed to be.

It didn't bother me that I was living day by day. By now I had gotten used to that. However, I was concerned that I might endanger the partisan group who had given me my papers and my chance to fight the Nazis in the first place. Under torture I might tell the Germans some little scrap of information that allowed them to hunt down my fellow conspirators.

I came to the inevitable conclusion that the only way to escape would be to somehow make my way into Romania. I knew just the way to do it, too. I finally stamped papers for myself! I forged my own documents that stated I had permission to freely travel from Dnipropetrovsk to the eastern border. I believe this would have been the town of Zmerinka, but it has been so long I don't recall exactly, and I would hate to be inaccurate about this. Anyway, I had only to fill the papers in with my name. I worked my last day wishing that I could say goodbye to Herr Zgoda and Maria, but on New Year's Eve I left in the dark, without a word to anyone. It was very cold and began to snow, and I said to myself, "I have to leave now. Tonight the soldiers at the borders will be drunk. I must go!"

I only brought with me a small satchel with a few personal items. It was not like I had much to begin with, but now I had only the clothes on my back. I left in a rush, but I was certain that I had those papers with me in the satchel. It was only when I got to the station that I found that they were gone! I was shocked and confused. How could I have lost the papers I'd worked so hard to forge, and that were to get me a little closer to freedom?

It was in the middle of the night, snowing, and very cold. I could have dropped them on the way, or God forbid left them in my room. I couldn't even remember if I had filled out the papers with my name! If I had, and somebody from work found them, then they would know what my plans were. I thought, "Oh my God, if these papers are found at my apartment then the Germans will track me down!" They would know I was a criminal. As an employee I was not authorized to stamp travel papers. They would soon figure this out and come looking for me. But there simply was not enough time to go back and search for the missing documents. Walking to the station took long enough, and the next train was due to come very soon. I had no choice but to continue, and hope that luck would come my way once more. I had no idea how I would finally get to Romania.

I walked up shivering to the train depot. The night man in charge at the station knew me as a girl from town. We had occasionally spoken a little Russian together, and I was convinced that he had no idea I was a Jew. By this time the storm had worsened. "What are you doing here so late on New Year's Eve, dear?" he asked me. "The snow is piled up everywhere, so the train won't be coming for a long time! If you've come to meet someone you'll have a long wait." I told him that I meant to travel, and he just shook his head. "You won't even be able to get on the train when it finally arrives," he told me, "no civilians can take the train going east because it is now reserved for soldiers only."

Well, I certainly wasn't in a uniform, and I didn't have any papers anyway. Still, I was determined to go. The night manager must have felt a little sorry for me, because he offered lots of information and stayed on the platform with me for awhile. When he made as if he would go back into his office, I followed him in, and said that I would wait for the train inside. He went about his business, and I settled into a chair by the door. When he had his back turned I slipped out the door to wait on the platform. I decided that when the train came I would try to sneak on somehow. I stood there shaking and looking down the tracks for the train, thinking, "I am going on this train no matter what."

I thought about how I would travel without the proper papers. It was necessary to have them, especially for the other side, because I didn't have a clue who I would encounter there. Everything was unclear and a big maybe. I was willing to take the chance, however. For better or worse, I had to try and get as close to the Russian troops as possible.

My heart began to pound as the locomotive finally pulled up. I was so afraid the train wouldn't stay long enough for me to slip on. When it finally stopped in front of me, what did I see? It was filled with nothing but German soldiers! I thought, "Oh my God, what do I do now? These Germans will never allow me to board!" While I was standing there trying to decide what to do, a man stepped off the train. I remember him very clearly even today. The train appeared to be filled with mostly lower-ranking soldiers, but he was different. He was some kind of an officer, perhaps a major. When he saw me standing there he said the same thing the old night manager at the station had said to me. "Young lady, what are you doing here in the middle of the night?" I don't know how I came up with the idea, but I told him that an aunt who had raised me was waiting for me in Romania, and that I was desperate to reach her because she was very sick. I was in the middle of telling the officer, and let me tell you he was quite handsome too, when suddenly I couldn't take it anymore. I burst into tears. I was so tired from the stress.

This officer said to me, "Fraulein, don't cry! I will try to help you. You come with me." He didn't even ask me about my papers. I walked with him towards the train, and he took my arm and steered me in front of him in a very polite gesture. The soldiers tried to stop him from bringing me aboard. I think that those soldiers on the train were jealous of his rank, and perhaps they resented that he had a woman with him. They said, "No women are allowed on this train!" The officer just opened his lapel to show his military rank and said, "She's going with me. Let her board!" He turned to me and whispered, "Let's go before we get any more argument." The way he spoke was very strong and confident, like he wouldn't take "no" for an answer. Everybody made room as we went up the stairs. I really don't know how I had the guts to do such a thing. Here I was a Jew, and

I was on a train full of German soldiers, just surrounded by them. It was like the times I walked around L'vov without my armband.

The officer showed me into his compartment, and we sat across from each other. The way he acted implied that in a way he was glad that he helped me. Now he had company for the trip toward the front, and maybe he wasn't looking forward to going there. It took about a half-hour to get to the Romanian side. The train was nearing my destination, and I went from one disaster to another, because the officer started asking who was going to accompany me to my aunt's house. How could I say that I didn't have anybody on the Romanian side to meet me? I stalled for time, saying that everybody was with my aunt, helping to care for her, but really there was no relative who was dying, and no family at all! Again I had to ask myself, "What am I going to do?" My mind was working like crazy. I had to come up with something to say. Finally we came to my stop, and that very kind officer accompanied me off the train! This was something I had not expected. He said, "I have to discuss some business with the train manager here. Please stay and wait for me."

IN HER RESEARCH on Jewish women who passed as Aryan, Lenore Weitzman learned of many accounts in which pluck and sheer nerve allowed for survival. One woman smuggling weapons into the ghetto made the decision to stride purposefully up to the Nazi in charge of searching suspicious bags, and proclaim that she was carrying eggs and butter. Although these items were also illegal, her ruse as a coy girl proclaiming a naughty deed was effective, and she was permitted to pass. For most of those performing illegal acts, however, luck played a vital part in success. The proper look, accent, and attitude were all essential to survival when a Jew attempted to "pass."[2]

With her Aryan looks, perfect Polish, and more than enough attitude, Nina possessed every quality needed to escape the fate of her fellow Jews up to this point. However, without the proper papers, and no place to call home, she left herself wide open to discovery. Nina had indeed been very lucky to have found a soft-hearted German officer to assist her in boarding the train. Now she faced the difficult task of excusing herself to venture off alone. The officer had proved to be a gentleman, and it was this trait that Nina decided to play upon in order to make her own way.

This officer was very cordial, and he told me to wait for a moment, but I was distressed to see that he was leaving me on the platform with his briefcase! I thought that maybe this would be a good time to run away and disappear from him. I had been so overwhelmed with what I would say once we got off the train that I didn't have time to think about this briefcase he suddenly handed me. There I stood, with my little satchel in one hand, and his case in the other. I considered leaving the briefcase on the platform, but that not only would have been unkind after all he had done for me, but dangerous as well. He might suspect that I had a reason to run. It seemed as if a very long time passed as the train stood there hissing at me, and still he didn't come back. I paced back and forth in a panic. Soldiers were everywhere, and the snow was falling harder than ever. Since it was New Year's Eve, most of the soldiers were drunk. A few rowdy ones stumbled by me, making some rude comments and advances, so I walked further away to stand under the platform light. I stayed where it could illuminate me, and in this way, staying in plain view, I thought that the men might not harass me. While I was standing there I pictured myself dropping the briefcase into the snow, and just walking away from the whole situation. "Let the officer think what he wants of me," I said to myself, "maybe he'll think I just got tired of waiting, or that some of my family had come after all."

I finally built up the nerve to do just this, but as I was getting ready to throw the briefcase, I saw the officer coming back! It was too late. My heart was beating like a little rabbit's as I handed him the case. I said, "Here is the briefcase you left with me." He took it and said, "I apologize for taking so long with my business. Do you know why I left the case with you? It was so you would know that I was coming back. I want to take you to your aunt's house. I didn't want you to think that I would leave you alone in the night." I have to admit, if those German officers wanted to be polite, if they wanted to be gentlemen, they most certainly could be. I thought, "God, should I stay with him until the next train leaves, and try to talk him out of it? What, what can I do?" He saw that I was upset and said, "What happened while I was gone? Are you all right?" I suppose there were tears in my eyes because I was so frantic. We were both standing under the light on the platform, so he must have seen that I was crying.

I looked right into his handsome face and made up another very good lie. I looked down at the snow and said, "I have to confess something. I feel that you must let me go to my aunt's home alone, please. If my family saw me walking up to our home with a handsome, young German officer…in the middle of the night, on New Year's Eve…well, my reputation would be destroyed forever. After all, my aunt is on her deathbed! You must understand that it would be inappropriate for me to show up with you by my side." If you threatened to kill me today I could not tell you where that idea came from. I had avoided the truth so many times that the lies I had to tell in order to stay alive came so easily.

He looked at me for a long time, and finally he said, "Are you sure you can get home by yourself all right?"

"Of course," I assured him, "I've gone that way many times. I could do it with my eyes closed." I gave him back his briefcase, and shook his hand saying, "Thank you very much for being so kind, and for being such a gentleman. But I have to go alone, I just know it." As if on cue, his train started up. He had to continue east, and the trains did not stay for very long in these small towns. We said goodbye and shook hands. He was a gentleman to the end. He didn't try to kiss me. He did absolutely nothing out of order, but was completely honorable. My entire family was dead for all I knew, and here I was standing with a handsome stranger, talking about the life of an aunt who didn't really exist!

The major got on his train, looking back at me as it pulled out, and I wondered, "Is it possible? Am I dreaming or did I really escape again?" It was like an angel had been watching over me. I had been very lucky throughout the war, but a lot of my success had to do with thinking on my feet. On many occasions I had to quickly consider my options, but somehow I was always able to come up with ideas that bought me a little more time. Unfortunately, it was important to remain alert in order to take advantage of every moment, and this was exhausting.

Maybe a little destiny was also in my favor. Perhaps I was meant to survive so that I could tell others about what the Nazis had done. At that moment all I knew was that it was snowing harder than ever, it was the middle of the night, and I had nowhere to go. I had only thought as far as getting to Romania. What I would do once I got there had not occurred to me. I walked around in a daze trying to get used to my new situation. I felt that I no longer knew if I was Jewish or not Jewish. Was I Polish? And what would my name be now? I had absolutely no identification and nowhere to go. So, I went and locked myself in the bathroom, and spent the night there. I didn't really sleep, but at least I was out of the cold. I certainly wasn't about to spend the night alone in the station with a bunch of drunken soldiers!

When I woke up in the train station bathroom the next morning I was cold and hungry, but I had a plan. Maria and I were once talking about how nice it would be to see Romania when the war finally ended, and she told me that if I ever found myself in that region I should look up her friend. I remembered her last name, Nikolajvna, and I knew that I was close to the Romanian border, in a town called Zmerinka, so I decided to find this woman. I didn't know exactly where she lived, and it ended up taking me a week or more to locate her. In the meantime I wandered around looking for work. Before I found Mrs. Nikolajvna I had nowhere to stay, so of course I was sleeping in abandoned buildings or in the woods again when it got warmer. I went to a little stream I had found and splashed around there to wash up on occasion. It was pretty cold, but it's unbelievable how you find a way to survive and get by. When I couldn't make it to the stream I stayed dirty and sweaty. Very often I smelled so badly that I couldn't stand myself. I had no change of clothes because I hadn't taken anything with me when I ran off to Romania.

Once I found a little work I was able to barter bread for a scrap of clothing, and in this way I got a skirt and blouse. At least I could now change into something that didn't look so dirty. Of course during the war nobody looked elegant or exciting; we were all a little disheveled. At least I blended in. I couldn't find work at some of the better places until I was cleaner and more put together. It would have been nice to have gotten a job at least as a maid or something, but I had to keep myself out in the open, in the fields or the marketplace. I went outside the city to find food such as apples or a potato someone had missed. I had to do this whenever I gave away the bread I had earned for other necessities.

The soldiers had taken most of the food as they passed through, and it had been cold and snowing, so foraging for food was not easy. In one field I found some carrots. There was no water, so I could only brush them off a bit before eating them. It's a wonder I didn't become sick from how unclean things were, but I didn't want to ask the locals for help. I kept to myself, and as soon as anyone so much as glanced at me I went off to hide in the bushes. I lived in my usual state of fear, and if I saw a person on the street that so much as looked my way, well then I crossed the street and went the other way. Everything was so abnormal and even today it seems strange to tell of these things. Now when I speak of that time in my life I wonder, "Am I making a story or did this really happen?" Yet, I know in my heart all of these things did happen. I was living as a homeless person does, and I was afraid to look anybody in the eye.

One day I cleaned myself up better than usual and found a job in a German employment office! I discovered that the Nazis had set up this place for people to check in each morning if they were looking for work. I went into this office and simply volunteered, with no papers or anything. They asked if I had secretarial skills, and I told them that I did, which was only somewhat true. So they gave me a desk where I was in charge of recording the names of people coming in to register. That's all I had to do, but it was good to finally have a job. The "office" was only a damaged boxcar converted into a work place. I used to get a little bit of bread every day for payment, and most of the time it wasn't much, but at least I didn't have to starve. They almost always had black coffee there, and that kept me warm and energized.

It is hard to explain how people just never had enough of anything during the war. There were a lot of people walking around like me going hungry. Utilities such as electricity, and even water, were not always handy. As for food, well everyone was strictly rationed. They handed out tiny amounts of food that was supposed to feed several people, but the portions were so small and barely enough for one. It certainly wasn't like the concentration camp or the ghetto, however, so I as far as I was concerned I would get by all right.

Through working at this registry I found out about some Jews who still lived in a nearby ghetto. When I processed them I came to learn that some of the people coming to register for work were Jews coming from this section of the city. I almost died when I learned this. They didn't have to wear a visible star armband as we were required to do in Poland. They had a special mark on their papers that allowed them to register for work, and this was how I discovered they were Jews. I was dying to find out where they were living and what kind of place it was, but I didn't dare to go there at first. I was afraid that I would somehow get trapped in that ghetto, and start all over again with hiding and running. As far as I knew it was not yet closed off to others. Germans passed through there as well as Romanians and quite a few Russians.

Most of the people around me spoke Romanian, which is a Slavic language. I didn't know this language well and kept pretty quiet. I didn't speak with hardly anyone about the ghetto, because I didn't want to show my interest in Jewish life. When I learned that some Jews had survived up to this point I thought of my family. Here was a ghetto that had not been destroyed, and the Jews were even allowed to look for outside work! I said to myself, "Maybe there is hope that some of my family is alive after all. Since I made it this far perhaps they did too." When I met my future husband I found out that he spent time in this ghetto. It never was liquidated, and because of this he remained safe and survived the war. But I'll tell that story a little later.

I didn't stay at the registrar's office for long, because a lot of people passed through there, and I thought that maybe someone from my former place of employment would come by and give me away. The two towns were not that far away from each other, so this was a possibility. I was so afraid of being discovered that I decided to look more diligently for my neighbor Maria's friend, and then leave for another job once I found her. I did find this woman, and thank God she allowed me to stay with her.

Again I was saved by the kindness of strangers. She was a wonderful lady, this Mrs. Nikolajvna.

Let me explain her name. The Russians would take the first name of the father and incorporate it into their last names. Her father's name was Nikoli, and she inherited it as a woman becoming Nikolajvna. She explained all of this to me, and I thought it was fascinating. She had a little one-room apartment, but there was no bathroom. She didn't have running water so she picked up water in a bucket from the town well, which wasn't too far. She was a sweet person, and spent most of her time taking care of her little granddaughter, Erichka. Her daughter, Tania, was not living there with them.

Tania was a very nice looking girl whose husband had gone off to the war. Unfortunately Tania ended up having quite a few encounters with German officers. Mrs. Nikolajvna told me that her daughter slept with some of these officers because they brought her food and drink. I don't know if she was particularly choosy about the officers she associated with, and really who am I to judge? During this time we didn't really know who would end up controlling the area, the Germans or the Russians. If the Russians returned they would punish people like Tania for being collaborators. It was known that the Russian soldiers would find women who had fraternized with the Germans and send them to Siberia as a punishment. It was whispered that sometimes they even killed these women. I think Tania was afraid that the Russians would track her down, and this was why she no longer lived with her mother but stayed elsewhere. I met Tania only a few times, and she was very nice to me. But the grandmother was in complete charge of taking care of the baby. Both Tania and her mother told me they didn't feel safe with her staying there. It was too dangerous for everybody.

THE REPERCUSSIONS for a civilian fraternizing with a German soldier during the Second World War could be immense. Although many women keeping company with a Nazi soldier or officer were doing so only as a way of obtaining food and other precious resources for their families, the eyes of their fellow townspeople were constantly upon them. Bitter over the loss of loved ones at the hands of the Nazis, these vigilante groups extracted revenge as soon as the opportunity presented itself.

Bannführer Alfons Heck spoke of his only wartime romance as a clandestine affair. Fabianne Mercurier, a local girl Heck romanced while stationed in Luxembourg, insisted on keeping a low profile whenever she met with her German boyfriend. To his dismay, the relationship ended before war's end. To her credit, Fabianne had been wise to keep their friendship secret, and to break off the relationship. Not long after they separated Heck learned the fate of any female who had dared to keep company with a German: "…I heard that women and girls in occupied countries who had become intimate with German soldiers were publicly shaved, spat upon and made to run through town under the taunting cries of 'German whores!' Some of these women shared the fate of thousands of males who were summarily shot without trial as collaborators…Although near war's end, almost everyone claimed to oppose us, the truth was that many more had collaborated."[3] There seemed no reason for Nina to pass judgment on Tania. No one knew better than she how people might misconstrue the reasons for associating with the enemy. For the time being, Nina focused on surviving the remainder of the war with her new family.

When I found Mrs. Nikolajvna I had been slowly starving. Mrs. Nikolajvna also found it difficult to provide food for herself and her granddaughter. There were few resources, but at least she had a place to call home. I was so grateful that she let me stay, because that winter was a cold one. At night we used to go to the railroad tracks to find old wood or any bit of coal that had been dropped, just to manage heating the apartment. At least we had each other. Zmerinka was not very large. It was a nice town that had been bombed in a terrible way, because it was an important connection between the west and the east. All of the trains came through there, so the Allies bombed the area quite frequently. By this point we were all getting used to hearing the big guns firing all around us, just like you get used to anything in life. We listened for them, but had no idea if it would be a German or a Russian bomb that hit us. Both sides were ferociously fighting around the area where we lived.

LIKE MOST CIVILIANS, Nina interpreted the signs around her to mean the war was drawing to a close. This did not necessarily mean that safety was ensured, however. With the Nazi armies on the run their behavior became increasingly rash and unpredictable. Soldier and civilian alike scrambled to obtain food and shelter. Making life still more difficult was Hitler's spiteful demand that nothing of worth be left for the advancing Allies. In Hitler's mind every decent German should go down fighting. Those who survived as a conquered people were not worthy of any kind of future.

The winter of 1944 was the worst in years, yet no provisions had been made to evacuate those Germans who settled in Poland during Hitler's glory days. Once considered noble servants working the land of a new German frontier, they now were forced to march through snow and ice with whatever they could carry away with them. According to William Woods, all forms of transportation were directed toward movement of German troops, leaving civilians to fend for themselves. "Motorized transport there was none," Woods wrote, "so the peasants used horses, and the horses, improperly shod, often fell on the icy roads, or floundered along for mile after mile belly deep in the snow."[4]

Those who had been repressed by the Nazis could take some pleasure in seeing their enemy's hasty and desperate departure. Woods found a record of Warsaw civilian Maria Bankowska, who saw from her window the exodus of German troops: "Across the river in Praga one could make out smoke rising into the still air...She could see damaged guns being towed, men marching without boots, wounded men limping along on sticks, men with horses and carts. 'It was a positively Napoleonic retreat,' [she said], a whole beaten army streaming toward Berlin."[5]

The frantic exodus of Nazi troops was soon replaced by an eerie stillness. While the awkward shift in power took place, those left behind waited in uncertainty. Of one thing they could be certain. Any army that replaced the Nazis was bound to offer an improvement in conditions. Nina guessed the tide was turning, but like every civilian in town, she could only hope the Allies were on their way.

We sensed that the Russians were gradually beating the Germans. We saw less of the Nazis, and the bombing had increased. We could see that the Germans were again running to the west, but we stayed put, hoping the Russians would soon liberate us. This meant that we had to survive the constant bombing. Even when the first Russian troops showed up the shelling continued. It was not as if all of the fighting stopped and we were safe and cheering for our freedom. These were the scenes they showed on newsreels, but the reality was quite different. Our world remained unstable for some time.

As soon as they arrived the Russians began to evaluate the situation in our little city, and as they had upon arriving in L'vov at the beginning of the war, they began to count people. They wanted to know specifically how many people were living in our area, and what their needs were. Because I spoke decent Russian I soon found another job helping the Soviets count everybody up. It was good to have a job again, but it was difficult and required a lot of walking.

I went from one place to another obtaining a basic count of each family. Today I believe this would be called a census, but I wasn't really as organized as that. I traveled for miles on my own two feet to get the information, but by then I was quite used to it. Unfortunately, I was undernourished and tired, so it took me longer than perhaps it should have. I came to one settlement that was rather small, and as I walked up to the nearest cottage I began to feel a little dizzy. I don't know what kind of a person I presented to the family who opened their door, but I am certain that I appeared thin, and a little ragged in the one dress I constantly wore. I was also, quite frankly, filthy. As I stood at the threshold I began to inform this family why I was there with my clipboard, when, wouldn't you know it, I fainted right at their doorstep! This was the second time I passed out in front of a peasant's house, and the second time the family showed me kindness. I suppose that I did a lot of fainting during the war, but I somehow always managed to get back up and start life again. Luckily this family took me in, and they seemed very worried about me. I was allowed to lie down on a straw mattress, and then they gave me a little something to eat. I think I was running a bit of a fever, because they wouldn't let me up again for some time. My eyesight was blurry, and my whole body seemed to be shutting down after all that I had been through during the war. My immune system had certainly been compromised, but it helped to finally have an opportunity to rest up.

I have to say that by this time I was so filthy I could smell myself. After I started to feel a little better I asked the people taking care of me if it would be possible to clean up a little. They said that they were happy to help me with this; however, they had no running water. Instead they heated some water in a big pot in their kitchen, and after doing this several times they were able to fill a big barrel. Once it was filled they closed the kitchen door and allowed me to take my first proper bath in a long time. Oh, it was wonderful! I was so happy to feel like a human being again! I was so thankful for this little thing they gave me. I am still amazed at the way I always found somebody with a kind heart to help me when I really needed it. I was very fortunate in this way.

I ended up staying with that family a full two weeks. After that time I felt strong enough to go back to Zmerinka. I didn't want to lose my job, and if my employers were still willing to keep me on I would have to prove I could still work. The peasant family made arrangements with a neighbor to transport me in his horse-drawn wagon back to my workplace. I was feeling much better, and I thanked the family as best as I could. How do you thank someone for saving your life? They waved to me until I was out of sight, and I never saw them again.

The man driving the wagon was also very nice, and he took me all the way back to Zmerinka. As soon as I could I found my supervisors and explained what had happened to me. They had been wondering where I had disappeared to, and at first they were a little suspicious about my story. I had to bring along the man who gave me a ride to confirm why I had gone missing for so long. Without him vouching for me they might have thought I deserted my position, or even that I was a spy. When the wagon driver helped to explain what had happened my bosses were very thankful for what that little town had done. As I recall they even got some kind of recognition for being so helpful. I could never live in a Communist country, but I have to admit that the Soviets were careful to recognize good citizenship. I was relieved to have my job back, though it did not last long.

It was only meant to be a temporary position, and when my bosses informed me that there was no more work I got a little panicky. I walked around town looking for work, and asked at the few open shops if they might hand out a little food for people going hungry. Eventually I came to a bakery. I thought, "Oh it would be wonderful to find work here! Please God let me get a job at this bakery so I can bring a little bread home to Mrs. Nikolajvna and the baby." I went in and, after finding the owner, asked if they needed any help. I couldn't tell if he was Romanian or Russian, so I spoke to him in Russian, hoping for the best.

Well, my luck continued and he hired me! He gave me the night shift, and I ran home to tell Mrs. Nikolajvna the news. That night around ten o'clock I started work, and I didn't return home from work until three or four in the morning, but I was elated to have a job that provided bread for us.

When I started working at the bakery I felt as if I were in heaven. It was warm there, and it smelled so wonderful from the bread baking. We baked white bread and rolls, which I believe were being sent to the soldiers as supplies. We never got any real salary. The owner didn't have much money because of the war, but we were allowed to have three or four pieces of bread each day. These were big pieces from a large loaf so it was very fair payment. The owner couldn't do much better than this because the Soviets made him account for every bit of flour and supplies. I never ate the bread right away, but instead proudly brought it back to Mrs. Nikolajvna and the baby. She could usually find time during the day to go into the neighboring fields. There she looked for potatoes and carrots to make a little soup to go with the bread. If we felt there might not be food the next day we put a little away. The baby started to look healthier and we were all happy to have one full meal a day. It was wonderful.

My plan to keep us all fed became a problem, however, because I wasn't eating enough to sustain myself at work. Although I was paid with bread from the bakery I always denied myself any of it until I could go home and share it with my little family. Even combining it with whatever we had, it was often only a potato or a little cabbage. It was anybody's guess what Mrs. Nikolajvna would find on her excursions into the fields. Sometimes she would get lucky, but as time went on there was less to add to our meals. One day I simply could not keep up with my work. Most probably I wasn't getting the nourishment I needed, and this made me weak. When they opened up one of the baking ovens, I felt that rush of heat and simply passed out! I was tired and overwhelmed, became dizzy, and hit the floor.

The next thing I remember is waking up on the bakery floor. The owner revived me, but he was concerned about my health. He very kindly gave me some water and forced me to eat a little bread, but it didn't seem to help much. I continued at the bakery for a little while, but I kept fainting to the point where it just didn't make sense to keep me on. After a while I sensed that I could be fired. The owner didn't know why I was passing out. I had kept quiet about sharing my bread with others. He didn't realize that I was spending my "pay" on two other people, so he came to his own conclusions. He thought my fainting was due to some sickness that might be contagious, and this was not a far-fetched idea. With everyone's resistance down, a lot of germs spread from one person to another. The conditions were far from sanitary, and disease spread through the passing troops as well. We were supposed to eat our bread right there at the bakery. I didn't want to get in trouble for taking mine home, and considered this job such a blessing that I didn't dare ask for extra to bring home to my friend. All during the war I was afraid of something, and I felt as if any moment I would be caught or arrested or shot for any little thing.

I needed real food, and had gotten too thin to be any good at such a physically demanding job. I couldn't blame the owner when he finally gave me my last payment of bread and said that I shouldn't come back. That night I went home with a heavy heart. As usual on my trip home from work it was very dark, and I had a long walk. I was concentrating on putting one foot in front of the other, when I heard somebody walking behind me. I thought, "Well, this has already been a very bad day. What can I expect now? Is someone going to now try to rob me of my last payment of bread?"

In my weakened state I suddenly became afraid that I would get beat up or worse. This was a strange feeling for me, because up to this point I had been through much worse and not felt so afraid. Perhaps I felt as if I had come too far to end up dead so close to the war's end. I didn't know who was behind me, or what they intended to do, so I told myself, "Well, Nina, you have to face whoever this is." I thought it would be better to see who was coming to hurt me, and try to do something about it.

I turned around very quickly and said in a strong voice, "Who is that behind me?" How silly of me to be so afraid. My so-called assailant was a late-night worker just like me! He was very surprised at my outburst, and he said, "Excuse me, but I'm not trying to hurt you. I've only just come from work!" I suppose what had scared me so much was that he had a lantern, and the shadows it cast made him look a little strange. I realized then that my nerves were worn out. The man must have sensed this as well, and he asked me, "Why are you walking around so late at night? You're just a girl!" I told him I was on my way home from working at the bakery. He shook his head and said, "Well, I'll walk with you so you're not so afraid." It was a little embarrassing, to tell the truth, but I appreciated the company.

He walked with me the whole way home, and I thought of how I had been walking through the entire war like a quiet little slave. By the simple act of turning toward what I feared and confronting it, I had finally made a choice. How do people say this in English? I "took the bull by the horn," and I was finally a little proud of myself!

When we reached my apartment I said to my new companion, "Thank you so much for walking with me. I am very glad that you came along." He asked if he should wait until I reached the door of my apartment, but it was late and I could tell he was tired. He was much older than I, and I didn't want him to get home later than he had to. We said our goodbyes at the corner, and I ran into Mrs. Nikolajvna's place to tell her about my adventure, and how scared I had been over nothing. Then I told her I had lost my job, and the reality of this hit me. I started crying, but Mrs. Nikolajvna said that everything would be okay. She would pray for all of us and God would provide. I knew that, like so many Romanian women, she was a religious lady. Oddly enough I never saw her go to church, but maybe her church had been bombed and so she had nowhere to attend a service. This was not uncommon. I knew that she was Catholic because she used to pray and cross herself all the time. I don't think she ever realized I was Jewish, and I had no desire to tell her so. Deep down in my heart I still didn't trust anybody.

Again it was time to find a job. I couldn't allow us all to starve, could I? The bombing hadn't stopped, but more Russian soldiers came in larger groups and continued to take things over. It wasn't official for a long time, but we began to feel free for the first time in years. It was strange how German soldiers started to disappear a little at a time and then...nobody. One day I went to the train station and saw that they were all gone.

It was a blessing in every way. But we were still starving and in a terrible situation. Every day I went looking for food or supplies with little success. We had no clear idea about how Hitler's little war was going. I learned a little by asking here or there. Occasionally I got up the courage to ask someone what was new. In this way I discovered that the Russian army was in complete control of our little city, and in fact they were working to establish a first aid unit. They were looking for workers, so I told myself, "This is perfect for me. I have to find work there!"

I located the Russian doctors and nurses, and learned that the first aid station was part of a mobile medical unit that followed behind the Soviet troops as they advanced. For the time being they were staying in our town, and they did need workers for cleaning and setting up a facility. Believe it or not, the building they intended to work in had been used as a stable! I suppose they had no choice because it was the only large structure in town that was still standing. The Germans had been using it for their horses, and let me say the Germans were a very clean people, but the stable they left behind was just that...a place to put horses. It still had manure in it, and it was cold and smelly.

I asked for and received a job helping them clean up the building. Like the other people in town who had come looking for jobs, I was elated to have found work again, and they wanted us to start right away. The bad news was that in order to help them establish this medical unit we would have to work under impossible conditions. Supplies were very low because of the fighting, so we had no choice but to use water from our local wells, which was ice cold. We also had no soap or rags with which to clean this place.

Not one of us working to clean that stable cared about these difficulties.

The Russians had liberated us, and things were looking up. We searched the town for any supplies left lying around. We found some coarse paper and went begging for rags. We all worked for over a week cleaning this place, and somehow managed to scrub the horse manure off the floors and walls. Again, the Russians couldn't pay us actual money, but they gave us a little bit of soup and bread, and that's all anybody wanted anyway. To this day I don't know how we did it, but we got that building clean enough to act as a mobile hospital. It is amazing what people can do when they are motivated by hunger.

Here I was doing the lowest of jobs, and I was just happy to have work. I had gone from a very luxurious life as a child to an adult life full of work. Yet I never saw things in that way. There were many people in my situation, and after all, as a Jew I was lucky even to be alive.

I happily worked along with everyone else until the mobile unit arrived to set up. Up to now everything had been about preparing for them. Now it was rush, rush, rush to accommodate the doctors and nurses. They came by train, and we had to unpack and organize all their supplies. We eventually took over another structure that operated as an office. I worked there and at the clinic for over two weeks before anyone began to ask for our papers. They soon started asking questions like, "Who are you?" and "Do you have any documents?" I had a different accent from my co-workers, so I knew they wondered about my background. I kept telling my boss that I left my papers at home, because nobody had initially asked me for them. I kept saying, "Please, I want to stay. I need the work. I will bring my documents tomorrow." They would not put up with this explanation for long, this I knew. What would I do now? I could only hope that if one door closed another would soon open. I have always believed that, with a certain amount of faith, this is how life can be.

The day came when they weren't interested in listening to any more of my pleading, and they said the next day I would have to produce my papers or not return for work. I thought that good fortune had served me again when that night, as I walked home, I found somebody else's papers in the street! They were just laying there right in front of me on the ground! It was a little passport, and even had a picture of a girl my age. I had no idea who this girl was who had dropped it, but I decided then and there to use these papers as my own, never mind that the picture didn't look like me at all.

I thought, "Maybe I can pass these papers off as my own and nobody will notice the inconsistencies." The first time I had attempted this, the Germans hired me with barely a glance at my papers. I already knew how to scratch out the name and put my own in. By then I was pretty good at forging such things. I had some experience. The whole idea was crazy, I suppose, but at the time I thought it was worth a try. The next day I went to work, and when they asked for my papers I gave them this document. I was so proud to finally have something to give them! I apologized for the poor condition of my papers, explaining they were all I had. They gave my documents to the big shot in charge of hiring people, and for the time being, allowed me to continue working.

Everything seemed fine at first. Then they started asking me questions. They wanted to know all kinds of things about my papers, especially where I had obtained them. I said, "Well, they are mine of course. I got them from officials in town." As it turned out my papers were very suspicious. For one thing they had been written in Russian, so I didn't know exactly what they said. I could speak enough Russian to get by, but their alphabet is different, and I didn't know how to read it very well. Clearly I was not the Russian girl in the photo. They challenged my statement, saying, "Oh no, these cannot possibly be your documents, they don't look right at all."

At that moment I was very angry at myself because I hadn't done my usual good job at forging. But I simply hadn't the time or the means. The people in charge were angry with me too. They said, "Well, what do we do with you now? Perhaps you are a spy!" The man who was my superior seemed to like me, and he stood up for me. He seemed satisfied with the work I was doing, and somehow was able to convince his bosses to let me stay in the mobile hospital until they figured out what to do with me.

I thought about it later and realized my big forging plan had been entirely stupid. Instead of taking chances like that I could have said that I had lost my papers when my house was bombed. They still might not have kept me there at the clinic, but at least I wouldn't be as suspicious a person as I now apparently was.

I waited to find out my fate. I was afraid of everything falling apart. I kept working, but was very quiet, and turned from any person who gave me more than one look. Finally I couldn't stand the suspense anymore. I went to my boss and told the truth. "You know, you were right, those really aren't my documents."

My boss said, "Do you know what the penalty is for forging documents? They send you to Siberia!" I knew what he said was true, but in my heart I hoped that I could escape deportation. I thought, "For heaven's sake. Here I was running away from the Germans all this time, and now I'm going to be sent to Siberia by the Russians! What have I accomplished?" My boss said he would see what he could do, and to keep on working. I was made to stay there under observation. I could not go home to Mrs. Nikolajvna, but they kept me fed, and the working conditions were getting better too.

Two days after I admitted my papers were false, I was told to report to the man in charge of things. Something was wrong; I just knew it. I walked to his office and stood there waiting to be told of my deportation to Siberia. The Russian officer in charge had my papers in front of him, and when I asked him if there was a problem he became extremely angry. "These are not your papers!" he yelled at me, "how did you get them, and where are your own?" I told him that I had already admitted to my superior that I had found the papers in the street, and used them because I'd lost my own. This officer would hardly let me speak, however. He warned me that I had no chance of working with them anymore unless I confessed completely. "Who are you, anyway," he asked me, "and what is your true name?"

I didn't know what to say, but I knew that I couldn't create a new lie. It wouldn't do me any good. I told him that I was Maria Kwasigroch, the name given to me by the Polish Underground. He began to yell something at that point, something about proving who I was. I should have been listening, but I didn't hear him very well. My mind was spinning, and to be honest, I didn't want to hear anything more he had to say.

Instead I waited for him to calm down, and then I asked him, "Can I speak to somebody higher up? May I speak to the person who supervises everything? I have something to say."

The officer was indignant over this, and he yelled at me, "Who are you to ask something like that? Of course you cannot speak to someone else. We'll have to watch you for a while until you decide to tell me everything. And let me assure you, we think you're a risk around here." They again refused to let me go home, and I was sent back to the laundry until they could figure out how to deal with me. Again it was implied that I could be sent to Siberia! I had survived a labor camp, a firing squad, and life on the run. So by now I was only thinking, "Well, who the hell wants to go to Siberia?"

I worked as hard as I could with the laundry, and as I folded linen I thought, "Who can I speak to? There must be somebody!" I asked around, and the other workers told me the person running our entire operation was a female Russian major. She was a petite woman, but tough, and very efficient about how she ran the medical unit. She was also a doctor. Then somebody told me that this major was Jewish! Imagine my surprise when I discovered that the main person running this medical unit was not only Jewish, but a woman as well!

I thought, "I must get to this woman somehow and try to talk to her." She had a reputation of being a good officer, intelligent, and very organized. I heard that she was very strict, but also fair, so what did I have to lose? I thought if I could only speak with her, somehow I could straighten things out. I didn't even know her name, but I was so desperate I just asked the nurses and other workers, "Where is the major who runs this unit?" I finally found a female assistant of hers, but she told me the Major was too busy to see me. I wanted an appointment, and as usual I was being a pest about it. I actually took the assistant by the hand and pleaded, "Please, when can I see her?"

I didn't even know if the Major could do anything for me, but I needed to try. Her assistant said that she would see if she could arrange something, and I held my breath. When you're so desperate you cling to any bit of news, and any little bit of information seems so important. I kept telling myself that it was fate that the Major was Jewish. "Maybe she will understand why I kept my real identity secret for so long," I thought, "and she might give me another chance." I was shocked when I finally saw her walk by, because she was not the impressive person I imagined, but very short, like I am now! I could tell, however, that although she may have looked delicate, she had an enormous amount of energy, and she ran that unit like a clock. As she brushed by me, I felt as if speaking to her would almost be like speaking to God.

I waited to hear from her assistant, but time dragged on. When I saw her one day speaking to a nurse I decided not to wait anymore. I stood there in front of her until she noticed me. I was a little intimidated, and wondered what I should say to her. Should I tell her that I am Jewish and give her my real name, or should I give her my Polish Underground name? As I was debating this in my heart, I at least got up the courage to introduce myself. I said, "I'm going to tell you something about myself, and please…you must believe that I am telling you the truth.

"I am Jewish," I proclaimed, "and I have escaped from the Nazis. I was in terrible danger from them when I worked in their labor camp, and later they tried to execute me. I managed to escape, and joined a partisan group, but they never told me their name, so I cannot prove this. I began working for them because they were able to give me papers stating I was Polish. They told me to find employment with the Germans. I obtained a position in a German outfit so that I could provide information to the partisans. I had no other choice in my efforts to survive. I am hoping that you will believe me, and allow me to stay here working. Please, I need this job."

I even told her how the Nazis killed my mother, but I didn't say anything about my father being imprisoned by her comrades as a capitalist. I only said that my entire family was missing, that I was alone, and that I wanted to work. I couldn't stop talking and crying. Finally I said, "I'm telling you honestly that no matter what job you give me, and regardless of the hours, I will do it. I promise you that there are no limits to what work I'll do, so long as my mind and body hold up. I would even take a job that could endanger my life. I don't care. But I cannot go back to the Germans."

Well, the Major listened, or at least she let me talk. She heard me pour out my heart and tell her my entire story. I was even a little surprised by my confession. After I finished blurting out everything, she asked how I had acquired my forged papers. I said, "I forged the papers, and perhaps I do deserve punishment for this. I realize what could happen because of my actions. But you must understand that I lost the papers the partisans gave me when I ran away from the Germans to get closer to the front. I'm asking for your help because I don't want to fall into German hands again. I would rather be killed right here and now. Couldn't you please just give me a chance to continue working for you, and I'll prove that I can be trusted."

This was the first time that I really spoke to anybody the truth about my survival. It had been bottled up inside me for so long that I felt a huge desire to pour it all out. Right away she said, "I am trying to be fair, but I have to admit that I don't trust you. I find it hard to believe what you're telling me, and maybe only part of it is true." I could tell that she didn't believe I was a Jew. People could never tell, and before this moment it had been a blessing. Now it had ironically become a problem! The major gave me hope when she said, "One thing is certain. We need strong people for the work we plan to do here. I will let you stay, but do not ever forget that you are under surveillance the entire time." The Major was not happy with me, nor was she anxious to waste any more time on me and my story. She let me stay only because they needed workers, and for this I was thankful.

I grabbed her hand and said, "Whatever work you have for me I'll do. No matter how hard it is, and no matter if the hours are long, I'll be there for the hospital staff." I said this with all my heart. I belonged to the Russians now. For the time being I couldn't go back to Mrs. Nikolajena's place. They were serious about keeping a close eye on me, and because I worked the night shift it really made more sense for me to sleep at the clinic anyway.

Soon there came a terrible amount of bombing. Apparently the war was far from finished. Real work at the mobile hospital had begun. Day and night they brought in more wounded soldiers. We started to work twenty-four hour shifts. They gave us a little food, but after a while there wasn't much water. There was no real lodging, so I slept on the floor, or wherever I could find a place to lay my head.

There was a Russian officer who was often at the hospital, and he always spoke to me when I passed by. Every time he saw me he asked how I was doing, and finally he inquired about where I lived. I told him that I was currently looking for a decent place, but since I had to stay close to the medical unit it was difficult to find lodgings. I really had been thinking about moving out of Mrs. Nikolajvna's place. It was a little too far from the mobile hospital, and besides this I was afraid that she would somehow learn that I was a Jew. I didn't know how she would react to this fact, and I would have been devastated if she turned me away because of it.

As I chatted with this officer I did not mention to him that, as a person under suspicion, I was required to stay at the hospital. One day he told me that he could find a place for me to stay that was closer to my work. Some of the Russian girls working at the unit saw this officer speaking with me, and I guess they became a little jealous. After all, I wasn't even Russian, so why should I get attention from this officer? I have to say that he was good-looking too. Anyway, one of the nurses eventually pulled me aside and told me this man was no good. She implied that he was something of a playboy. I didn't bother to tell her I had already decided to avoid him. I was still nervous about people I didn't know, especially with my superiors watching me as if I were a spy. I was also a little uncomfortable around men because I had little experience with them. I admit that I liked the attention this officer gave me, but I came to suspect that he might not have good intentions. Perhaps he might even have been sent to see if I was a spy. For all I knew this officer's intentions were no better than those of the Ukrainian Gestapo man who had offered to help me find Ziun.

I found ways to put off this officer, yet it seemed almost a shame. He was very nice to me, and he seemed to be a gentleman. Herr Zgoda had been good to me, and the German officer on the train as well, but they had not been aware of who I really was. In my mind I had been treated decently only because of who I pretended to be, not because of who I really was. After escaping east and living on the run I had become more like a frightened animal than a young lady. It was true that I had managed to survive and find work again, and Mrs. Nikolajvna's kindness had helped to make me feel secure again. But I had not been treated like a real person in some time, much less like a real lady.

By the time I met this Russian officer I had finally begun to feel a little bit more like a human being. I no longer had to lie about my identity, and I had a job that allowed me to clean up a little, and I was getting tired of being so lonely. While I was working for the Germans I had no choice but to keep to myself. This provided a sort of protective shell around me. Now that I could be myself, I began to recognize how alone I really was. It would have been nice to have a little companionship, and this man had never given me any real reason to doubt him. Still, I felt that I could not take the chance. I again closed myself off, averting my eyes from the handsome Russian officer and working twice as hard to take my mind off my loneliness.

I tried to be as polite as possible when he kept offering me these places that he knew of that I could rent. I could no longer put him off, so I lied and said I had found my own room close by. Well, wouldn't you know it, he then offered to take me home! What could I do? I made some excuse about having to work late, and hurried off before he could say anything, but I don't think he believed me.

I was completely mystified over why this man continued to offer his help. I thought that he couldn't possibly think of me as someone he might take out on a date. If you were to see how I looked at the time you would agree. Because of the food available at work I was not as skinny, but I was still thin enough to have lost my curves. My clothes were stained and not holding up very well. The only thing going for me I think was my complexion. I was a little proud of it, and the other girls even asked how I kept my skin so rosy and nice. Frankly, I was lucky to find a place to wash up most of the time, but I managed every now and then. Anyway, I think the officer finally got the message when I told him that my duties at work had increased. I couldn't even think of moving and had to remain on the hospital premises. "I have to be close in order to work the night shift," I lied to him. I had no nighttime duties then, but I didn't know any other way to put him off. After that he let me alone.

WHY DID NINA PUSH AWAY the handsome officer's advances? Though she had admitted she enjoyed his company, and was starving for companionship, she continued to believe she was better off alone. The once lively and affectionate girl had ultimately survived the war by maintaining a distance between herself and others, and she found it a difficult habit to break. Avoiding romantic entanglements seemed to come naturally; she had yet to fully convince her superiors she could be trusted.

I wanted desperately to prove myself to the Russian female officer. One night she ran into me coming from the medical building. It was around midnight, and she wondered why I was there. I replied that I was going to work! I believe she had decided that I was okay by then, because she smiled at me for the first time, and told me to have a good night. Once things quieted down I was able to leave the hospital for a day or two. I went to Mrs. Nikolajena's place and told her what had happened, and why I disappeared for a while. I cleaned up and rested a bit, but returned to work as soon as possible.

The Russians now trusted that I wasn't a spy, and I wasn't going to let them down. I continued to work, and when I had more than a day to rest I slept at Mrs. Nikolajena's. The Russians even allowed me to occasionally bring supplies from work to our apartment. I must have really convinced my superiors that I was okay, because one day they offered to provide me with a gun for protection. Can you imagine me with a gun? I cannot say for certain if I could have ever used it. Maybe if I saw one of the Nazis who had killed my family I would have. The Soviets felt I would have been safer going to and from work with a firearm, because walking the streets was becoming more dangerous. There were many different people running around, including German soldiers in disguise trying to escape west.

I really didn't want to carry a gun. In my current state of mind I might have been tempted to turn it on myself. I still had occasional thoughts of suicide, and my only real concern was if I was unsuccessful I might cripple myself in some way. Anyway, I never accepted the gun, and though my superiors felt I was being foolish they didn't press the point.

We worked away and the wounded kept coming. Their uniforms were full of blood, and because we were handling them so much we were also covered with it. I don't know where I found the energy and ambition to keep going. I continued to work beyond my limits, and there was plenty of work to do. Zmerinka was shelled often by what was left of the German forces. We were constantly being hit day and night. At four o'clock in the morning or in the middle of the night, we never knew when they would start up again. I often wished I could go somewhere a little more peaceful, but I had accepted work with a traveling medical unit and had to remain close to the fighting. The wounded men they brought us were often without arms or legs, and sometimes we didn't have enough bandages and supplies to help them. Many times we had to wash out our old bandages and reuse them. Those of us who had been so happy to find work now struggled with our limited training and supplies. We could only do so much because we weren't trained professionals, so we prepared the wounded for surgery, doing our best at applying first aid.

I don't know how the Soviets managed to push the Nazis away from us, but they were ultimately successful. The day finally came when we were able to rest for a full three days. We didn't have much to eat, they still could only give us a little piece of bread and maybe some soup, but at least we weren't starving as we had been when the Germans pulled out. When the Nazis were in control, food was hard to come by. With the Russians in charge we didn't have to worry about starving completely, much less being killed or abused.

AS OUR CONVERSATIONS LED US into the last days of World War II, Nina began to repeat certain stories to me, unaware that we had already recorded them. I would stop her and repeat the story back to be certain I had recorded every detail. Upon pointing this out she would inevitably make the same comment:

> You know, perhaps I have told you this story before. But I have to point out that by repeating myself, this only proves that what I'm saying is true. If I was making things up then the stories would change I think. A lie is mixed up and gives itself away, because you forget how you put it. But when you're telling the truth...maybe it's not always the same words, but the idea and the meaning are the same. Some

people don't want to believe what really happened during the war, but I'm here to say that it did!

Nina said this to me more than once and I never doubted the accuracy of her stories. Although she complained about forgetting bits and pieces of her younger life, I found her memory to be exceptional for a woman in her eighties.

There was always more to tell of the long and dangerous days she experienced as the war slowly drew to an end.

One day I was walking home after some very long hours of work. I was tired and not really paying attention to where I was going. I suppose you could say that I was schlepping. This is a very appropriate Yiddish word to describe how I was walking with very heavy feet. Suddenly I saw somebody working on, of all things, a streetlight. I thought, "What is this guy doing, trying to get the light to work when a bomb or bullet is only going to put it out again?" I dragged myself up to this lamp post and watched the man work for a little while. When I see a picture of it in my mind I think I must have looked half-dead, and I have to laugh. But I was curious to see what he was doing, and as I looked up the man winked at me! I remember it like today.

I said to him in Russian, "What in the world are you doing up there?" He said, "Well, I'm fixing the light!" I could tell that he had an accent, but he brought it up first. "Hey," he said, "you're not Russian." I spoke Russian and German fairly well by this time, so I suppose I was a little put off by this comment. But I discovered the reason he mentioned it at all was because he thought I might be Polish. When he asked where I was from and I told him that I was born in L'vov, Poland, he immediately came down the ladder! The man said with some excitement, "I know of L'vov! I have a very good friend from there, and he has been trying to find family and friends."

This man was so happy to have found somebody from Poland that he stood and talked with me for some time. "My friend works with me from time to time," he explained, "and I respect him so much that it would be an honor to help him find a fellow Pole. My goodness, he would be so happy to meet someone from his hometown! He's always talking about it." I really didn't feel like meeting anybody, especially since I was such a mess, but this man would not let the idea go. "Gosh," he insisted, "you just have to meet him!" Here I was looking as if I had just slept in the gutter, and he wanted to introduce me to a man with who knows what kind of character.

This was all I needed. I don't think this man knew that I was Jewish, and it never really came up in the conversation. He only said that his friend's name was Josef, and even when I did meet Josef I didn't realize he was Jewish. We Jews were accustomed to keeping these things to ourselves, and I suppose old habits die hard. Anyway, I argued with this man about meeting his friend. I said, "Oh, no, I just can't do anything socially right now. I only have time to get a little rest, and then I go back to work."

"I won't take no for an answer," this man told me, "you have to meet him." I simply smiled and started to walk away, but this man was so persistent. He yelled after me, "I'm going to bring my friend by to meet you."

I saw this electrician on a few more occasions when I walked home from work. Each time he insisted I meet his friend Josef. "He's very lonely for someone from his hometown," he kept telling me. Maybe destiny was working for us, because finally one evening I ran into this electrician while he was working with Josef. He was so excited to be introducing us at last, and I had to hand it to him, he managed to stop me long enough to do so.

"Here is the girl I was talking about," he said to Josef, "she is from L'vov just like you. Perhaps you know some of the same people!" I seriously doubted this, and I stood there trying to make small talk and feeling very uncomfortable. I cannot tell you my first impression of Josef, who would eventually become my husband. I was not really a normal person at that time, so I think meeting anybody new would have made me nervous. I have to say that it was good to converse in Polish with someone, and to share a few memories about L'vov. He introduced himself as Josef Morecki, but we really did not exchange any other personal information. There had been so much bombing the night before, and we both had certain responsibilities, so we had very little time to chat. I did manage to explain to him about my work with the casualties from the front. I didn't tell him where I lived at first, but when he said that he would like to see me again, I agreed it would be nice. He wished to talk with me about L'vov some more, and he asked about my family. I sort of ignored those kinds of questions. I was very afraid to give any information about myself to anyone.

———

Josef came up with the idea of helping me out during the next bombing. He said to me, "The one thing I want to do is to make certain you are safe during the shelling. I know a place that is safe, and I can take you there the next time the bombing starts." I agreed to go with him under those conditions, and this is when I gave him my address, though I didn't really think he would show up.

I told Mrs. Nikolajvna about meeting Josef, and about his offer to take us to safety during the bombing. She shrugged and said, "Go ahead and bring him over and we'll see." One day, soon after meeting him, Josef showed up on our doorstep. I introduced him to Mrs. Nikolajvna, and then Josef said, "Who is this charming little girl?"

"Oh, she's mine," I lied. This just popped into my mind. I don't know why I said that Erichka was my daughter. I was thinking that maybe nothing is ever going to be serious between this man, Josef, and me, so it won't matter if I lie a little bit. Maybe I thought that he would only help all three of us if he thought they were my family. Anyway it just came out of my mouth that Erichka was mine, and Mrs. Nikolajvna didn't argue with me. I didn't feel good about the lie, because I was starting to like Josef. Unlike other men I had encountered during the war, I didn't want to push him away. I just wanted to help my little temporary family, and maybe pretending that Erichka was my daughter was necessary in order to get help for her and her grandmother. I also thought that maybe he would respect me more if he thought I was a young mother. Perhaps it would make him more willing to help us.

Josef said that it was a pleasure to meet them, and that any time the shelling began we should wait for him a while, but not for long. If he didn't show up he told us to go into the nearby fields outside of town. "I suggest that you go into fields when trouble starts up," he politely told us.

"It really is the safest place, because there are no targets there that the Germans wish to destroy." I told Mrs. Nikolajvna it might be a good idea. Josef knew the territory very well, and he explained how we should get there if he could not take us. I remember thinking at the time that Josef was very resourceful.

Before he left that day Josef said to me, "Remember, if you go into the fields and lay under the trees, you're more likely to come out of this war alive. I'm only telling you this because you seem like a nice person, and I wouldn't want you to get hurt. You have to think about the child too. What if a bomb hits your house?" I couldn't argue with him. I had become too exhausted to argue about anything. I couldn't even think straight because I was always so tired. If somebody suggested any little thing at this point I would have gone along with it. All I cared about was keeping my job so that we wouldn't starve. I told Josef that it would be fine for him to come when the bombing started. I still thought he was a little crazy for going out of his way for us. I also could not be certain he was right about running into the fields to avoid the bombs. It sounded a little silly to me.

Well, that very same night the Russian medical unit where I was working was partially hit by a bomb. The building was almost completely destroyed, several patients were killed and some doctors as well. Apparently some renegade Germans had tried to destroy a railroad track nearby. Releasing bombs over a target was not an exact thing, and they must have miscalculated the distance. Maybe they didn't care that they were in danger of hitting a medical unit, who knows?

I was on my way to work just before the medical unit was hit. When I heard the bombs falling in the direction of my work place I turned and ran away. In the middle of all this bombing I somehow reached Mrs. Nikolajvna and Erichka. We talked things over for just a few minutes and decided that Josef had a pretty good idea after all, so we headed for the fields to wait until the shelling stopped. We hid in some kind of an irrigation ditch covered with grass and branches. Other people were trying to get off the road and hide there as well, so I suppose we weren't the only ones with this great idea! It was not as if the ditch truly afforded us any extra protection, but it made all of us feel a little less like targets.

On this particular night Josef could not reach us. He was stuck somewhere else for the entire evening until the very early morning. The next day I went to see if the people at my medical unit were all right, but things looked very bad there. The wounded were placed in a structure that had not been hit, and I was put in charge of taking bloody uniforms off of the dead and dying. We were desperate for cloth, so we washed the dirty clothes to use as bandages. It was horrible to see the suffering in peoples' faces, and to have the smell of blood surrounding us once again.

For months the fighting had gone back and forth, but we still felt the Russians were winning. The Major had not been hurt in the bombing that destroyed our little clinic. But she must have been assigned to another unit, because soon afterwards she left along with some of the other officers. I also noticed that the officer who had offered to find me a place to live was gone, yet this came as a bit of a relief. I never did feel completely comfortable around him.

I secretly wondered if Josef had survived the recent bombing. I was worried, because as I walked home from the medical unit destruction I saw massive graves being dug for all the people who had died in the shelling. This was not a very big city, and it appeared that the population had been affected in an immense way. Everybody had lost a friend or loved one. Maybe Josef had been killed as well. That very evening, however, he showed up. When he saw me he said, "I told you that they would be bombing our little city more. You simply have to continue going into the fields when this happens."

Well, every single evening after that day, Josef came to gather up me, Mrs. Nikolajvna, and Erichka. The little girl could not run fast enough once the shelling started, so Josef picked her up and carried her on his shoulders. One night as we lay crouched in the woods, waiting for the bombing to stop, he let me in on a little secret. He told me that he knew good and well that the people in my home were not my own family! He never believed my little lie. As he held little Erichka he said to me, "She is not really your daughter, is she?" Of course he had figured this out from the very beginning because she didn't look anything like me. She was blond with blue eyes, a beautiful Russian girl just like her mother Tania, and I looked nothing like her. My hair was light brown, and my eyes brownish-green. I told Josef that he was right, and that I had lied because I wanted to be sure he would help all of us to safety. I knew that it sounded silly, but Josef let it go, and didn't act as if my lie had disturbed him.

The guns continued to fire all around us, until one evening Josef again did not show up. We were really worried about him, because the shelling that night was especially bad. I didn't know what had happened, but I prayed that he hadn't been killed. The last time I saw him he was wearing big, beautiful boots. He had always worn them on our excursions to the field, and the first time I commented on how nice they were he informed me he got them when he was a big shot in the ghetto. Don't ask me what he did to survive in this ghetto, but it was the very same one I had learned of as soon as I reached Romania. I believe Josef was involved in some way with the black market. He knew how to sweet talk and manipulate. He also had lots of friends because of his generosity. He could fix anything, and make anything possible, and people trusted him. He had these qualities.

Some of his partners in the ghetto disagreed with his generosity. They didn't want to share what little profit they made, but Josef always tried to get extra supplies to the people living around him. He would say to these partners, "If we have bread, then those going hungry around us should also have it." Because of this he was rather popular. Apparently he had become friends with a shoemaker, and this man made his lovely boots as a gift for Josef's kindness. You see, my husband was a sharp dressed man even then.

Well, the night of our terrible shelling, he was still asleep. Before he could get up to help us a shell hit right where he was sleeping. He rolled away when he heard it whistling toward his apartment, and it just missed him. After the dust cleared he looked over to where he had set his boots. The bomb had not hurt him, but his boots had been blown clear away! Eventually he showed up to tell us the story. He said to me, "My boots went down with everything else in my apartment." I gave him a pat on the back and said, "Well, be thankful you were not in them at the time. At least you still have your feet!"

The shelling went on for around four weeks. When it had settled down again Josef came with sad news. That night he arrived at our apartment and said, "I have not come to take you into the fields this time. I have come to say goodbye." I couldn't believe it. I had begun to care very much for Josef, but I was too shy to tell him this, and was still acting as if he was a mere acquaintance. I tried not to show how upset I was by his announcement. All this time I never so much as gave him a hug, even when he showed up after the night he lost his boots. I wanted that night to hold him and say, "I am so happy that you are alive!" But I was scared to feel close to anyone. I had spent so much time losing people I cared about, and everything still remained very uncertain.

I didn't know if Josef and I had a future, so I didn't know how to act. There had never been anything spoken between us that could be considered romantic. We spent most of our time running from the bombs. Josef never indicated how he felt towards me, but I sensed that he at least liked me. He had been a gentleman, and a very faithful friend, and now here he was telling me goodbye. He explained that he was going with the Russians to fight on the front close to Berlin. He told me that German boys as young as ten years old were being drafted to fight the Allies, so things were getting very desperate for the Germans.

"When are you going?" I asked, trying not to sound very concerned, and he said his unit would be leaving right away. At this bit of information I could no longer hold my composure, and I began to panic. "Take me with you!" I suddenly suggested. The idea of accompanying Josef to the front seems crazy now, but at the time it didn't seem like an unusual request. I had done more dangerous things, and I was used to working at the front. I pleaded with him, "I want to go with you, and I can be ready to leave in two minutes."

"I can't take you with me," Josef said. "They drafted me, not you. You're a woman!" I wouldn't hear of it. I had heard of Russian women helping on the front from the people at work. But Josef would not listen to my request. All he could say to me was, "You are not a Russian, and I will not allow you to get in harm's way." He was starting to become angry with me, so I got angry too.

I was hurt that he wouldn't take me, and I said something very mean. "Fine then," I yelled at him, "I refuse to say goodbye to you! I'm not even going to speak to you anymore!" Oh, I was horrible, and I cannot believe he still cared about me after I said such things. Maybe he understood that I was just afraid of losing him. All these years I had been taking care of myself with no help, and no emotional support from anyone. Once I met Josef I felt that I finally had someone who truly cared about me. He had been my only protector during this lousy war, and I did not wish to be separated from him. I had let my guard down and begun to care about someone, and that person was about to disappear in front of my eyes.

I had my back turned to Josef, deciding that if I stayed angry at him it would not hurt as much to see him go. I would not cry and beg anymore. Josef said goodbye to Mrs. Nikolajvna and gave Erichka a kiss on the cheek.

Then as he was walking out the door he turned around and said one last thing to the stubborn girl who would not speak to him. "If we survive," he told me in his strong voice, "I will find you." And with this he left. We never so much as shook hands. I was alone again, and when the last of the bombing started up we waited in the fields, where I could not stop thinking of him.

TO NINA, Josef's departure was yet another example of a loved one's abandonment due to the war. Though her anger toward him was misdirected, it was understandable that she would protect herself from further emotional trauma by turning away. Nina always spoke of this moment with regret. She told me of her fear that she might never lay eyes on her new love again.

With this last, cruel assault on her soul, Nina resolved to make her way back to L'vov in the hope of finding any member of her family.

CHAPTER VIII

Breaking Away

(1944)

NINA HAD VERY LITTLE TIME to lament her brusque behavior toward Josef. She soon learned that her medical unit was moving west, in the same direction as Josef's military unit. The idea of traveling closer to L'vov greatly appealed to Nina, and she immediately left with her Soviet employers. Once again, with no concrete plan to guide her, she allowed her instinct to direct her actions, hoping she would eventually reach her hometown. Nina willingly said goodbye to Zmerinka, her only real regret being that she could never properly thank Mrs. Nikolajvna or give a parting kiss to Tania's baby girl, Erichka.

Not long after Josef was recruited to fight with the Russian army, I found out the hospital where I worked was to be relocated. We had to go where the casualties might be, so just like that we packed up everything to follow the army west by truck or by train, whichever was available. If I wanted to remain employed I would have to move with them.

I never had time to properly say goodbye to Mrs. Nikolajvna and the baby, Erichka. I came to work one day, and found the officers packing up what was left after the bombing. They directed us to get into the trucks with them, and everything was in such chaos that I had no choice but to do as I was told. I felt badly that I could not see my little temporary family one last time, but I thought maybe I would be able to check in after the war ended. Of course this never happened, and to this day I don't know what became of them. Anyway, we had our orders, and I had no choice but to be as flexible as always. Remaining flexible had allowed me to survive throughout the war, and I was not going to change my strategy at this late date.

So off I went again, and I was excited to learn we were heading west toward L'vov. They transported us in cattle cars, which is a little ironic to me now that I know that this was how Jews were taken to concentration camps. For all I know some of my family were sent to their deaths in a cattle car just like the one that took me back towards L'vov. The Soviets in charge tried to accommodate us, but there were few supplies available and so it was a difficult journey. Whenever the train stopped the local people sold us produce, and we got by on that for a while.

As for me, well, I was not complaining. I was part of this military hospital unit, and I was still determined to do my best. I believe that most of the other people traveling with me felt the same way. We were part of a Russian medical unit now. They seemed to appreciate us more than the Germans ever had, and we were doing our duty by working for them. We traveled west for some days until our supervisors chose a new site.

We settled into work once again, this time in a field outside of some little town. We put up operations there in order to avoid any more damage from the intermittent fighting that continued on and on. There were fewer casualties because we were not as close to the front, so instead we spent a lot of time getting organized and giving more extensive care to those patients who needed it.

As usual I kept very much to myself, even when some of the other workers asked me to join them for a break. I spent a lot of time alone, and it made me think of one instance when I went against my own rules of avoiding people. One night I lay there recalling to myself an incident that had occurred just before we pulled out of Zmerinka. It was that period of time when there had been terrible bombing around us. It was pretty clear that Russia had liberated every area we passed through before, but it was still sometimes dangerous getting around. A co-worker told me one day about a little party they were planning on having in the middle of town, just some sort of religious celebration, and she asked me to meet her there.

I felt as if I could use a little fun, so I went. I was alone on the street looking for this friend, when I saw a Russian officer stop his jeep. He leaned out and asked me if I needed a lift into town. He spoke to me in Russian, and asked where I was going. "I don't know really," I responded, because I didn't have any clue exactly where the party was. This officer offered me a ride, and to my surprise I said yes! He had a different kind of uniform; his lapel and arm had badges that showed he was high ranking. I also knew he was of high rank because he had a very nice car. I was lonely beyond belief, and any companionship would be a welcome relief. I wasn't worried about whether or not it was safe to go off with this officer. Somehow I felt that he could be trusted.

Besides my confidence that the officer would be a gentleman, a ride in an automobile was a real treat for me. I was tired of walking miles and miles just to get the slightest thing done, and the idea of riding in a real car was very appealing. I stood there like an idiot thinking things over one more time, until he motioned to me and said, "Okay, hop in." We drove around a bit until coming to where his friends lived. He wanted a good meal, and he said that I could join him. I wondered how close we were to the neighborhood party, but I went along because I was so hungry. When we arrived at his friend's home they welcomed me very nicely. They greeted the officer with respect and admiration, and they treated me like an honored guest. When we sat down to eat I could not believe my eyes. Before me was more food than I had seen in years! I was grateful to these people for including me in this absolute feast, but I was uncomfortable with the situation. I began to understand that the officer's friends thought we were a couple, like a boyfriend and girlfriend. Because of this I was a little too embarrassed to eat much of the food.

I was surprised to see that the meal took so long, until very late in the evening. Then the officer's friends suggested that we spend the night. I tried to object, but he didn't want to drive home at such a late hour. He made the decision for us to stay, and I got more and more nervous. I was in an absolute panic when they put us in one room together to sleep! They knew that I was not Russian, but they didn't know the true nature of my relationship with this man, so I couldn't really blame them for doing this. I wanted to run out of that room and head home on foot.

The officer prepared for bed, and as he was taking off his belt that held a gun I made a move for the door. He stopped me and said, "Don't worry; I am only taking off my gun. I'm not going to get undressed and you don't have to either. We can lie together on the bed to sleep, but I promise I won't touch you." He must have seen the doubt in my eyes, because he took his gun and put it in the middle of the bed, saying, "If it makes you feel better I'll put my firearm between us. If I make so much as a nudge, all you have to do is grab the gun and shoot me! As for now, I am tired and you must also be exhausted. So lie down and get some sleep."

Well, what could I do? I still wasn't sure that I could trust him, but I had nowhere else to stay that night, so I lay down. He was true to his word and left his gun between us. I wondered if he was going to shoot me once I fell asleep, but I was too tired to care. He never took his clothes off, and I didn't take mine off either. He even kept his shiny boots on! I eventually rolled over and fell asleep. I was sure he would get angry if I didn't. Sure enough he didn't touch me the whole night.

WHEN NINA RELAYED THIS STORY to me I was reminded of the tale of Camelot. As a way of proving his chivalry, Lancelot laid his sword between himself and Gwenivere, leaving the choice of crossing over to him up to her. Though Nina's situation was hardly as romantic as that, the Russian officer had made his point. In deference to Nina's honor he maintained his distance through the night, his gun remaining a border between them. Nina awoke refreshed with her innocence intact.

I slept well, and in the morning we thanked the officer's friends for their kindness. We got back into the car and headed back to my unit. Halfway through our trip the officer had a little discussion with me about how risky things were for a young woman alone. He actually chastised me for being so naïve, and he cautioned me, saying, "If it had been any other man in last night's situation, I don't think things would have ended up the same, do you?"

I had to admit that I had been a little stupid about taking a ride with a virtual stranger, but I had truly believed no man could possibly have any interest in me because I was so thin and disheveled. The officer reminded me that anyone could have easily beaten and raped me. I realized then how foolish I had been. When we arrived at my unit the officer stopped his car, and then turned to give me a final dressing-down. He said that I should be more careful, and not expect everyone to be a nice person.

I thanked him as I got out of the car, and went to work thinking about how I should be more cautious. Even so, if an opportunity came to get me back to L'vov I had every intention of taking it, whether or not it put me in danger. At that time the depth of my morality was so shallow. I had been through so much that by then I was simply going through the motions of living. I was like a…what do you call them? I was like a robot. If that Russian officer wanted to kill me that night I would have said, "Fine, do what you want with me. I just don't care!"

By this time the war had really affected me in such a way, and I wasn't a whole person. I had been hated by Germans, Ukrainians, and my Polish countrymen. My family had been taken from me and I had been surrounded by the enemy. Even after successfully presenting myself as a Pole, I had never felt entirely safe. Here and there people had shown me compassion, and I had been lucky enough to happen upon them in my most desperate moments. But I had been left utterly alone at a very young age. This was hard for me, because I had been sheltered as the youngest child. Now I realize that my tragic situation, my loneliness and my desperation, caused me to do crazy things during the war. I was always ready to die, but almost by accident I survived. I wanted to kill myself many times, because I felt so strongly the need to get out of my entire situation.

I couldn't share my fear or sadness with anyone, and I didn't trust my own shadow. I didn't know where to go and whom to turn to. My life had been so torn up that I no longer had any real incentive to continue other than to track down family who might have survived. My experience with the officer woke me up, and the fact that he thought enough of me to give warning about my stupid choices made me realize I had to respect my own life. I knew the time had come to be more careful, and I have to admit that his attention made me feel a little more alive.

Anyway, I had very little time to feel sorry for myself, or to think back on what I may have done wrong in Zmerinka. Before long our mobile medical unit was on the move again. We were all put on a train going toward Warsaw. All of the workers tried to peer out the door to see if any towns going by were familiar to us. I recognized more and more as we continued west, and I sensed we were getting close to my hometown. I heard one of the workers say, "We're coming to a big city!" Well, I knew by then we were going through L'vov. My heart nearly beat out of my chest, and I wanted to jump out of the train that very minute.

I thought of nothing else for the remainder of the trip except how I would leave the unit to go looking for my family. The Germans had been pushed out of this part of Poland, so I thought I would be relatively safe. I could have asked to be excused from work and explained that I wished to find any surviving relatives in my hometown. All of us workers certainly deserved some time off. We had been on our feet or on the road for many months. Still, I was afraid that the Russians might deny me this opportunity. They desperately needed workers, and besides, if they still had doubts about whether or not I was a spy they might never let me go!

We settled into a little town to continue our treatment of soldiers, but every day was sheer torture because I knew we were close to my home. I couldn't concentrate because getting back to L'vov was such an obsession for me. I would have done anything to get there, but whom could I ask for help? I said to myself, "Well, I am always on the run, so why not make one more try?"

One day I slipped away without a word to anybody. I ran to the station and waited for a train going in the direction of L'vov. The whole time I was afraid someone from my unit would come looking for me. I had to ask around about the trains' schedule, and every time I spoke to a Russian I thought they might arrest me simply because of my accent. Here I was without any documents again, and naturally I had no money to live on.

Luckily my situation was nothing new, so I found a way to improvise. Instead of trying to get on a passenger train I decided to use the cattle cars just as my medical unit had. I found out when there would be empty cargo cars going toward L'vov, and I slipped on while the train workers were not looking. I selected one big empty boxcar and hid in the corner where I couldn't be found. I don't know how long I was on this train, but once during a stop I heard someone coming, maybe to look inside the cars! I ran out of my car and hid in the trees until the train pulled out without me. It was once again time to walk, and I did so for what seemed like forever.

I wondered how I would ever make it back to L'vov. I estimated it was still some forty kilometers away, and I needed some other transportation besides my two skinny legs. I didn't have a car or even a bicycle. My feet were so tired and swollen from walking, and I couldn't go on that way. I kept telling myself, "I must keep moving. Maybe someone in my family is alive!" I stayed close to the tracks in case another train came along, and sure enough I heard one slowly going by. I hopped on and was traveling again in luxury. The train moved painfully slow, and I believe I was in that particular car for days. I was tired and hungry, and could only go to the bathroom when the train stopped. Oddly enough I had to go less and less. I guess I was getting used to the train's schedule. It's strange how the body shuts down to accommodate one's situation.

I slept whenever I could, and I was in a deep dream when a strong light forced my eyes to open. I don't know who was more surprised, the man shining a lantern in my face, or me at the sight of him! He was an old man, so I wasn't really very afraid of him, but I was concerned that he might throw me off the train. He was a train worker, and he demanded to know what I was doing in that car. When I found my voice I heard myself telling him that I was trying to get to L'vov and find my family. I was dirty and hungry, and must have looked pathetic. "Why don't you travel in one of the passenger cars?" he asked me, as if it were that simple. Normally I would have fabricated some story as I always had before. This time I decided not to deny who I was anymore. "I am a Jew," I told him. I felt sort of defiant when I said, "Even if I had the money to travel I could not be sure that someone might not try to kill me!"

I saw pity for me in the old man's eyes. He gave me another look and he walked away. I thought that he would just leave me alone to travel as I had, but he came back before the train pulled out, and gave me some bread and a little water. He even told me how far I had left to go in order to reach L'vov. Again, I had been saved by a complete stranger. I felt rejuvenated by this, and as the train continued on I had so much hope. All I wanted was to get back home and find a relative or acquaintance. I thought, "I know I will find somebody! I couldn't be the only one, and certainly God would not have let me survive without a reason. There has to be somebody waiting for me, and I'm going to find them!"

I knew my mother was dead, but I wasn't certain about what finally happened to my father. If he was sent to Siberia perhaps by now he had been released. Maybe my older sister Lina and her family found a way through the war as I had. As for my middle sister, Helena, there was less hope in me for her. I had the feeling that she couldn't have survived. I don't know how she might have died, but she wasn't strong like my older sister and me. I simply never expected to see her after the war, and the thought of her suffering made me sad. But the rest of my friends and family…well, who knew? Certainly anything was possible.

NINA FELT HER BONES RATTLE as she suffered through the jolting cattle car ride to L'vov, feeling both anticipation at reaching her hometown, and dread over what she might or might not find there. Like many survivors, she held out hope that certainly someone from her family must have come through the Nazi gauntlet just as she had.

After years of living in fear and trepidation as a Jew hiding behind a false identity, Nina was in no hurry to let down her guard.

I knew I would have to be careful once I reached L'vov. The Poles still hated Jews, and they were afraid that any of us who returned would want to reclaim their property that was now back in their control. The killing wasn't as open as when the Germans were in charge, but Jews did wind up dead even after the Nazis left. I later learned that 180 people were killed when they returned to the town of Kielce. It was around 1945 and the local citizens killed these refugees.

I FOUND RECORD of a pogrom which occurred in the Polish town of Kielce on the 11th of July, 1946. A correspondent of a Jewish publication in London investigated and reported seeing, "…36 terribly mutilated bodies, with battered faces, crushed bones, broken legs and limbs almost torn off."[1] Though far from the numbers Nina recalled, the manner in which these survivors were murdered reminded the few Jews left in Eastern Europe of how precarious their situation was. Hitler was dead, but his twisted ideology remained in the hearts of many Europeans, German and non-German alike. In spite of the Allied presence, many Jews felt their lives were in danger, and were desperately making plans to leave for countries overseas.

Like other survivors, Nina had no reason to believe anti-Semitism had disappeared in her homeland. She was fully prepared to encounter Poles who were bitter and unchanged in their anti-Semitic attitudes.

During the war the Jews were scattered everywhere, all of them taken from where they had lived, in some instances for centuries, and placed in camps. Most of these camps were in Poland. After the war people tried to go back to the cities and towns where they had been born and spent most of their life. The main reason they returned was in the hope that they would find a family member alive and waiting there for them, just as I was trying to do. Unfortunately, many of the locals got it into their heads that we were returning to reclaim all of the property stolen by the Germans, Poles, and Ukrainians. It was true that all of the Jewish homes and businesses that hadn't been demolished were taken over by the Nazis and later the Poles, but this was far from a priority for most surviving Jews.

The locals rarely wasted time asking questions, and usually took matters into their own hands. Some were of the opinion that if Hitler couldn't finish the job of killing Jews completely, well then they would. I heard this with my own ears. In the towns I passed through I heard people sneering, "Look how many Jews are coming back! Hitler didn't do a very good job!" Even though I had long considered myself a citizen of Poland, I knew these were not my countrymen. The war was over, but Jews and Poles were enemies.

THE ABANDONMENT of their Polish heritage seemed to be a byproduct of war common to many Jewish survivors. It is understandable that a people once loyal to Poland no longer felt an allegiance to the country that allowed for their almost complete obliteration. Survivor Hedva Gil described the reasoning behind the decision to discard her Polish identity for one that was completely and defiantly Jewish. She explained her childhood and adulthood as involving: "…three nations: Jews, Germans, and

Poles. My family was very assimilated and we lived among Poles; this assimilation was an ideology that I abandoned during the war, and I could not become Polish again after the war after having denied my Jewishness for two years and once I had seen how different my fate was from that of my Polish friends. As a child, Poland was my beloved homeland—I saw myself as a Pole even if I did not deny the fact that I was Jewish. I love the Polish language, literature, folk songs…But I chose to return to the Jews. And I did this with great enthusiasm."[2]

Even more disheartening to Nina was the hypocrisy shown by those claiming to be devout followers of the Christian faith. Working at the L'vov hospital under the supervision of Catholic nuns had given her a sense of sanity at a time of havoc and uncertainty. Witnessing the actions of the "good Christian Poles" now caused her to question the worth of those values the good sisters tried to emulate during those first days of war.

I was disgusted to hear anti-Semitic remarks even from those who considered themselves "good Catholics." If someone ever said to me that all people who go to church and call themselves Christians are compassionate I would have to disagree with them. Not all so-called Christians are faithful to their religion and what it's supposed to teach them. I encountered hateful people who went to church on a daily basis, and they had no problem hurting us or benefiting from our misfortune. Quite a few of these people even assisted in killing us.

Hitler would have done anything to eliminate Jews because he was a madman. What really appealed to many Poles and Ukrainians were the material rewards behind our disappearance. Once Jews were out of the picture they could take over many fine homes and businesses. This greed underlies every action against us. Those of us who had resources were envied by those who did not. A lot of Jews had money left in Swiss banks, and at first these accounts remained untouched. I knew that my father had money in some of these banks, but of course I could not produce documented evidence. I barely had the clothes on my back, so what could I do about collecting my family's financial holdings?

All I could remember was what my father said to me just before the war. He told me about the Swiss accounts, and also that he had purchased several bricks of gold. He must have sensed that there would be hard times coming, and he thought enough to try and put something away. He hid this gold in the ceiling where our chandelier hung. It wasn't even noticeable that he had hidden it there, and I thought he was very clever to do this. I have no idea if this gold fell into German or Polish hands, but when I went back to see our apartment it was gone. It was long after the war, and the Russians had divided our big apartment into three small ones. I went in to see the old place and of course, no chandelier. I barely recognized the place, and I never went back to number ten, Kopernika Street.

MANY JEWS WHO HAD TRUSTED their belongings to Gentiles found their former friends and neighbors reluctant to return anything of even remote value. Hard times bred a selfish mentality, and a strange sense of entitlement seemed to have taken hold among those with any resources. As Nina would soon encounter with the Ravitsky family, any surviving Jew seeking out his property could encounter a range of uncomfortable situations. A non-Jew would often deny having held the property at all, and pressing the matter might lead to open hostility.

Knowing they remained vulnerable to attack, many Jews simply walked away from whatever material goods they had left from the Nazis' devastation. Survivor and L'vov resident Leon Wells discovered upon liberation that: "Many of the Poles didn't like the idea that even a few Jews had been saved. These survivors could be witnesses that the Poles had collaborated with the Germans in destroying the Jewish population. Others, who had taken over Jewish houses and belongings, were afraid they might have to return them."[3]

Nina had survived the war with virtually the clothes on her back. Having at last made her way to L'vov, she headed for the one part of town where she might find both food and a familiar face: the open market. Here a weary population did its best to buy and sell the meager produce and meat still available. At the market Nina happened across Hania, the faithful servant who had been treated as family by the Grütz clan. By this time, the daughter of Hania's former employer had become quite thin and ragged. Looking nothing like the happy and vibrant girl Nina had once been, Hania at first did not recognize the frail creature calling her name.

When I arrived in L'vov I immediately began to look for any familiar face I could find. I didn't know if I would ever see Josef again, but I hoped that, if he made it through the last days of this war, he would track me down. In the meantime, I struggled to survive in my hometown. I lived on the streets as usual, and was barely managing because I couldn't find any work.

One day I found myself in the marketplace of L'vov. I had nothing with which to buy food, but I hoped to find something to trade. I had no idea where I would stay that night, but I was getting so used to living by the seat of my pants that I wasn't particularly concerned by this. I knew I would manage somehow, and I was prepared to again sleep on the street. "Big deal," I thought, "at least I am alive and at last in my hometown."

L'vov was built in such a way that it surrounded the marketplace. This place where food and other goods were sold was called the *Rynek*. Somehow, after all these years, the peasants were still bringing milk, eggs, cheese, and chickens for sale there, as well as things like cloth and wood. It had been that way for many years, and on a certain day each week they would sell whatever they managed to grow or produce on the farm. I was alone in the marketplace, naturally, and with my usual guard up. I stood there in a daze, surrounded by people, when all of a sudden I heard a voice that reminded me of my childhood. After six or seven years this was quite a unique occurrence, believe me! I turned in the direction of the voice, and saw a woman standing close by. I couldn't believe it. I thought that certainly I must be dreaming. It was Hania, one of our former servant girls. I never really expected to see anyone I knew there at the market, so it took me a moment to get over the shock. I ventured up to her and said, "Hania?" I felt as if by saying her name the dream would be over, and she might disappear.

She looked back at me and asked, "How do you know my name?"

I didn't want to scare her off, so I carefully said to her, "I think I know you from before the war!" We stood there looking at each other, until I asked, "Don't you remember me?"

"I'm sorry, but no," she replied, "who are you?" Well, the way I looked you can imagine what she thought. My clothes were little more than rags, and I was desperately thin. I probably looked old and sad compared to what she remembered as the young Nina she had cared for. I told her my name, but even this didn't register with her at first. She said my surname out loud, "Grütz, Grütz," trying to recall how she knew it. The war had been long and hard for everybody. The days before the war were like a vague dream to us all, so I suppose my name wasn't ringing a bell.

Looking as horrible as I did, I have to admit that it felt strange to remind her she was once a servant for my family. I was ashamed, in a way, to tell Hania she had once been under our employ. After all this time, and all that had happened, I didn't know if I had the right to say these things. Besides feeling uncomfortable over this, I was also very aware that we were now considered a Communist country. I had always thought of Hania as a friend, but now I wasn't sure if it was all right to speak of her as our former servant.

I remembered that when the Russians took over, my mother told her that we couldn't keep servants anymore. "I'm not leaving you," Hania announced to my mother at the time. "I'm not telling you to go away, or not to live with us anymore," my mother replied in an attempt to calm poor Hania down, "but it must be as if you are truly a member of our family. You cannot stay in the capacity of a servant." Hania had never learned to read or write because she came from the country, and her parents were quite poor. My mother had been good to her, and she really was like a member of our family. Naturally we didn't wish for her to leave, and she didn't want to go. Hania stayed with us all the way up until the German invasion. When the Russians moved us out of our apartment she tried to help us though the period of time when we all lived in one room. There was nothing she could do when the Nazis came looking for us, however, and we lost track of her shortly after scrambling for a place to hide.

Now Hania stood before me, and I didn't know how to tell her my story. How could I explain how Mama died and my entire family had disappeared? It all seemed too overwhelming, so I simply stood there feeling stupid.

I hesitated in explaining too much anyway, because, as I said, I didn't wish to offend her. I realized she was waiting to learn some news, so I slowly explained, "You know…before the war, before the Russians came, you worked for my mother, Rosa." When I began to explain about Mama, and how things were before the war, I could see Hania slowly starting to remember. Recognition appeared on her face along with confusion. The girl who had worked for us was now a young lady, and I looked like a beggar. It was a very strange situation for both of us. I asked, "Don't you remember that you used to call me *Dozia?*" This was the nickname she gave me years ago.

With this bit of information her eyes suddenly became very wide, and she said to me, "Yes, of course! I called you *Panienka* Nina?!" You see, in Poland if somebody was sort of a patron, or employer that you respected, you preceded her name with the word *Panienka*. It is like "Miss."

"How are you, Miss Nina?" she asked me.

"Forget all that," I shrugged, "I am no longer a Miss. Just call me Nina because everything is different now." The memories overwhelmed us, and we embraced in a big hug! It felt so wonderful to finally have contact with someone I knew, and that embrace melted away a few years of pain and loneliness.

"Where are you staying?" she asked me through her tears. I remained silent because I was too proud to tell her I had been living on the streets. By the way I looked she must have guessed as much. She took me by the arm and proclaimed, "You're coming with me to my house!"

What could I say? I certainly was not going to argue with her. I was too tired and hungry to do anything but let her take me down the familiar streets to her home. We talked the whole way, filling each other in on how we had spent the years of war. Hania found help and shelter with distant relatives and managed fairly well. I told her a little about my life, but I was too tired to go into much detail. I was so happy to have found her that I barely noticed how many buildings lay in ruins on either side of us. Poor L'vov had been such a beautiful city. Now it seemed very sad and tired, just like me. But I now had a true friend from the old days. From now on things would improve, I was sure of it!

Hania let me stay with her for well over a week. My kind friend gave me food and even found some decent clothes for me to wear. She had a job during the day, but when she could take time off she went to the market and purchased food for us and even remembered my favorites! She cooked so many familiar meals for me it made me a little homesick. During the course of my stay I learned that Hania had managed to save some precious memories of my family! She took me aside shortly after I moved in, and she said, "I have something special for you."

We sat at her little kitchen table, and to my amazement she spread pictures of my family out before me! She said, "These are photographs of your family that I was able to collect after you were forced from the apartment. I wasn't certain that any of you would ever return, but I couldn't stand the idea of leaving your photos behind. I saved them just in case one of you made it home alive, and now I am so glad that I did!"

I remembered all of the possessions we had lost to the Russians when they took over our home. When the Germans forced us into the ghetto Hania was also treated very roughly. Because she wasn't a Jew she was not sent along with us, but she had been forced to leave our place with very few possessions. Naturally when we were evicted there was very little we could take with us, so we left the photographs behind in order to carry some clothes and extra food. These we needed to survive, and we had to put aside our sentimental feelings for other things. The fact that Hania thought enough of us to save a few of our photographs meant so much to me.

She actually sneaked back to the apartment after the Germans took us away, and quickly grabbed what she could before being discovered. It was so sweet of Hania to know that if we survived we would want those photos more than any other material thing. It was amazing to have these photos, because so many Jews were left with nothing but the pictures in their mind of lost family members. I looked at the images of my mother and sisters, and it dawned on me that I would probably not see any of them in the flesh again. When the pictures had been taken we were all so happy. I looked at Mama's photograph for a long time, and felt so many emotions rush into my soul. I thanked Hania for her precious gift to me.

She and I shared those last days of the war together simply pleased that we had found each other. We didn't know a thing about what was happening throughout the rest of the world. When I ran off to L'vov I thought only of running. Once I made it to my hometown the only thing on my mind was finding my family. I searched one street at a time, but I found no one.

NINA WAS EXTREMELY FORTUNATE to have retrieved any family photographs. Few Jews survived with any tangible memories of their lives before the war. Most of those who managed to avoid the Nazis throughout the war by "passing" as ordinary Poles were forced to discard any proof of their former lives as Jews in the process. Tragically, they often found themselves the sole survivor of their families. Without photographs, heirlooms or any proof of their heritage, any victory felt over surviving the Nazi death squads soon became empty. Having outlived their loved ones, their struggle now seemed almost pointless.

Nina did her best to maintain a positive attitude and she continued to search for her own family members. Without the help of Hania she may have wandered the streets of L'vov hungry and alone and easily fallen prey to those Poles eager to take advantage of a vulnerable refugee. With a roof over her head and some semblance of health seeping into her body, Nina attempted to do her part for the dear woman who had taken her in.

Hania tried to do everything possible to make me happy; she even insisted on making up my bed for me every day before leaving for work. With Hania's meals in my stomach I began to put on weight and get some color back in my face. I couldn't believe all the food! There were a few times when I got a stomachache because I just wasn't used to it. I enjoyed staying with Hania, and it was very comforting to sit and talk with someone from my past. The time came, however, when I felt well rested, and I had the urge to move on. I thought perhaps I should search beyond L'vov for my family. Hania looked very sad when I told her that I should move on in this venture. "Why can you not look for your family during the day, then return here?" she wanted to know. I told her that I needed to stand on my own feet. Hania tried to talk me out of leaving but she knew I had to go. She had been the first real link to my former life, and finding her had been a godsend.

Even after the war I used to think that some day a member of my family that had survived might find me. After a few years passed I couldn't live under those kinds of delusions. I could not bear to think that I hadn't looked long enough, or well enough, to find someone. It would have driven me crazy. But early on, right after the war ended, I still had hope. I was tired of feeling so alone. This was the only time during the war that I didn't look diligently for work; I only concentrated on finding people who had once lived in L'vov as I had.

I did manage to find some relatives on my father's side. I was walking on the street and just ran into an entire family that had survived! There before me was the father, mother, and two daughters. The man was married to one of my father's cousins. They were happy to see me, and they allowed me to stay with them for a while. I continued to go out looking for family. Almost everywhere you looked was a Jew searching for people. If anyone saw a familiar face they almost dropped from surprise! Automatically one felt the need to walk over and ask, "Are you *Amchu?*" That's a phrase that we used in place of "Jew." If someone responded to that question we knew that they were Jewish. One could then proceed to ask after relatives or friends they might know. It was like a signal we developed to keep from getting hurt by the Poles who still wished to hurt us.

It was important to stay with relatives, no matter how distant they might be. My father's relatives, though unfamiliar, were the only family I had. They went into hiding for a very long time, and it changed them. They came from a small town, and there they told some neighbors, "If you hide us, you may keep our house." A lot of families were doing that once the Germans marched in. They would strike up a bargain with people that they knew, and offer to give them jewelry or other possessions in order to stay alive. It was a very dangerous game, but people were desperate enough to do anything. I was happy that my relatives survived the war, but I longed for my own family. I continued to search, and at the same time I hoped others were looking for me. I didn't want to leave L'vov, because I wanted to make it as easy as possible for them to find me. I was still unaware of the Jewish organizations that offered assistance in locating family members, so I stayed in the town of L'vov, where my family would know to look first.

THE MIXED EMOTIONS Nina felt upon liberation were a familiar reaction to survivors' wartime experience. Without a home or family, few survivors felt any more security than they had during Nazi occupation. In her research of Jewish survivors and the psychological effects of the Holocaust, Marion Kaplan wrote of the difficulties Jews faced directly after liberation: "Those who spent the war in hiding talk of great joy during the first days of liberation, followed by the harsh reality of the mostly futile search for friends and relatives. In contrast, those who were liberated from the camps discuss the great physical weakness they had to overcome, and their exhaustion and inability to feel joy. Many of these [survivors] emphasize that liberation for them was not a happy time…it was actually a moment of great difficulty."[4]

With a feeling of confusion over where she now belonged, and a desire to reunite with anyone from her past, Nina went in search of the family that had given her shelter during a time of need. Plodding the streets of L'vov that were familiar to her, she was able to locate the Ravitskys.

I eventually went in search of the Ravitskys, the family who had sheltered me after my brother-in-law asked me to leave. I did track them down, and I spoke to Mr. Ravitsky personally, but it was difficult to express myself. He was extremely happy to see me, but he and his family were in a different situation than my own. They were in a big hurry to leave the Russian side of Poland, and they really didn't know what life had in store for them. They were now in their seventies, six or so years older than when I last saw them. Time doesn't stand still for us even when a war is on.

So much had occurred since I last saw Mr. Ravitsky, and I was sort of, as they say, "shell-shocked" from all that had happened. Nevertheless, I tried to show my gratitude for his hiding me during the first months of German occupation. He seemed genuinely glad to discover I had survived, but I was uncomfortable. I cannot even explain why, maybe it was because his entire family was intact, while I had lost everybody. I was still very guarded and angry. Because of this I couldn't show the proper amount of appreciation.

After hearing about each other's adventures and generally getting caught up, there was a lull in the conversation. I stood there awkwardly in front of his house until I finally remembered to ask about the few personal items I left with him before departing from the safety of his home. When I left I had next to nothing much in the way of clothes or memories. I reminded Mr. Ravitsky of the two small boxes containing the meager possessions I had left. When I was running from the Nazis there was so much confusion and uncertainty, and every day I expected to disappear to wherever the rest of my family went. In anticipation of this I packed my little boxes so they could be easily transported. I was always in transition somewhere, and these were the only family memories remaining.

At the time Mr. Ravitsky had happily agreed to watch over my things. Now he seemed a little put out that I was asking about them. He did tell me, however, that he still had my things set aside. I don't know even if I would have had any use for the things in those boxes, but as I said, they were all I had left of my past. I was just looking for some material thing that represented my life before the war. I also wondered if there was anything of value that I might sell in order to survive while I continued to search for my family. I have no idea what it was that drove me to get those boxes back, but I believe it was because they were my only link to my younger and happier pre-war days.

I soon got the feeling that Mrs. Ravitsky was not happy about my request! She greeted me along with her husband, but judging by her reaction she was quite unhappy about my desire to get my boxes back. She became almost indignant, and there was no question about it, she didn't want to return my things! Maybe she felt it was an imposition to dig around for them, or maybe she was hoping to keep them herself, though there was really nothing of value there. The Ravitskys gave me most of what they could retrieve from the boxes. They had repacked some things because one box fell apart over the years. I don't even remember if I used those personal items for any significant purpose. It was just a sentimental thing to seek them out in the first place. I parted comfortably with the director, but not with his wife. Perhaps she believed I was acting in an ungrateful manner, although that was not my intention. I don't remember if I told Mrs. Ravitsky that I still had the rosary beads she had given me.

I really should have, because they represented a gesture to me that meant, "I want you to survive." It was my obligation to say something to her, but to be honest, after passing my things off to me Mrs. Ravitsky didn't stick around. She marched off in what I assumed was anger.

I couldn't really understand why she was mad at me. I stood there for a few moments trying to think of what to say to Mr. Ravitsky. I could tell he was in a big hurry. He and his family were anxious to leave for western Poland. The Russians were allowing people to leave if they didn't wish to stay in a Communist country, but there was little time to do so.

It seemed as if Poland was always being divided; it happened after the First World War, and afterwards as well. I also planned to leave, so there wasn't much time to look for family or friends. I considered Mr. Ravitsky a friend, so it seemed right to find him and see how he was doing. Unfortunately, after what I had been through, I didn't know how to express this. Instead I simply gathered my things and left. Later on I felt that I shouldn't have even asked for the boxes.

Mr. Ravitsky and I didn't part very well because of this encounter, and I blame myself for this. I should have been more appreciative of what the Ravitskys did for me. Perhaps I should not have asked anything from these people who had helped me so much in my time of need. Years afterwards I wished I could have recognized the Ravitskys as "Righteous Gentiles." This is how surviving Jews reward people for showing mercy during atrocities such as the Holocaust. You would have them proclaimed righteous, and then plant a tree in Israel in their honor. By the time I learned of this possibility I had no idea where to find the Ravitskys. It is impossible to find peace with yourself after such a situation, because you recognize it as a missed opportunity. Mr. Ravitsky deserved more than the few words I gave him.

———

There are so many questions in my mind for which I have no answer. Why did I do some of the things I did, such as the way I acted with the Ravitskys? Why did I survive and the rest of my family perish? I have given up looking for answers to many of these questions. Sometimes when

I pray to God I ask, "Could you help me to be a better person?" I don't know if God hears me, or even if I have any right to ask such a thing. I can only hope that by mentioning things like the Ravitskys' kindness toward me things will work themselves out. I speak of my own mistakes as a way of admitting that I was in no way a perfect human being. Who knows why I was allowed to live when others like my mother were killed? This is one of those questions that remain unanswered. I didn't know how to feel about my encounter with the Ravitskys.

AMONG THE MANY complicated emotions survivors experienced was the distinct feeling of guilt over outliving relatives, and anger at having to justify their very survival. Confusion about their Jewish identity was only natural in those who had "passed" during the war, while those who had survived the camps had difficulty feeling any emotion at all. The overwhelming need to speak of their experience was all too often pushed aside in favor of forgetting the wretched past with all of its painful memories. The business of rebuilding their lives preoccupied the survivors for a time. This method of coping affected surviving Jews for years to come, and often resulted in depression as well as an inability to move beyond their wartime experience.

While Nina adjusted to life in Russian-occupied L'vov, a determined young man made his way east looking for the girl who had refused to say goodbye to him. Released from his responsibilities as a Soviet soldier, Josef made the hapless search for his friend as he had promised her he would. Somewhat put out over what he perceived as Nina's cavalier attitude toward the value of their relationship, Josef never discussed the difficulties he encountered in his attempts to find his lost war time love. Josef's success in locating the transient Miss Grütz in war-torn Poland was nothing short of amazing.

I did not know it, but while I looked for my family, Josef began to look for me! The war was coming to an end, and so the Russians allowed him to return to L'vov. Unfortunately he had a terrible time tracking me down. This I will explain later. First I must say how my husband grew up, and how he came to meet me in the first place. He had a background very different from my own. Josef Morecki came from a small city in Poland called *Skole*. Although it was tiny compared to other places in Poland, it was a beautiful location, and Poles considered it something of a resort. Surrounded by mountains, Skole's clean air and beautiful forests drew tourists in the summertime to spend their holidays in the various cabins and hotels available there.

Josef was born in 1912 and was the youngest child of his family just like me. He had two sisters and two brothers. Sadly, his mother died in his arms when he was only around seven years old. She was only twenty-seven or so, and died of either tuberculosis or pneumonia. It was fairly common at this time for people to die of these illnesses, so I cannot recall which it was that ultimately killed her. According to Josef, his father was a very intelligent and religious man. The Morecki family had their own home, and Mr. Morecki made a good living. He was a very decent and responsible father, but he wasn't very loving. Josef loved his father, but from what I understood they were not particularly close. My husband used to say that his mother was more that type of person who could express love, and she loved Josef very much. I think he was a cute little boy, and maybe a little mischievous.

When his mother died Josef was forced to grow up very quickly. He didn't like school very much. He loved mathematics, but he did poorly in both history and writing. He didn't particularly like to read, and when he was a boy, reading literature or studying anything besides arithmetic was like poison to him. God forbid he should make any effort in these subjects. He always pretended to be sick on the days he had tests in those classes.

But when it came to mathematics, he had a mind like a computer. I remember in our closet he had only two shelves that he ever used, and this was where he kept his books on our finances. Our bookkeeper in California would always shake his head after looking over the books. He would say to my husband, "Josef, you don't really need me. Every time you show up with your records and information there's nothing for me to do. It's all been completed by you!" My husband could remember figures from years ago, and he never needed a pencil and paper to figure things. He did it all in his head, which amazed me because I was always terrible at that sort of thing.

He could have finished school, but he hadn't the patience for it. I think another one of the problems Josef had was that he wasn't very obedient. He had very good common sense, and so he felt he knew the proper thing to do most of the time. But he could not deal with teachers telling him what to do and how to do it. Josef had his own way of doing things. When his mother died he began to go into little business ventures with his friends. He could buy something for five cents and sell it for ten. My husband's head for numbers was already working to his advantage by that time.

His father insisted that his sons attend Yeshiva School, but of course his youngest son didn't like it. Josef kept up with his religious studies until he was about fourteen. Then he made the decision to move out on his own. The eldest Morecki sister was married, and living in the big city of L'vov at the time. So Josef said to his father, "I'm not going to live here with you anymore. I think it would be better for me to move to L'vov in order to make a living for myself." He informed his father that he would be living with the eldest sister just long enough to save up money for his own place.

Josef's father didn't like the idea, but my husband had made up his mind. He assured his father he would be fine living on his own, and said, "I'm strong enough to do this, so please do not worry." Well, who could argue with my husband? Josef was the youngest, but his father couldn't deny that his son had a head for business, even at the young age of fourteen. He also knew that when Josef wanted to do something nobody could stop him. Even before this little declaration of independence, my husband had proven that he could provide for himself. He was a good boy, but he had to be honest with his father. His mind was not on the Talmud or school.

Josef went to stay with his sister in the big city until she had a baby. His brother-in-law was good enough to help him out in the beginning. This young couple was not wealthy, but they made a decent enough living to give my husband a start. Josef got his first real job selling snowshoes. In Poland you really need these, and he was able to get a position in a store that specialized in them. By the time he was seventeen he was already managing the store. He worked there for two years, and learned everything about galoshes. More importantly, he learned how to order and ship out the merchandise. Josef took very good care of his customers, all the while learning about the wholesale end of this business.

He didn't like to talk about the old days too much. I found out a little at a time about how well he did in this job. I also learned that he was a lady's man, no question about it. He was a gentleman, and very charming, so women were just drawn to him. As a young man, my husband had girlfriends right and left.

———

When the war started Josef was about twenty-one or two. Josef lost everybody, his whole family. He didn't like to talk about the war very much, so I actually know very little about his past. I know that when the Russians came into Poland my husband was already in an important position as director of some large retail store in the shoe department. He didn't know Russian, and he didn't have the patience to learn it. According to him, there simply wasn't time. Even so, the Russians allowed him to continue working for them. He and the Soviets understood each other because they spoke in terms of numbers, and when it came to mathematics Josef really knew what he was doing.

Here is a little secret about my husband. He was what people call "claustrophobic," and when the first series of bombs dropped he refused to go with his family to the cellar. Josef could not stand the idea of a building falling in on top of them. He was stubborn about this to a fault, and even during an Aktion he would not hide in a cellar. On one such occasion he actually waited in an apartment with a gun he had managed to acquire, fully intending to shoot at least one Nazi before they killed him. He escaped that roundup, but during another he was caught, and they hit him so hard on the nose that it forever affected his sense of smell. He told me he didn't regret it, however, saying he would rather stand up to the Nazis than be caught like a dog in the street. When he told me this story it seemed so strange that he wouldn't seek out the proper shelter, particularly during a shelling. When bombs are falling on top of you, the cellar really is an excellent place to hide. Josef had what Jewish people call "chutzpa."

My husband didn't have any idea what had happened to his loved ones. He left part of his family in L'vov and others in Skole, but he never heard from them once the Germans invaded. Some neighbors wanted to help him go into hiding. Apparently it could have easily been arranged, but for some reason Josef declined to take them up on this kind offer. Instead, he took his chances with a transport that was taking Polish and Ukrainian people to work in a part of Russia taken over by the Germans. He wanted to join this group because it placed him closer to the front.

Just as I surmised, Josef thought that working in this area might afford him an opportunity to escape to the Russian side. He decided on his trip east that he would pretend to be a regular Pole, much the same way I had. He had a little money, and a very expensive gold watch. This was called a "Patek" watch, and if you ask at any jewelry store about these watches they'll tell you they're still considered the very best a person could buy. At this time only well-off gentlemen wore them, and Josef thought that if things got tough he could sell this watch for food or transportation.

He made it as far as Romania, to the town called Zmerinka, and he managed to mingle with a group of Polish workers collecting at the train station. There were quite a few who wanted to go east. It became common knowledge that if you offered to assist the Germans in some sort of work, you might get better treatment. There my Josef stood on the platform, waiting for his train, when one of these Polish workers came up to have a little chat. This man stood close to Josef and said, "I wonder what people would know about you if you took off your pants," just like that!

Now anyone else would have thought this man was out of his mind, but Josef knew what he was implying. One could prove a man was Jewish by showing that he had been circumcised. The *B'ris* ceremony is an important religious ritual for Jews, but during this time most Polish men went uncircumcised. The man looked at my husband's watch, and he said, "That watch would be nice to have."

My husband tried to put the man off, acting as if he didn't know what was being suggested. He said, "If I take my pants off, you would have to take off yours as well." But this Pole wouldn't let things go, and he kept looking at my husband's watch. Josef didn't want trouble, so he took off his beautiful watch and gave it to the man.

When he related this story to me, he said that giving up that watch was like giving away his heart. To him it meant security and a future. Besides this, it had taken him a long time to earn enough money to buy such a fine timepiece. It represented all of his hard work, and Josef wanted to buy his freedom with it. But in such a situation, what else could he do? He would have to manage in some other way. God knows what this watch would be worth today, but I know it cost a pretty penny back then. I always hoped to someday replace this watch for my husband. It was my dream, but I could never afford it. I did find a band like the one he described for the watch. It was twenty-four carat gold. I saw it in a shop in Palm Springs, California, and I said to myself, "If I don't eat for the rest of my life, I will buy this for Josef." My husband had lost so much during the war, and I felt that he deserved this. Eventually I was able to purchase the watch and a nice band for him, and he was so surprised!

NINA WAS CORRECT in her estimation of the worth of Josef's timepiece. 18 karat gold Philippe Patek watches are sold today for up to $69,000.[5] To have been such a success in business that he could have purchased jewelry from the Patek Company is an indication of Josef's talent with finances.

Unfortunately, the good luck he experienced in business did not hold out for Josef in his attempt to escape for the eastern border. Jews running from the Nazis were constantly concerned about encountering Poles bent on exposing them. Jewish men had the additional worry of carrying with them the one identifying mark that could easily give them away, circumcision. In her investigation of Jews living on the Aryan side of Poland, Lenore Weitzman found that a Jewish male in such a situation was, "very conscious of [their] physical vulnerability and was careful to avoid undressing and washing in the presence of other men." She also discovered that because of this physical disadvantage, "men…were more reluctant to try [to pass], just as Jews with other distinguishing physical or social characteristics, such as dark hair, or a prominent nose, or a distinctive accent, were afraid that they would be identified."[6]

Josef Morecki took this latest setback in stride, and set about the task of finding a place to wait out the Nazi Aktions. This would be essential until he could formulate another plan of escape. As fate would have it, the idea of where to stay came to Josef in the unlikely form of a child. Nina told the story as it had been related to her by her husband.

Josef handed his beautiful watch over to the man threatening to expose him. Because he was in such a hurry to gloat over his little prize the man completely forgot my husband was even standing there. Most probably he didn't truly understand the value of this watch. Back then a lot of people didn't have jewelry like that. When that greedy man became distracted by his new piece of jewelry, my husband took the opportunity to disappear. He never got on the transport train at all. Instead, he just walked the other way down the platform. He saw a little boy cleaning shoes, and decided to sit by him for a time. Josef needed a place to think of some new plan, so he sat down to have his shoes cleaned just as a way of blending in. The little boy made conversation with him, and my husband noticed that he said a word that would only be understood by a Jew. It was sort of a slang word, and my husband looked at this boy and asked, "Are you Jewish?" The boy replied that, yes, he was. "And are you okay living here?" my husband asked. The boy said yes, and mentioned he had moved into a ghetto where nobody bothered him. I think this was well into 1942 when the Nazis had already begun to ship out large groups of Jews, and quite often simply executed them on the spot. Josef was very surprised to hear of a ghetto that was still in operation. He thought that this might be a good place in which to disappear until he could think of another escape plan. He asked the boy to show him the way to this ghetto. My husband said, "Come, I'll give you some of my change if you'll just show me where your neighborhood is."

Off they went, and my Josef spent the rest of the war in that area of Zmerinka. He was never assaulted there, and was able to live in relative peace. It was on the Romanian side, which was still under control of the Germans, but it was so close to the Russian border that they never got around to liquidating that particular ghetto. I suppose it was too small of a group for the Nazis to bother with, and the Romanian people insisted on controlling that part of town.

Before long, Josef became a very big shot as a trader of material. He made good money, and apparently he had a number of girlfriends! He worked away, hoping one day to search for any surviving members of his family, but he never saw a single one of them again. By the time Josef was in this Romanian ghetto, the concentration camps were in full operation. Like my husband, I had no clue these extermination factories even existed. We didn't learn of them until after the war.

After being released from the Russian army, Josef came to the conclusion that his family was gone. Josef himself lived and worked in the ghetto until towards the end of the war. I suspect there was much more to his story, but he refused to speak of it with me. I think he wanted to forget the war years, and I know for certain that he believed it was bad for me to remember them.

JOSEF MORECKI was of the firm belief that the less said about the war and its tragedies, the better. As a pragmatic man, Nina's husband masked whatever residual pain was left over from the war with the work ethic that had served him so well over the years. Intent on leaving the European continent to pursue a better life, Josef managed to find Nina, and eventually convince her to accompany him overseas, as his wife.

I found work here and there while in L'vov, but steady work was hard to come by. The only promising position came when I was offered a job working at a radio station. The people in charge of this station were part of the Soviet-controlled broadcasting system. One day I dropped by to see if there were any available positions, and they were very encouraging. The manager really liked me. He said I could do some kind of broadcasting because I spoke proper Polish. I decided to turn him down, however, because I knew it would be a long-term job, and I didn't want to stay in a Communist country.

I soon began to think of leaving my hometown. It was 1945, and I hadn't seen Josef for over a year. It was pretty clear that my loved ones were not around, so I left L'vov, and went to the city of Katowitz to look for my family there. I heard there was an organization from America working in this city that assisted Jews in finding family members lost during the war. Many Jews in the United States were frantically trying to locate family they'd not heard from since the war, so they formed an organization by the name of "UNRRA" (United Nations Relief and Rehabilitation Administration) to research lost loved ones in Europe. I was not anxious to leave L'vov until I heard of this group. I realized, however, that I could no longer rely on my own methods of finding my family, and I wanted to see if this organization could help me.

I thought of Josef often, and I wondered if he would be able to find me if I left L'vov. I remembered him saying that if he were still alive after the war he would make his way back to me. While I had been running and searching he was not so much on my mind, but now I thought that it would be nice to see him again. I told myself that even if he had survived, it was very unlikely he would find me. I believed that Josef would be like everything else in my life up to that point. For years I had lived with so much fear and uncertainty, so I assumed that, like everyone I had ever really cared for, Josef would simply disappear. I was afraid that the more I thought about him, the more I would go to pieces. I drove thoughts of him from my mind, instead considering him a pleasant memory. Unfortunately, other than Josef I had no dreams of my future, and very few prospects.

Katowitz was very far from L'vov, but I felt there was no point in searching for loved ones in my hometown any more. All I had on my mind was finding family, and I immediately sought out the UNRRA offices. There was a long line of people on the same sort of mission, and I took my place expecting a long wait. Before long I heard a familiar voice behind me. Just as I had been surprised to hear Hania at the marketplace, I was amazed to hear this voice, because it most certainly was coming from my second cousin Hedda! I turned around and there she was! I ran to her, and she threw her arms around me. We were both ecstatic to see that a small portion of our family had indeed survived. Hedda told me that her father had also survived along with her younger sister. Both of them were living in another city, and the whole family planned to relocate somewhere out of Poland.

Hedda was searching for any remaining relatives with the help of her boyfriend. It was wonderful to see my cousin alive, and while in Katowitz we spent time together before she left to rejoin her family. It was difficult not to be jealous of Hedda, because I was quickly losing hope of finding any of my direct family alive. Upon registering with UNRRA I was given some food parcels, but my stomach could not handle more than a little food at a time because this was all I was accustomed to. Even now I don't require a lot of food. I rarely eat breakfast, and I'm not usually hungry until after noon. I suppose this is one of the habits left over from the war.

I asked a lot of questions at UNRRA, and the people working there informed me of certain places I could stay. Apparently when the Allies began marching toward the city all of the Germans left in a big hurry. They had been staying in some of the nicest places in town, and many were homes once owned by wealthy Jews. They ran off so quickly that most of the food and furnishings were left behind. The Jews registering with UNRRA were directed to these abandoned places as temporary shelter. I found an apartment that I ended up sharing with three other people. One was a man who had escaped a "death march" from his concentration camp. Before the Allies arrived the Nazis wanted the camps cleared so that very little evidence of their atrocities could be discovered. This included moving out any remaining survivors. The man staying in our apartment had been stripped of every piece of clothing, and then loaded onto a cattle car. As he was marched to the train he noticed that any prisoner too weak to continue was immediately shot where he stood. Knowing his strength was leaving him this man decided to take his chances, and when the opportunity came he simply jumped from the train completely naked! How he survived naked in the woods he didn't say, but he was clearly affected by the experience and didn't like to speak of it. I got to know him fairly well, and I believe he was involved in some kind of smuggling operation, because he usually had food or basic materials to contribute to our little group, and there were very few ways in which to acquire such things.

Our group got along well enough, and we all spent the majority of our time searching for our loved ones through UNRRA. At one point I went with my roommate to investigate the other empty apartments. We walked into a place we thought was deserted, only to find a very nervous German lady in the kitchen. I suppose that, like many other Germans, she believed we were out for revenge or something. Upon seeing us she began to tremble, and then in German she kept saying, "Forgive me! Forgive me!" At first we were confused by her words. Why would we automatically blame this old woman for killing our loved ones, simply because she was German? We tried to tell her we had no intention of hurting her, or even of staying there in her home, but she wouldn't listen. She kept pleading with us saying, "I'm leaving right now. You can take anything you want from here!" It was actually a rather disturbing display, and we wanted nothing more to do with her, so we quickly left.

I was still in the process of looking for relatives in Katowitz when Josef finally tracked me down. He must have first sought me out in L'vov, because he knew we had this place in common and it would be the first place I would try to reunite with family. I have no idea how he then found me at Katowitz. I only know that when I opened the door and saw his handsome face I almost died. I thought that I must be dreaming. It took him a moment to smile at me, but he finally did and said, "I'm here!"

It was as if heaven had opened up a door for me! We embraced and I invited him in. It was so wonderful to see a familiar face and a handsome one at that. At first he was angry with me, because I hadn't left word with anyone in L'vov as to where I might be found. I felt badly about worrying him, and I had no explanation as to why I had been so careless. At the time I was only concerned with getting to Katowitz, and many other details simply slipped my mind. I did not tell Josef that I had really doubted he would try to find me if he survived the war. How could I explain this way of protecting my already battered heart?

We sat down with a little coffee, and Josef finally asked me, "Why did you run off without any word? How was I supposed to find you anyway?" He accused me of doing it on purpose, and he said, "I told you I would come looking for you. Why didn't you give me a better idea of where you would be?" I sat there with a stupid expression on my face and told him I was sorry, but I had been in a big hurry to leave. This statement really did not impress my future husband, and to get back at me he never revealed how he knew to look for me in Katowitz. We were too happy to have reunited to argue the day away. He wouldn't completely let it go, however, saying to me, "You gave me a very hard time. Don't ever worry me like that again. If you do I swear I'll leave you." There were plenty of instances afterwards in which I worried him half to death, but he never did leave me, and I always felt loved and protected by Josef.

We gradually learned that the war had ended, but it wasn't as if people in Poland decided all of a sudden to tolerate those Jews who had survived. All of us were pretty much on our own. When they liberated the camps they simply told everyone to go back to where they came from. This was not quite so easy, because the Germans had transported Jews from all over Europe into the camp. From what I learned, most of the prisoners couldn't even communicate with each other, because they all came from different countries. How was everybody supposed to reach home when it could be hundreds of perilous miles away? Many Jews we met didn't even speak Polish. How would any of them find transportation, or even know in which direction to travel?

Even if one spoke the language, it was dangerous for a Jew to travel in Poland. In some towns the locals might rob or even kill a Jewish refugee. Well, Josef and I had been through too much to allow that to happen. My husband said to me, "That's it! I'm not staying one extra minute on this continent if I don't have to. We survived Hitler and now we're expected to survive our own countrymen? We will find our way west, and take the first boat overseas."

At first I argued with him about his plan. I told him that I didn't want to leave until I found out what had happened to my family. Besides this, it didn't seem right to take off to who knows where when we were not even married. There never seemed to be any doubt that Josef and I wanted to stay together. Marrying would be the natural progression. Josef promised to find a way for us to do this legally. He worked on this while I kept checking in at UNRRA. I was intent on looking for my loved ones and had registered with other organizations as well, such as the Red Cross. Like Josef, I no longer had any love for Poland or its people, but I dreaded the idea of leaving without word from my family. What would happen if my sisters or even my father were found and I was out of the country? I might never connect with them.

Knowing that Josef was determined to marry me as soon as possible so that we could be on our way, I became a little nervous. I was still trying to figure out how I felt about him, but I learned how much he cared about me when he offered to take me to Warsaw and register at an agency there. One of the better places Jews could use in finding missing family was in Warsaw. Josef said he would do all he could to help me, and he was a man of his word. "We'll go to every organization there is if necessary," he promised, "I want you to at least know what happened to your loved ones." He knew what it meant to lose your entire family. We shared that kind of sorrow and perhaps he felt that finding a member of my family would be like finding one of his own.

One thing was for certain, Josef knew what he was doing. I had such confidence in him that I let him do the thinking for both of us. This would have been unacceptable before I met him. I never trusted anybody with decisions, but I knew Josef was clever and sincere, and frankly I was very tired of doing all the thinking. Once Josef found me in Katowitz he would not let me out of his sight. He insisted that we marry then and there, because he wanted to protect me, and make certain that everything was done in a respectful way.

Our wedding ceremony was quite simple. We married in 1945 on a Sunday, some time in September. I remember it was just before the Jewish holidays. A Jewish wedding requires ten people to be present, and the couple must declare their desire to be together. Josef dragged in some people from the street to act as witnesses. There were ten strangers standing around to hear our statements. I don't even think they were all Jewish! There was no wedding band for me, but later on in America Josef gave me a lovely ring that I wear to this day.

During the ceremony we said our own vows, and then obtained a document written in Hebrew that made it legal in Jewish law, and I think we were lucky to find a rabbi. We later obtained an official wedding document in Vienna. Josef was wonderful about doing what he could to ensure we were united, but he was also very strict. He said, "Either we get married right away, and we travel where I decide, or we go our separate ways. It took us a year to find each other, and I don't want to lose you again simply because we're not man and wife!" It was a very difficult situation. He wouldn't go anywhere with me until we got married, and I desperately wanted him to take me to Warsaw. Still, I hesitated for just a moment because marriage seemed like a very strange idea to me. I had been on my own for so long, and I wasn't sure things would work out between us. Josef insisted on marriage or nothing, however, and he had a knack for getting his way. So I agreed to marry then and there, and I was never sorry. In my heart of hearts I never doubted he was the man for me. From the minute I met him I felt his power and strength. For the first time since the beginning of the war I allowed someone to really take care of me.

MARRIAGE WAS ONE WAY survivors chose to reintroduce some sort of normalcy in their lives. Bonding with another survivor made practical sense for a number of reasons. By forming a union with a man, female survivors were better protected and ensured of a partner with similar goals. The idea of marriage was appealing to many Jewish women who struggled on their own throughout the war. Survivors shared the experiences of watching their loved ones die, withstanding near starvation and beatings, and dodging Nazi roundups. Many survivors felt that only a Jew who had been through similar tribulations would truly understand the way in which they now viewed life.

In her research of Jewish women living among forest partisan groups, Nechama Tec noted that an official ceremony need not have taken place for such unions to exist. She found that, "When a man and a woman shared a tent or a bunker and acted like a couple, others began to treat them as married. It has been estimated that about 60 percent of the adults lived as couples. Most former partisans say that these 'marriages' were stable and lasted a lifetime."[7] Although they had also been recognized as a couple, it became very important to Josef that he and Nina exist officially as man and wife.

After our little wedding ceremony we made our way to Warsaw. My husband was such an honorable person. From the minute we got together in Katowitz we had to stay in a bed together, but he didn't touch me. After a little while I actually wanted him to try something. He was attractive, and by then I was feeling very comfortable with him. I was still a little scared of what intimate relations would be like, but I felt ready to act like a wife to Josef. He remained a gentleman, however. We were not physical until I was completely healthy and we had private and comfortable accommodations. I don't remember one occasion when I asked him about making love. From that day on he made a joke that he didn't stay with me out of adoring love. He said that he married me out of pity! "You were so skinny and pathetic," he would laugh, "I couldn't very well leave you on your own in that condition, could I?"

We both knew he was kidding. I would laugh and say, "You know, this is a very good reason to get a divorce! If I am so pitiful, and you are so generous, then perhaps it is time to correct this generosity!" Josef never grew tired of teasing me on this matter: how he married me because he felt sorry for me. I let it go until one day, after we had been married for some years, I asked him about how he really felt the day he asked me to be his wife. By then we had a baby girl together, so I took to calling him "Daddy." "Daddy," I asked him, "I have always been very curious about something. Why is it that we were alone together so often while traveling to Warsaw, but you never tried anything with me? You never even tried to kiss me without permission."

I don't know why this question had always been on my mind. It was not as if Josef and I had a romantic setting during those post-war days. We never undressed while we were sleeping in the woods, because you never knew when you had to run from the locals. We never knew when one of our own countrymen, disappointed with the war's outcome, would try to kill a Jewish refugee. There were even German soldiers walking around out of uniform, so we were vulnerable. While we were in Warsaw we stayed on our guard, and we didn't stay very long because we didn't feel safe. There was no time for Josef and I to be alone together, let alone even to imagine some sort of honeymoon. We left right after registering with the Jewish organizations.

I had always been so curious about what went on in Josef's mind during this time, and after I pressed him for an answer he admitted, "I was attracted to you, certainly. But I intended to marry you right away. I was very serious about you, and I would never touch a woman I respected as much as I did you, certainly not before I had made an official commitment."

I admired Josef for this, and even while we went to Warsaw and back I knew he was doing his best, even risking his own safety. It was a terrible thing to ask someone to go all the way to Warsaw and wait through the long process of registration. The journey was dangerous, and we had a difficult time finding food and shelter there. Each day went by without a word from the agencies, but it was wonderful not to be alone anymore. I no longer felt the constant pressure of quick-thinking and standing on my own, and I came to rely on my new husband. Before long I just let him call the shots. He was a strong and smart person. Whatever he wanted to do I went along with it. This was why I agreed to travel out of Poland when he decided the time had come. We had exhausted all resources in finding my family, and we needed to leave before any more problems came about.

Fortunately, while in Warsaw we discovered there was safety in numbers. Josef found some other couples who also wished to travel west, and we banded together with these other Jews in order to safely travel through each town. The group fluctuated in size as people left or joined up with us, but the core remained the same; four or five couples, all in their late twenties and intent on leaving Poland. One couple wanted to go to Canada while another wanted to make it as far as the Swiss Alps, and the rest of us wanted to eventually end up in Palestine. I remember the names of the people we traveled with the most, however. Regina and Max were a couple, and then there was Wanda and Marc. Wanda was also from L'vov, but younger than I. There was also a single man in our group who was quite young.

The two strongest men in our little band were my husband and Marc. Together these two were very capable, and they naturally fell into the role of leaders. They learned that the Allies were formulating ways for "displaced persons" to return home, but to do so refugees had to travel to central gathering points. Only after registering at one of these stations could one leave the country. Our initial group of twenty-one trickled down as people left to make their own way. By the time we reached western Poland it was just Josef and me, with a few other couples.

We had a very difficult time going. We had next to nothing in the way of possessions, because we had all been in hiding one way or the other. Our pooled resources did not amount to much. Josef and Marc learned that there were quotas of people being allowed out of the country. Certain nationalities had higher numbers set in this quota, and one additionally had to prove they no longer belonged in Poland in order to leave. We were eventually successful in our endeavor by becoming Greek. Somehow Josef found out that the Allies had a sort of regulation that stated Greeks were to be some of the first to travel in large numbers out of Poland. All one had to do was make their way out of Poland, then register to leave. After that, the Allied armies would see to it that you were taken back to Greece, simple as that. What kind of transportation you got to Austria was your own worry. Who knows why the Allies decided on this regulation, or even if it was simply a rumor? All I know is that we were on our way out of Poland as soon as Josef and Marc could make the arrangements.

It was up to these two men to find a way of proving we were Greeks! It was decided that we should all say that we entered Poland as Greek Jews, transported by the Nazis just like everybody else. Josef and Marc believed this would work because, after all, what Greek Jews leaving the country would have papers indicating their nationality? Everybody was stripped bare of all personal items upon entering the camps. As we made our way through checkpoints, we tried not to speak to each other. We were afraid the authorities guarding the borders would figure out we weren't Greek by our accents. The twelve of us needed to keep our mouths shut as we approached each checkpoint.

Josef and Marc did quite a bit of gesturing to explain where we wanted to go. Speaking Polish would have given us away, and we certainly didn't want to attempt speaking Greek! Our luck changed for the better quite soon, however. Somehow along the way my husband managed to obtain documents that allowed all of us to continue west without so much trouble. He never told me how he acquired these papers, and for all I know he made them himself. The officials at the border were all Poles supervised by the Allies, so they never questioned the fact that we were Greek.

It turned into the perfect plan, because few people spoke the Greek language, and everybody was in too big of a hurry to bother with a bunch of skinny Jews leaving Poland. The whole thing was rather amusing, because when I glanced at our papers I saw that my husband had written in certain spaces in Hebrew! I believe he did this just so they could look foreign to the officials. Because the officials hadn't studied Latin or the classics, they assumed this exotic writing was Greek! We made it across each border, and halfway through managed to get a ride on a sort of shuttle that took people to work. Finding transportation such as this was a rare occurrence, however, and we spent quite a bit of time walking.

TRANSPORTATION IN POST-WAR Europe was indeed a hit and miss operation, particularly for civilians. Going any significant distance required a combination of ingenuity and luck. William Woods described the haphazard manner in which refugees managed: "Those who lived in the cities had to travel by railway, mainly in unheated goods wagons or, if by road, in open, snow-covered trucks, but these often became stranded for lack of fuel. One saw people who had yoked themselves into sledges, carts, perambulators, even overturned tables loaded with their possessions."[8]

Luckily for Nina, Josef and Marc were very capable of finding ways to transport their group. Working together, the two men could be a very persuasive team.

One night I remember we were able to get a ride on a truck. Josef and Marc flagged the driver down to ask for a lift. I don't even remember seeing the truck until it was right beside us, but I was so grateful because it was raining and very cold. As usual, it was a desperate situation, and we simply had to find shelter. Josef told the driver that he must find a way to fit all of us in his truck. Oh, what nerve my husband had! The driver took one look at our group and said no, he didn't want to take us. He wanted to get home to his family. But Josef was adamant, and he spoke to the driver in a very convincing way.

My husband had beautiful blue eyes, and when he looked at a person they could tell Josef meant what he said by his eyes. He could be very intense when the situation warranted it. He said to the truck driver, "Look, do you want to stay alive? You take us on your truck, or suffer the consequences; it's either one or the other." He wasn't fooling around. We were desperate, and he had to be aggressive in order for us to survive.

Josef had had just about enough of being treated like dirt. All during the war we had been abused. Even animals had received better care than the Jews, and my husband was not going to stand for it anymore. "Look here," he said to the driver, "you see this bulge in my pocket? I don't want to alarm the ladies, but it is a gun, and I am not afraid to use it! I would have no trouble shooting you and driving this truck myself. I don't wish to hurt you, but we can no longer walk, and we are getting a ride with or without you!" Well, Josef didn't have a gun of course, but the threat worked, and I don't think the driver was very happy about it. Usually one or two people ride in the front seat of a truck like that, but the driver let us decide how to do things. Four of us crammed ourselves into the front seat with him, and the rest of us in the back. Soon we were on our way, and we covered quite a few miles in relative comfort.

———

There was very little shelter in the way of barns or deserted houses, so as we were making our way west we usually slept under the stars. We rarely found any food in the fields, so we were terribly hungry most of the time. When we came to the occasional city food was in even shorter supply. We experienced a terrible gnawing in our stomachs that was impossible to get used to. I had known hunger many times during the war, but this was particularly bad because we knew we were so close to real freedom.

LIBERATED JEWS like Nina and her group had to use extreme caution while making their way west. The potential threat of encountering anti-Semitic Poles in each town and forest remained, and few survivors lived under the delusion that Allied victory made them truly free. Leon Wells wrote of the peculiar camaraderie that existed between Jews who "shared a similar fate." "It seemed that this was the 'normal' life," Wells explained. "The non-Jewish world continued to be strange to us. We lived in our own world. We didn't talk about those we had lost or how it happened. One's own family was few among millions."[9] Traveling in large groups held the added advantage of intimidating non-Jews when the occasion arose. Wells stated that he had no qualms over demanding food from Aryans who "now lived in Jewish apartments and had taken over our furniture." When he confronted a woman who had betrayed his mother to the Germans, thereby causing his mother's death, this neighbor who had once had good relations with the Wells family told Leon, "It wasn't Hitler who killed the Jews; it was God's will, and Hitler was his tool. How could I stand by and be against the will of God?"[10] Wells became angry and indignant over his fellow countrymen's lack of remorse for the Jews' fate, and he decided that these Poles, "owed us at least a meal a day."[11] Nina's group of refugees made do with whatever food could be scrounged and whatever transportation became available. When necessary, they also used intimidation in order to persuade the locals to assist them.

We traveled in all different ways. We walked through every forest, and we once went by a horse-drawn cart. A peasant took us as far as he could in this manner, until we came to a lake. The lake was very big, and it would have taken forever to get all the way around it. We were simply left there to figure things out for ourselves, hungry and tired while it began to get dark. None of us could bear the idea of sleeping in the woods again, so the men went to find a place to stay for the night.

We were close to the border where a lot of Germans lived. This was because during the First World War many Germans moved east, and then remained there even after their county's defeat. We used to call them *Volksdeuche*. When Hitler took over he gave special preference to these folk. A lot of them spoke only German and kept their German traditions. At the same time they were living in Polish territory.

On this particular night my husband and Marc happened upon a family living in this area by the lake. The women in our group were told to rest a bit while the men explored, but after only a couple of hours our men came back and said, "Up, let's go!" The other ladies and I didn't really expect them to find shelter. "But where are we going?" we asked them. "Don't worry," they assured us, "we have a place to sleep and even something to eat."

We women were not about to argue. It was not very restful to sleep in the forest every night. On the way the men explained that we would be staying in one of these settlers' homes. Apparently Josef and Marc had knocked on one family's door and said, "We have a group of people who are homeless from the war. We are going west and need to stay the night. We also need a little food." When our men were told that nothing was available, my husband said, "Fine, if you won't help us, then you might not leave this place alive. I don't care anymore about what is right and wrong. We have families to care for, and if you won't give us a bed then maybe you won't have that bed either. Maybe you'll never sleep in it again." I must explain that Josef was not a violent man, and when he came across as threatening at this time he was bluffing. But if he were forced to act on behalf of the group I believe he would have done whatever was necessary to protect us. He must have been pretty intimidating because this family allowed us to stay the night.

It was clear to me that those German settlers didn't like the idea of our staying there, but they were too afraid of us to say no. It was strange to me how they appeared to be so terrified when we were the ones who had been assaulted so often by their countrymen. We would have been justified in extracting some kind of revenge for the loved ones we lost, but this was the furthest thing from our minds. Anyway, as long as we had shelter we didn't care what these people thought. The couple spoke to us in German at first. My husband could speak German as well as I could, but he said to these settlers, "No, it was our people who won the war. We'll speak Polish while we're here. For years we were forced to speak your language as well as Russian, so now it's time to speak our own language."

The settlers spoke Polish to us from then on. An elderly German woman brought us a big pot of cooked potatoes and sour cream. We hadn't seen food like that for years, and we had a feast that night! We kept asking for more and ate until our stomachs hurt. Luckily there was no meat; otherwise I am certain that we would have gotten sick. Jews from the concentration camps died from eating too much food right away, but our bodies were not quite that emaciated. We could manage a plate or two of potatoes, and then worry about the stomachache later.

I have to admit that before the war I was never that fond of potatoes. Maybe this was because of the incident with the dog, I couldn't say for certain. Mashed potatoes still are not my favorite dish. But I don't think I've ever enjoyed a meal as much since that night! This family had managed to keep up their farm fairly well, so there were lots of vegetables in this stew. They even served us some good sauerkraut! When the Germans started to clear the table we said, "Don't throw it away! We'll take the leftovers with us somehow!"

NINA LAUGHED at this and, taking my hand, looked at me intently.

Sweetheart, I hope you never have to experience such hunger. Most people could never understand what it feels like. Knowing real hunger changes you. That food meant a lot to us, and I felt very grateful to these Germans. I was actually a little shocked at how my husband spoke to them, and as we prepared for bed I said to him, "There is no reason to be so harsh with this couple. They were kind enough to take us in, and after all they are innocent people." Josef explained that at first they had no intentions of feeding us. He had no problem being direct with them, and he actually became very angry with me at this point.

"Did any of those Germans during the war ask you if you or your family were innocent before they started killing?" he asked. "If you don't like the way I speak to them you can stay with them! Haven't you had enough of their prejudice and cruelty? Look around you. These Germans have homes, and farmland, and enough food to eat! They have everything our families once had before they decided to kill us off. You need to remember this!" I could not argue with him, and I didn't bring up the subject again. Exhausted and full from the meal, I instantly fell asleep, but Josef and Marc took turns guarding over all of us throughout the night.

The settlers must have believed they had no choice but to help us. They would have been too afraid to complain to the Russian, English, or American soldiers who were then in charge of all the territory in Europe. They knew that, as Germans, they couldn't complain about anything and get much sympathy.

We were thankful for all of the Allies' help, but anxious to get into the American territory of Austria because we heard that the Americans were doing the most to help Jewish refugees. Of one thing we were certain: we weren't going to follow the orders of a German anymore. We also had no desire to live in a Communist country, although we felt more secure seeing Russian soldiers in every town. Germans were especially afraid of the Russians, because Soviet soldiers could be quite rough. Everyone knew that while they were advancing toward Moscow the Nazis had been very cruel to the civilian population. Apparently, the Russian soldiers were giving back to the Germans exactly the same treatment. German women were afraid of being raped, and much of the Germans' supplies were taken by Soviet troops as they advanced to Berlin. As for the German settlers who put us up, they ended up being fairly decent.

We woke up well rested, and had the leftovers for breakfast. The women in our group wanted to stay a few days more. It was hard to leave a place that provided food and a bed. But the men insisted we leave right away. Even though they had initially tried to turn us away, the Germans had been nice to us. So we thanked them and left. We had been polite and appreciative, but I clearly felt that the German settlers were glad to see us go. I think they were a little worried we would stay longer. This was not our intention and really, we never would have hurt them. It seemed sad that things had come down to this level of distrust on both sides.

When I speak of how we managed to survive by giving empty threats of shooting people I hope readers do not misconstrue our situation. As Jews who had struggled more than anybody we were prepared to do and say just about anything to survive. Those German settlers had lived a life of luxury compared to what we had been through, while we Jews had nothing to lose. We had been left without families or any possessions. We didn't have any money, and even if we had managed to save any there was nothing in the stores to sell. Let's say I was hungry, and I went begging for just a piece of bread. Well, there would be no place for me to beg. People like us had no alternatives. Those lucky enough to live on farms were surviving better than others. We were on the road, and so we never had enough. Whatever food we happened across we had to eat as much as possible because there was really no way to take it with you. The men knew the desperate situation we were in, and they acted accordingly. Marc, for example, was a very clever man. He and Josef made a good team, and this is why we made it safely to Austria.

We women were not supposed to say anything about how we had survived on the road like that. The men instructed us to forget everything once we reached the American Allies. But how can you forget any part of the war? Even after leaving Poland the feeling of hate I carried inside me was overwhelming. I was also exhausted and weak from all of the experiences. Through all of this my husband was my shield. I trusted him in every way. If he had said to me, "Okay, it's time for us to die," I would have agreed. Even though I made it through the war, if I had not reunited with Josef I am sure I would not have survived liberation. I had become so tired of my life and the struggle, especially when I returned to L'vov. When I spent so much time there looking for family and not finding any I thought, "What does my life amount to? What was it all for? If I cannot find my family what is the point of living?" In a way, Josef saved me from myself.

We traveled for days, until finally we were able to hop onto a train going the rest of the way to Vienna. It was not a passenger train, but one that transported cows and horses or cargo. We sneaked up to it at night, and the men pried one of the doors to the cars open. The car was large enough for all of us, but it was not a pleasant experience. The livestock had been removed, but it smelled as if cows were all around us. We slept as best we could, but I know we smelled horribly for days afterward.

The next morning we were afraid of being discovered by the conductor. Josef felt that we were coming up to a town, so when the train slowed down the men jumped out and the women went after them. Each man tried to catch one of the ladies jumping off, but when my turn came I was afraid to jump. My husband and I were the last ones on the train, and one of the younger men ran along the tracks waiting to catch me. I couldn't make up my mind when to jump, so finally I yelled to Josef, "Push me!" and he gave me a shove. I almost broke my neck in the process, but I was off that train, and Josef came down after me. I ended up with some bad bruises, but it felt good to be on solid ground again. In total we had spent around two months making our way to Austria and the Displaced Persons camp.

NINA AND HER COHORTS were among those Jewish survivors who had successfully maneuvered their way through a land ravaged by war. Although their lives had become more secure, they remained wary and cautious. A whole new life of challenges awaited Nina, yet with Josef by her side the recently wed Mrs. Morecki at last felt she had a reason for living.

The hope of finding any surviving members of her family rapidly fading, she now set her hopes on forging a new life with her husband in a country that promised freedom and a chance to prosper. In Nina's mind that place could only be Palestine. She once again began to dream of traveling to the holy land. Josef, in the meantime, immediately set his sights on acquiring the funds with which to leave Europe far behind.

(Above) DISPLACED PERSONS
Left to right top: Regina, Wanda and Nina—Left to right bottom: Max and Marc
Group shot of Nina and cohorts who traveled from Poland to Austria posing as Greek Jews.

(Above) NINA IN SALZBURG
Nina Morecki, no longer hiding or pretending, in Displaced Persons camp. Salzburg, Austria, 1946.

(Above) D.P. NINA
An exuberant Nina recovering in the Displaced Persons camp. Salzburg, Austria, 1946.

(Above) JOSEF COMFORTS NINA
Josef comforts Nina while she recuperates in the
hospital. Salzburg, Austria, 1946.

(Above) HOSPITAL RELEASE
The official form releasing Nina from the hospital in
Salzburg, Austria, where she spent much of 1946
recovering from a multitude of ailments.

(Left) NINA AND JOSEF, D.P.s
Nina and Josef Morecki rest in an Allied-assigned
apartment for Displaced Persons. Vienna, Austria, 1946.

(Above) SALZBURG TRAIN
Nina is escorted to a train bound for Vienna so that she might seek medical treatment from a specialist. Salzburg,
Austria, 1947.

(Above) SALZBURG GANG
The Moreckis celebrate liberation with fellow Jews in 1946. Using his Brownie camera, Marc snapped this photo of fellow expatriates who made their way from a still dangerous, war-torn Eastern Europe toward Allied forces in Austria. Pictured left to right: Regina, Max, Nina and Josef Morecki, and Wanda.

(Above) NINA AND WANDA
Nina, Wanda, and an unidentified friend. Salzburg, Austria.

(Above) JOSEF IN SALZBURG
Josef Morecki, 1947, taking in the sights of Salzburg, Austria, while awaiting permission to immigrate with Nina to America.

(Above) NINA AND JOSEF AT PICNIC
A much healthier Nina and Josef enjoying the outdoors. Salzburg, Austria, 1947.

(Above) NINA AND JOE AT THE BEACH
Josef and a recuperating Nina taking in the sun. Salzburg, Austria, 1947.

(Above) SALZBURG ACQUAINTANCES
Nina at far left with friends she met while at the Displaced Persons camp in Salzburg, Austria.

(Above) JOSEF IMMIGRANT
Nina's husband and ambitious new American citizen, Josef Morecki, New York City, 1949.

(Above) NINA IMMIGRANT
Nina Morecki, Displaced Person, in Salzburg, Austria, 1946.

(Above) MORECKIS AND FIRSTBORN
A new generation is begun. Nina and Josef Morecki, proud parents showing off their new daughter, Rosalyn, New York City, 1948.

(Above) NINA AND KIDS
Nina with daughters Rosalyn and Carol in New York City, around 1954.

TE OF IDENTITY IN LIEU OF PASSPORT

AMERICAN CONSULATE GENERAL, MUNICH GERMANY

Date Mar. 19, 1947   16419

1. This is to certify that   Dozia Nina MORECKA   , born at
(name in full)

Poland   Lwow Jan   XX   on 24th
(country)   *(town)*   *(district)*   *(day)*

of December   1920   female   ,   married
(month)   *(year)*   *(sex)*   *(marital status)*

, intends to immigrate to
(given and maiden name of wife)

United States.

2. He (she) will be accompanied by Josef Morecki, husband, born Dec. 14, 1912 at
(Here list all family members by name, Lublin, Poland: Wigdor Grutz, father, born
birthplace and date, together with citizen- at Ztoczow, Poland in 1888: Polish citizens.
ship of each)

3. His (her) occupation is   XXX

4. DESCRIPTION

Height 5 ft. 2 in.

Hair brown Eyes brown

Distinguishing marks or features:

none.

SINGLE JOURNEY ONLY:

5. He (she) solemnly declares that he has never committed nor has he been convicted of any crime except as follows
My internment was due to racial persecution and not because of any crime.

6 She is unable to produce birth certificate, marriage license, ~~divorce papers and a photos card~~ for the following

reason(s)

I hereby certify that the above are true facts, proper photograph and description of Myself.

Dozia Nina Morecka
(Signature of applicant)
Dzoia Nina Morecka.

Subscribed and sworn to before me this 19 day of Mar.
1947.

Thomas A. Moore
(Signature of consul)

Travel passport to the U.S., 1947.

(Above) IMMIGRATION PAPERS
Nina's identification and travel passport permitting her to immigrate into the United States, 1947.

(Above) GIRLS ON SOFA
Morecki daughters Rosalyn and Carol, New York City, 1951.

(Above) NINA AND JOSEF IN BEVERLY HILLS
Nina and Josef posing outside their Beverly Hills, California, home in the mid-1960s.

(Above) BEVERLY HILLS HOME
The Morecki family in front of their Beverly Hills home, early 1970s.

(Left) JOSEF RUNS HOTEL
Josef Morecki in the mid-1960s. Owner and operator of the Hotel St. Moritz in Hollywood, California.

(Below) JOSEF'S AWARD
Placard given to Nina's husband, Josef Morecki, by the "Meals On Wheels" volunteer program in appreciation for his work in the Beverly Hills neighborhood, early 1970s.

(Right and below)
MORECKI ANNIVERSARY
Nina and Josef Morecki celebrate their thirtieth wedding anniversary. Beverly Hills, 1975.

(Above) **NINA IN ISRAEL** | Nina with family including daughter Carol. Israel, 1973.

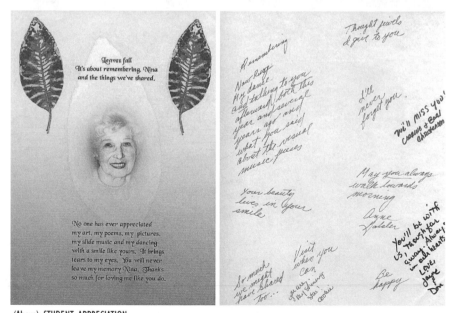

(Above) **STUDENT APPRECIATION**
A scrapbook page autographed by students whom Nina visited during one of her speaking engagements. Letters, poems, and artwork are often given to Nina in appreciation of her efforts to educate young people on the Holocaust, and speaking in favor of tolerance.

(Above) NINA SPEAKS
Nina speaks of her experience to high school students, Carpinteria, CA, spring 2005.

(Above) COHORTS
Colette Waddell and Nina Morecki at work.

PART FOUR

Building a New Life

The fighting was over, and weary Europeans began the difficult task of gaining some order amidst the war-induced chaos. Millions of people had been torn from their homes and way of life. A new term was found for these drifting souls: "displaced persons." As a small part of this group, surviving Jews presented a unique challenge to the Allies, because few wished to remain in their homeland.

While various organizations scrambled to find placement for the remaining Jewish population, the Moreckis languished along with other "D.P.s" in hastily constructed camps. Unfortunately, the D.P. label did not necessarily guarantee a full belly or adequate shelter. It would take time for the Allies to determine how to best distribute aid. Nina and Josef made their way among the throngs of homeless Jews seeking a way out of Europe.

CHAPTER IX

"Displaced Persons"

(1945-1959)

BEDRAGGLED AND THIN, Nina and her companions had completed the long trek west to Austria. Under the guardianship of British and U.S. troops the Moreckis could now focus on basic needs such as food and shelter. Enlisting the method of following their instincts that had been reliable thus far, Josef and Marc tracked down the American-based relief organizations that ultimately provided them assistance and temporary asylum. In regard to the damage done by Allied bombing, Austria had fared somewhat better than Germany. However, as in every other European city, food and other supplies were extremely limited. Picking through the massive warscape of rubble and corpses, dazed civilians rummaged for what they could to get by.

We were so glad to be in Austria because we knew the Americans and British were in charge of this area. We heard that the Americans treated Jews like human beings, so we were anxious to get as far west as possible and find them. All of the territories had been divided up between the three powers of Russia, England, and America, but we knew that there were still Germans around who could hurt us.

When we finally arrived in Vienna, it was a little like a ghost town. Most of the Germans who once lived there had run off further west. And they left everything behind. Many beautiful apartments were completely empty of people. We found a nice one and stayed there for about three weeks. It was wonderful to have a bed to sleep in, but there was absolutely no food. Not only was the city dead, but the stores were all empty, and we were again slowly starving. In order to obtain any necessity one had to have something to trade. Somehow my husband managed to find a pair of shoes, which he traded for a can of sardines, and that was our entire meal for the day!

I will always associate Vienna with hunger. It was rough going in Vienna, and before long we concluded that we would be better off in a smaller town. An American soldier working for the Jewish Relief advised us to go to Salzburg where a Displaced Persons camp had been created. We left the next day and made very good time. When we arrived in Salzburg we found the D.P. camp, but things were still very primitive. At first we slept in the local stables, but then I was used to this kind of accommodation! They gave us little sacks to sleep on in a little room, and it was better than nothing.

By now our little group consisted of only three couples. Wanda and Mark were not yet married, but Josef and I were now husband and wife. I do not remember the other couple very well, but we stuck together and it served our need for protection and scavenging for things. The D.P. camp at least provided some food, and our entire group received coffee and soup once or twice a day. We stayed in the stables for a little over a week and worked with the Jewish authorities to receive aid. The organization was under American supervision, and they were trying very hard to improve our condition. They eventually set us up in some rough sleeping accommodations, but for our three couples it was very small. In one room we had a set of bunk beds. Josef and I had a top bunk, which provided some privacy, but it was very cramped.

After asking around a bit we learned that there were a lot of vacant homes around this area just as there had been in Vienna. Believing that the Soviet Army was coming, most of the Germans fled to who knows where. The Jewish organization worked at placing people within these homes that had been abandoned, and most of them were very nice homes. Things began to get a little better, and we were placed in an apartment with a little kitchen. All three couples had their own rooms, and this was quite a luxury. We were still living on soup and coffee, but the Americans came over from time to time to see if we had everything we needed in the way of soap and water. The men in our group began to look around town for extra supplies. Every now and then my husband would show up with some kind of luxury for me. I have no idea how he did this, but one day he gave me a sandwich with meat in it! I didn't know if it was kosher, most probably it wasn't. But at the time we weren't being picky. I looked at that sandwich and asked my husband, "How on earth did you find a sandwich with meat?" Josef never would tell me where he got things. He only said to be a good girl and get some weight on me again.

THE MORECKIS were fortunate to have found lodgings that many refugees would have considered luxurious at the time. Surviving Jews were one group in particular left after the war with virtually no place to go. Grenville described the sad fate of these people as "the most pathetic DPs, who sought their home but were prevented from going there. [The Jews] longed to enter British-controlled Palestine."[1] Nina also dreamed of immigrating to the Holy Land. Josef, however, made no promises. He turned his attention to providing for his wife in any way possible. Trading on the black market was one way to acquire goods in post-war Europe, and with his skill in finance and trade Josef Morecki would certainly have learned how to engage in this activity with ease. Industrious refugees could swap whatever they had with others in an effort to "trade up" to a more valuable item. Even the Allies joined in, using the new currency of cigarettes as exchange for war souvenirs and other goods.[2] Not content to wait for Allied assistance, Josef decided to take the matter of arranging departure from European soil into his own hands. Leaving Nina in the care of their friends, he sought out ways to circumvent the painfully slow bureaucratic jumble of applying for exit visas for himself and his new bride.

Josef decided to go back into Vienna to ask the authorities there about how we might travel to Palestine or America. My husband no longer felt safe on the European continent, and he wanted us to immigrate as soon as possible. While he was gone I became ill. I was already very thin and malnourished from the war, so I think my resistance was down quite a bit. I had a temperature so high that I became completely delirious. Soon I developed a rash, and the people living close to me started to worry that they might get it as well. They decided to enforce their own little quarantine on me in case I was contagious. Josef was gone, so they took it upon themselves to take charge of me, and I don't believe they were very nice about it. This group of friends with whom I had spent so much time and hardship resolved to basically get rid of me. They fashioned a kind of stretcher and carried me out of the apartment. There was a kind of field where they left me there with some water, only checking on me from time to time. Can you believe it? I later learned that I had contracted scarlet fever, but at the time no one had a clue what was wrong with me, or what to do.

When my husband came back from Vienna he became very angry with our roommates. "Where is Nina?" he asked them. "What have you done with my wife?" They explained that I had become sick, and when they showed him where I was, all alone in that field, he gave them a real piece of his mind. "What is wrong with you people," he yelled at them, "she survives the Nazis and the war, and now her friends are trying to kill her?" He told me this after I recovered. I was so ill when he found me that I barely recognized him, and when he asked me questions I just lay there without saying a word. My husband stayed with me in that field all night holding my hand. The next day he searched for a hospital, asking some people at the camp to help. Explaining the situation, he said, "My wife is very sick and in desperate need of medical assistance. Is there any way you can help me move her to a hospital?"

Rummaging up a stretcher and some volunteers was not easy. He had to be so insistent with the officials at the camp, arguing with them about helping us. He had to resort to threats, saying, "If we don't get my wife to the hospital and something happens to her I'll kill every one of you! We're taking her now to a doctor, and I will not take no for an answer!" Finally he dragged three or four people from the D.P. camp to fetch me and off we went. I thought I was dreaming when I heard him say, "We've got to save her!" I was shivering from chills brought on by the fever, and just as Josef arrived I began calling out his name. This upset him so much that he threw himself on top of me to keep me warm. "Don't worry," he whispered, "I'm here now and I will protect you."

Finally I was transported to a hospital in Salzburg, and by the end of that day they discovered I had scarlet fever. They tried to separate me from Josef, but I didn't want him to go. The doctors told my husband to stay out of the room, but when the nurses tried to enforce this rule he almost broke the door down. He only settled down a little when they began to take care of me. When I became more coherent I begged him to do what the doctors said. I suppose they intimidated me a little because they were all German. I was still afraid of Germans, and I felt they might try to hurt us in some way if we didn't follow their instructions. For all I knew some of those doctors and nurses had worked at a concentration camp. We had begun to hear stories of these horrible places, and after spending time in the camp at Janowska I knew that at least some of them must be true.

My husband was not so easily intimidated. After finding me in that field he was determined to keep his eye on me, and as soon as the nurses left the room he came back to my bedside. Strangely enough, even after spending so much time with me, sometimes lying right beside me, Josef never contracted my scarlet fever. He made certain that I was well cared for, and he risked his own health to ensure mine. For example, at the D.P. camp we were lucky to get a cup of soup a day, but my husband not only gave me his, but he found ways to provide even more food so that I could regain my strength. When the American organization handed out packages of extra food Josef never opened his allotment. He saved up as many as he could, and then he brought them to my doctors as a bribe for better care. These local physicians were starving as well, so Josef would say to these doctors, "Here is a little something extra to help you survive, and to ensure my wife is well cared for." Soon Josef learned it was even better to trade these packages for luxuries like soap or chocolate. My husband was a wonderful businessman in these ways, and I truly believe I would not have survived if he hadn't been so clever.

WHILE AWAITING PERMISSION to leave Austria, Nina Morecki battled several illnesses. In addition to scarlet fever, she suffered from dysentery, meningitis, and painful boils brought on from infection. Ailments such as these, along with typhoid and a number of other infectious diseases, were common among Jewish war refugees.[3] The problem of infection was compounded by cramped conditions within the D.P. camp. Nina's resistance had been further compromised by traveling from one stressful situation to another amidst bouts of starvation. The final long journey to Austria took its toll, and after years on the run her body staged a revolt, beginning with scarlet fever. This began as a bad sore throat that was soon followed by fever, headache, nausea, and a spotty rash on her upper torso that eventually spread over her body.[4]

Amebic dysentery is brought on by ingesting food or water that contains parasites, and is prevalent among a population with no access to clean water or proper food storage. The symptoms can be life-threatening and range from abdominal pain to diarrhea, fever, and passing blood. The patient experiences a lack of appetite and consequently an inability to maintain a healthy weight.[5]

Nina might very well have contracted meningitis during one of her stays in the hospital. This inflammation of the spinal cord causes fever, chills, malaise, headache, vomiting, stiff neck, a deep red rash, and inability to tolerate bright light.[6] Nina's body was rapidly shutting down, and with such health concerns she could do little more than rest and await her husband's visits.

While she succumbed to the process of physical recuperation, Nina experienced a release of new emotions. Preoccupied with the daily struggle to survive throughout the war years, she had effectively ignored the pain and feelings of abandonment that followed each family member's disappearance. Now as she lay on clean hospital sheets, missing Josef terribly, the veneer of competence and strength Nina presented for seven years crumbled away. Doubts and insecurities temporarily pushed aside finally made their way to the surface, forcing Nina's first steps to the long road of recovery and acceptance.

I stayed in the hospital for about six weeks or more. Perhaps it was my fear of losing the one person left in the world who loved me, but when Josef wasn't there in my hospital room I would cry and cry. Strangely enough, during the war I couldn't shed a tear. Once they took my mother from me I simply couldn't bring myself to cry, not for the longest time. After surviving the war and marrying Josef, I rediscovered the ability to cry, and I now found myself unable to stop.

Any little thing set me off. Josef had to leave every now and then in order to obtain travel papers for us, so I tried to control my insecurities. But as soon as he left my room I again cried my eyes out. The doctors didn't really have the time or facilities available to treat my little break-down. Only when my husband showed up again would I be all right. I struggled with my quarantine because it left me alone without even a roommate. Thankfully, my scarlet fever did not mean I was completely isolated. There were some little babies also infected who received treatment on my ward. Most of the nurses were German, and so at first I was afraid of them. But they must have known how lonely I was, because at night they brought the sick babies to my room and allowed me to hold them! This got me through the loneliness and I regained my will to live.

I was very ill the entire time I was in Austria, so some of my memories from that time are a little cloudy. I recall, for example, obtaining my first really nice piece of clothing since the war. I had just been released from one of my hospital visits, and I was still trying to recuperate, so it was advised that I visit a specialist in Vienna. I went by train because these rails had remained intact after the bombing, and it felt strange to be traveling by myself for the first time in a long while.

I boarded the car all right, but I couldn't put my valise on the rack above my seat. I was still quite weak, and after it fell, a man who was sitting close by assisted me. We struck up a conversation, and he turned out to be a doctor who practiced in Vienna. I was very much interested in his work because I had wanted so badly to study medicine before the war. He was some kind of a surgeon, and when we arrived in Vienna he helped me locate the specialist I needed. I was afraid to tell my husband about this encounter, because I didn't want him to think that anything inappropriate happened. Of course it was nothing like that. This kind man simply wanted to help me, but as I said I was very insecure at the time. I told the physician very little about myself, and I certainly never mentioned that I was a Jewish survivor. The wartime memories were still fresh in everyone's minds, and as a Jew I was still afraid. I continued to pretend to be a Polish Gentile, and I held a deep resentment toward the Germans. I wondered why they were walking around as families when I had lost mine. Every German represented to me the crime committed against my people, and I had to wonder if they would ever have to answer for these crimes.

The specialist I saw was helpful, and he prescribed some medication that would restore my strength. I left his office and decided to look around a bit before heading back to Salzburg. American soldiers were everywhere now, so I didn't feel quite as vulnerable. I came to an open market where locals were selling whatever little thing they had, and somehow I stumbled on a lady who was selling a dress. I can't remember now exactly how much it cost, but I could tell it was a quality gown. The woman was asking for much less than it was worth, and I mean next to nothing. Maybe she was desperate to purchase food, but her eyes lit up when I offered to buy it. The transaction was quick, and after the lady wrapped it in some paper I carefully placed the garment in my handbag. I could not believe my luck, because this dress was gorgeous. It was black and very elegant, with embroidered sleeves. It looked as if it had come from Paris!

When I took it back to the apartment to try it on it fit perfectly. I was very slim at the time, and I still had good posture. My mother had always encouraged me and my sisters to hold ourselves very straight. The whole effect of the dress was quite nice. I was pleased with my purchase, and it felt wonderful to have one good dress, even though I had no place to wear it. Josef liked it on me as well, and he purchased accessories for me on one of his visits to Vienna: a purse that I still have, and the material to make a nice hat. I kept thinking, "Where the heck am I going to wear these things?" It was not as if my new life would be anything like what I enjoyed in pre-war Poland. I had no social events or outings planned! But I held on to the ensemble, hoping for the best.

———

Once my health improved I was officially discharged from the hospital and returned to the camp. I remember how strangely people acted in the D.P. camp whenever Josef introduced me. When they found out we had just gotten married they were quite angry with my husband, and they would say to him, "Why did you marry a *Shiksa*?" You know what it means to be called a "Shiksa"? Nowadays it simply means a non-Jewish girl, but back then it could also be the term for a girl who didn't come from a good family. Because I didn't look Jewish they thought my husband had taken on a Gentile wife. This was an insult to many Jews at the time because there had been so many of us killed off. There was a strong feeling that we should stick together and rejuvenate European Jewish culture. Most of us wanted to have families again, and producing babies seemed like the best way to ease the tremendous blow our people had suffered. Looking like a Gentile had helped me to survive the war, but now it was working against me! Josef brushed off these comments, however, and he accused the Jews who made them of acting as racist as the Nazis.

Josef and I were assigned a very nice place once inhabited by a German officer. We lived with three families in this very large apartment with individual rooms to sleep in, so the conditions were not as cramped. Josef traveled outside the city to find some kind of temporary work, and once more he returned with a little money. I hadn't felt good the whole week he was gone, but I was managing. Unfortunately the day he returned I had fallen completely ill once more. He came home early while I was still in bed, so he did not realize right away that I was not well. When he walked into our room I tried to pick up my head to say hello, but I couldn't do it! My head just fell down back onto the pillow. Josef asked what was wrong, but to my surprise I just couldn't respond. So right away he knew something was wrong again, and he arranged for a doctor to come see me.

When the physician asked me how many fingers he was holding up we discovered that I was seeing everything in double. Off I went again to the hospital, and it was determined that I had, of all things, meningitis! Who in God's name knows how I managed to get this illness, but I lay on my stomach for six weeks while they drew fluid from my spine. It hurt so terribly, and I was often unconscious from the medication they gave me. I suppose that I was fighting some sort of infection off during the whole process, because soon after being admitted to the hospital they discovered boils under my arms.

I had to lay a certain way for some time to rid myself of these ailments. I was very low on iron, and therefore incredibly weak. I sensed long before this that my body was not receiving the proper nutrients. I had had very little to eat at the beginning of the war, and even before entering the ghetto I lost my period completely from a lack of body fat. Then when I was on the run I ate whatever I could find in the forest. Once I found work with the Underground things were a little bit better. Still, the Germans had first pick of food, and I could only purchase a little here and there, so this manner of hand-to-mouth living continued even during the years I was a "regular" Polish girl.

Even for those lucky enough to work for the Germans it was very difficult to get food, and almost impossible to come across fresh fruit or vegetables. Huddled in my cold little apartment I often thought of those lovely oranges my mother made certain I had during my youth. I really didn't pay much attention to my health during the war. Clearly something was wrong, but I was too preoccupied with basic survival to worry about it. As the war was coming to a close there was absolutely nothing to eat. Everybody was just scraping by, and the soldiers helped themselves to most of the resources as they passed through. By the time Josef and I arrived at the D.P. camp we were all very thin. I suppose that many of us were lucky to recover at all.

The doctors got my meningitis under control, but the infection under my arms was becoming worse. I even started to swell up a little bit in other places. The doctors performed two separate operations on the infections, and this made me feel like a rag doll. Eventually I was well enough to return to the apartment, but I still made many visits to the hospital. This was because, as it turned out, my body was fighting off an additional infection caused by one of the surgeries! They ended up digging around and finding a tiny piece of gauze left behind in the wound of my left arm. Apparently my muscle had closed up over this gauze, and became infected all over again! Let's face it: the conditions of hospitals in those days were not the best. The staff was overworked and tired.

Here I had survived the war, and now my own body was going to kill me. One Saturday I was scheduled for my final surgery, an appendectomy, and I lay on the gurney, waiting for someone to fetch me. The hospital still lacked the proper equipment and was low on medication and doctors. There were days when a surgery would have to be rescheduled because the physician decided to run off and reunite with his family or find food. Just before my scheduled appendectomy I began to feel a little better. Josef was waiting with me, and I turned to him and announced that I had had enough of the hospital. I didn't want to have this operation the doctors claimed I needed. I was still the same kind of girl who didn't want anything to do with illness, or being confined to bed, just like when I was sick as a ten-year-old.

Josef said, "No, you should have the procedure as they advised. I don't want to have to bring you back here after you become sick again." I told him, "I will be good, I promise. I won't complain about anything!" So he took me home, and I never did get my appendix taken out. To this day I don't know if it ever should have been removed. Maybe it was a misdiagnosis. All I know is that I never went back into a European hospital again.

———

In all we spent about a year and a half in Salzburg, first living in the D.P. camp, and then revisiting it for supplies once we were assigned apartments in the city. I spent most of my time at a hospital called Landeskrankenhouse, but my treatment included going to Vienna a couple of times to seek help from the specialist once I was healthy enough to travel. It sounds very bad when I list all of the illness I experienced directly after the war, but really it wasn't all that unusual that I was so sick. Everybody was getting scarlet fever at the time, especially in the D.P. camp. We were all so thin and worn out.

I felt better with Josef around, and though he often left to check on the progress of our immigration papers, he always came home at night to be with me. Once he even managed to bring me flowers! This would normally be an impossible task, considering all the countryside around us had been bombed to hell. I was so pleased and amazed at his gesture.

Dying of curiosity, I finally asked him where he found flowers. "From the cemetery," he said with a little smile. I hope the person buried under those flowers understood how important it was for my Josef to borrow their arrangement. I have to say, he was a clever man. I kept my promise and got better so that we could leave Europe for good. I was always afraid of getting sick again, but Josef would say, "We will deal with things when and if they come." He was so confident in my regaining perfect health that I began to believe in it myself. Before long I was better, and we were ready to leave the continent that had left us with nothing but painful memories.

We had all the arrangements worked out to immigrate to America, but I still thought we should stay a bit longer to look for family. Josef was anxious to leave, however, and he said, "If the authorities find any of our family then they'll look us up. If anyone contacts us I promise you that I will personally go to get them and bring them back to you." We had received word from my aunt in America that she could sponsor our immigration there, and my husband was determined to go. This aunt, my mother's sister, was the one who once offered to take me to the States when I was a young girl, and Josef was very encouraged to hear from her. He felt that we would have a real chance to make a new life in America, and he was in a hurry to start.

I understood my husband's impatience to put our past behind us, so I agreed to prepare to leave while he took care of the paperwork.

Like many Jews, we had initially wished to settle in Palestine. We were preparing to do so, but while we were waiting for permission I had become very sick. To make a long story short, we could not go at the time we were scheduled to officially apply. Being an energetic man my husband instead registered us to leave for America, knowing that I had family there. I did not remember my uncle very well, but I recalled how much my aunt Erna loved Mama. They were very close sisters just as Lina and I had been, and I had always remembered Aunt Erna's visit just before the war when she offered to take me to America. By the end of the war her husband's family business had grown quite successful, and the Messing Bakery was becoming well known for quality products. When Josef contacted the Messings about sponsoring us as immigrants to the United States, she wrote back saying that they would be happy to help us. Even though I'd had my heart set on Palestine I became excited to see what was left of my family living clear across the ocean.

———

Even as Josef worked to obtain our paperwork I remained too ill for such extensive travel. I did my best to get better, and once I received a clean bill of health from a physician we were permitted to leave for the U.S. It was not an easy thing to immigrate to America. They would not let you into the country if you were contagious with anything. We'd heard stories of how the authorities at Ellis Island were turning people back after failing their physical examination. We had to have our health approved by a doctor, and then we had to be counted as part of a quota of certain nationalities they were fulfilling. Finally, we had to have a sponsor. With all of these things in place we held our breath until we got on the boat leaving for the States. We were concerned that if things fell through we might be sent back to Poland. Not only did we not wish to live in such a hostile country, but now that it was a Communist state we might not have another opportunity to leave!

Initially the authorities had only provided papers for me. This was because my aunt didn't realize I had married, so when she was contacted she approved sponsorship for only one person. Josef urged me to go alone, but I flatly refused, saying to him, "There is no way I am leaving you behind now that we have found each other! You're not getting rid of me so easily." So Josef readmitted our request and eventually everything worked out so that both of us could immigrate. I still have the papers showing us registered for the trip to America.

We traveled from Salzburg to Munich, then to a port in Bremen. That's where we boarded a military ship used by the Allies during the war. I leaned on Josef as we boarded the ship together. I was still very weak, and in my heart I secretly prayed we could someday end up in Palestine, but here was our first real opportunity to leave, and Josef had no intention of letting it pass us by. The boat was packed with refugees, most of us skinny and tired, but elated to be leaving. I was just twenty-two years old.

NINA CONFIDED that she left Europe with conflicting feelings. While still innocent in many ways, she felt emotionally much older than her years. Losing her family had taken its toll. Starvation, beatings, hard labor and an isolated existence had produced a rabbit of a girl, darting from one hiding place to another. Out of necessity she pushed her pain deep within. Confronting her own death at such a young age forced Nina to operate on instinct. This, along with luck and sheer will, had allowed her to survive the war. Dealing with sudden betrayal and surprising salvation, each close call put the young Nina more on edge, until suicide actually posed a more pleasant alternative to the daily struggle for life. With a previously undiscovered talent for acting, the young woman raised in affluence in a traditional Jewish home "became" a quiet, hard-working little Polish girl.

Nina had lived in constant fear that she might be discovered as a fraud by the Germans working alongside her. Steely resolve, along with some very brazen lying, had brought Nina to the eastern front and relative safety. Now with a husband and savior in Josef she left a sad and shabby continent.

Nina was as worn out and damaged as the homeland she was leaving. Tired and war-weary, she happily allowed Josef to decide their future, and she tried to mirror his confidence in building a new life in America.

When we traveled to America it was on an old Navy ship. I remember that I boarded that ship with my head still bandaged from a recent stay at the hospital. I decided that I was tired of being sick and took the bandage off as soon as we pulled away from the dock. We were grateful for the transportation, and we knew this was all the Americans had available to send us, since every other ship was in service to the troops. There were some places where you could shower, but we were all too weak to go down to these little closets.

The smell of sickness on that boat was awful. People became seasick and had to vomit into the ocean. Before long the stench was tremendous. It was degrading in a way, but not purposely so as the Nazis had humiliated us. Anyway, I really didn't have time to think about such inconveniences. I was too preoccupied with keeping up my strength. We were on this dreadful boat for over four weeks, and all during that time everybody was ill at one time or another. I spent a lot of time throwing up, saying to myself, "If I have to go through one more day of this then finally it's time for me to die!"

The first day on the boat my husband was the "big hero." He gloated about it to me and said, "I knew you would get sick. What else is new?" I can laugh about it now, but I was so disappointed in myself. Josef was teasing me, trying to make me feel better, but he was right. He had seen me sick so many times after the war, and now here I was ill again. The ship made good time going to the America, but it felt as if time dragged on forever. I don't remember much about the journey, such as what kind of food was available, because I was so ill.

In spite of the conditions everybody was excited to see the last of that damn European continent. Excuse my expression, but after what we had experienced this was how most of us felt. We were looking forward to living in a free country. Some people were going to stay with relatives, and some were receiving help from American friends. We were going into the unknown, but it was new and had to be better than where we had been. Some people were heading to the States because other places had fallen through for them, while others had been longing to go to America all their lives. The expectations we all had were huge. All anybody wanted then was to stay in one place and recover from the war.

Once we were underway my husband became restless. I suppose standing around watching my face turn green lost its appeal, so he decided to look for someone on the ship who would like to play cards. He was very good at card games, and he felt that this would be a good way to amuse himself. Somehow he found another group of men who were playing poker. They were playing for real money, and Josef could not resist trying his luck. All he really had that was worth anything was his cigarette case. Believe it or not he had won it in a previous poker game. It was made of twenty-four carat Russian gold. Well, easy come, easy go I suppose, because he lost the game in which he used this case for a bet! He felt very badly about it because he was planning on selling the cigarette case in America as a way to obtain starting-out money. It would have been worth about five hundred dollars back then, and that was a lot of money to us. Oh, he was so furious, and when he returned to check on me I knew by how he was acting that something was wrong.

Maybe he was trying to keep me from worrying, because for the longest time he didn't tell me we were traveling to America as penniless immigrants. Things became worse for my poor husband, because the day after his big loss he became seasick just like me! At that time men and women were sleeping in different places on the boat. This was done out of respect, in order for the women to be comfortable. I was on the top level resting, and when Josef didn't come to visit me in the women's area I knew something was wrong. When I learned that he was ill I became very worried, and I thought, "What on earth is to happen next? Will anything ever be right with our health and our fortune?"

Eventually Josef told me about the lost cigarette case. It was after I was feeling a little better, and naturally I got angry with him. I said, "What did you think, that nobody but you would know how to play poker on this boat?" Back then I was still very angry. I tried to stay mad at Josef, but my husband was so sick I soon realized all he needed was for me to look after him for a change, and this is what I did.

———

I don't remember the exact date of when we pulled into the New York harbor. Perhaps it was May 6th or 7th in the year 1947. I do remember that it was late in the evening, and a little scary. On Ellis Island they looked us over and checked our documents. They even examined our eyes to look for some kind of illness that was common amongst European immigrants. We collected our pitiful luggage—only a satchel for each of us—and were released to go out on the dock to find our sponsors.

When I saw my aunt waiting for us she looked older, but certainly not as sad and ruined as my mother had before she was murdered. We embraced, and I introduced her to Josef, but everything felt very new and uncomfortable. After my aunt vouched for us to the authorities she led us out to a taxi and off we went. We were so exhausted by this time, and to be honest even a little dehydrated. We had been traveling all the way from Europe on a ship that was many years old, and had to be one of the ugliest, most uncomfortable and disgusting ships ever built. Most probably the enemy would take one look at it and sail the other way! I was happy to see the last of it.

We arrived in May when the weather was beautiful, so our hopes began to lift a little. We drove along the water, and the whole city looked wonderful to us. My relatives took us to some hotel downtown, and they left us there. We rested until the next day, trying to come to our senses.

My aunt and uncle had done well for themselves in America. They were quite wealthy, and we were thankful that they agreed to sponsor us until we could get on our feet. I don't mean to sound ungrateful, but we were a little confused over the hotel where they placed us. They must have known that we lost everything in the war, and so we were dependent on them in an almost embarrassing way. But if we had known that we would end up in this particular hotel we might have tried to find something on our own. It was dirty and in a very bad part of the city. As immigrants we felt a little frightened to be in this hotel, but we were just off the boat and had no choice.

It was not like Josef to sit around and think about such things. We had to immediately start thinking about how we would support ourselves. Neither of us could speak English, so we learned what we could from my Aunt Erna who translated for us. When she first came to America she hired a private tutor to learn the language, but I couldn't speak one word of it. I learned the hard way, just by studying the English dictionary and listening to other people's conversations. Josef caught on very quickly, and eventually his English was so good people couldn't even hear his Polish accent. He was also much braver than I was at the time. After he looked around our hotel room he told me he wanted to go out and see what the neighborhood was like. He told me to settle in while he did so, and I poked around the hotel room to see what was what. I looked into the cupboards and drawers, and I even checked the sheets and blankets. Everything was a little dingy and overall the room was quite disappointing. Frankly I was scared to sleep there, and I had slept in some pretty bad places. I remember it was somewhere on Seventy-Fourth Street, and the whole neighborhood seemed to me a little dangerous.

I was thinking about opening my satchel, when suddenly I heard something move across the floor. I looked down and saw one mouse and then two dart past! They were running out from the cupboard where I had disturbed them. Instantly I was reminded of something that happened to me during the war. This was when I was working with the unpleasant German woman as a sort of secretary. I was to make certain that if the soldiers made it to our post they collected all of the mail belonging to them. The men received things from relatives all the time there, and many of the packages were weeks or even months old. I used a roll-top desk that could be opened and closed, with little cubbyholes in it. These compartments I used for storing the older parcels. We closed it every evening with a lock so that nobody could take them, just in case there was something of value enclosed.

One day I decided to clean things up and get more organized. Germans are considered the cleanest people under the sun, and I wouldn't have anyone thinking we Poles couldn't keep things nice as well. I suppose I should have known that families were sending the soldiers things in the mail such as cookies and other sweets. People are bound to do this during any war. These packages often sat for months until the recipient showed up or had been listed as deceased. Apparently the local mice found a way to chew into some of the parcels and got into the soldiers' treats. As I was sorting through things I interrupted a little rodent dinner party, and these mice scattered everywhere, including up my arm!

I started to scream and tried to run out of the room, but the German lady I worked for was intent on showing me how a soldier woman should act. She told me to stop making such a commotion as they were only mice and could not hurt me. All I could think of was the disease they might be carrying, but my boss said I was making a big deal out of nothing. She made me feel so stupid that I had no choice but to resume work and hope I wouldn't run into any more of the horrible things. Soon after that I was transferred from her department, and I no longer had to worry over what she thought of me. But having these mice jump onto me was a horrible experience, and I never forgot it.

Well, when I saw these mice in my hotel room it all came flooding back, and I started to scream. I couldn't stand how the memory brought the war right back into that dirty hotel room. I jumped onto the bed and continued to scream until other residents came out into the hallways to investigate. The mice had been scared away by then, so nobody knew what was wrong with me. They had no idea what I was screaming about as I was yelling in Polish! This continued on with people trying to get me off the bed, but I was convinced that the mice were all waiting for me on the floor, and I held onto the bed for security.

Amidst all this commotion Josef returned to our room, but he couldn't grasp what was happening. There I was surrounded by strangers who were grabbing me and trying to get me off of the bed. They were speaking a strange language, and they seemed angry at me. Once I saw my husband

I began to settle down. At least he was somebody I knew and trusted. Josef looked at me and asked, "What are you doing on top of the bed?"

I caught my breath and pointed to the floor saying, "Mice, mice, mice!" The people around me finally started to understand. Probably they had mice in their rooms too, but they were used to seeing them. Eventually my husband convinced me to come down from the bed, and that was when I started to cry. I said to him, "I don't want to stay here! I'll even go back to Poland if we have to, just don't make me stay here!" I couldn't stop weeping.

It took me a couple of hours to compose myself. Josef calmed me down, but he knew that it would take a very long time for me to fully recover from the war. I had so much hurt and anger in my heart, and now part of that was directed toward my relatives. Here my aunt and uncle were millionaires compared to us, but they felt it necessary to put us up in a filthy place swarming with mice. I never did gather the nerve to ask them why they did such a thing to us. I didn't want to hurt my aunt, and so we ended up staying there for over a week while my husband looked for better lodgings. The only saving grace was that my aunt truly seemed to love me in her way. After Josef and I became more settled she spent more time with me, and she was quite nice in her own way.

There was one moment when she was quite candid with me. We were speaking once about how I wanted to go back to Poland, and I suppose her conscience got the best of her. She said to me, "You know, God has been very good to me. I wouldn't know how to thank Him for all the blessings we have living in this country." She went on to say, "I know how much you wanted to go with me to America when you were just a girl, and after the war started I was so worried about you. I said to myself that if I heard from you there was nothing I wouldn't do to bring you back here. I never forgave myself for letting your mother talk me out of bringing you to the States."

It was strange that she never asked me about my wartime experience. Neither she nor anybody in her family ever asked about the Nazis or what they did to my mother. Not one of them had any questions about the war, absolutely nothing, and this has always puzzled me. Perhaps it made them uncomfortable.

What made things still more difficult was that Josef did not wish to discuss the past either. If he even sensed I was thinking about the war he tried to put a stop to it. Whenever he felt that I was becoming sad or reflective he became concerned. He knew that I had been especially affected by the loss of my mother. Even if I went off somewhere to cry in private he sought me out to say, "Look, you're thinking about the war and crying already! I don't like to see you upset."

I said to my husband, "What difference does it make if I am crying on my own. It doesn't affect anybody."

"It affects me!" Josef would say. "And I cannot stand to see you this way. If I ask you not to think about the war then you should do as I say. I am your husband, and I don't believe dwelling on the past is good for you!"

This angered me at first. I thought, "Well, am a slave that I have to do everything my husband says?" But as time went on I understood more and more that he was only trying his best to care for me. He wanted to protect me from anything that might cause me pain. Even early in our marriage I knew he was trying to help me to recover in this way. So I tried to stop thinking about the war in order to make Josef happier. He had saved me in so many ways, after all, so why shouldn't I do as he said?

Anyway, I really didn't have time to feel sorry for myself. I wanted to start looking for work in order to help improve our living conditions.

MORE THAN ONCE I suggested that, had she been allowed to express her sorrow, Nina might have experienced healing much sooner. "I am not sure that I could ever be entirely healed from what happened during the war," she offered, "but I do think it would have helped to let things out a bit." Unfortunately, it was not uncommon for Jewish refugees to remain silent about the war years. Friends and family did not usually encourage such discussions. Men felt inclined to be especially stoic in order to "get on with life." With this in mind, Nina set about helping her husband establish a home for them in America, all the while hoping to become closer to the only other people she could claim as family.

I never spent much time with my uncle, but I visited my aunt as much as I could before she died. Even after I found a job, she encouraged me to take the subway to her home once I finished my shift. Since I had very few living relatives I wanted to stay close to my aunt. I came to like her in a special way. She liked to do little things for me, such as purchasing for me a dress or hat. Sometimes I wish I hadn't been so stubborn in refusing her generosity. But I was often too proud to accept these little gifts, and really Josef and I wanted to do things on our own.

Our first full year as immigrants was in 1947, and that November we were invited to the home of my Uncle and Aunt Messing for Thanksgiving. All of their children, now grown with families of their own, were present for the occasion. I had never seen such a feast! I think there was more food on that table than I had eaten during the entire war! We pretended to have a nice time, but it felt very strange to have all that food available to us at one time. To tell the truth I wasn't even hungry because of the sadness I still carried over from the war. These people were family, but I must say my cousins were insensitive to what Josef and I had experienced during the war. They were a bit rude in the way they put off the hardship and struggle we had suffered. It was as if they didn't want to recognize it, and I felt uncomfortable around them. What bothered me most was the fact that everybody avoided discussion over what happened to the Jews in Europe. This had been true even in the D.P. camps. It was as if people wanted to lock away the whole experience and pretend that it never happened. I felt this silence was very unhealthy, and consequently many survivors like me experienced emotional problems that followed them for the rest of their lives.

Strangely enough, I think I more enjoyed the meal made by the German peasants who were forced to feed us when we were making our way to Vienna. Maybe it was the pleasure of knowing the Germans were afraid of us for a change. Maybe it was because we had finally gotten a chance to clean ourselves up a little bit after living so long on the run. I remember Josef insisted that we do this as a way of regaining some confidence in ourselves. Whatever the reason, I thought back on that meal with more pleasure than this reunion with my relatives. Josef and I tried so hard to be polite, and I felt badly for subjecting my husband to my cousins' bad behavior. This was my family after all, but I felt as if I still had nobody but Josef to really love me. My relatives basically ignored the subject of our loss, and they didn't realize how difficult it was for us to see such a big family celebrating, while we had lost every parent, sibling and friend.

I had prayed for a family during the High Holidays, but this was not what I had in mind. When I heard of people who had lost a loved one in the armed forces, it made me want to tell them how fortunate they were not to have been left entirely alone without any family at all. Perhaps this is too harsh, but I felt it would have been preferable to have had the opportunity to fight as a soldier than to live in fear of execution for any little thing. If I overheard a person speaking about a parent they had not seen in a while, and how they were coming for a visit, I became quite jealous. Because of this, weddings and birthday celebrations were always hard on me. During the war I tried not to remember the holidays and was too preoccupied with survival to even recall my own birthday. I had to come to terms with the fact that my life would lack certain experiences that my mother and sisters had enjoyed.

Even after being in the U.S. for some time we never saw any books or heard any discussion about what the Nazis did to us. The word "Holocaust" did not even exist at the time. Still, many people knew what had happened to the Jews, and so it seemed strange to me that this part of modern history was even ignored in American schools! Teachers talked about World War II, but said nothing about the concentration camps and killings. It was like some dirty little secret. There were a few programs about it on educational television later on, but very little else. It was not in the consciousness of what you would call the mainstream population. And so we all pretended we were fine and ignored the pain in our lives.

I am sad to say my relatives in America didn't really help to ease this pain, and it was difficult for me to understand them and the way they did things. For example, one of my cousins came by the hospital when I gave birth to my first beautiful daughter. Here was a girl from an extremely wealthy family, and she brought the strange gift of some diapers. It was not as if I didn't need the diapers, and I don't mean to sound ungrateful. It just seemed such an odd gesture because there were so many other things the baby really needed, such as a carriage or even an inexpensive little blanket.

Encounters like this made me very unsettled, and I resolved to stay as independent as possible. I didn't ask them for help, and focused on adjusting to my new home. My husband and I worked hard to adapt as new American citizens. We were intent on building a new life and felt that we really only needed each other to do this.

At first I was very unhappy. I felt we had made a mistake, and would have gone back to Europe if Josef had allowed it. I was very resentful of our situation because we had not gone to Palestine where I really wanted to live. I never brought this up to Josef, however. I knew that it would make him feel badly, and he was doing the best he could. I was still a little weak, but I have to say that as soon as we entered America my health improved. Emotionally I was not so healthy, and those who had not lived through a war, and witnessed the attempted extermination of their people, would never understand. Even after some years in the U.S. I continued to be careful. Perhaps it was just as well that my relatives never asked me about the war, because I couldn't explain how I carried the experience in my heart every day. The unlimited freedom, for example, took some getting used to. For years I had been pretending to be somebody I was not, so I remained a little paranoid around people I did not know. This fear followed me around for a long time.

The first time I saw a New York City policeman I froze. Going for a walk one day I saw one on the street, and his badge and jacket reminded me of a Nazi SS man. I had trained myself to be invisible to people of authority, so my first instinct when I saw this policeman was that if he came up to me I should be ready to act as if I was not afraid of him. I couldn't shake my fear of uniforms, and I had to turn my head away from policemen for some time.

I was also uncomfortable if new acquaintances asked me about myself.

I wouldn't offer the information about who I was. I felt as if I were still successfully hiding, and could not shake the expectation that, if discovered, I might have some sort of problem. Nowadays I become a little angry if people tell me that I don't look Jewish. I say, "Do you think that we all look a certain way? Do you believe, for instance, that every Jew has a hooked nose?" As an immigrant, however, I wanted to hide the fact that I was a Jew. I'm not proud of the way I acted, but I understand now that it was a reaction to what I had been through. I continued to prepare myself for any catastrophe, and this habit took time to fade away. I'm still a little jumpy in certain situations because of what the war did to me.

NINA SUFFERED from symptoms of post-traumatic shock common to survivors of the Holocaust. Because the subject was taboo in most circles of family and friends, Jewish refugees were forced to deal with their feelings in a vacuum. A situation considered by some as quite normal could suddenly trigger memories of war, leaving the victim embarrassed and confused. Survivor Tomasz Sobanski echoed Nina's discomfort over many of the same everyday occurrences. When interviewed by William Woods, Sobanski admitted to a lingering paranoia even twenty-five years after the war; "he cannot bear for anyone to walk behind him in the street. He steps aside and lets them pass. Even a tram conductor coming toward him in uniform makes the palms of his hands sweat."[7]

Episodes of anxiety aside, Nina maintained a positive outlook, and in the Banners found surrogate parents willing to assist the young Morecki couple as they acclimated to America.

Life finally began to improve for us when we met Max and Rosa Banner. They were an elderly couple and distant relatives to my uncle through marriage. The Banners were not well off, however; they needed to rent out one of the rooms in their apartment just to get by. This was a stroke of good fortune for us, particularly since the Banners were wonderful people and treated us very well. I liked Rosa immediately because she had the same name as my mother, and she was just as kind.

Thank goodness for this kind couple, because they were our only real friends. Our first twelve years in America were spent in New York, but for such a big, crowded city Josef and I made few acquaintances. Strangely enough there was not really a community of refugees like you hear about other immigrants developing. We went through the procedure at Ellis Island, but we never socialized with other Jews who came over after the war. For one thing we were too busy looking for jobs!

When we found work both Josef and I put in as many hours as we could to save up our little nest egg. I occasionally saw my aunt, but I had no real social life. Not long after we had become established in New York, Josef and I were invited to my cousin's wedding. Finally I would have an opportunity to wear the nice outfit I acquired in Vienna! Rosa had some factory experience working as a seamstress, and she used the materials Josef purchased to make a hat for me. It seemed so long ago when he presented the handbag and hat fabric to me, though it had been a little under a year.

The entire outfit came off beautifully. I only had to buy a pair of shoes. I didn't wear cosmetics at the time. I couldn't afford such things, and I really didn't know how to apply them. When I was a girl I never saw my sisters wear make-up either, this just wasn't done among the girls we knew in Poland. Most of the women my age were now wearing makeup, and because of this maybe I didn't look as American as they did. I didn't care about this because I was accompanied by my good-looking husband. We splurged to buy Josef a new suit that made him look so handsome. We went to that fancy wedding and for the first time in years we both felt presentable. We were proud to be man and wife, and we went to my relatives' wedding with our heads held high. I didn't want the rest of the family to look upon us as poor refugees. We would persevere, and I intended for them to see how strong we were together.

Josef and I were happy together, but there was a period of adjustment. In the beginning there were certain challenges to being a young wife. When I first met my husband I learned that he liked meat, potatoes and soup like the rest of us, but how was I to provide these dishes? As a child I never learned to cook because we had a woman hired to do this. During the twelve years we spent in New York I was constantly working. We needed to keep our strength up, and we had enough money to buy a few groceries, but neither of us had the time or knowledge to prepare meals.

Luckily for us Rosa stepped in to help. The Banners always took such good care of us, as if we were relatives. If we helped with purchasing the food Rosa promised to prepare meals for all of us. We all sat down to eat like a small family, and I didn't have to learn how to cook the entire time we lived in New York. Rosa was like a second mother to me, God bless her, and she really made it possible for me to work. I was in heaven because I didn't have any obligation to actually go shopping or prepare anything. This allowed me to look for work, and I was anxious to begin as soon as possible. This was a habit left over from the war. Working made me feel productive, and now that I had a chance to really make a difference with my earnings I could not wait to find a job. Though I didn't speak a word of English I had high hopes!

We lived with the Banners on the East Side, in one of the poorer sections of the city. After being there only three weeks I found a job in a place that made and sold candy. In the very beginning my husband couldn't find a job. For two or three months he looked, and I think it was frustrating for him to see that I found a job only weeks after we arrived.

Finally Josef found work in New Jersey. Unfortunately he had to travel two hours there and then back again in the evening! He left the apartment at four o'clock in the morning in order to arrive at his job by six. Naturally he was exhausted all the time, but he was pleased to have found work. This job was at a meat-packing factory, and he did well on that job, but I knew he wouldn't be there for long. My husband was the type of person who worked well independently, and he preferred to be his own boss. Josef and I devised a plan in which we would live on my earnings, but save up his so that he could go into business for himself.

Exactly six months after my husband was hired his boss approached him and said, "Josef, I want to make you a foreman. You have been an efficient worker, but you are too smart to waste on simple labor." Everybody knew that my husband had a real ability to organize and complete tasks. Josef thanked his boss for the offer, but informed the man that he planned on going out on his own. His boss cautioned him, saying, "This is a good position I am offering you. Are you sure you know what you're doing?" Josef appreciated his boss's concerns, but once my husband had an idea there was no changing his mind. We saved every penny of his salary in order to start his own business as soon as possible.

I was happy for Josef, and for him I tried to adjust to living in America. He was such a good man, though I must say that he had a temper. I often found myself trying to calm him down over some little thing. "Daddy," I would say, "will it do you any good to make yourself so upset?" This made me remember my Mama's stories about how grandmother settled her husband down, and later my mother had the same skill with my father. I learned from them how to deal with my husband's personality. Whenever he became too angry over something I said, "Why are you allowing yourself to be so irritated? Just walk away from the problem until you settle down a little."

Only on rare occasions would we go out to dinner with another couple. Usually it was just to celebrate a special occasion, and I remember how he sometimes became annoyed by the bother of it all. It's not that he didn't like to be social, but if he was tired or stressed he could be moody in this way. Josef would complain, but when I convinced him to do it for me he was more understanding. We really loved each other very much. Besides dealing with his occasional moods, I also had to hear from him how wonderful America was. I would nod and try to hide my yearnings for Palestine.

I was not as impressed with the U.S. as my husband. I felt that Americans were unfriendly, but I later realized this was not true. Because of my poor English they just couldn't understand me, and this made having any real conversation very difficult. Once I learned the language it was easier to connect with people. I never had the chance to go to school to learn English, but I became competent in it. Even now my English is not the best in the world. When we first came to the U.S. Josef still spoke with me about the idea of ending up in the Holy Land. He was even a member of an organization that assisted Jews wishing to immigrate to Palestine. He became disappointed with the organization, however, and dropped out, while secretly I still longed to go.

I HAD ALWAYS ASSUMED that Nina deferred to her husband in every way. His word was final, so I thought, not only because Nina felt protected by Josef, but because she still considered herself a traditional Jewish woman. This was a logical assumption since Nina always stressed how much she respected, and depended upon, her husband.

I came to learn that this was not necessarily the case. As I had with every word put on to paper for my friend's memoirs, I sent this chapter to Nina for approval. Before long I received the corrections I anticipated with notes written by Nina in the margins of my manuscript. Typically the corrections were made in blue ink, with the unmistakable penmanship of a European student. The loopy-loop cursive was often difficult to make out. In this instance, however, it was very clear what my friend wanted me to adjust in this chapter. Where I had typed that Josef "…went on to start his own business," Nina made a note in capital letters. She had crossed out the sentence stating that Josef had "…saved up enough money to start his business…" and in the right margin replaced it with "WE had saved up enough money…"

Apparently Nina was no shrinking violet where her worth was concerned. Although she held her husband's intelligence and financial know-how in high regard, she definitely saw herself as Josef's partner in marriage. On the otherwise pristine, white paper was a subtle and striking statement. Nina loved and respected Josef, but she made it very clear that her contributions equaled those of her husband. In these little ways I was constantly reminded of Nina's strength of character.

My husband went into the import/export business, and right away he acquired his own label. He had never been in this kind of work, but he was not afraid of trying something new. When he first told me that he left his job at the meat factory I was just dying in my heart. But I didn't dare to say anything. I thought, "My goodness, what are we going to do? Now there is only my paycheck to rely on." He must have sensed this doubt from me and said, "Don't worry. Everything will work out and we'll get by." He was tired of traveling so many hours just to work for someone else, and I couldn't blame him. Still I was scared, and he picked up on it. When he sensed my doubt his old temper flared up. We had an argument and he said, "You don't believe I can be successful in my own business? I need to take certain chances if we are to get ahead. I need your emotional support and confidence in me, not your doubt!"

I went off to a separate room to get away from his anger and to cry. But as I sat there alone I realized what he said was true. I had taken risks all throughout the war and never had a problem with it. No matter how risky my actions were I never gave it a second thought. It seemed different when I was on my own with no responsibility to anyone else. There was only my own welfare to consider. Now I didn't want anything to ruin my relationship with Josef or our time together. I decided to put on a brave face for my husband, and sure enough we got through the first difficult weeks until his business prospered.

We had close to two thousand dollars accumulated to start his venture. There was a place he wanted to rent on Orchard Street that could serve as an office and warehouse. In order to do this he needed all of our savings, because he also had to buy merchandise. Josef went through a few partners until he found some he could trust to work as hard as he did. Then he found two reliable men who contributed an additional six thousand dollars to the business.

It took time to become established, but soon the business was well underway. We put away all the money generated from his little company, and I did my part by supporting our daily needs with my job. This I knew how to do very well. I was a full-timer and worked overtime whenever it was offered. I always offered to work Saturday nights so that I could get time-and-a-half payment. A lot of girls didn't want to work on Sunday as well, and they knew that I would fill in for them if needed. I always worked on Christmas. When I began with the company they had seventy-five stores, and when I left after twelve years they had around one hundred and eighty including stores in Brooklyn and Long Island. When I wasn't working in my neighborhood I worked in these other stores.

I worked very hard at my first job in America. Initially I didn't speak English, but I knew that if I paid attention I could learn the language. It's so funny to me now, I had learned German as a child, and I studied Russian very quickly in order to find work during the war. Both of these languages helped me to survive. Suddenly English was the language that would provide a better life. I never had time to take an English course. Instead I used the dictionary and asked my co-workers many questions. They were very patient and good to me in this way. I remember that the first phrase I learned in English was "May I help you?" I would say it very carefully, and pronounce each word as clearly as possible.

After going through so much during the war, it seemed a little thing to learn another language. Josef was also determined to learn how to speak English well in order to conduct business more efficiently. Together we quickly learned the basic rules of the English language, and then began to improve our vocabulary. At times I became lazy and just wanted to speak to my husband in Polish, but Josef became angry if I didn't at least attempt the words in English first. We both knew it was important to assimilate into America this way, and we eventually gave up speaking Polish altogether. Even when we had children we rarely spoke our native tongue.

Working at the candy business for twelve years was the longest I had ever been employed at one place. It is easier to stay in one position if you aren't running and hiding from people intent on killing you. After six years they wanted to make me a manager, but I said no to this opportunity. By then I had two daughters, and I wanted to spend as much time with them as I could. I could not possibly put in the extra hours it would have taken to be a manager; however, I was very flattered by the offer.

I will always remember how good my employers were to me. I am not trying to say that I was a brilliant person, but I was pleased they at least thought I was smart enough to manage a very busy store. I know for certain that I was hard-working. I did enjoy my days off, however. I really looked forward to sleeping in on those mornings, because a normal work day for me didn't end until way after dark. I usually worked two different shifts, one from nine a.m. to six p.m. and another from one p.m. until ten. Once I had children I had to get up early on my days off to prepare them for school. I never went to bed before one in the morning just out of habit. The days that I could sleep in until ten or eleven I felt like a queen! On those days my husband would bring me a little coffee or something for breakfast, and then he would take the kids to Coney Island for the day. Sometimes they went to a movie instead, but he always made certain that I had a little time of my own in order to rest. I cannot tell you what this meant to me, because later in the afternoon or evening I had to work until twelve at night. I usually worked that late on Sundays as well.

I will say quite honestly that I knew the name of every single piece of candy in that store. I suppose I appeared pretty enthusiastic, and I did take on some responsibilities that were pretty serious. For example, the manager and I were the only ones who had a combination to the safe. Every evening all of the money and register tapes had to be counted and stored. I committed that combination to memory because I was too afraid to write it down! If the combination got into the wrong hands it would be a disaster. My husband always offered to pick me up when I was working late, but usually I declined his offer. He was just as tired as I, and I wasn't afraid of walking at night. After what I had been through during the war I felt very safe even in a bad neighborhood in New York City. Every night I put the money in the store safe and went straight home, happy to have work and a place to live.

BY ACQUIRING A JOB in New York City Nina became part of a burgeoning work force created by the influx of refugees and returning of U.S. soldiers. As a married woman who spoke little to no English, Nina could not hope for much in the way of position or wages. As stated in The American Promise, a text that examines the history of the United States: "When women took jobs [in America], they entered a sharply segregated workplace. The vast majority earned their paychecks as clerical and service workers, factory operatives in light manufacturing, domestic workers, teachers, and nurses…and because they were female occupations, wages were relatively low."[8]

Yet business was good in post-war America, and there were jobs available to women of Nina's class. Because of a strong U.S. economy she was able to join the ranks of females who found work in roles traditional to their gender at the time: "The growing clerical and service occupations swelled the demand for female workers, and women moved into the workforce during the 1950s at a rate four times that of men…Moreover, the largest increases in employment occurred for married women and women with children…increasing numbers of women sought a second family paycheck to allow their families to take advantage of the new commercial abundance."[9]

Like many European expatriates making their way in the States, Nina was anxious to improve her situation. She was an immigrant eager to help her husband in obtaining the "American Dream." By uniting their efforts they drew closer to economic security with the hope of soon starting a family of their own. This presented still more challenges for Nina.

When I first became pregnant I don't think I was truly prepared. We didn't even consider starting a family until we had been in America for three years. I relied on my husband to decide when we might be financially ready. As immigrants we really could not afford to have children, and my husband knew how to ensure I didn't get pregnant. He was a little more educated in those kinds of things; let's just put it that way.

At first I was still very sick from the war. I probably could not have conceived anyway. Josef wanted me to be healthy and strong before taking on any other responsibility. He knew that it would be impossible to talk me out of working, but he really treated me like a princess in other ways. Josef was my husband, my best friend, my lover and even a father figure to me at times. I had been alone for so long during the war that having a husband like Josef was a small miracle. Before starting a family we also had to consider how it would affect Max and Rosa. They had a three-bedroom apartment but it was not large by any means. They stayed in one room, their son stayed in the other, and Josef and I stayed in the third bedroom. We paid them forty dollars a month for the room, and I know this helped a lot until their son went to college.

Rosa was wonderful. When she saw that I could find work so quickly she insisted that our arrangement include meals. This was when she offered to cook for us, and I have to say she made it so much easier for Josef and me to work and save money. We started to think about having children when Rosa spoke to my husband about it. She told him not to worry about any inconvenience, and she assured Josef that she could help out, and so we shouldn't feel that starting a family would be a problem. What a dear woman she was. Rosa said, "Look, your wife is in her mid-twenties already. It's time that you tried to have a baby so don't be shy about it!"

When he heard this Josef didn't waste any time, and soon I became pregnant with my first daughter, Roslyn. By the time I realized I was with child I could not decide if I was as happy as I should be. I struggled with horrible morning sickness without knowing what caused it. I thought to myself, "Whatever this flu is I have had enough of it!" Of course I didn't know what to expect. My mother and sister weren't around to tell me what was going on, or how my body was changing. I finally confided to Rosa that I wasn't getting my period, and that I felt very sick all the time. She then explained to me what was happening and how to deal with it. She even took me to her family doctor in Brooklyn, and he proclaimed that, even though my health had been so compromised by the war, I would probably have this baby.

If it weren't for Rosa I don't believe I could have made it through that first pregnancy. She helped me with the constant "morning" sickness, which to be honest lasted all day. I wanted to continue working as long as I could, but how could I function if I was always running off to vomit? The people at work allowed me to stay on the job as long as I liked, but it was very difficult. The first six months nobody that I worked alongside even realized that I was pregnant. Back then we didn't discuss such personal things with everybody.

I had a lot of different emotions during this time. I wondered if Josef and I were truly ready, and I wished my mother and sisters could have been there for me. I put myself under a lot of pressure to do well at work, because I knew we would need the money for the baby. The other ladies at work eventually learned that I was pregnant, and they did their best to help me out. When I finally started to show they insisted that I do everything in the back of the store so that I could at least be more comfortable. The boss agreed this was best, and said to me, "Don't worry, Nina, back here you can train all the girls how to make the candy baskets and other gifts. You can teach them how to take inventory and be very useful to us even though you are sitting down for a change!" Everyone made me feel so useful, and I was so grateful for their kindness that when I thanked them I just started crying.

AS THE BIRTH of her baby drew near, Nina grew painfully aware of the void left by her mother and sisters. Without the benefit of an older female generation Nina had no idea what to expect from the birthing process. With little time to contemplate her new situation, and with every effort focused on staying at work for as long as possible, Nina pushed aside all thought of what awaited her after her nine-month term.

I think maybe I would have liked to wait longer to have a baby, but life doesn't often work that way. I was only happy about being pregnant about three weeks before delivering Roselyn. By that time I had finally stopped working and was resting at home. I tried to clean up the apartment a little in order to keep active. I went for walks quite a bit too, and I remember taking one of these walks in October. It was a beautiful sunny day, and I sat on a bench for a while. For the first time in years I was very peaceful. For once I wasn't thinking about the past. I wasn't thinking about anything except how beautiful the day was. That day it seemed that I had everything I once dreamed of. I had a nice husband who was good to me. I knew that I really loved him, and not just because of the support and protection he gave to me. At that time I think I realized how ready I was to have my baby, and three weeks later I did.

I remember like today when I gave birth to little Roselyn. It was a Monday night, just before our High Holidays, and it was raining. My husband wasn't home, but Rosa was in the kitchen baking some sweets. I started to feel pain and realized that I was having contractions! I immediately ran to Rosa for help. I told her, "I think that I need to go to the hospital." She had this blank expression on her face, as if she couldn't believe what I was saying. She was taken so much by surprise that the first thing she thought about was the cookies in the oven! She yelled, "Wait, wait, if we leave now the cookies will burn!" Here I was barely able to stand, and she wanted to wait for her baking to finish?

"No, Rosa," I told her very clearly, "I don't just need to see the doctor. I think I am going to have the baby!" Well, she took all the cookies out of the oven, almost dropping it, and we prepared to leave. I don't know why, but I didn't have a thing ready for the hospital trip, not even have a raincoat, and it was pouring outside! We finally made it outside to the curb, and Rosa motioned to passing cars. Eventually a taxi stopped. She told the driver that "her daughter" was having a baby and we needed help.

We got in the car even though the cab driver looked as if the last thing he wanted in his cab was a woman about to give birth. Maybe this is why he drove us so quickly to the hospital. The nurses took care of me from there. I looked back at Rosa standing in the hallway. As they wheeled me away I suddenly felt so alone. I had never been to any kind of class that gave instruction about having a baby. I didn't have a clue what to expect. In a way I was acting as if somebody else was having my baby!

I still couldn't speak English very well, so I assumed the word for nurse was "sister" because in Poland this is what we called nurses. Most of the hospitals in Poland were run by the Catholics, and I remembered that the nuns I worked with were always referred to as "sister." When the maternity nurses placed me in a room to rest I really felt as if the baby would be coming any minute, so I began yelling in English, "sister, sister!" But nobody came in to help me. It was so disturbing. I felt as isolated as I had been when I had scarlet fever, because there wasn't a soul around me. Griping my stomach I went out into the corridor, and there I saw a small group of nurses. They were sitting there drinking coffee, having a nice little break. I yelled to them, "I am in pain. Please help me, sisters!" One of the nurses said, "I'm not your sister!" I guess she thought I was delirious or something.

It was true that I had no idea about what was going on with my body. I can laugh about it now, but I was crying hysterically at the time. They called the doctor, but since it was so late in the evening there would be some time before he arrived. To make matters worse it was raining very hard. When he finally arrived the doctor did not bother to explain to me what was happening during the birthing process. I was afraid to ask him any questions. I had made the mistake of calling the nurses "sister," so I was afraid they would laugh at any of my stupid questions. I didn't know how to handle the situation at all, and I felt like a lost child. The physician on call wasn't a gynecologist, but at least he was a doctor, so I suppose I should have been grateful. They took me to the delivery room and put me in those strange stirrups. Then they threw a sheet over me and injected some sort of sedative to get me through the pain.

By twelve o'clock midnight I finally had my baby, and the doctor told me that everything was okay. My daughter was small, but normal. I went to sleep after that, totally exhausted and not waking up until the next day. Even then I was a little confused, and still so afraid of the staff. I thought that they were being mean to me because I was Jewish. Any person of authority made me nervous in this way because of my memories of Europe. I was still in the dark about the birthing process as well. I never realized that my water had broken, and I didn't understand anything about the umbilical cord. This confusion remained up to the birth of my second daughter. I was still rather unprepared because she came so soon after my first.

After Roselyn was born my husband showed up at the hospital, and he was so happy to have a daughter. He wasn't disappointed as some men were who wished primarily for a son. He even said after Roselyn was born that he would like to have another girl. What can I say? He was a lady's man, so he loved having the girls around.

———

When I returned to the apartment I thanked God that Rosa was there to help me. She was as close to a mother that I could ever have hoped to have. It seemed that all through my life I was able to find people who cared for me in my most desperate moments. Maybe in this way my mother was taking care of me from heaven. Sometimes I think that she was putting good people in my path so that I would have the love that she wanted to give me.

As I said, it was not long before I had my second daughter, Carol. Both Max and Rosa helped out enormously with the children. Words cannot describe what a blessing they were to us. After school let out, they met the girls, took them home, and fed them a little snack. Sometimes my daughters would play outside, or when I got off work I would take them to the park. Max and Rosa always kept an eye on the children while Josef and I worked. To my daughters this couple was really "grandma" and "grandpa." The beautiful part of it all was that my kids couldn't have been in better care. I knew whom they were with and what to expect. Max and Rosa truly loved my daughters, and I knew this was a real blessing.

When they got older we sent the girls to a Jewish parochial school. At first I wondered if we should even remain practicing Jews. I remembered that during the war I wanted to be anything but a Jew. Maybe to be a cat or even a mouse would have been preferable. While I lived in the ghetto I promised myself that if I survived the war, I would be anything but a Jew.

But Josef brought me back to my senses on this subject. Once when I told him that being a Jew meant nothing but pain to me he chastised me, saying, "How can you ever think such a thing? It would dishonor the lives of our parents if you refused to embrace the faith of your ancestors!" At that point I knew he was right, and so we agreed to raise our girls in the Jewish faith. I even kept a kosher home, just as my mother had. Another good reason for sending the girls to parochial school was the quality of education it provided. We wanted them to have a well-rounded knowledge of the world, and to speak English properly. At the same time they were taught Hebrew and religion. The school we decided upon was called Bat Jacob, and I believe it was on Grand Street. It was an all-girls school. Best of all it was very close to where we lived downtown.

WHILE NINA DID HER BEST to spend time with her two young girls, she also realized that without a second income she and Josef could never hope to get ahead. Without the assistance and generosity of the Banners, the Morecki family might have been forced to struggle and live in less desirable housing. Without Rosa's assistance, Nina would certainly have had to stay home to care for her daughters on a full-time basis. The Banners made it possible for both parents to earn enough money to contribute to the household as well as send their girls to one of the better schools in the city. Both Nina and Josef hoped their efforts would eventually lead to their children attending college, and to later become professionals in a field of their choice. The war caused Nina's dream of becoming a doctor to be brushed aside. Now it was her wish that her daughters have the education she and her mother had been denied. The Banners became adoptive grandparents to the Morecki girls, and both clans formed a family that functioned surprisingly well.

Max and Rosa were happy to have small children in the house. Their own child, Abraham, had moved out and eventually became a lawyer. When we came to stay with the Banners Abraham was just finishing high school, but as a young lawyer trying to establish himself it didn't look like he would be producing grandchildren any time soon. Max and Rosa played with my girls, and cared for them out of love, not obligation. I was able to resume work, and my husband improved on his hosiery business with his partners. They were refugees like him, and somehow they decided to go into this line of business. We had to borrow a little bit more to match the amount contributed by the other partners. But my husband promised that we would have that loan paid off in a year, and this is what occurred almost exactly to the day. We began to put a little money away from my paycheck as well, I made sure of it. Sometimes my husband wanted to spend a little, but I said, "No, Daddy, it's not our money until we pay off the loan." Before long his business was thriving. He even had his own line of stockings that were very nice. I still have a box of them somewhere. These weren't like the pantyhose they sell now, but were regular stockings held up with garter belts. It's a little sad now that girls don't dress up like that anymore. In those days even young girls dressed like ladies.

Financially speaking we were doing pretty well by the 1950s. My husband was the outside man, negotiating deals outside the office. He could easily run the office and factory as well, but he ended up being the representative of his business. This was just his way. Even at parties he became the focus. He was so much fun, and people were drawn to him. My husband was always the bartender, and the party wouldn't be in full swing until "Joe" arrived. He had such a sense of humor we used to call him Bob Hope. My husband used to travel to Philadelphia quite often to get merchandise. But by the mid-1950s he made a deal with his distributors. He wasn't in direct competition with them, so he thought they wouldn't mind giving him larger orders. This ended up benefiting everybody, because with better access to supplies his customers were able to order more.

Josef was very creative this way, and he began to get a reputation as someone who could increase business. The big companies agreed to increase his orders because he always made certain to pay them as soon as he received merchandise. Both my husband and I felt strongly about staying out of debt. If we didn't have the money for something we simply didn't buy it. We always put money away for bills because we didn't feel it was ours to spend. This was how Josef ran his business as well. There was a periodical that rated companies like his at the time, and we were always on the top of the list. Not bad for such a small company.

———

As time went on Josef and his partners realized it was time to work more on exports. The three of them separated the business into retail and wholesale. The wholesale business involved only the New York area, and they decided to expand it. One partner wanted to go out of the country to expand there. As I recall he was a very religious man who even insisted the business remain closed on Saturday. My husband had his passport in order so he offered to go along with his partner overseas, but this man insisted on going alone. To make a long story short, this partner ended up stealing from the company. He got caught smuggling diamonds of all things! It was very strange how he went about it, and I don't feel comfortable giving the details. The point is that my husband felt so betrayed. He had been good to this man, and really took care of him as if he were family. When I think back on it now it's no wonder Josef developed a heart condition from all of the stress.

I spoke up in anger over his partner's crimes, but Josef never did. He tried not to discuss business concerns at home because he preferred to relax with his family. I always said to him, "Daddy, I want to know what's going on. When I find out later that something's wrong with our business it only hurts me. It's as if you are hiding things from me." He only told me not to worry and that he could handle things. At this time I didn't appreciate why he did this. Later I understood that it was a good idea. Josef had some wonderful qualities. He wasn't a highly educated man, but he had such brilliance and ambition. He was also very kind. The more I spent time with my husband the more I cherished and idolized him.

I still hurt from what had happened to me during the war, but I always managed to push the pain aside for my family's sake. And what did I have to be unhappy about? I had two beautiful daughters and a wonderful marriage. It felt good to no longer have to control everything in my life. During the war I had to be so strong and make so many crucial decisions. With Josef it was a relief to give these pressures over to someone stronger than myself. I knew I could trust my husband's decisions because he always did whatever was best for the both of us. I enjoyed my job, and with Josef taking care of all of our finances I felt very secure. To be honest, I didn't even know how to write a check. Josef paid our bills, and quite frankly I was very busy being a wife and mother. These were the things that made me happy, and I felt as if I could not have asked for more in my life.

———

Then one day Josef decided that we should to move to California. He was discouraged over the dishonesty his partner had displayed, and he wanted to make a fresh start out west. He had this idea of conducting business out there that sounded very lucrative, but I really did not want to move. I broke the news to the people at work, and they offered me a very nice option. They knew I didn't want to leave New York, so they offered me a grace period of four to six weeks after the move. I could come back after that amount of time and still have my old job back. That way if things didn't work out in California, well then I still had a good income waiting for me back in New York. They were very kind to do this, and I really appreciated it. They even called once to ask how things were going and if I would consider coming back. Believe me, there were times when we first arrived in California that I wanted to take them up on their offer. But I respected my husband's desire to stay in California and make a go of it.

NINA'S ADVENTURE of moving west was filled with personal doubt and trepidation. Fresh from New York City, the Moreckis became part of the 1950s wave of suburban transplants. With a rising gross national product they made up the 60 percent of U.S. population now recognized as "middle class." At a time when four out of five families owned television sets, washing machines, and refrigerators, American prosperity appeared to have reached an all-time high, and with it the desire of young couples to own a home in the new "bedroom communities."[10] This style of life had its advantages: the homes were far from the congestion of the city, and neighborhoods were situated in pleasant and clean environments with access to good schools.

Yet they also presented unique challenges to newcomers. Uniform housing developments reflected the homogenous population within, and access to small businesses and rapid transit was limited. For a former city dweller, adjusting to suburbia was difficult. For a Jewish refugee already struggling with repressed emotions left over from the war, it was an incredibly lonely experience. James L. Roark and his colleagues describe in their text how residents often traded the unique identity their old neighborhoods provided for the security and opulence of suburban life: "Although suburbs fulfilled many of the dreams of their inhabitants, they contributed substantially to a more polarized society. The suburbs isolated women, many of whom spent their entire days with children and other mothers."[11]

In an effort to support her husband's wishes, Nina resigned herself to her new living situation. Though she now enjoyed her own home complete with access to the latest in domestic appliances, she had lost the ability to venture out beyond this new world. City transportation had made it unnecessary for Nina to obtain a driver's license. She now began to feel that her new home was a remote island far from any of the shops, libraries, or synagogues she could frequent in the city. Her isolation was made more apparent with her new role as "housewife." No longer could Nina enjoy the social aspect of a full-time job or the vibrant cultural life available in New York City. With time on her hands, she found herself slipping into the past and all of its painful memories. Unwilling to indulge in self-discovery, Nina went beyond creating a pleasant home for her husband and children, and set her mind to discovering ways of interacting with others in her community.

PART FIVE

One Door Closes, Another Opens

And so a new chapter in Nina's life loomed ahead. Trading the role of a savvy New Yorker and working woman for that of West Coast housewife, Nina attempted to ignore the residual depression and anxiety left over from her wartime experiences. Determined to embrace her new living situation she held fast to the notion that, so long as she had the love and support of her husband, all would go well in their latest endeavor to be nurturing parents and prosperous Americans.

CHAPTER X

One Door Closes, Another Opens
(1959-1988)

LIFE WOULD INDEED BECOME simpler for the Morecki family. The children flourished in school, and Josef's earning ability grew more secure. For the first time in many years Nina enjoyed a quiet existence surrounded by family. Sadly, however, Josef's eventual retirement would usher into Nina's life one of her greatest tragedies, that of losing her soul mate.

When I met and married Josef life took on a completely new meaning. I felt responsible for someone other than myself, and even as Josef looked after me, I also took care of him. The reason I adored him so much was because he supported me in ways that went beyond financial responsibilities. I was always able to find work and to make enough money to support myself. I knew that I could make my way quite nicely, especially in America. I might not live in luxury or under the best conditions, but I knew how to find employment and how to work hard.

What I needed from my husband was a partner who could understand, shelter, and protect me. I allowed him to make decisions because he knew how I felt about things, and I always felt he respected me. Josef meant the world to me. It has been suggested that my husband took the place in my heart left empty by losing the people I loved at such an important time in my young life. But I certainly don't think this is true. Josef was a very good father to our children, but to me he was a friend and husband. I really didn't have any close girlfriends, and this was true for most of my life. I had acquaintances, but no one special to complain to like some women have. I honestly felt that I had nothing to complain about, not when it came to Josef.

My husband knew that it was crucial to raise our children in a stable environment, and he felt that California would be healthier and provide more opportunity for them. In our old Manhattan neighborhood the buildings were getting renovated, so there was commotion in that respect. Then once the buildings were fixed up the owner felt justified in charging more rent! Max and Rose really didn't want to deal with such a situation, and they also wished to help their son out more. They had a little money to purchase a duplex where they could live together with their son and his family, and we didn't want to get in the way of their plans. The Banners were too kind to put pressure on us to move, but we sensed that it was time to try and make it on our own as a family. The apartment we had called home on East Broadway was getting too small for our little family anyway.

Although I was apprehensive about leaving New York, deep down I agreed with Josef that it was time to make a big change. We knew some people from the D.P. camp who had moved to California. My husband got in touch with them and expressed his interest in moving out west. These people were willing to help him with starting up a new business, and very kindly offered us a place to stay until we became more established. Josef was always very confident in his decisions, so he immediately liquidated the business in New York, splitting the profits with the remaining partners who had been honest and decent. We took a bit of a loss, but we had enough of a cushion to settle in California. I kept my doubts to myself, but I was extremely unhappy and afraid over the move. It was in my nature to be cautious, and I suppose the war had produced in me a feeling of "expect the worst and hope for the best."

This attitude was nothing new to Josef. He tried to assure me that everything would be fine, but he was intent about getting us ready. I said to myself, "I have to trust my husband; no matter what he decides to do it will be best for the family." He had worked so hard at his business in New York, and here it had ended in such disappointment. The problem with his partner had not been his doing, and I didn't want him to be discouraged with my attitude as well. I tried to be cheerful about the move, because when Josef had a plan it was best to just go along with it. I tried to ignore the personal torture I felt inside about leaving people who had been wonderful to me. Our plans to move weren't even definite at first, so it was tempting to just ask Josef if we could stay. But I felt this would make my husband angry, and this was the last thing either of us needed.

It is strange to think back on it now, because I remember that I hated New York at first. When we got off the boat as immigrants I felt misunderstood and unwanted by the Americans and my remaining family. For the first time in my life I felt lost in a big city. While packing for California I reminded myself that I became quite content in New York once I got used to it. It would be the same when we settled in the West Coast in 1959. I had difficulty imagining a better place than New York City, however. We had lived there for twelve years after all. I suddenly realized how much history we had in our little place with Max and Rose. I felt established and safe in New York City. The west was a big mystery.

———

Just as I had when I came to New York, as soon as we arrived in California I hated it. Just as soon as the plane landed in Los Angeles I wished for my husband to change his mind and take me back to the East Coast, but we stayed put. The kids were still young, and I worried that they might not adjust well to the move. They had led a sheltered life much as I had when I was young. I still had not spoken to them about the war. At that time I simply didn't feel it was appropriate to discuss with young children. Anyway, there wasn't any time for that kind of discussion.

I wanted to support my husband's vision, whatever it was, but it was difficult for me to adjust to this new life. The main problem was that out west everybody lived in the suburbs. This was supposed to be the big American dream at the time, but I hated the suburbs as soon as I saw them. All of the homes looked alike, and there were no stores within walking distance. I had grown up in a city and felt comfortable with it. Even during the war I had lived in places like Zmerinka and Dnie Propetrosk, and though they were not as large as New York City they still had all I needed. Even today I feel free in the city, and maybe this is because during the war I felt more anonymous and safer in such places.

Small towns make me feel... how should I say it...claustrophobic? In the suburban home Josef found for us I felt as if I could not breathe. I also liked the freedom in New York of going wherever I wanted on the subway. I never got lost taking this kind of transportation and I loved the convenience. I often took the subway to Forty-Second Street just to see all the different people there. New York had become a part of me, and now I was in sunny California feeling like a complete foreigner all over again. I tried to hide my disappointment from Josef, and attempted to settle in.

Another problem I had with California was that for the first time in years I found myself without employment. My husband was looking for someplace to set up his business, and this took time, so I was often left with nothing to do. I was dying in my heart every day Josef called to let me know he was heading home. I was always afraid of losing Josef in a car accident, and being left on my own in a strange place with two small children. I know it sounds silly, but I would think about the different circumstances I could find myself in if I lost my husband. I had been so utterly alone during the war, everyone I cared about disappearing one at a time. So I suppose I fell into some kind of automatic "what if?" After all, thinking ahead had always kept me prepared for any catastrophe. It was a symptom left over from the war.

THIS HABIT of "preparing for the worst" was a personality trait I shared with Nina. My husband's job also required that he travel extensively, and I sometimes could not help playing out in my mind various scenarios of disaster. No matter how much I chastised myself for allowing such negative thoughts to creep into my brain, I could not help but imagine it was better to emotionally prepare for any possibility. I may have inherited this morbid reasoning from my mother. While my father flew missions in Vietnam she raised four children, along with managing our yearly moves from base to base. No matter where this strange habit originated, it was one I could understand and never fault Nina for experiencing.

Like my mother, Nina refused to allow her new situation get the best of her.

My husband continued to look into employment opportunities, including one in San Diego where he had been offered a managerial position. An acquaintance of my husband mentioned a place for us to live in Fairfax that was not too expensive, and another suggested Beverly Hills. This was where we finally settled. Initially we never thought about living there, but we were told that the schools in this area were some of the best schools in the country! I had never heard of the place. In New York we lived in rather a bad neighborhood, but our girls could easily walk to their parochial school, which was one of the best. Like me, my husband knew nothing of Beverly Hills, but he decided that we should look into it. While investigating the location we learned that most of the people living in Beverly Hills were wealthy, and so the community could afford to provide quality teachers and staff. I was a little hesitant about living there in such an expensive neighborhood.

The one house we found available to us was not very big. It had only two bedrooms, and it needed some work because it was a little old. But the elderly couple living there was anxious to move. Their adult children wanted them to move closer and receive more care, so the price on this house was unbelievable. The down payments were next to nothing. It was officially just inside the borders of Beverly Hills, in fact the garage portion was actually considered part of Los Angeles, which I thought was funny. Making ends meet would be tough at first, but buying this home would allow us to provide the best education for our girls. As Jews who had been denied access to most of the universities in Poland, we felt it important to take advantage of every educational opportunity that America had to offer.

Eventually my husband established himself in the business he was familiar with, which was importing hosiery. Even so, we were trying to save as much money as possible. I don't know how Josef worked it out, but we purchased this place and it became our new home. Our mortgage was laughable compared to today's prices, only one hundred fifty dollars each month! The girls initially attended one of the four little grammar schools, and then ended up in the local high school. I thought the high school was one of the most beautiful buildings I had ever seen, and facts are facts, they hired only teachers who had been trained at the highest level. Most of the parents who sent their children to this school were lawyers, doctors, and other professional people.

I didn't know how to drive at this time, and no other form of transportation was available. So I felt as if I were cut off from real life. In the suburbs at that time there were no real bus lines to take people anywhere significant. There were a couple of people that I knew who would give me a ride on occasion, just to get around town, but I didn't like to bother them. It was a struggle for me to hide my disappointment in California and suburban life. But I was determined to make the best of things for my husband's sake. I had also to be positive for my children. They were smart kids and I didn't want them to pick up on how unhappy I was in their new home. It might make them afraid of starting their new school, and it was already a big difference for them to move from a parochial school to a public one. The institution they attended in New York had a very good reputation for providing a solid education. It had been expensive to send them there, but somehow we managed.

When we moved to the Los Angeles area we found the best school was in Beverly Hills, and there things were very different. For one thing it was co-ed, which had not been the case in the parochial school. Children were still pretty innocent back then, but I still preferred the protection and focus an all-girl class provided. My girls always behaved properly, but they were very, very pretty if I must say so myself. Roselyn was a little beauty, and her younger sister Carol was very outgoing and active. Roselyn always tried to act very grown up, like a little lady. It was funny how my youngest defended her. When they were very small I gave them both their own little parasols, and Carol decided to use hers like a sword. She would point it at any other kids who teased Roselyn and say, "Don't you ever, ever touch my sister or I will hurt you!" She was a little cowboy, that one.

Both of my girls are still very organized and tidy. They keep nice homes and are such good and loving mothers. I am so very proud of them, and thinking back on things I suppose moving to California did not harm or upset them. As for what had happened to me during the war, well, I thought speaking of it wouldn't do them any good, so I kept the pain to myself, as usual. Deep down in my heart, however, I was always questioning why I had lived while others perished in the war. I always asked God, "Why did You save me?" Once again there was little time for feeling sorry for myself. My days as a wife and mother required that I wake up early and go to bed late in the evening. I was happy not to have much time to think about these things.

ONE STRONG EMOTION shared among Holocaust survivors was that of guilt. Whether they attributed their survival to personal strength, clever decisions, or sheer luck, many Jewish refugees walked away from the war with the same nagging question, "Why me?" Why had God spared them while their family members perished at the hands of the Nazis? Many found comfort and a temporary peace in the distraction of raising their own children and establishing themselves in their adopted countries. Far from Poland and the bitter memories it represented, Nina was able to put aside the pain that threatened to overwhelm her in the D.P. camp. As the job of keeping home and family became less demanding, however, Nina would find it more difficult to keep the sorrow from welling up inside her.

In his attempt to understand the difference in suffering based on gender, Lawrence L. Langer interviewed a Jewish woman who experienced emotions similar to Nina's as a recovering survivor. During Mr. Langer's interview the woman explained: "I've been liberated thirty-five years, going to be this month—April fourteenth [1980]. And as I get older, and my children are all self-sufficient and no longer at home, and I am not busy being a mother and a wife, and I can be myself—I have given a great deal of thought to how I should conduct myself vis-à-vis the Germans, how I should feel. Should I hate them? Should I despise them? ... I don't know; I never found the answer....But sometimes, when you are uprooted, and bring up children—I'm talking as a mother and a wife—and there is nobody to share your sorrow or your great happiness. Nobody to call up and say something good happened to me today: I have given birth to a beautiful daughter; or, she got all A's; she got into a good college. I mostly remember when holidays come, I have tried to preserve the holidays as I saw it at home, transfer it to my own children. We have beautiful Passovers like I saw it at home. But the spirit is not there....there's something missing. I want to share it with someone who knows me really."[1]

When the long days in her new California home caused her to reflect on the tragedies of her past, Nina found her role as wife and mother a welcome distraction. Desperately wishing to present a comfortable home to her family and her husband she focused her attention on domestic duties. To fill the empty hours Nina searched for activities that would allow her to assimilate into her community.

My girls settled in nicely, but I was restless, and looked into volunteering at their school office just for something to do. It also helped me to become acquainted with people in the area. I eventually obtained my driver's license, and Josef purchased a little car for me to drive around. It only cost us one hundred and fifty dollars, so the price was right! I have to say that the car was a little shabby. At first Josef suggested something newer, but I liked this car and insisted we get it. "Well," my husband laughed, "you can be certain that nobody will hit you. The way this car looks they'll avoid you like the plague!" I found a little part-time work here and there, but these jobs were not ideal. It was difficult to time my quitting time with the girls' return home from school. I felt that working at their school could accommodate my daughters' schedule, but I had to be persistent and was refused many times before the administration finally found something for me. This was why I had to start as a volunteer, but after a couple of months I was doing part-time work there. It was not very challenging work but it kept me busy.

Believe it or not I actually stayed there for twenty years. The pay wasn't great, but the hours were such that I could be home for the girls after school. I wanted to help them with their homework, and I felt it was good to know what they were doing after school. To help them become more comfortable in their new neighborhood I encouraged them to bring their friends home with them. We had an open house, with milk and cookies or crackers waiting there for the kids every afternoon. As my mother had done with me, I made an effort to know who my girls' friends were. As newcomers to America I didn't want my daughters to be teased or branded as refugees.

As it turned out nobody gave them trouble for being immigrants or Jewish, but there were other adjustments to make. Most of the children in

Beverly Hills had the things one associates with money, such as nice clothes and cars. We were not as well-off, but I made certain my girls had every opportunity to fit in. They were both fun and bright, which made them quite likable. To my relief things went smoothly and my girls seemed happy in our new home.

On the other hand, I had some things to learn. When we moved to California I didn't know how to cook a thing, so I just tried to make what my husband liked and learned as I went along. I never liked to cook very much or do housework. I preferred a regular job that would bring in money, but I also realized that learning how to cook would benefit my family, and this was when I decided to keep a kosher home. Since both Josef and I had lost nearly all of our family in the war we felt tradition was important. If we didn't give our girls some sort of link to their ancestry, then where would they receive it? It wasn't as if they could go to their grandparents and ask for family stories or anything about Jewish culture. We knew eating kosher was healthier, and I would also bring a little more tradition into our lives. I used two separate sets of dishes for certain types of food, and I tried to purchase kosher food whenever possible. The point was to introduce to them Jewish traditions while they were young.

ALTHOUGH NINA WAS WORKING part-time, she now felt pressure to conform to ideals popular in the 1950s regarding gender roles. Women were encouraged to create an oasis of domestic bliss for their hard-working husbands. Home economics books and films gave instruction to high school girls as to how they might keep a pleasant home, and a woman was to "admire the manly things" about their spouse, recognizing his "superior strength and ability."[2] As late as 1963 books such as Helen B. Andelin's *Fascinating Womanhood* were used as a reference for the young bride. Amidst the suggestions of cooking and cleaning, women were directed to: "Prepare the children….They are little treasures and [your husband] would like to see them playing the part. [He] will feel he has reached a haven of rest and order, and it will give you a lift too. Greet him with a warm smile and show sincerity in your desire to please him. Listen to him…remember his topics of conversation are more important than yours."[3] The general consensus among both men and women at the time was that a good wife should cater to her husband's comfort, and in this way the woman herself would experience immense personal satisfaction.

The idea of fulfilling her role of dutiful wife and mother was not altogether lost on Nina. Her own mother had managed to do both, all the while maintaining her family's factory store. Mrs. Morecki, however, did not have the benefit of domestic help, and without Rose Banner's assistance in caring for her girls she could no longer hope to work the hours she had in the city. Settling for the less lucrative position available at her daughters' school, Nina did her best to be a "proper" wife and mother in post-war America.

Life went on in California and I learned to adapt. My husband made friends easily, and he met some nice people who he sometimes invited over for little dinner parties. We enjoyed socializing over dinner because that was the European style. Back then people did everything in their homes, and we wanted to recreate this warm custom. I learned to make a few fancy dishes for these evenings. Unfortunately when the guests left there were always lots of dishes, pots and pans to clean up. "Oh, I'm so tired," I would complain to Josef, "I'll just clean up tomorrow morning." My husband could never stand the idea of leaving a dirty kitchen.

"Sweetheart," he would say to me, "if you're too tired to clean up tonight you don't have to. But I'm going to do it."

I couldn't allow such a thing, of course. "You work every day, Daddy, this is my job and I will do it, but can't we just let it go for now? We're both tired and need to go to bed."

But no matter how many times I argued with him his response was always the same. "We have never left a dirty kitchen before; now that we are doing well it's not a good time to start. Our house should reflect how much we care for it." I tried to see his point. Anyway, things went quickly when I did the washing and he did the drying. Like many families at this time we didn't have a dishwasher. Even if I had one I wouldn't know how to use it.

Josef was such a good man in so many ways. We were alike in that we both wanted to do volunteer work, so he looked for some way to help people in our neighborhood. If you can believe it, he was the first person to establish "Meals on Wheels" for the Beverly Hills area. Nobody thought to do this before, because the general belief was that all of the families in Beverly Hills were well off. This was not the case, and my husband did not like to see any of his neighbors doing without. He helped to organize programs in which some of the more desperate families received daily meals. He also worked with others in the community to arrange meal delivery for those who were just experiencing temporary financial problems.

It was a constant surprise to me how people living outside our area thought Beverly Hills was nothing but mansions and movie stars. We lived there for thirty-seven years, but our house was modest, as were the homes around us. We were lucky to have found a heck of a bargain. A lot of the other homeowners had simply inherited their places from their parents. It was strange to see the transformation of the neighborhood, with huge estates popping up everywhere. There were families that were really struggling, and these were the ordinary people of Beverly Hills.

My children seemed to like going to a co-ed school. I had never been educated in one, but I suppose it was good for my girls. Maybe I was so innocent about the facts of life because I went to school only with girls (although I did use my imagination later on to figure things out). I grew up so differently from my daughters, and I don't regret that. But I wanted my girls to experience a normal American life, and if that meant sharing a school with boys, well then that was all right. Josef and I still kept a close eye on them to see that they didn't get into trouble, but they had both male and female friends just as I did as a youngster.

I think the real difference in our upbringing was that, as they grew older, my daughters didn't have to deal with the hatred and fear that goes along with racism. I couldn't help warning them, "Life is very unpredictable, girls. It is important that you appreciate the freedoms you have now and fight for them if they are ever threatened!" My daughters really didn't know at this time what I had gone through during the war, so at first they sort of shrugged their shoulders at my warnings. I was determined to protect them from any pain, however. I would say very seriously to them, "Whatever happens to you in life, whether it is good or bad, I want to be the first one to know about it. I will try my best to understand." Of course, girls keep things from their mothers, but I really did try to have open communication with them. Life for young women was different in America, and I tried to keep up with the changing times.

Our little home in Beverly Hills was comfortable, and my family seemed okay. Other than fighting off bad memories from my past, I was comfortable too. I enjoyed raising my family and found ways to stay productive. I made an effort to remain attractive to my husband to keep things romantic. I remained fairly slim and tried to dress properly on the evenings we went out. Like any housewife, there were days that I didn't want to bother with fixing myself up. But Joe went to work every day for us, so why not let him come home to a pretty wife? I felt that it was my responsibility to look nice for him. I was proud of my husband for being such a good provider and father, so when he suggested this or that I didn't mind complying. If he liked one outfit on me better than another one, what did I care? I thought it was nice that he noticed and cared about what I was wearing. Joe and I got along very well, and our marriage lasted because we adjusted to each other's needs.

I have only one slightly negative thing to say about my husband's personality: he had a bit of a temper. I argued with him over things in the very beginning when we got married. Even as a young girl I had been headstrong, and when I married Joe I remained this way. I didn't understand how to deal with him when I couldn't get my way. There were some arguments when I would become exasperated and ask, "Why don't you listen to me for just a moment?" I didn't like to give in on anything, and I always tried to explain my point to Josef. "No explanation is necessary," he would tell me, "I don't want to hear any more." And that was that. This made me so frustrated! Many times I just went out for a walk in order to settle down. What made things worse was the fact that he hated to see me cry. It may sound like a contradiction, but my husband thought that expressing my feelings this way was what actually made me unhappy. He never wanted me to suffer as I had during the war, and he felt that if he insisted I never cry then I would automatically be happy. Bless his heart, he never understood how crying might actually help me to feel better. I needed the release it provided, but I held it in for his sake.

As the years went by I realized that this was simply a compromise I had to make for our marriage. I told myself, "If I do the few things Joe asks of me then our marriage will be peaceful." I decided that trying to get my way with my husband might make him fed up with me. What would I do if he decided he'd had enough and leave? Gosh, I could not live without him, and I knew that Josef didn't want that either. We could eventually come to some compromise, but I learned what made his temper flare up, and on those occasions I would say, "Yes, Daddy, of course you're right." If I felt strongly about something I just found a way around it. In this way our time together was peaceful and satisfying. When I was young many marriages survived in this way.

I have to admit, when I began to share my story with students I left these things unsaid. It would not have been appropriate to discuss such personal things with young people. Any time I spoke at a school it was with certain goals in mind. I wanted only to make it clear to the students how hatred can destroy lives, and that they should be vigilant in fighting racism. There seemed no reason to bring up the more sensitive things about my life. Anyway, I wasn't married during the war, so I never offered information about it. No one heard about my life as an immigrant and a young wife in America, and I have kept it private until now.

It is particularly difficult to speak of my husband's illness and eventual death. I don't recall some of the later years of my marriage, perhaps because I don't wish to remember losing Josef. I can't keep it in my *kope*. Do you know what that word means? It's a German, or a Jewish word for "head." The war years still come back to me clearly, but when I think back on when Josef became ill I sometimes get events out of order.

I do know that my girls grew up and graduated from Beverly Hills High School without any problems. They were both bright, independent young ladies, and they did very well in school. They went on to their own adventures and eventually created families of their own. I was about fifty-one and my husband not much older when we became "empty-nesters." We were still young by today's standards, and we kept active. My friends often commented that I looked much younger than my age. It was not long, however, before Josef's health began to fail a little. He became tired more easily, and could not do as much. It was around this time that he had his first heart attack, and that really scared me.

Before his attack I learned my husband had high blood pressure, and do you know who the first one was to discover this high blood pressure in my husband? It was my gynecologist! Dr. Mistachkin was very bright, and whenever I had some physical problem I could get a straight answer from him. When I sensed that Josef was not feeling well I brought it up with my own doctor.

"Dr. Mistachkin," I said, "I think there is something wrong with my husband, he hasn't been his usual self." He advised me to bring him in sometime for a check up. Can you imagine? My husband would never have agreed to go to a ladies' doctor, so I asked him to accompany me on one of my visits. Josef and I were planning on taking a trip, and I somehow convinced him I needed to drop in on Dr. Mistachkin's office before we were to leave. While we were there the doctor asked Joe how he was doing, and bless his heart he managed to get the facts out in the open. He checked my husband's blood pressure and strongly suggested a visit to a general practitioner.

No matter how much a person insists that they are fine and healthy, reality will have the last say. Regardless of how long someone with an illness wants to pretend all is well, if they're sick it becomes obvious. My husband tried very hard to assure me he was fine, but I recognized his health problems. It started with high blood pressure, and then other symptoms started to show up.

NINA WAS RIGHT to be concerned about her husband's physical well-being. If left unchecked, high blood pressure (hypertension) can lead to the damage of blood vessel linings, particularly in the heart, kidneys, and eyes. Complications include, among other ailments, enlargement of the heart, congestive heart failure, and stroke. Josef would require an immediate and thorough physical exam so that a physician could determine whether a change of diet, medication, or further monitoring would be necessary.[4] Unfortunately for Nina, her husband was not the most cooperative of patients.

I was so worried about my husband and I urged him to go see our doctor. All the time Josef just put me off, saying, "Honey, I'm okay. Don't worry about me." In the beginning I let the matter drop. But when his health didn't improve I felt that I had to press him on the topic. I knew he was trying to hide that he didn't feel well. When I brought this up he became defensive, asking, "Are you telling me how to feel now? What are you trying to do, put me in an early grave?" These were ridiculous statements, of course, but Josef was trying to get me off the subject in this way. He hated being told to slow down. I agreed with him just to calm him down, but I was not about to give up.

"I'm sure you're fine," I said, "but I'm still going to make an appointment with the doctor just in case." When I arranged the date and time of his appointment he insisted he was not going. "Oh, shall I cancel the appointment then?" I asked him. I tried to be agreeable, and with this sort of diplomacy he eventually went to a physician. The doctor wanted to continue seeing Josef over the course of a few months, but my husband still tried to be the one in control. There were a few times when I had to call and reschedule his appointment. The nurses at our doctor's office knew how difficult it was for me to get Josef in, and they always managed to accommodate me.

SYMPTOMS OF cardiovascular disease can appear suddenly and often indicate a grave condition that can result in heart attack. Once it is determined that bypass surgery is necessary, survival depends on the patient's health at the time of surgery, patient age, and the extent of bypass being performed.[5] The Moreckis were faced with a dire situation; however, if Josef had any doubts or misgivings he wasn't revealing them to his wife. Nina would not be fooled, and she realized from the beginning the seriousness of her husband's condition. At the risk of upsetting him she made it her business to watch Josef very closely, and monitored his health in every way possible.

Whenever I felt that Josef was overdoing things I called the physician to say, "Please, Doctor, don't let my husband know that I contacted you, but I am concerned for his health. Could you just have one of the nurses call him? Perhaps she could say that he has an appointment we already had set up long ago. Maybe you could tell him that you were reading his x-ray and he should come in for the results."

I was determined to keep my husband healthy, and I could be pretty devious in finding ways to do this. Sometimes this was not easy. Josef was a very smart man, and he began to ask if I was behind some of these schemes. He would get a look in his eye and ask, "Why did the doctor call me out of the blue?" What else could I do, for goodness' sake? I knew the man was sick and that he needed help. As much as his health could be in my power I wouldn't let it go, even if he wanted to. I wanted only to keep him with me so we could grow old together. The doctor was my ally, and he reminded Joe every time he could that I was doing the right thing.

Once it was determined that my husband had heart problems I began to mark every symptom he had down in a notebook. I also noted his medication and when he took it. I kept a sort of diary listing everything my husband ate and any symptoms he had. I had begun to do this for my own examinations just because it seemed like a good idea. I thought that it would be a good idea for Josef as well to help the doctors if ever they needed information about his condition.

I eventually had to learn how to cook meals for Josef that were healthier for his heart. Unfortunately, Josef and I loved crackers and bread. We liked these things even more than cake. Like many Americans at the time this kind of food was included in most of our meals. It wasn't helping my husband at all, so I decided to limit these. I remember there was only one health food store in the city. Things were different back then. People were not as interested in organic food or low sodium meats. I asked the woman at the health food store what I could cook for my husband for his hypertension, and she was very helpful. I spent hours learning about health food and different ways to prepare it.

Whenever Josef went in to see the doctor I went with him because he would not pay attention to what was said. At least I could write things down and make sure he followed instructions. This constant attention only annoyed my husband, and one day he asked, "How come I never go to your doctor with you, but you are always coming along with me as if I am a child?"

"Well," I explained, "when I have a doctor's appointment I have a list with me showing all my symptoms from A to Z. But when you have an appointment you only say, 'Doctor, I don't know what I'm coming here for. I feel perfectly fine.'" I didn't want to imply Josef was incapable, but I had to be realistic about things. I knew he was sick, and if he wouldn't take care of his health I would do it for him.

My husband was a proud man, and when the doctor told him to take it easy for a week or so he asked, "Why should I stop working if I feel well enough to keep going?" He made a big joke out of my notes, saying, "Oh, my wife is again writing down every little thing I should do. God in heaven, why did I have to marry somebody who thinks they are a nurse? For everything she has an explanation, from little things to nothing. I have a little heart attack and she makes a big deal about it." I know that he was trying to reassure me with his humor, but it angered me right down to my soul. I tried to reason with him and I continued to keep an eye on his health. I learned from our doctor that we were overdoing things like salt, so for the first time we had none of it in our food. I knew that we would have to change our whole way of eating, and this was not always easy because my husband reached for the salt shaker the minute he sat down to eat.

It was around this time that Josef decided that he would like to try out a new profession. This was when he purchased and operated a hotel in Hollywood called the St. Moritz that became very popular once he improved upon it. It had seventy-eight rooms; however, when Joe bought it the place was nearly always half empty and close to bankruptcy. He promised me that it would be full by that New Year's Eve, and sure enough it was. When my husband set his mind to something he always did well, so even though he didn't know a thing about the hotel business he developed the skills for it. He handled most everything concerning the hotel and turned that place around. Needless to say, Josef did not want to even begin thinking about retirement. In the meantime I was being very careful with money for when that time finally came. I understood that Josef dealt with a lot of stress at work, but he didn't want to retire. He wanted to accomplish more, but I knew that the pressure of running a big hotel wasn't good for him.

One day he began to rub his arm on the left side, and I knew this might mean a heart attack. I always watched him very closely which bothered him to no end. "Daddy," I asked, "what are you doing? Is something bothering you?" He pretended to look up at heaven and said, "I can't even rub my arm without her giving me some diagnosis! Help me God; my wife is trying to control me!" I laughed and let it go. I had to be very careful with Joe because his ego got in the way of admitting he could be anything but strong. He continued to make every excuse to avoid seeing the doctor. One day he even said to me, "Well, I already know what is wrong, so why should I go and spend good money to hear the same old thing from the doctor about my health?"

I don't think that I was the only one who thought that Josef was a good-looking man. Because he was also very confident this made him twice as attractive. So there were times when other women noticed him, and you know he really was a gentleman if ever he was approached. This happened sometimes when we went out dancing. We both enjoyed this, and Josef was a very good dancer.

After his heart attack I worried every time we went. One night we were out at a local place that had a dance floor. If we danced with other people from time to time this was fine because we trusted each other. Dancing with a different partner was perfectly acceptable, and this was not my concern. On that particular night when a woman asked him, "Would you dance the next dance with me?" I thought twice about allowing it. I knew that Josef would be too polite to deny the lady a dance, but this was a polka, and that sort of dance is very fast. After a polka people generally become hot and out of breath. My husband's heart was not up to this kind of strain, and I knew it. I tried to be casual about stepping in, and I was able to get him off the floor. Josef sensed something was going on, however. He said to me, "Why did you embarrass me like that? I was only dancing one dance with that woman and you could have gone out on the floor with a partner as well."

"Listen to me, Daddy," I scolded him, "I am taking care of your health because you don't seem to know how. You feel as if you are still a young man, but you have to accept that your body is not as young. I need a husband, not the glamour of fancy dancing. If we have to stop coming here in order for me to keep you around another year then that's what we will do!" When it came time for me to put my foot down I remained strong, even though it was breaking my heart to tell Josef to slow down. I normally would not stand up to him in this way, and I did not wish to humiliate him, but what else could I do? I didn't want anything more than to have time with my husband, and for that I would not give up too easily.

Our doctor was still concerned about Josef's health, so after a few appointments checking his blood pressure he sent my husband to UCLA. There they established that he had a genuine heart condition, and we were given instructions on how to deal with it. I continued to keep an eye on him, and there were a few times when I was very worried about his symptoms and insisted he go to the hospital. He put up his usual arguments, and would always say, "You cannot force me into an ambulance when I am perfectly fine!" This kind of behavior caused me a lot of concern. How could I care for my husband if he continued to deny his condition?

Josef was only fifty-seven when he had his first heart attack, and it frightened me very much. I remember that we were both home that day in 1971, and he called to me from the other room. He looked very bad, and this time he went to the hospital without any argument. I had never seen him in such pain and looking so vulnerable. It was frightening, and that night I cried as if I were putting my sorrow out there to I don't know who, to God maybe.

Josef recovered from that first heart attack, but afterward he still wanted to go to work at the hotel. His stubborn attitude did not keep him from having a second attack. The doctors at UCLA had warned him to be very careful, but exactly a year to the day after his first, he had a second episode. The night before was a Monday. He didn't feel good, and my heart was telling me this was a bad sign. I knew that he was very sick this time. I went to the kitchen to make one of my secret calls to the doctor, and he told me to get Josef to the hospital right away. I knew something was wrong when Josef again went willingly without complaint. He only grumbled a little with the same old, "This is the last time you're taking me to the hospital." For Josef to experience another heart attack was just too much for me to bear.

When the doctors determined that my husband had endured his second heart attack they agreed it was time to do something aggressive. They wanted to keep him at the hospital in preparation for surgery, but Josef didn't like this idea at all. I said, "Daddy, sweetheart, I love you with all my heart. I'd do anything for you. I just don't know how else to care for you. I'm not a nurse and I'm definitely not a doctor. So maybe it is time to follow instructions from the professionals." I pleaded with my husband to cooperate with the physicians.

One of the physicians advising us was a female doctor, and she understood that I was struggling with a stubborn husband. She told me, "Whether your husband likes it or not, you should keep him here at the hospital where we have the equipment and staff to help him." I asked her if a night nurse could come to our home, but she made it very clear that a stay in the hospital was in order. After all, it wasn't as if they could just wheel in oxygen for Josef. He needed very specialized care. His heart was that bad.

We learned that if Josef had a third attack that would be the end. Both my husband and I finally agreed that he should get a bypass procedure done, but thinking about Josef undergoing such a dangerous operation was almost too much to bear. I died a little every day wondering if he would survive it, but I knew we had no other choice. If he had another attack he would certainly die.

The doctors could not promise anything, but they did tell me that surgery was our only chance for keeping my husband alive. I don't know how I kept my doubts from Josef, but I had to be strong for him. My youngest daughter was already married by that time and the eldest was also living her own life. They were there if I needed them, but I felt it was up to me to care for their father.

At this time bypass surgery was still considered quite serious. Surgeons had not perfected the procedure as much as they have now, particularly for an extensive bypass, so I was very afraid for my husband. It would be dangerous, but both Josef and I decided that surgery the right decision. Joe was impatient to get on with his life, so he was all for having the procedure done right away. We arranged for it to be done immediately, and went together to the hospital. Just before the operation he tried to convince me to go home. The nurses were preparing him for surgery and he said, "Look, this is going to take some time and I don't want you just waiting around. You have enough to do at home and somebody can call you there if I need you for anything." I told Josef I would go home, and I could have walked from the hospital to our house. It wasn't far and we had made the trip by foot many times. But I had no intention of going home until I knew he would be okay. The whole time we were acting as if the operation was no big deal, I was dying inside. I could never have waited at home to find out how things went. Josef would never know it, but I stayed at the hospital during his entire procedure.

As they were preparing him for the operation I went out into the hall because I didn't want my husband to see how anxious I was. As I waited outside his room I tried to hide that I had been crying, but I suppose I looked terrible. I straightened up and put on a confident face as they brought him out for the operation. It was very difficult, but I smiled and said that I would see him soon. This is the kind of positive attitude he wanted from me, and I pretended to be as fearless as he was because I loved him so very much. "You should just leave," he said, patting my hand, "once they bring me back I'm just going to go to sleep anyway." He said this in an attempt to keep me from worrying all night, but I knew that if I went home I would never sleep. "Yes, Daddy, of course," I lied, and they wheeled him away. I prepared to spend the night in the waiting room. I was friendly with some of the nurses by then, and they gave me a pillow and a little blanket so I would be more comfortable, but I never really slept.

Initially the doctors planned to perform a triple bypass. But when they looked more closely at his heart it was determined that he needed a quadruple bypass! While I sat there worrying, a lady who was waiting as well asked me, "What are you so nervous about, dear?" "Well," I explained, "my husband is having quadruple bypass surgery and this is very serious. I'm so worried he won't make it through." "Listen, don't worry," she said, "the doctors know what they're doing. If they decided now is the time for the operation then you have to trust them." I was trembling at the thought of it, but she said to me, "There is no need to be so terrified. My husband came out of it all right, and your husband can enjoy a fuller life after his operation." She reassured me, saying, "I know a few people who have had this surgery, most of them men. They all recovered and felt wonderful afterwards." This woman eventually left, and I tried to keep her comments in mind. The whole time I was making what might be considered a selfish little prayer. I said to God, "Whatever Josef's condition is when he comes out of his surgery, please allow him to stay with me because I cannot live without him. If I have to be his nurse for the rest of his life I will accept that over losing him."

The surgery took five hours and things were a little touch and go for a while, but he made it through all right. According to the doctors' reports my husband's vital signs were "under control." I peeked into his room afterwards, but he didn't see me. It was enough for me to see him alive and resting, so I went home to shower, relieved that Josef had survived.

I never told my girls anything but what was absolutely necessary. They had their own lives and responsibilities, and I didn't want them to worry. When they asked about their father I said he was "just fine," because what good would it have done to worry them? Once the doctors permitted visitors the girls came to see Joe, but he would not let them stay long. He never liked us hovering over him when he was sick. While our daughters were there I stayed in the shadows a bit so he wouldn't feel fussed over, and I slipped out of the room when the doctors did their examinations. The next day as I sat by my husband he winked at me, saying, "You know, honey, I don't need you here. I need you in the bedroom maybe, but not here!" I could not believe that after surgery he could joke with me like that, but he had always been a comedian, and this probably helped him to get better.

The bypass procedure gave my husband another fifteen or so years. Not long after the surgery the doctor came by while my husband was in the bathroom. The doctor just smiled at me and wrote with a marker directly on the pillowcase that read, "Joe, you are doing fine. Go home!" The doctors knew my husband hated being in the hospital, and as soon as he learned he could leave, Josef began to pack right away. "Don't you dare suggest to the doctors that I should stay here longer," he warned me. I have to admit it was good to have him home, but he still needed a lot of care and at first could barely walk. The doctor recommended little strolls to build up his strength, and so we did it together. We went for a walk every day, and in time he was fully recovered. It was just as if nothing had ever happened to him except for the scar on his chest. Once things got back to normal it was even harder to get Josef to slow down.

JOSEF'S IMPATIENCE over his ill health is understandable considering the physical and emotional strength he exhibited during the war years. As a very young man he had shown himself to be an independent thinker and self-sufficient. According to Nina her husband was accustomed to handling any situation, and was immensely pleased that he had been able to provide for his wife and children in America. Josef Morecki survived a turbulent childhood, and as a young man dodged endless Nazi assaults during the war. He had done his duty as a Soviet soldier, and made the treacherous journey out of post-war Europe. For such a man it must have been incredibly frustrating to discover his body could no longer keep up. Nina did what she could to keep her husband in good health. Josef resumed his frantic schedule, yet in some matters he wisely deferred to his wife's wishes.

My husband ate the healthy kosher meals I made, and the walks we continued to share every afternoon kept him in relatively good health. We still went dancing some nights, and everything seemed hotsy-totsy after the bypass operation.

His surgery changed the way I looked at things, however. For example, I couldn't help thinking how Josef or I would handle things if either of us died suddenly. I wanted to donate my body to science, but I did not know if this was something people of our Jewish faith should do. As for Josef, well of course he would not even speak of what sort of ceremony he wanted. He thought that he would live forever. I, on the other hand, happen to be very practical about such things. I like everything in order, and it bothered me that questions like these had not been resolved between us. I finally managed to get him to discuss with me what to do if either of us passed away.

This was when I told him that I wanted to donate my body to research. He had never heard of such a thing, and I think my request really surprised him. "Daddy," I explained, "I understand if you do not wish to do this, but I would really like doctors to use my body for research. Maybe this could one day help someone like the doctors helped you." I had recently learned of a Jewish man we knew who donated his body to research, and at first the idea disgusted me. I don't know why it had such a tremendous effect on me, but later I began to wonder if it was a good idea after all. I thought, "I don't know where any of my family is or how they actually died, but I keep them in my memory. Family members can still honor a relative who has passed on whether there is a body to stand over or not. Why arrange for a grave when nobody really benefits from a useless body lying in the ground? Why shouldn't I instead give my body to research?"

I couldn't make up my mind one hundred percent about it, so I asked a rabbi whom I liked very much if this was a possibility. One day after temple I pulled him aside and said, "Rabbi, please forgive me. I have a rather unorthodox question for you." I had to be clear because I am not Orthodox but a conservative and so not extremely traditional. Here I was all dressed up, and perhaps too young to be asking such a question, but I was so curious. When I explained the idea to my rabbi he gave me a long look, took my hand, and kissed it! He was so kind and gracious about it. "I tip my hat to you," he said, "I think this could help the living, and if you want to do this you should. Even if it's not so traditional it's a wonderful idea." I felt good about the decision after that. I know that if I died today I would leave a decent set of eyes, and unlike most people my age, I have excellent hearing. I can still walk three or four miles any day of the week, so I know the rest of my body is in pretty good shape. I have a donor card and a reference to this in my will. It pleases me that I will still be educating people even after I die!

Josef had been very successful running his hotel in Hollywood, and he wanted to resume his regular work schedule after the surgery. But eventually he had to face the fact that he couldn't keep up like he used to. We argued for some time over whether or not he should retire. I finally put my foot down, and he never really forgave me for that. I couldn't live with the fear of losing him, however. "I don't want your money," I explained to my husband, "I want you by my side. I don't want to lose you and I feel you have provided enough for us. I could live on bread and water and be very happy so long as I have you next to me. Forget all of your big dreams. I don't want or need any material things. You're going to give up work entirely and we'll manage. I'll work if I have to." I even told him that if he continued to operate his hotel he wouldn't find me at home when he returned every evening. "You either retire or I leave, because I cannot stand to worry about you anymore." I thought my forcing the issue might prolong his life, but like many men Josef hated the idea of retirement. He was only in his sixties and still full of life, but I knew his health would suffer if he kept working. He finally agreed to retire in 1974.

NINA AND I often spoke of the difficulties we shared in keeping pace with our husbands and their ambitions. Though we both agreed it was beneficial to have a strong man as a partner in life, it could also be a hindrance. We shared the opinion that ambitious men oftentimes pursue a goal to the exclusion of all else, particularly their own well-being. I wondered if I would face my years as an old woman alone as Nina had. People tend to persevere under such conditions, if not to carry on with their own lives then for the sake of their adult children.

Yet the effort of putting on a brave face comes at some cost. For Nina the constant worry over her husband's health took its toll. After listening to the tapes of our first interviews my friend decided that, of all things, it was her voice that gave away her age and the hardship she had endured over the years.

I was happy to tell Colette my story, but I hated hearing her play the tape recorder back during our interviews. It sounded so different from what I imagined my voice would be. When I heard myself on the tape recorder it reminded me of a woman selling fish in the marketplace! I am pleased, however, that I had the opportunity to tell others about my life. I don't consider this work a book on history, or even particularly a memoir. It's more a lesson, especially to young people, on how to live. My purpose in revealing details of my past has always been to educate. I want to encourage young people who read my story to do their very best to embrace life. It is important to persevere in difficult circumstances. Young people especially need to know that when they encounter hardship they should fight through the feeling of "why is this happening to me," and focus on moving forward. When a person succeeds in this way it gives them a feeling of ecstasy.

I also wanted to express how important it is to remember one's heritage and culture. I grew up in an atmosphere that honored Zionism. I remember in our home we had the most beautiful poetry from Dr. Herzl, the Jewish doctor of philosophy who started the Zionist movement. He wrote that "the only salvation for Jewish people is to have their own homeland." This movement caused Jewish people with the means to buy land in Palestine. My father thought it would be better to go and actively acquire a piece of the homeland, so he purchased a lot in a small city between Jerusalem and Tel Aviv. I was raised with these Zionist beliefs and I accepted them. Having been raised in such an environment my desire to visit Israel was overwhelming. My Auntie Dincia and her husband sold the family business and almost everything they owned to go there when it was still part of Palestine. Their last name was Gotblie, and they brought their four sons, leaving a married daughter behind.

My aunt died before I could go to visit her, but I always dreamed of seeing the Holy Land. For years afterward I promised my children that I would show them Israel. I finally convinced Josef to take me after he had recovered from his bypass surgery. He knew that I had been dying to go, even though I never told him my heart had been set on living there instead of America. I think that maybe I would have been truly content in Israel. I never developed a strong feeling for America as I had for Israel. I eventually made good friends, and I appreciated the enormous opportunity the United States offered, but I never felt completely comfortable in America. Once my daughters were grown I thought of asking Joe if we could perhaps relocate to Israel. But I knew he wasn't ready for such a big change, and since most of my life required that I remain flexible I put aside my dream of living in Israel for my husband's sake.

We couldn't actually make the trip until 1973. Our younger daughter accompanied Josef and me, and I was so excited to see it for the first time with her. My first impression of Israel was overwhelming. We knelt and kissed the ground when we arrived. We stayed only one week, but I loved the freedom I had there to be a Jew. Josef and I looked for and found the empty lot that my family purchased so many years before. There was nothing there, just land. It seemed so sad to see it empty because it would have been nice to build a community there. This kind of communal living, known as kibbutz, was a wonderful way to give young people wishing to settle in Israel a real start. These little communities helped establish the Jewish state. The lot my family once owned was in a prime location, not far from the ocean, and I wish I could have reclaimed it and lived there.

I loved Israel as soon as I saw it, and I felt as if I could truly express myself there. The focus on education there is tremendous. There seems more ability for people to give their children a good education and therefore a good future. We visited the beautiful university there, and like most of the buildings it is kept up very nicely. I was amazed at how much the Israelis had developed their country in such a short time. It is a very modern place and well run. They built places that protected people from the outside elements, with solar energy and other modern innovations. The Israelis have great insight on what is required to live comfortably there. We visited one or two kibbutzim, and noticed how they kept those places very clean. This can't be easy considering how rough the conditions can be. During our stay we came to understand how important it was to support the kibbutz organization. I learned that Israel's medical organizations were some of the best, and hearing this made me think again how wonderful it would be to live there. It would have been easier to look after Josef's health.

Unfortunately, things are not perfect in Israel. I recall meeting a French girl there who was in terrible shape. She had been living in Jerusalem, and one day while lunching with a friend in a restaurant a bomb went off. Her friend was killed instantly, but she was taken to the hospital. It was a miracle she survived. She decided that after she recuperated she would speak throughout Europe and America about how Israel needed assistance in the face of such violence. "Everyone knows about our difficulties with Palestine," she said, "and in a war we understand there are always casualties. But I do not understand why the Palestinians attack innocent people who have nothing to do with the war! This is why I speak on behalf of Israel." She was a very articulate young lady, and she made it clear that the situation in her country was not black and white. "I'm not saying that the Israelis are always right in everything they do," she explained, "but I do believe that it is wrong for any civilians to suffer." She was a very powerful speaker, and a beautiful woman in spite of her injuries.

My husband was also impressed with Israel, but I knew that he would never want to live there. Naturally I said nothing to him of my dream, but it was difficult. I made a resolution with myself instead to accept my life as it was. We stayed there for some time, and then went on to visit Italy, England and Greece. The entire trip took about four weeks, and when we returned home my husband still seemed healthy. But not long after our return he began to have problems with his stomach. He didn't want to worry me and so never mentioned his discomfort. I never even learned what all of his symptoms were, but at some point he complained to the doctor about them. The doctor suggested a specialist, and he scheduled an appointment on Yom Kippur. The doctor wanted him to keep the appointment even though it was one of our High Holidays, so we left straight from temple. Even after we saw the specialist they weren't certain if Josef had an ulcer or something more serious. More tests were needed and we saw many different physicians. As usual Josef was always angry when I made him keep these appointments. "Why are you always schlepping me to the doctors," he would complain, "when you can see that I am perfectly fine?" But I could see that he didn't feel well. Finally it was determined that my husband had cancer of the colon.

COLORECTAL CANCER is known among physicians as "the silent killer" because it produces no symptoms other than perhaps a slight change in bowel movements, constipation or diarrhea. Once the tumor is detected it is almost always too late for treatment, giving the disease the dubious distinction of being the second leading cause of cancer death in the United States.[6] Regardless of the cause, Nina held out hope that the doctors had removed her husband's cancer in time, and that he would survive this latest assault on his health. Once again she kept vigil at the hospital and waited, as ever, to hear good news.

You can imagine what the news of Josef's cancer did to us. My husband had to endure surgery once more, followed by chemotherapy. When the doctor told us about the cancer there wasn't a big decision whether or not we should go ahead with another operation. The surgery could kill him, but if he didn't have it he would almost certainly die.

A whole new set of specialists evaluated Josef. They had to be sure about removing specific parts of his intestine because taking out too much might have made things worse. This could not be determined until they actually went into surgery. Whichever way you looked at it, the situation was not good. After the first operation they had to go in another time. That surgery seemed to last for an eternity, and I was convinced that Josef would not survive it. It was only supposed to take two hours, but the nurses came out every so often to tell me it would be another hour and then another, until I thought I would lose my mind from worry. The more they looked at him the more they found wrong.

It was agony to see my husband suffering so, and I felt very alone. My youngest daughter in Claremont lived the closest to us, and she came to check on us as much as she could. My other daughter lived farther away, in Carpinteria, a small town just south of Santa Barbara, California. She called every night, saying, "Mom, should I come? I can be there in a few hours and I wouldn't mind waiting there with you as long as you need me." I always said, "No, sweetheart. There's nothing you can do here. I'm just sitting and waiting." How could I ask my girls to put their lives on hold when there was really nothing to do but sit at the hospital? It would only distress them to see me so nervous and scared, and I felt it would be better for all of us to wait and see how things were going to turn out. Josef wouldn't even know they were there, and besides they both had big responsibilities of their own. My youngest daughter had a baby girl at home and was pregnant with my grandson, and my older daughter had to work and care for her family as well. It would have been pointless for my daughters to stand around waiting at the hospital. Especially since Josef's last surgery took seven hours! He ended up coming through things all right, and when we got him home we tried to live a normal life. He felt better some days more than others. I could tell that this illness affected him in an even bigger way than his heart had. The doctors could not be certain they had effectively eliminated all of the cancer, and he was tired much of the time.

Josef was never one to give up on life, and he was determined to do things with me that we both enjoyed. Sometimes we traveled to the desert because we liked the warm weather, and there was a small Jewish community there where we could do things with people our age. We often got a room at Desert Hot Springs, California, with a little kitchen where I could cook his special salt-free meals. I could make a chicken with just some garlic powder, pepper and a little thyme or paprika. Even when we had people over they all wanted the salt-free dish because I was able to make it taste so good. It was never any trouble because at this time we were not eating much anyway. We were busy staying active, and we felt it was healthier for us to stay on the slim side.

In spite of Joe's illness I remember those days in the desert as such a good time. We went swimming in the morning, and then had our coffee. Sometimes I made a little compote with orange, tangerine and apple to go with it. We went for long, long walks and enjoyed the beauty of the cactus flowers and fresh air. It was always cool first thing in the morning, and so very quiet. We passed by all the pretty homes and said "good morning" to people who recognized us because we visited so often. The desert was good for Josef and I, and life was easy there. He actually seemed to be enjoying his retirement.

In the evening my husband played cards while I went back to the pool. Whenever we visited the desert I practically lived in the water. When the air was warm the pool felt so refreshing. Later Joe would meet me at the pool, and we enjoyed the beautiful night sky. It was so romantic it felt like a dream! On Saturdays we went to the big temple that had been built to accommodate the Jewish community. It was a lovely building and the rabbi was a very good speaker. We also attended potlucks and played board games with friends. Sometimes when we were home in Beverly Hills I would become depressed over my husband's illness, and when he sensed this he said, "You know where we're going? We're leaving for Palm Desert. Start packing."

"Have you made a reservation?" I would ask him, because often his decision to go was quite spur of the moment. Somehow he always found us a place, and we found ourselves settling into our usual room. On one of these occasions my determined husband spent four hours looking for a place to stay. We decided to spring for a room at one of the bigger hotels, and on the way to this hotel we saw a woman working in her yard. My husband just asked her out of the blue if she had an extra room she wanted to rent out, and she agreed to accommodate us! She had a little pool, and she let us use her kitchen as well. What luck we had that time. Yes, the dessert always worked out for us because we were happy to be together and forget all of our problems.

I loved Josef with all of my heart, but like any marriage ours took some compromise and work. I never knew a more confident man, but this also meant he was a little arrogant. I was sometimes so timid that I know it drove him a little crazy. Joe liked to get on with things, not discuss them too much. It was sometimes hard for me to understand my husband, but luckily I came to realize early on how to listen to his good sense about most things. Josef was like a strong hand guiding me and this is what I miss the most. "Yes," he would say after we discussed something, "We are doing it such and such a way." Once he even asked me, "What would you do if I was not here to make decisions?"

"You know, Daddy," I answered, "I wouldn't be here without you. I refuse to even think about life without you." Maybe this was why we complemented each other so well, because together we felt we could accomplish anything. Without him I feel almost like half a person. Even today I cannot quickly make up my mind about things like he did.

When he died I really wanted to die too. I planned on it, but for some reason I never did commit suicide. It was not a spontaneous decision like the ones I made during the war. Instead it was an obligation I felt to stay around for the people I loved. It would have been easier to take a few pills and join my husband, but I didn't want to do that to my family. It was an effort to get through every day, however, and boy did I suffer without Josef.

RECALLING THE DAY of her husband's death was extremely difficult for Nina. Reliving the pain of his passing seemed even more dreadful than calling to memory the death of her beloved mother. Perhaps her feelings were still raw from the experience, but it was clear that continuing through life without the one person she had come to trust completely changed Nina forever.

It has always been difficult for me to speak of my husband's death. I lost him in the spring of 1988. We were both only in our late sixties and enjoying our life together. We had just come back from one our trips to the desert, and I could tell that my husband still wasn't feeling well. I had made an appointment to see the doctor because my back was bothering me. Josef was due for a check up, so we planned on going in for appointments together that week. My eldest daughter dropped by to visit and noticed her daddy was not his usual self. When he went to lie down she said, "Daddy doesn't look well at all. I know something's wrong." Her comment made me wonder if we shouldn't go to see the doctor that very day. Josef brushed off the idea when I brought it up, and insisted we keep our appointments as scheduled.

The next night was a Sunday, and he said he wasn't feeling well, so I immediately went to call our physician. Unfortunately Josef saw me and said, "Who are you calling? It had better not be the doctor! Do you want to put me back in the hospital so soon?" I didn't want to upset him, so I agreed we would just keep our regular appointments. Mine was for the next day, and I thought Josef should go in my place, but as usual he said, "Honey, I'm okay. Don't worry about me. You should go because you haven't been feeling well either. What good would it do if you get too tired? I want a little time alone anyway. Just go and I'll be fine." I still didn't like the idea, but I agreed and walked to the doctor's office because it was so close. I wanted to clear my mind and come home with a smile on my face for Josef.

On the way home from my appointment I wondered if Joe and I shouldn't go out for dinner. Perhaps a different atmosphere might make my husband feel a little more like a human being. "We haven't been out in a long time," I thought, "and it would be good for both of us." I stopped at one of our favorite restaurants to see if they could get us in late that afternoon, and to ask if they could make an entrée that was salt-free.

When I arrived back home I called out to Josef, but when he didn't answer I had a very bad feeling. I ran into the living room and found my husband lying on the floor. Once I saw that he was not moving I panicked. Throwing myself on Josef I tried to shake him and wake him up, but his beautiful blue eyes were closed. I kept crying and rocking him, saying,

"No, this cannot be happening!" I screamed then screamed some more, weeping over and over, "Daddy, Daddy, Daddy!"

But I knew he was gone. And that was that. I'll never forget how alone I felt at that moment. We never got to say good-bye to each other, and again in my life I did not have closure. I lost my entire family without the benefit of one last word, so for Josef to die while I was out…I have to say that it was more than I could bear.

My neighbors heard me crying but never investigated because they didn't know exactly what to think. Perhaps they thought my husband and I were having an argument, though we never fought in such a way. I eventually stumbled to the phone and tried to call the doctor. I couldn't get through to him, so I called my daughters. I don't even remember who I reached first, but everybody came as soon as they could. They took me to another room, the bedroom I think. I was tearing myself away from them, because they wanted to take away his body so that I shouldn't see it. However, when I reached the room where he had been he wasn't there anymore. Oh, how I was yelling! This was when I first had the idea of committing suicide. I said to myself, "I'll never forget this moment, and I don't want to live with it." I was so overwhelmed, and being with Josef was the only thing on my mind at that time. With Joe's death it was as if he was still there but I could not reach him. All I could think was, "I have to go with my husband. He needs me!" I honestly think that if my family hadn't come right away I would have found a way to join him.

My youngest daughter's husband came immediately to the house, and he began to look after things I could not handle in my state of mind. Everything was a blur after that. The timing of it all was so tragic, because my eldest daughter and her fiancé were to be married that week on Saturday. Josef would have been upset if they changed their date because of him, so I insisted they go ahead with it.

I couldn't help remembering how weak my husband felt during his last days. He had asked me, "How will I be able to make the wedding if I'm this tired?" I don't really know what was going on in my husband's heart. Maybe he knew what was coming for him. I said, "Daddy, don't worry. If you can't drive to the wedding they'll take us. Everything will work out." I know that this was childish, but I never really talked with

Josef about the possibility of his dying before me. Other than agreeing on what sort of memorial services we would each like, we never spoke about what I should do if he passed away. The idea of life without him was impossible for me to grasp. It is strange how I was so intent on discussing donating our bodies to science, yet I refused to consider other practicalities of death.

Looking back now I realize that having such a conversation would have saved me a lot of pain, and I recommend it to any married couple. Before Josef passed on I was only vaguely aware of our financial situation. I hadn't a clue about managing taxes or bills. At first I didn't even try to deal with such things because I was still considering suicide. I remember that I was actually disappointed there were no high buildings in our neighborhood, because it would have been handy to simply jump out a window. I could put up with a lot of things, but not my husband's death.

In spite of all that had happened to me as a young woman, my husband's passing was the biggest tragedy of my life. I dealt with the disappearance of my family, and I even accepted my mother's death in my own way. But Josef's death was different somehow. My daughter went through with her wedding ceremony, but in the end I couldn't bring myself to go. I was such a mess. My youngest daughter took me to her house to stay because she didn't want me to be alone, and I spent a lot of time with my grandchildren.

I don't remember the particulars of closing up our house in Beverly Hills. We transferred all the funeral arrangements to Claremont, and the rabbi there very kindly took care of everything. What a speaker he was, what a genius. I knew him from a wonderful temple in Los Angeles. We liked to go Friday nights with some friends because his services were so beautiful. My daughter took care of everything after her daddy died, and I think that the love I had for my family was all that kept me alive. I didn't want to give my daughters the pain of losing a father and mother at the same time. We all needed each other so badly. We had a small memorial service, keeping it small and private. I tried to remember the happy times with Joe, how he loved a good movie and how he loved life. Even now when I see people dancing I think of him. I thought, "If this is dancing then Josef could show these people a thing or two."

There are many qualities I loved about my husband. He was so well-informed, constantly keeping up with current events by watching the news or listening to it on the radio. Josef didn't read many books, but he was a wonderful conversationalist. For my sake he kept the Jewish traditions, but ultimately he believed in his own ability to pull us through things. He always said, "God will help you if you help yourself and remain strong. All God expects from us is to love each other."

Luckily for me my husband had his papers in order before he died. He never used a desk, only two shelves in the closet where he kept all of the bookkeeping. The man he hired to do our taxes would say, "Joe, everything is in such order. What do you need me for?" And here I didn't even know how to write a check! It was as if I had lived in a dream world, and when Josef died I certainly didn't want to learn how to take care of things. Eventually I moved back to my home in Beverly Hills, but my youngest daughter always checked up on me. It was difficult for me to be in the house without my husband, so in the daytime I just walked around the neighborhood.

This was not easy, those first years after Josef's death. In many ways this experience was more difficult than surviving during the war. I was younger and stronger then, and almost subconsciously I did things that allowed me a greater chance of survival, such as keeping to myself. Being alone after Joe died was not good for me, however, so the same tactics could not work. As a young person I was also a bit more careless. No one could suggest to me that what I was doing was good or bad. I did whatever came to mind, and most of the time I wasn't concentrating on the actual fight for life. I went only from one moment to the next, and made decisions that affected my life on the spur of the moment. I didn't dwell on, "Shall I do this, or shall I not?" As a young woman I wasn't responsible for anybody, and sometimes not even for myself. I just looked at life as if it were a roulette game, and didn't really have time for self-pity.

When Joe died I absolutely felt sorry for myself, and it was difficult getting through each day. We buried my husband's ashes and placed a little inscription on his plaque, and there I went every week, sometimes twice a week. After a while I couldn't cry anymore. I had used up all of my tears. I spent plenty of time talking to Josef, however, saying, "Daddy, why were you so selfish? Why did you have to go off by yourself? Couldn't you take me with you? You always said that you would never leave me. Why did you allow me to depend on you so much? Why not take better care of yourself so that we could grow old together?"

But I never got an answer, and I felt lost in everything I did. My daughters encouraged me to get professional help, but all I did when I visited the grief counselor was cry, so I stopped going. I am actually a very private person, and I didn't like expressing myself in such a personal way to a stranger. I managed to somehow fill my days, but the first night I had to sleep alone I couldn't even bother to undress. How could I sleep without Josef?

Fortunately my neighbor was very kind to me. She had never been married and had lived in her home for forty-five years. Once in a while I passed by her house and waved to her, and sometimes I brought her fruit from our house. We had a lemon tree and grapes, and to take my mind off things I sometimes baked her honey cookies. With all my visits she became something of a friend. She had just had eye surgery so we took care of each other. I told her how I could not face sleeping alone in my bed anymore, and she suggested I spend evenings with her. So every single night, the minute it started to get just a little bit dark, I went to my dear neighbor's house. I really appreciated it because at night the darkness seemed to creep into every corner of my house. I always told her not to bother making up a bed for me, but she insisted on setting out a nice pillow, sheets and blankets. At six o'clock in the morning I straightened everything up and returned to my own home. This went on for about two months.

My younger daughter knew I was lonely. "Mom," she said, "I want you to come here to stay. We're not that far away." But I told her I wanted to work things out on my own. There were certain things I had to get used to. I still experienced moments when I did not wish to live. If somebody had offered me a simple little cup of poison that allowed me to sleep forever, well, I might have accepted it. Instead I waited for life to feel worthwhile again.

One evening I was preparing to go to my friend's house to sleep, but something delayed me. Perhaps it was a telephone call, but I'm not certain. Anyway, I suddenly realized it had already become dark outside. That was when I thought, "I can no longer run away from my own house every night. I have a home and I belong here." I slept on the sofa bed until I felt comfortable enough to sleep in my own bed. It was as if my heart was telling me, "You could not do this before, but now you can." Sometimes I didn't sleep the entire night, but it was a step in the right direction.

After some time I began to feel like a somewhat normal human being. At least I was starting to think about what I should do with my life. I eventually learned to function as a woman living alone, but I feel the loss of my Josef to this day. I have always been grateful to have my daughters. My family is important to me, but nothing really takes the place of a spouse.

I remember the first time I went to the grocery store after my husband died. About three months had passed, and I decided to try doing ordinary things. When I went to the market I saw an elderly couple in the aisle. They were holding hands and shopping together, just talking about what they needed. Well, I walked out of that market crying so hard that people came up to ask if I was all right. I was almost hysterical, and I thought, "Well, I'll never go shopping again. That's that!" I had to work through these kinds of things on a daily basis.

I have to admit, I still wasn't taking very good care of myself. Once I became sick with shingles. At first I assumed I was just fatigued from the death of my husband. I wasn't eating properly and was down to around ninety pounds, but at that time just looking at food made me feel ill. On the day I felt particularly tired I had an appointment with a real estate lady. I wanted to make some changes in my life and was thinking about selling my house. The lady called that afternoon to say she could come around five o'clock. I remember hanging up the phone, but after that I fainted. I still had my old habit of fainting at the strangest times. I know that I made it to the floor, but everything was very fuzzy after that. Luckily the real estate lady called me back to ask for directions to my home. The ringing brought me back to a state that was somewhat conscious, and I managed to reach the phone from the floor but could barely speak. The real estate lady asked, "What's wrong with you?" I suppose I answered something incoherent, and she said, "I'm coming right away. Try to get to the door and unlock it for me."

I was in the kitchen at this time, and there was a very long living room that I would have had to cross to get to my door. I couldn't stand up, and at first I just curled up in a ball on the floor. After laying there for a while to regain my strength I crawled to the back door. I used the last of my strength to push open the screen door and waited there for help. I feel badly that I cannot remember that lady's name, but bless her heart she arrived only minutes after I got the door open. She wanted to call an ambulance, but I told her I would be okay once I ate a little something. Here we were complete strangers, and this kind woman was trying to help me as if I were family. She looked around the kitchen for food and finally found a little bread. She said, "You're probably dehydrated and have low blood sugar." She was right and I felt much better after eating.

I had my usual luck with kind strangers. Believe it or not that woman spent the entire night with me! She called my daughter the next day and even offered to stay another night, but my daughter stayed with me. She took me to the doctor where I was diagnosed with shingles and a very high temperature. My daughter insisted I stay with her, and her husband carried me like a baby into their house. What a mess! I stayed with them until they began to prepare to move out of state. They wanted me to come with them, but I felt it would be better if they settled in first; after all, they had a brand new baby boy to care for. At this time I thought quite a bit about how much Josef would have enjoyed his grandson. I would have given half of my life to see Josef play with his grandchildren, but I did not say this to my daughter. Because of me she had taken almost a year and a half prolonging the decision to move. Eventually they moved to Massachusetts, but I wanted to do things my own way. My eldest daughter lived in Carpinteria, which as I mentioned is a beach town about ten miles south of Santa Barbara, California. I stayed with her while looking for a place of my own in that area.

SPEAKING OF her husband's death left Nina exhausted. Perhaps it was a relief to have finally released this memory, and I tried to be sympathetic without offering the usual trite advice about healing or moving on from the pain of her past. It was clear to me that, for Nina, Josef's passing had indeed been even more traumatic than the war years. Far from being a cathartic process, I believe that relaying the details behind his death merely opened up emotional wounds afresh.

Nina never avoided the subject of her husband or how she valued their relationship. Now, however, I could see that Nina harbored a special heartache for Josef. Once more my friend had, for the benefit of our project, brought back to life the spirit of a loved one. This she did willingly, never flinching from my questions and demands for detail. Yet it was not at all pleasant for her to recall those dark days. I prayed that, through our project, we could at last put Nina's sadness in its proper place, or that she might, for just a moment, forget her loss.

$\mathscr{N}ina\ \mathscr{S}peaks\ \mathscr{O}ut$

(1988-2005)

THERE ARE PLENTY of examples in which historians attempt to decipher the phenomenon of "remembrance" among Holocaust survivors. I have cited a good number of these historians, and in their work are revelations that run the gamut of explanations about why survivors feel the need to tell their stories to others.

This book, however, was never meant to be an academic interpretation of Holocaust survivor behavior. All I could determine with any assurance was that, in Nina's mind, survival carried with it a responsibility to educate others about the effect of hatred upon society. Ironically, my friend was not able to fulfill this responsibility until after the death of her husband. Like so many of his contemporaries, Josef felt that by restricting his wife's discussion of the war years, he was preserving whatever innocence and joy remained in her heart. However, by insisting that Nina repress her wartime memories, he also denied her the right to deal with them properly.

Josef's passing was a terrible loss, yet with his death Nina finally stumbled upon a way to remedy her past.

After Josef died I had no idea what I wanted to do with my life. My daughters discussed it until I became quite sick from the topic. I finally said to everyone, "There is no rush to make decisions concerning me. I can take care of myself!" Perhaps I was being unfair. They only wanted to help, but I only wanted to chase everybody away. I didn't want to face Josef's passing. If I thought about my future it would mean admitting that he was truly gone.

It was 1988 when I moved from my home in Beverly Hills, and I'm still not certain it was a good idea. I had always heard that when a death or tragedy occurs in your life you should do nothing for at least a year. Maybe I was vulnerable and easily influenced, but advice and suggestions were valuable to me at such a time. If I had stayed in Beverly Hills I wonder if I would have eventually been content with a quiet life there. I could have found a roommate, or volunteered at the Holocaust Museum in Los Angeles. Then again, if I had not moved I would not have met the people who encouraged me to speak of my wartime experiences, and this was ultimately my survival. Needless to say I had difficulty adjusting to my move north. It had not even been a full year since Josef's death, but I was undecided about what else to do, and so I accepted my oldest daughter's invitation to live temporarily with her in Carpinteria. I left the business of what to do with my home in Beverly Hills to my family, and they rented the place out, furniture and all.

Typical of me, I at first didn't really like my new town. I could not make friends and felt very isolated. During those first few months I became so desperate that, walking along the beach one day, I had my final suicidal thought. I considered drowning myself in the ocean. The thought of throwing myself into the ocean seemed quite appealing at the time, and I thought, "Well Nina, why not just keep walking into the water until you can no longer move? The beach is empty so nobody will notice. At least this way you will finally know peace."

I was actually on my way into the waves when I thought of my family. My girls had done so much for me since Josef died, and after all they had lost their daddy too. "Do I have the right to do something like this to my daughters? Is it right to take away their mother as well?" My girls had no grandparents or extended family, and I hadn't realized until that moment how alone they were. Up to that point I had only been thinking of myself. I suddenly felt ashamed and realized how such a selfish act would have devastated my family. So I turned around and walked home.

THE GRIEF ONE EXPERIENCES over the loss of a spouse is very personal and extraordinarily painful. The usual practice of keeping her emotions in check proved very unhealthy for the newly widowed Nina. Out of desperation to bring their mother out of her depression, her daughters suggested a change her residence. Nina apathetically complied. Comforting thoughts of suicide continued to haunt her, however, and she withdrew within herself, banishing all thoughts about the future. Nina's loss of appetite and inability to sleep compounded those lingering feelings of despair.

Perhaps the best remedy for Nina was to focus on the needs of others. Nina's grandmother, mother, sister Lina, and husband had all found great satisfaction in volunteer work within their communities. Research suggests that the elderly benefit most from this type of activity, giving them a sense of purpose and a longer, more productive life.[1] The family tradition of helping others would be just what Nina needed to find purpose to her life.

I continued to have problems with adjusting to my new life, and I thought, "How could anyone think I would be happy in this town? There are no temples, only churches. Where am I supposed to meet people?" My daughters were typical American girls, so they seemed to make friends easily no matter where they went. I remained a little self-conscious about being an immigrant. I still had my Polish accent and always felt a little different because of it. On top of all this, I was still mourning my husband, and so I didn't seem to have the energy to do anything.

My daughter Carol was very supportive during this time. She would call and check on me quite often, and she suggested that I find a different place to live besides Carpinteria, perhaps Santa Barbara. I am sure that my eldest daughter Roselyn wished for me to snap out of my depression. In the meantime she had to go to work every morning, and eventually I became tired of sitting around in discontent. Around the year 1990 I began to take little walks around town just to get out in the fresh air.

On one of these walks, I had a life-changing experience. It was a Thursday morning and there was to be a grand opening of a supermarket in the middle of town. I went off by myself to see the new store, and afterwards headed home through a neighborhood filled with pretty Victorian homes. All of the children were in school, so the streets and sidewalks were very quiet. I came to a little church where I slipped on something and fell. I suppose I wasn't paying attention, as usual I was thinking about Josef, but I really fell down hard! At first I didn't feel any pain, but when I tried to get up I found that I couldn't move an inch. I didn't know it then, but I had broken my arm in two places. The pain coming from my shoulder was so bad I went in and out of consciousness. I must have lay there for over an hour without any help.

Finally a Hispanic woman came by. She didn't speak any English, and as she looked down at me her first thought must have been that I was drunk! All I could do was moan, and we were by a beach where homeless people sometimes liked to drink. Maybe she thought that was my story too! She finally realized I was in pain and ran off for help. An ambulance arrived and I was taken to the hospital in Santa Barbara where they learned I had broken my arm and shoulder. I stayed in the hospital for a few days, but it took about five additional weeks before I was healed enough for physical therapy. Thank God for my daughter. I don't know what I would have done without her at this time.

The doctors decided that my arm would not heal properly in a cast. Instead they fashioned a sort of sling that allowed more movement, though this was very painful. Soon enough the doctor told me I could work with a physical therapist, but only on one condition. "It will be very painful," he warned me, "but your muscles have to work through this discomfort to gain strength. You must do exactly as you are told by the therapist or else agree to have immediate surgery." I still wasn't over my fear of doctors. But I certainly had been through enough surgery as a refugee in Vienna, so I told him, "I will do anything you say."

I spent the next six months crying my eyes out as the therapist told me to reach and pull on a rope. I would pull and cry, pull and cry. It hurt so badly, but I remembered what the doctor promised, and sure enough I got better. I think this dramatic experience caused me to snap out of my depression. It may seem strange, but breaking my arm caused me to find purpose again. With my husband gone I had let my physical self go because I wanted to die also. Working with the physical therapist helped me to regain confidence in myself and my abilities. Josef continued to be on my mind, but now I saw things more realistically. When my arm healed I felt that if I could overcome such an injury, then maybe I could also do something meaningful with my time. I remembered that after Josef's retirement he had taken on volunteer work almost full-time. It seemed to satisfy him so much, and I wondered if I shouldn't give it a try. But what particular volunteer work should I do?

As soon as the doctor pronounced my arm completely healed I went to the community center in my town where I met Toni. I explained to her my interest in working with other people my age, and asked, "How the heck do you get acquainted with anybody around here?" Toni was a bright lady and I liked her immediately. She had worked hard to achieve her goals, and she had everybody's respect. She tried to place me in work that allowed me to meet people, and I did. Still, it did not entirely relieve my loneliness.

Soon after meeting Toni I went to a local restaurant for a bite to eat. I was feeling very down about Josef's death, and when I went to the ladies' room I found that I just couldn't stop crying! It bothered me that my depression came on all of a sudden, but I could not help it. I tried to collect myself, remembering how I had been determined to turn my life around. After wiping my eyes I walked back to my table. I passed two ladies who recognized that I had been crying, and they asked, "What's the matter? Don't you feel good?"

I was surprised they had even seen me, and I tried to put them off, saying, "Oh, it's nothing special. I'm just in a lot of pain from an accident." This was partly true. I really was still hurting physically, but the pain in my heart was worse than in my arm. I didn't want to tell strangers my problems and tried to walk away, but instead of letting me go on alone they said, "We're all having a cup of coffee. Join us!" "No," I said, "I really don't feel like it. We don't really know each other..." They stopped me in mid-sentence and said, "Well then, this is a good time to start!"

These ladies were so kind, and God bless them for being so persistent. I ended up sitting with them and sharing a little about my life.

They seemed very interested and likable, and soon I became part of their group. From then on they made a point of picking me up each morning for a walk on the beach. I began to look forward to seeing them, and I enjoyed going for those walks in a place where I had just recently contemplated suicide!

The fact that my daughters were so devoted to me also kept me going. My youngest daughter, Carol, who had moved to Massachusetts, knew that I wasn't adjusting well to my new home, and she finally said, "Mom, you have to keep your spirits up. How can you have any energy to spend on your grandchildren if you let sadness overwhelm you? Why not move to Santa Barbara and start a new life? That way you'll still be close to Roselyn, but you'll also have the freedom of a little place of your own. You're going crazy just wandering around Carpinteria." I had to admit that this was true, and eventually I found a place of my own in Santa Barbara. My daughters helped me get settled in, and things began to get better.

This was when I decided to really put everything into my volunteer work. Toni found something suitable for me, and I enjoyed my work even though it meant driving from Santa Barbara. I received a lot of nice certificates for my volunteering at different places, but I would have done it without any recognition at all. I felt useful working as a volunteer, and I met more people because of it. For example, I became acquainted with a German lady who was a very accomplished piano player. She put on wonderful little concerts in her trailer-home. Even though I learned she immigrated to America before the war, I suppose I should have felt strange associating with a German. I can't explain my reaction to her except to say that this woman was very kind to me and so I responded in a similar way. Maybe losing my husband caused me to look at things at little differently. Anyway, social activities like these seemed to make life interesting again. I found reasons to go out, even taking up an exercise class.

Through my volunteer work I met a Japanese-American woman named Masa. She and I were in our early seventies, and we became good friends. Unlike me, she spoke freely of her past, and she began to tell me about her experiences during the war. I had never heard of "internment camps." I only knew of Japan's nervy move of bombing America! But Masa told me that during World War II many Japanese-Americans were put into special camps. Apparently the government was concerned over some of these people becoming spies for the Japanese. It seems silly now, but people were very paranoid at the time. Masa told me that she and her family were suddenly treated as suspicious foreigners. The camp where she stayed was not pleasant, but of course it was nothing like the camps created by the Nazis for Jews. She said to me, "Yes, it was difficult being taken from my home and forced to live in a camp built in a harsh environment. We had so little to do. This was frustrating for me because I was a young woman. We did not have the same advantages and opportunities of other Americans, but we were never hungry or beaten, and we weren't forced to work."

Masa also told me that she spoke about her experiences through a Mrs. Elisabeth Chowning at Carpinteria High School. This teacher developed a good program for senior students that allowed them to learn firsthand about the past. Mrs. Chowning was currently trying to expose the students to people who had lived through World War II. It was at this point Masa asked, "Could you tell me a little bit about your own experience during the war? I noticed that you had an accent and so I assume you are not from here."

"Oh Masa," I said with a shrug, "my experience was so different from yours. I don't think you want to hear about it." I think Masa knew I was having trouble overcoming my past. Maybe she suspected that I had had a tough time during the war, even though I hadn't told her anything about those years. I tried to make it sound as if nothing unusual happened to me, but Masa persisted in her questions. She tried to make me open up a little, saying, "Your experience must have been worse than my own. We were taken from our homes and put in a very unpleasant area. But at least for me it turned out to be a good thing. I met my husband there!"

I saw pictures of Masa when she was young. She was very pretty, and she must have been so much fun to be around even if it was in an internment camp. Her marriage lasted many years, and her children grew up to be successful, kind people. Masa didn't bear a grudge against the American government for what they did to her and her family. She received compensation and I think that helped a little bit. I suppose I can understand why Americans were afraid of the Japanese living among them. Wars change people in this way.

My friend continued to ask me about the war, until one day I finally opened up. It was really the first time I ever told someone all about what I had gone through. I spoke to Masa for about an hour, telling her how I lost my family and a little bit of how I survived by pretending to be a Gentile Pole. She was amazed and I think a little surprised that I had let her in on so much.

"That English teacher at Carpinteria High School, Mrs. Chowning, is interested in people who lived through the war," she reminded me. "You should speak about your experiences with her." I let the topic drop until one day Masa mentioned that she was going to speak at the high school. I personally felt that my experiences during the war were too traumatic and gruesome for young people to hear. I thought that it would be wrong to expose even high school students to such a thing. My early years as a Jewish immigrant gave me the impression that everyone wanted to forget what happened during the war. Watching my family disappear, my mother's death, and my time in a labor camp were horrible experiences for me to remember. Who would want to hear about these things, and for that matter why would I want to relive it?

I made it very clear to Masa that I didn't wish to speak to Mrs. Chowning's class. "No," I insisted, "it's out of the question. I've never spoken in front of a group, and people won't be interested. My husband and relatives didn't want to hear me speak about the war, and nobody else will either." I firmly believed that, at least in America, the subject of what happened to Jews during the war was taboo. After I explained this to Masa and was clearly all talked out my friend said, "Goodness, that is a shame! Now I am certain that you should talk to the students and tell them this big secret! I know that it was the most tragic time in your life, but they should know what it was like for Jewish people in Europe, even if it is an unpleasant piece of history."

I just shook my head. "Really, Masa," I insisted, "let's not discuss this any longer. I don't want to go back to that time. Please just let it go." She made as if the discussion had been laid to rest, but then later she called the school and spoke to the English teacher about me, and can you believe it, Mrs. Chowning called me the next day! She introduced herself and said, "I have to meet you, Mrs. Morecki. Why not come to the school and just tell me a little about the war?"

I tried to put her off, explaining, "Oh, I couldn't possibly come. I have too much to do here in Santa Barbara." I tried to get out of it by telling her I had no transportation to the school.

"Well," she said, "we'll just have to get you here somehow. If it's difficult for you to get to the school then we'll send someone to pick you up." Anyone else would have given up on me, but not that Mrs. Chowning. When she said something was going to happen, well that's how it was going to be! Before we finished our telephone conversation she suggested I speak alongside Masa, just to be comfortable. I told her that I wouldn't come if this was the plan. So Mrs. Chowning agreed that my first visit would be as an observer only. She made me promise to at least show up and refused to take no for an answer.

Well, what else could I say? "Of course," I told her, "I would love to hear Masa speak."

That night as I lay in bed I thought, "What if the students ask me about the war? I can hardly make sense of it myself, how could I possibly speak to a room full of young people about those years?" Even with these misgivings, the next morning I went along as promised. By now I was a little intrigued but I still didn't want to speak in front of the class. Among other things, I was afraid that the students wouldn't understand my accent. I told myself not to worry because it had been made clear to me that I would not speak.

Masa presented her story and I sat to listen. She did a good job explaining things to the students, and after she finished I assumed we would go home. But Mrs. Chowning turned to me and said, "Now it's your turn!"

I couldn't believe it! This lady would not give up! I couldn't very well argue with a teacher in front of her students, but words cannot describe how nervous I was. My palms began to sweat, and I walked up to the front of that classroom with shaky legs. After all these years of forced silence I wasn't prepared to speak, and I wondered if I could do it. Mrs. Chowning just put her hand on my shoulder, smiled and softly said, "Well, you have walked all the way to the front here, so you have to say something. You're not going to embarrass me in front of the students by refusing me, are you?"

She didn't really give me the opportunity to say no. She looked me straight in the eye and said to the students, "Mrs. Morecki will tell us a little about the war as she experienced it. Nina, tell us something about what you went through."

"I have tried so hard to forget the war," I whispered to Mrs. Chowning, "how can I remember anything now?"

"It doesn't have to be any prepared speech," she assured me, "and you don't have to tell things in order. Just say what's in your heart." She pushed me in front of that room full of students, and I started my speaking career.

Well, I was in a spot. I don't know how I did it, but I swallowed hard and started to speak. As I heard myself explaining what my life had been like just before the war I thought, "Nina, what are you doing? This teacher must be wrong. You don't know whether or not these young people want to listen to such things." But I kept speaking anyway, almost as if I was in a dream. I told them a little about my family and my childhood, and then began to speak about Nazi crimes.

If I had known at the time that I was speaking to a senior honors class I couldn't have continued. Most of the students planned on going on to universities or colleges and they were so bright. I may have been using poor English at times, but Mrs. Chowning seemed pleased, so I must have been clear enough to her students. It felt strange to be giving my version of a war that had happened long before any of these students were born; however, as I went on, I could see that they were actually very interested! They were old enough to grasp the details, and apparently they wanted to know more, because once I finished they had millions of questions. Somehow, when they started asking me those questions, my memory clicked in. I found that I could recall details from my past that had eluded me before. With their interest and Mrs. Chowning's encouragement I spoke for a long time.

When I felt that I had said all I could, I simply stopped talking. I stood in front of the students not knowing what to do. Mrs. Chowning saw that they were still enthusiastic, so as a good teacher she took advantage of their interest and suggested that they make a project out of my story. She asked if they could put my experience down in writing, and this was the first time the idea ever came up. I agreed that that would be all right, and as I was leaving Mrs. Chowning came up to me, saying, "Oh, Nina, you have to come again to speak. It would be so good for next year's students to hear your story."

I have to admit that I felt better after finally speaking about the past. It was as if a huge weight had been lifted from me. Even if it was only for a short time, it felt good to have been relieved of this burden. I told Mrs. Chowning that I would definitely think it over. To my surprise and delight the students sent me letters of appreciation for my time with them, and they all commented on how excited they were to work with me on their new project. As it turned out they did a beautiful job with it, and at the end of the year they invited me to a big graduation party! It was in one of the student's private homes, and I was treated like an honored guest. I have a photograph of that day, and every time I think back on it I am still very moved that the students treated me so well.

That day after I spoke Masa winked at me and said, "I knew that you would be good at this!" She was right. I didn't mind it a bit, and I felt a certain amount of satisfaction telling others about those years. I began to present at the high school more often, and I discovered that I actually liked to speak in public. It seemed to come very naturally to me, and now I felt as if I could do something important with my time. I never felt as if my life had any real meaning until then. I had been a mother and a wife, and I loved my family, but once Josef died I thought, "What's the use? What do I do with myself now?"

Now, I wanted to help others understand about the victims of war and prejudice. I no longer felt as if I was living day to day. Speaking to the students that day in 1993 gave me purpose and a new perspective on life. I began to have interest in the news and in the world around me.

I went to a program one night to hear a man give a lecture about the city of Baghdad. He was very intelligent, and he spoke of the centuries-old culture of this city. Here was this man with I don't know how many Ph.D.s, and I had the nerve to ask him a question. "I also think that history is very important," I said, "but it has been neglected compared to the fields of science and mathematics, computers, or even English." I asked him, "With more emphasis on the subject of history don't you think our students could better their lives a bit more and apply the lessons of past mistakes?" Well, everybody started to applaud, which really surprised me because I thought this was an unpopular idea. I suppose some people think the same way after all.

When young people write me letters of thanks for speaking at their school they often tell me how different it is from learning about the Holocaust using books or films. When one hears history from the source it really makes a difference. In a way it is proof that history is flesh and blood. Hearing somebody speak of how they survived something like the Holocaust helps young people to appreciate and cherish life. I always emphasize how important it is for us to tolerate each others' differences. This means we all need to try and understand different cultures, including the wide variety of religious beliefs that exist in our world.

I once met a man who questioned me about how Catholics and Jews were different. He taught at a parochial school where I was speaking, and he asked, "Why did so many people wish to persecute the Jews? We believe very strongly in Moses' Ten Commandments, and aren't they the kind of ideals that Jesus was preaching?" What I do know is that until we can, without fear, embrace our differences, we can never live happily together.

BY SPEAKING about her Holocaust experience, Nina could begin her much-needed healing process. As with many Jews, survival brought for Nina a detrimental combination of shame and despair. Giving voice to the calamities she endured at the hands of the Nazis allowed her not only the opportunity to validate her experience, it also gave her purpose.

Educating younger generations in lessons she learned from the Holocaust is a goal Nina continues to share with survivors worldwide. During her research on the effects of Holocaust memoirs, Elisheva Baumgarten discovered that the survivor's story is ultimately, "…Written for members of their families, the author wants his or her grandchildren to close the book with an understanding of where their grandparent fits into all they know about the Holocaust, and how this piece of the past fits into the present they know."[2] Nina tentatively began her own attempts at educating young people about the Holocaust by speaking in local high school classes. As she gained confidence in her abilities as a public speaker, she accepted more invitations to enhance young peoples' knowledge of World War II and the Jewish experience during that period of time.

Since that first time that I spoke in 1993 I have gained so much. Young people look at life differently, and they interpret my story in ways that never would have occurred to me. Many of them remark that they are touched and changed by how I survived. I am pleased that they connect with both the sentimental as well as the intellectual part of history. In 1995, the students of Mrs. Chowning's English class even helped to compile my story. It was written up by my friend, Alice White, as a sort of open letter to young people. Perhaps they are intrigued because mine is a sort of living history. I also believe that young people are more aware of the damage racism can do. Another Holocaust could easily occur, and the students I have spoken to want to be prepared to combat such a thing.

I feel a deep connection with young people because when I went through the war I was around the same age. Speaking to an older audience is a little different. The adults ask completely different questions, and I wonder if perhaps they would be more interested if I spoke also about my life as an immigrant or a working mother. They might find the story of my husband's passing and how I coped as a widow more compelling. The younger students take things very much to heart, and when they write to me their letters mean so much. Sometimes they even add, "I'll never forget you."

So this is the way it all started. Speaking to students about the war has become my obsession. It was so unexpected, but after all, many things were completely unexpected throughout my entire life. I didn't expect to lose my family, and I didn't expect to live through the execution the Nazis attempted on me. I didn't expect to survive the war by working with the Underground, and I certainly didn't expect so many examples of kindness from complete strangers.

But there you are. It was hard for me to recall those dark years, but I now look forward to my speaking engagements. I am so pleased to meet so many young people, and I value each generation for what they bring to our future. Unfortunately, genocide still exists around the world. If I can reach just one young person with the message that we must fight against it, then my family's disappearance and my survival will count for something. It feels somehow essential to my soul that I share my story. And yes, it is my time to do so.

BECOMING A PUBLIC SPEAKER on the Holocaust did not immediately appeal to Nina. Only with great effort and courage could she bring herself to discuss the war with others. Nina's feeling of success had always been generated through her ability to find work. It would take time for her to embrace the idea that these speaking engagements could become the most satisfying work of all. Inevitably our discussion would lead to what young readers could learn from her story. Their future was and is her primary concern. In the process of educating young people about the Holocaust, Nina rediscovered herself and found what she believed to be the purpose of her survival.

L'Chaim, To Life

(1880-1935)

AFTER COMPLETING Nina's story I wondered whether an epilogue would be necessary. After all, once we covered her youth, the war years, and her experience as a wife, mother, widow, and public speaker, had we not said everything there was to say about Nina's life? But my friend wished to express more about her personal legacy of the Holocaust and how it came to define who she is today. She dedicates her later years to keeping the memory alive of what had happened to her family. But this she does with the souls of future generations in mind, trying to focus only on important facts, while at the same time delivering her information with a healthy sprinkling of anger and deep sincerity.

I stopped asking Nina questions. It was time to be silent. After a pause of some length, she offered up her own summary of reflections about how she had managed to cope with her past, and described her hopes for the future.

I know that the war has changed me. Even now it is difficult for me to see the homes of other people my age because they have memories hanging everywhere. My identity from the time before the war seems almost completely lost to me now. There is almost nothing that I can point to and say, "This is from my family and our home," except for the few photos that our housemaid Hania saved. There are times when I look at a picture of my family, or a place that meant something to me long ago, and I wonder if I was really there. It is all like a dream until the sorrow or the joy comes back.

When I look at the few photos I do have I often feel such torment. Did I ever participate in that life, or was it someone else who had the lovely family and home? I think of all that I wanted to accomplish as a young woman and realize I never had the time or opportunity to do anything but survive. Naturally I am proud of the family Josef and I created, but I always wonder if I should have done more with myself.

When I think back on the years that I survived the war my mind is like a carousel. To recall details is much more difficult now than it was even two or three years ago. I'm so afraid that in a few months I will forget everything, and that is why I am in such a hurry now to reach a larger audience with my story. At the risk of contradicting myself, I have to say that I do not speak about my past with the people who live in my apartment complex. Most of them don't even know that I'm Jewish or anything about my past. One of my neighbors is a lady from Poland, but we didn't speak of what we had in common for a long while. She finally came to me one day and said, "I liked the atmosphere of our temple in Poland. I used to go with my husband." I never even realized she was a Jew! I don't know why, but after learning she was I never asked her for details about her past, or what happened to her husband. I simply assumed that she was as private about these things as I am. Maybe this is a trait left over from the war, but other than the young people I speak to at schools, I am not very open with people. People say I am like a closed book and I say, "Yes, I am closed off, because in the past this sort of behavior was essential. My life depended on it."

I DO NOT BELIEVE that Nina is the same person who fled Poland to start a new life in America. The war had left its scars, this cannot be denied. But there was more to Nina than her Holocaust survivor identity. Yes, she happily took up the cause of educating others about her experience, but did this mean Nina wished to be seen as a survivor first and foremost? Even at the end of our interviews I had many unanswered questions. Had the constant pressure to deny her true identity as a young woman completely erased the person Nina had been before the war? After liberation, had she felt a certain obligation to heighten the Jewish identity that once encumbered her very survival? The Nazis spent the entire war proclaiming Jews were worthless. Did the constant barrage of propaganda ever once diminish her desire to claim the faith of her ancestors? And finally, had the guilt she carried for surviving actually caused her to shy away from her Jewishness?

Ultimately I came to understand that there were no pat answers that explained Nina's personality. My friend was more than a sad byproduct of war. Though she carried the scars of every hardship and terrifying encounter brought about by the Nazis, she had actually moved beyond it long ago.

After speaking to a group of students, a boy asked me what I would do to Hitler if I had him in front of me. I like to think that revenge is not slumbering away in my heart, so I suppose I wouldn't pull out a gun on Hitler and start shooting. What good would that do? I can guarantee you that Mr. Hitler and I would have a very long discussion, and I really don't think that I would stop until I received an apology from him. I am very stubborn in this way. But after all, Hitler thought he was doing everyone a favor by killing Jews. He looked at us as if we were vermin.

According to the Nazis there were certain characteristics that Jews had, and that was supposed to make them easy to weed out from the rest of the population. I didn't have the hooked nose, or even the manner of speech that a lot of Jewish people had, and maybe that was what really saved me time and again. Anyway, the whole concept of generalizing people in such a manner is ridiculous to begin with. If we were all alike then how would Hitler explain Jews like me? What does that do to the Nazi theory that Jews are one way and Aryans another? If one cannot distinguish between a Jew and the so-called "Aryan," then how are they truly different?

When I first came to America I would have denied my Jewish heritage to any stranger who asked me. This kind of thinking still affects me, and I still wonder if that is the first question they ask of themselves when they meet me. When I was growing up in Poland it was not uncommon for people to wonder, "Is she a Jew?" upon meeting me. So even now I sometimes ask myself, "What is wrong with you, Nina Morecki? Why are you trying to deny who you really are?"

AMONG HOLOCAUST SURVIVORS, identity confusion can be one of the most tragic byproducts of their experience. Many victims struggle to resolve these conflicting feelings, and they often find themselves either playing down their Jewish heritage, or proclaiming it whenever possible.

Nina continued to grapple with her Jewish identity even as we completed her memoirs.

Maybe I have not completely come to terms with what happened to me during the war. This thing about Jewish identity is not only something that affects me. I once went through the Museum of Tolerance in Los Angeles, California, and the guide presenting various displays was around my age. She shared her thoughts as a survivor, saying, "You will never know what it was like to live through such a thing." People wanted to take her picture, but some of them hesitated. They talked among themselves, and I heard a few people saying that the guide didn't "look Jewish"! It just strikes me as ironic that those of us hiding during the war were forced to deny our heritage, and now we have to convince people that we truly are Jews who survived the slaughter!

A few years ago I met some people who were represented in Steven Spielberg's film, "Schindler's List." I remember one man in particular. He was from Krakow and had practically been the right-hand man to Schindler. Once this man had settled in America he established a very fancy shop, in my neighborhood on Beverly Drive, no less. He sold lovely leather goods from Italy, and one day I happened to go in. When he heard my accent he said, "Oh, I am from Poland too!" We talked about our home towns and later met each other's families.

At first we didn't talk about being survivors. We just didn't approach things like that back then. Later when Mr. Spielberg's film came out I felt it was a good idea to tell stories such as these. Maybe it would bring people who had never heard of the Holocaust to really think about this part of history. Before the Spielberg film was released it seemed as if the media felt that point in history was too ugly to expose. Naturally it is important for projects like these to awaken the public to the reality of what happened during the war. But it also allows some of the quieter survivors a sort of license to speak out. Nowadays people do not understand this, but each survivor has a different story, because each of us had a different upbringing and personality. This meant that each and every survivor had a different reaction to things that happened during the war that was unique to them.

My only criticism with Spielberg's film is that it did not show how bad things really were. This was most probably because a modern audience cannot tolerate viewing the constant slaughter of human beings. If Mr. Spielberg depicted this in his movie then nobody would stay for the entire film; people would become revolted and turn away. I believe Mr. Spielberg's goal was to send an important message through film about this man Schindler, and this he did very well. Perhaps now people can begin to understand how the Nazis took away more than our family and friends; they took away everything that was consistent in our lives.

Before the war we had hopes and dreams. Our lives were fairly reliable and safe. Once the Germans took charge we all expected to die at any moment. Most Jews could not even properly mourn the passing of a loved one, because we didn't know how they were killed, or even if they were truly dead. The experience of watching people disappear left a permanent hole. Seeing the Spielberg film helped me to recognize how the war affected me in these ways.

Giving my story to Colette to make into a book was good for me on many levels. Primarily, the work became a sort of victory over the Nazis, and it made me feel stronger somehow. I didn't mind too much reliving things during our interviews, because it reminded me of how my mother told stories about her past to me. Sitting down to discuss the war and everything that happened afterwards also allowed me to unload my sorrow a bit. Certainly it was a chance to talk about the war more philosophically.

Telling my story was a personal choice, and this was important to me. Victims of the Holocaust were not given the choice to live or die. Situations were imposed on us, and those who survived were extremely lucky. There were small attempts at resistance, I suppose, such as those who fought in the Warsaw ghetto. But individually we were powerless. Even if one personally made the choice to take a stand he or she then ran the risk of endangering others. In retaliation and as a deterrent, the Nazis executed everyone around a Jew who acted in defiance.

Some people say that we were led like sheep to slaughter, but I don't think this is true. Jews had dealt with racism before, and expected things to go much the same way as it had in the past. We believed that if we cooperated with the government, and toughed things out, then the pogroms against us would eventually die down. By the time we realized this would not be the case, the Nazis had completely taken away our rights and dignity. Once we were forced into ghettos and cattle cars we were reduced to something lower than human beings. It became very clear that we were trapped with no real way out. This is why survivors spend the rest of their lives wondering why they were spared while their loved ones perished.

I told myself while I was in the Janowska labor camp that if it was meant to be, I would survive. I am now glad that I did manage to make it through the war. I know that I have been blessed by my children, and I had a good life with my husband for a long time. Still, at the time of my struggle I didn't know that I would have these things to be thankful for. One cannot deny that there is sorrow in life, for some more than others. But I am proof that there are good reasons to persevere. At times it would have been much easier to die, and I actually had to come up with excuses for going on with life. To be honest, even now there are days when I wonder if I should go on.

But every life has a purpose, and I refuse to sit and dwell on what happened during the war. I try to remember what I learned from it, and then help to educate young people accordingly. Instead of remaining bitter over what happened to me, or feeling resentment toward people that have hurt me, people who have probably died long ago, well I go for a walk and clear my mind of it. I try to appreciate life.

Still, I have to ask, "Why, why was I chosen to be saved? And can I forgive?" Colette has asked me if I could ever find it in my heart to forgive the Nazis for what they did to my family and me. Usually whenever forgiveness is brought up I try to avoid the subject. I worry that my experiences during the war have turned me into not such a nice person. Carrying around such hatred is unhealthy, even if it is well deserved. I avoid words such as "killing" and "hating." What matters to me is that others understand and respect what my people went through. I believe this is what all survivors wish for.

THROUGHOUT OUR CONVERSATIONS Nina and I spoke frequently about religion. I was very interested in knowing how someone like Nina could survive without some resource of spiritual strength. There were times this question came up when she spoke publicly, and Nina answered that overall she had remained true to her Jewish faith. Privately, however, she admitted that there were times she felt incapable of recognizing God at all. After all she been through it was understandable that she would, at the very least, be angry with Him. As a Christian, I was curious to learn how she dealt with her relationship with God, a relationship that, because of the war, had grown complicated and unsatisfying.

My friend expressed that she was glad to have been raised as a Jew, and by all accounts she loved the Jewish traditions her mother maintained in their home. However, during the war Nina often felt abandoned by her God. Hiding her faith had been a taxing exercise on her already weary soul, and she felt that posing as a Gentile had somehow compromised that faith. Once in America, Nina was able to freely practice her traditions. Raising her daughters in the religion of their ancestors became very important to her, and she enjoyed following her mother's example of keeping a kosher home.

Unfortunately, without the benefit of openly examining her past, Nina struggled to have a personal relationship with God.

When I was younger I believed in God. I knew how to keep the traditions, and I wouldn't have dreamed of marrying a Gentile boy. But I was not raised to pray, for instance, like a Christian would pray. The war changed everything, but you can bet I had plenty of conversations with God, and afterwards I was angry with Him. After the war my feelings about God and my Jewish faith were unresolved. Josef and I raised the girls in the Jewish religion, but I had no Jewish friends while living in Carpinteria, so there was no way to attempt to restore my faith. Because I had no other way of connecting to people, I went to the Church of the Nazarene around 1992. The ladies who invited me to have coffee with them attended this church, and I enjoyed listening to the different speakers there, but I remained unmoved by the service. Perhaps it was some kind of rebellion against God, but after a while I didn't want to attend these services. I also did not wish to hurt the feelings of my friends or the pastor, however.

I began to think of ways to manage this. Some of the ladies couldn't attend services because they had small children to look after. I thought that maybe I could help by watching the little ones while their mothers attended the sermon, and I became very good at this. One of the babies could wake up an entire neighborhood with his crying! I became especially close to him, and every Sunday we played together. When his mother brought him to me I would say, "Hello honey! I love you and I'll take good care of you." His mother couldn't believe how her baby boy stopped crying when she handed him to me. She thought that I had some kind of magic touch. Anyway, this was more satisfying to me than going to the service.

One Sunday I went into the sanctuary of the Church. Nobody had arrived yet, and I was alone. I stood there at the foot of the big cross positioned on the wall. As I gazed up at Jesus on the cross he looked down on me, and we had a little talk. "You know," I told Him, "on account of your being crucified we Jews have suffered so much." I suppose I wanted to put the blame on Jesus. In my heart was such a strong sorrow, and I could not get beyond it. "People do things in your name," I informed Jesus, "but so often things end up exactly the opposite of what you preached. Why don't people understand what you said? Your words were beautiful, but many people twist them to hurt others!"

Something happened in that moment. I felt a kind of connection as I stood there giving Him a piece of my mind. All of the fear and pain I had kept to myself during the war was choking me. Every bit of anger and hurt came out of me while I spoke to Jesus, and I suppose I was speaking to God as well. I realized how angry I had been with God for taking the people I loved away from me. Was I meant to suffer because I was Jewish? The thought infuriated me, so I ignored God as a way of rebelling against Him.

Suddenly I felt empty. "I don't want to come here any more," I said out loud, but there was no answer. I stopped going to the church immediately after that, and for a while I didn't feel anything at all. Eventually, however, I found a local temple and began to think more about my own religion again. I started to come to terms with things little by little. I said to myself, "I am a Jew, and I always will be." I continued to enjoy having coffee with my lady friends, but I never said anything to them or anyone else about what had happened when I was alone in their church. I didn't want them to know about my little argument with Jesus. This is the first time I have ever spoken about it.

So people might ask what I think of my Jewish faith at this point in my life. I go to temple when I can, but even now I am sometimes angry with God. When I think of what hell might be like, I think of those years during the war. It has gotten to the point where I refuse to feel guilty about speaking of it anymore. As I said, for a long time the Holocaust was a dirty little secret among my people, and I think it was unhealthy to keep our suffering buried within our hearts. This kind of behavior made me question God. How could there be answers for me if nobody wanted to discuss this topic in the first place? Still, I continue to turn to Him. Perhaps it is the way I was brought up, but something will not allow me to let Him go. God allowed me to survive, but there are still days when I think I would rather have gone with my family. If I was spared in order to tell others about what happened during the war, then it has been a responsibility that is sometimes very hard to take on.

NINA BEGAN to softly cry as she spoke. Up to this point I never clearly understood how bearing the burden of giving testimony as a Holocaust survivor weighed heavily upon her slender shoulders. It seemed unfair to have placed my gentle friend in such a position. What would Nina's fate have been had she not been born a Jew? All of her dreams and aspirations might have been realized, but would she be the same person? Was it Nina's spirit that drew me to her, or the stubborn will she developed over the years as a means of survival?

I had already decided that the war had not changed Nina's character, but it did leave a mark of sadness upon her soul that would never be completely erased. With every missing member of her family, portions of Nina's heart were also taken away. A youthful abundance of hope and trust in the future had been replaced by a pragmatic acceptance of life's limitations. Nina saw this as a flaw and she lamented its effect on her.

So, what does anyone really know about God? Is He a Christian, or a Muslim, or even a Jewish God? Why would He allow so many to perish in the Holocaust, and why would He decide to let someone like me survive? I prayed so often and so bitterly to Him, yet it seemed as if He never heard me.

Religious people say that God is present even in the face of tragedy. I don't know about that. I'm not educated in theology, so I cannot say. Christians have told me that life is a struggle between good and evil, but I have decided I don't believe in the devil. I only believe that people have a choice between the two. I have asked rabbis and priests why we suffer. I have a friend who is an Episcopalian priest, and every time we get together I have this same question. He says to me, "God has certain plans for you and your people. Regardless of what happens, you will always exist. Look how many nations have risen and then fallen. Still the Jews survive. There must be some meaning to this." When I tell my friend that it would be better for God to hurry up with this plan we both have to laugh. Life would be unbearable if we could not find humor over things we cannot understand.

I want to tell others what happened during the war as a sort of warning of what prejudice can do to people. I continue to challenge racism because this irrational hatred is such a concern to me. I know that having my story written might not change things, and eventually I will have to leave the final project up to fate. I only want to explain to everyone, and especially to young people, how World War II and the Holocaust affected so many human beings. It created a sick society. I actually spent very little time in a camp compared to other Jews. But the experience changed me right down to my heart. After the war I heard of Jews who had nervous breakdowns, and I can understand how the pressure could finally get to them. Everything we had been brought up to respect—our principles, our religion, and the sense of right and wrong—was called into question. The Germans destroyed our feeling of unity and humanity. I never want another generation to experience these feelings.

I still feel some resentment. When I heard that the Berlin Wall came down, well for a while I thought that it should remain up. I can say a few things about being walled up. Why not let the Germans, who took my family from me, feel what it's like to be separated from others? Well, not all Germans are the same, and I think the time has come to let these thoughts go. My aim is now to speak out against discrimination and genocide, not just for the Jewish people, but for every human being.

Well, I have told my entire story now, and it feels good to have finished it. We had some difficulties finishing this project. There was the problem of my memory for example. It was not always as strong as I would have liked. I am certain there are some little incidents that I have forgotten to tell. Colette went over things again and again with me, looking at each experience from different angles so that we could be assured of the facts. It was a challenge and sometimes very painful. I tried to give up most everything in my life that was fit to print, but I did not wish to touch upon some things. I feel that it is my business to bear the pain of what happened, and I chose to keep some of the more personal parts of my life private. Colette and I have given this book our best efforts, and expectations of it are cautiously optimistic. My greatest hope is for it to reach a large audience, and perhaps to change the way people think.

When I read the stories of other Holocaust survivors I realize they provide a lot of detail. I am different from them in two ways. First, I began to tell my story rather late in life when my memory was not as fresh. I am also different from many other survivors in that I have told my story from childhood to the present. Colette and I discussed what might be interesting for people to read, and she believed that the story of my life as an American immigrant, wife, mother and speaker, were as important as my story as a Holocaust survivor.

At the end of all of this I am reminded of a saying we have in Poland. I do not know how this translates exactly in English, but it goes something like this: "On the end of the tongue sometimes lays the whole word." It means that one must be careful about what is said. Some people are very open. They say, "Oh, I must share with you my every thought!" I could never really be like that. Colette once told me something she learned from her Native American friends who live on the Navajo Reservation. They have a tradition of keeping part of their stories to themselves. They never tell one person everything they know about their history or religion, because then that person would have too much spiritual power over them. To me, this makes good sense. I realize that I am taking a chance in revealing so much of myself in a book. But then, haven't I always taken chances?

When Colette turned off her tape recorder to finally say my story-telling was all captured and complete, it felt very strange. We worked together for so long, and I enjoyed our time together. It seems a little sad to say it is all over. Still, another part of life comes to replace what has passed, and I look forward to hearing what people think. And so, for now I will say *Dibitainya*. That is Polish for "Good-bye," but what it really means is, "I hope to see you again."

I would also like to say "L'chaim." In Hebrew this means "To life." I think it is best to end the last chapter of my story in this way. Because with all the tragedies that occurred in my past, I think ending the telling of it with this salute better suits my friends and family whom I lost. It is a phrase of hope to the living, and by meeting each day with enthusiasm we honor those who died during the Holocaust. As a young girl I loved life. I loved to dance with my friends before the war, and I especially loved to dance with Josef before he became ill. Now, even if I am tired, or I feel like staying home, I try to go out and experience new things. You might say that even now, if someone offers a social outing I try to accept, even though without Josef it is ultimately unsatisfying. I try to remember how much he loved the dance of life, and so I continue this "dance."

WITH THE LAST of our interviews completed I too felt at a loss. I would soon be immersed in the huge task of compiling Nina's vignettes, and finding historical data with which to frame her story. With the monumental task of reviewing Nina's life behind me, I saw the next phase of work looming ahead. The interview process had been both fascinating and difficult. I disliked having to imagine my friend in her most vulnerable and hurtful moments, but at least I had been there to hold her hand. I was astounded at how much we had learned about each other. Nina was surprised to learn she still had tears to shed over the loss of her family. I could not help but be moved by her stories, no matter how many times I had heard them. Though she refused to wallow in pity, there were moments when Nina could barely stand to recount certain episodes of her life. There were also times when her eyes twinkled with mischief, and soon she would have me laughing over some remark or ironic twist of fate. With her delightful sense of humor Nina was always able to bring us both "back to ourselves."

Nina and I keep up our friendship to this day. After sharing so many memories, disappearing from each other's lives seemed unacceptable. We had laughed and cried together over the most intimate of thoughts. Our bond was centered on conversation. It was what brought us together from the very beginning. Discussing the world and all its intricacies, endless telephone vigils and occasional weekend visits—these were pleasures neither of us could give up.

As for Nina's memoirs, well... all that could be said has been said. The end of our interviews signaled the end of our relationship as storyteller and historian. It was sad to see our days of reliving the past end, but my friend had told me many times that when one door closed on her another always opened. I knew Nina was right. Every end ushers in a new beginning, and as we place her story in public view we wait to see the results. All that could be recalled has been laid out on these pages. Perhaps now Nina can see the meaning of her survival.

I could never really know the pain and fear my friend experienced during the war. Only another survivor might come close to understanding her loss and her struggle. I am certain, however, that while the Nazis took her family, at times her dignity, even her very identity, they never could take her memory. By holding fast to those memories, and later revealing them to generations of young people, Nina has brought to light many Nazi atrocities, and brought back to life those whom the Germans had hoped to exterminate.

Perhaps Nina survived to do just this, or perhaps she survived simply because she was too stubborn to die or go mad. The reason no longer seems to matter. The Nazis attempted to put an end to my friend Nina Morecki. Who would have thought that a tiny little Jewish girl from L'vov, Poland, could ruin their plans in such glorious fashion?

As our work nears its end I realize that I am not the same person who showed up at Nina's door with tape recorder in hand. I now know that, along with the importance of asking questions, is the acceptance that some questions in life can never be answered. Nina never claimed to be any stronger than the average person, nor did she regard her actions as heroic or even clever. I once heard a quote that struck me as appropriate in summing up the life of Nina Morecki. During one of his sermons, my church's Pastor, Harold Bussell recalled a statement made by his great aunt, Madame Couleru: "Trials prove nothing. Pain is inevitable. But endurance and victory are optional."[1] These words I leave to my dear friend Nina Morecki, who not only endured, but has very clearly emerged victorious.

Acknowledgments

NINA WOULD LIKE TO RECOGNIZE the following people for their support and assistance.

Thanks to my friend, Masa Sato, for encouraging me to speak of my wartime experience for the first time. Without your urging, the idea of sharing the pain of those years with young people might never have occurred to me.

To my daughter, Carol Oberg, for supporting my vision to share this story with others, and for assisting me in every way throughout the most difficult times of my life.

To Alice White, for planting the seed of making my life story accessible to young people in the form of an open letter.

To Mrs. Elisabeth Chowning, my deepest appreciation for insisting I speak to that first room of hopeful young faces. Because of your insistent nature I eventually came to understand the worth of expressing my feelings to these bright students.

To Casey Roberts, yet another fine teacher at Carpinteria High School who carried the torch once Mrs. Chowning retired. Your unflagging support and friendship have meant the world to me. Your students have been a delight and I enjoy meeting them still.

To the Reverend Canon Brian Cox of Christ the King Episcopal Church, Santa Barbara, California, I express my gratitude for your sensitivity toward my culture and my religion. I have learned so much through our friendship, and will always value it.

To Dr. Harold Marcuse of the University of California, Santa Barbara, a million thanks for introducing me to your college students. I truly appreciate how you shared your passion for Holocaust history with me, and how you allowed me to tell my story to a larger audience.

Every single person I have mentioned here has made me feel loved and part of an extended family. I am blessed to have met each of you.

Colette's Acknowledgments

FIRST AND FOREMOST I wish to thank Nina Morecki for sharing her life with me, and for trusting me to develop her story into a piece of work that we both hope will touch many lives. Thank you, my friend. You are an exceptional colleague and a true inspiration.

I would also like to thank my friend and mentor, Larry Manson, who taught me to see history from every angle and to always treat the past with respect.

I could not have completed this book without the constant aid of Dr. Harold Marcuse. Harold, I deeply appreciate the part you played in bringing Nina and me together. Through your teaching I gained a better understanding of the Holocaust and the manner in which this event affected so many people. What a delight it was to pore over maps and textbooks with you.

I greatly value those who participated in furthering Nina's and my mission of reaching as many people as possible with her story. Among those who contributed to our project I wish to especially thank Casey Roberts for his camaraderie and support, and Carol Oberg for her acceptance and trust in me to develop her mother's story. I would also like to recognize my editors Ilene Segalove for her advice and amazing insight, and Catherine Viel for her immeasurable support and keen eye. Thanks also to Dee Dee DeGelia for her endless hours of photographic work. My publishing consultant Ellen Reid deserves enormous credit for shepherding this book to completion. I am grateful for every member of our team, and appreciate your talent and especially your patience.

A special tip of the hat goes out to my family; children Raven, Casey, Rhianna and Carly, my Da' the Reverend Daniel Pike and my sisters Charlotte and Caroline. You have all taught me one of the most important skills in life…how to laugh at myself.

Finally, I wish to express my love and respect for the love of my life, Ross Waddell. I am very fortunate to have been blessed with such a wonderful life partner. I thank you from the bottom of my heart, Blue.

Nina's Chronology

Although some dates pertaining to Nina Morecki's personal history are supported by documentation, most are approximate according to her memory of past events. Historical dates concerning World War II and the Holocaust were obtained from Landau, Ronnie S. *The Nazi Holocaust.* Ivan R. Dee Publishers: Chicago, 1994, and from Weber, Louis. *The Holocaust Chronicle.* Lincolnwood, Illinois: Publications International, Ltd. 2000.

Circa 1880—Nina's father Viktor (also spelled "Wigdor") Grütz is born in Zlochow, Poland. At that time Zlochow was part of Hungary. His family later moves to L'vov, Poland, where his father operates a soap and candle business similar to that run by the family of his future bride.

1885—Nina's mother, Rosa Roth, is born in L'vov, Poland (other Polish spellings are "Lwow" as well as "Lwiw," the Ukranian "L'viv," and German "Lemberg").

1908—Nina's older sister, Lina, is born.

1909—Nina's middle sister, Helena, is born.

December 14, 1912—Nina's future husband, Josef Morecki, is born in Lublin, Poland. His mother dies in his arms when he is seven and by the age of fourteen he moves to his sister's home in L'vov and finds work selling galoshes. He eventually becomes the director of a large retail shoe store.

December 24, 1920—Nina Grütz is born in L'vov, Poland.

1926—Nina begins public schooling.

1930—Nina prepares to enter *gymnasium* after being bedridden for nearly a year with an infection in her joints that weakens her heart. Private tutoring is provided to facilitate her advancement to the next year's level of schooling.

1931—Lina marries Bernard ("Buzio") Tanne, a physician.

January 30, 1933—Adolf Hitler is appointed Chancellor. Nazis take control of German state.

April 25, 1933—Law against the Overcrowding of German Schools discriminates against Jewish teachers and students, barring from the school system in Germany.

August 2, 1933—Germany's President Hindenburg dies and Hitler combines the offices of chancellor and president, declaring himself "Führer," or "leader."

1935—Lina gives birth to Nina's niece, Alma.

September 15, 1935—Hitler issues the Nuremberg Laws, revoking citizenship and restricting life for Jews living in Germany.

1935—Helena marries Leopold Frostig, an attorney.

March 1936—Nazi ideals begin to become popular in Poland. Hitler's influence is felt as pogroms targeting Jews increase in Nina's native country.

1937—Nina's aunt Erna, uncle Leon, and cousin Miriam visit from America. They stay for nearly a year. Nina is invited back to America for a visit; however, Rosa Grütz insists her daughter remain in Poland.

March 12, 1938—Germany's push west brings about the Austrian Anschluss, allowing the spread of Nazi doctrine and causing the exodus of many Austrian Jews.

1938—Nina applies for university in Italy and Palestine. She is accepted into the pre-medical programs of both schools, and ultimately chooses the university in Palestine. She begins to fulfill the requirement of competency in the Hebrew language.

June 14, 1938—Hitler issues an order mandating that all Jewish-owned firms in Germany register with the Ministry of Economics. This move eventually allows the German government to confiscate Jewish businesses. By November of that year, Goering oversees the "Aryanization" of all Jewish businesses, and Viktor Grütz must relinquish all control over his holdings in Germany, with no compensation.

August 22, 1939—Hitler reveals to his top generals his plan of liquidating the Polish people in order to make room for German settlers in his *Lebensraum* program.

August 23, 1939—A non-aggression pact is made between Germany and the Soviet Union. Hitler agrees to allow Stalin to take the eastern portion of Poland in the coming war, while Nazi troops march into the western areas.

September 1, 1939—Germany invades Poland. The Nazi Einsatzgruppen begin to execute Poles and Jews. By the 3rd of September both Britain and France declare war on Germany. By the 21st the Nazis begin to dissolve Jewish communities within German-occupied Poland. Jews are forced into the poorer sections of every city—areas which will eventually become walled ghettos.

September 17, 1939—Soviet troops invade Poland, advancing west just short of the city of L'vov.

September 28, 1939—After three weeks of almost continuous shelling, eastern Poland is subjected to Soviet rule.

Early October–November, 1939—The Soviets confiscate the Grützes' luxurious apartment. A Russian officer takes up residence there while Nina's family is forced into a small room located on the top floor of the building.

Nina's father begins to train Russian workers in the manufacture of soap and candles. As Nina explains, Viktor Grütz "knew something was boiling in the kettle," and that when he was no longer useful to the Soviets he would be imprisoned. Nina eventually finds work in a Catholic hospital. The nuns encourage her to pursue an education in nursing and allow her to briefly work in the surgical ward. After some months Nina senses she will be replaced by the Soviets, and leaves to seek out more reliable employment.

Winter, 1939—Nina takes evening courses to study Statistics and the Russian language. This leads her to a clerical position (which lasts several months) in which she assists in gathering information for the Soviet's "Five Year Plan": a reorganization of labor that is to facilitate the transition of business from private holdings to Communist control.

November 23, 1939—In western Poland, Nazis issue orders forcing all Jews to wear a Star of David badge that allows for easy identification. By the 28th Nazis in German-occupied Poland dictate orders through newly formed Jewish Councils, or Judenrate. By the 12th of December camps are created throughout western Poland where Jewish men between the ages of fourteen and sixty are required to perform heavy labor.

February, 1940—Nina's father is arrested as a capitalist and jailed without privilege of family visitation. To ensure against her own arrest Nina relocates to the L'vov apartment of her aunt Mialcia. Rosa Grütz moves in with Lina and Bernard, where Nina visits as often as possible.

June, 1940—The family receives no further word of Viktor Grütz. It is assumed that Nina's father has either been sent to Siberia or was executed while in the L'vov prison. Nina stays temporarily with her aunt Mialcia while Rosa Grütz goes to nearby Drohobycz to live with Nina's cousin Lusia.

January 20, 1941—High Nazi officials meet in Berlin to organize the deportation of all Jews within German-occupied Europe to a system of labor camps. It is here at the "Wannsee Conference" where the "Final Solution" to eliminate Jews through hard labor or outright execution is developed. By October of 1942 the first deportations begin to the Auschwitz concentration camp in eastern Poland.

June 21, 1941—Hitler breaks the non-aggression pact with the Soviets by launching an offensive into eastern Poland.

June 30, 1941—Poland is completely subjected to Nazi rule as German forces push further east and into Russia. On this day Hitler's troops mark their entry into L'vov by beating many of the Jewish populace to death. Nina recalls this as the day in which a local synagogue is set on fire by the Nazis, trapping and burning the Jews inside at worship. It is also at this time that Nazi officials confiscate Bernard's EKG machine; however, Nina's brother-in-law continues to practice medicine and analyze EKG readings for the benefit of German officers.

July 25–27, 1941—Ukrainian citizens of L'vov accost thousands of local Jewish men and women. Two thousand are killed to avenge the 1926 murder of anti-Semitic Simon Petliura by Shalom Schwarzbard.

September, 1941—Jews in L'vov are ordered to relinquish all valuables to Nazis at collection stations within the city. Rosa Grütz returns to live with Lina and Bernard soon after.

November 8, 1941—The Jewish ghetto within L'vov is established.

November, 1941—Nina's mother leaves Lina's apartment to engage in her weekly practice of prayer in a local Jewish cemetery. She is never seen again, though it is suspected that at the age of fifty-two she was part of a round-up (*"Aktion"*) of those Jews considered too elderly or too young to work. Nina witnesses an SS mass shooting near the cemetery that day and slips into depression. She becomes ill from two weeks of malnutrition; however, after Bernard chastises her she rallies and continues her fight to survive. Even so, the loss of her mother will bring about thoughts of suicide for years to come. Throughout the winter Nina lives a transient existence, traveling first to cousin Lusia's where she finds work as a store clerk. After only two weeks she returns to L'vov, spending most nights with Lina and Bernard and occasionally finding work in the ghetto, which has not yet been completely closed off.

December 7, 1941—The United States enters the war after the Japanese attack Pearl Harbor, Hawaii, and Clark Field in the Philippines.

December 10, 1941—America declares war on Nazi Germany and Mussolini's Italy.

Winter 1941—Nina's sister Helena goes out to run an errand and disappears. The family assumes that she was captured during an *Aktion* and deported for labor. She is never seen again. While visiting a camp archive many years after the war, Nina finds Helena listed as a prisoner under her maiden name.

Winter, 1941 or early 1942—Nina and her remaining family members learn of an announcement made by occupying German forces that "he who helps a Jew will be treated as a Jew." (also see entry for April 11, 1942) All Jews in L'vov are now given instruction on how to create a white Star of David armband according to German specifications.

January 20, 1942—Nazi officials meet at an estate in the Berlin suburb of Wannsee to decide the fate of Jews living within every region conquered by the Reich. In less than ninety minutes this group, headed by Reinhard Heydrich, creates the "Final Solution" involving the extermination of some six million Jews.

February, 1942—Nina's brother-in-law Bernard learns of an upcoming round-up of Jews, or *Aktion*. He sends his wife, Lina, and child to the countryside for safety while Nina continues to travel from their apartment to the ghetto. Lina and Alma are never heard from again.

March 16, 1942—SS troops begin to carry out the "Final Solution," now known as Operation Reinhard, with a goal of the complete liquidation of Polish Jewry. Jews are transported to death camps situated throughout eastern Poland where executions take place.

March, 1942—Once again Bernard learns of an *Aktion* scheduled for the neighborhood where he has been permitted to live and practice medicine. Depressed over the idea of seeing another loved one disappear, he sends Nina away for good to fend for herself in any way she can. Nina never sees her brother-in-law again. She finds temporary lodging with a family friend by the name of Ravitsky. She stays for three weeks in the Ravitskys' attic, but fearing she will endanger the family she leaves to wander back into the L'vov ghetto, which is soon closed off entirely.

Late March, 1942—The deportation of fifteen thousand Jews from L'vov ultimately results in their execution at the Belzec death camp.

April 11, 1942—"He who assists a Jew will be treated as a Jew." A German proclamation is issued in L'vov, warning Poles against assisting Jews.

Spring, 1942—Nina is assigned to cramped quarters within the ghetto, and is shuttled for some months to a series of work details. Eventually she is permanently transported along with other able-bodied ghetto residents to Janowska Labor Camp. There she takes part in factory work and later hard outdoor labor.

Late spring, 1942—Nina escapes execution and wanders the nearby woods for an undetermined amount of time. She eventually collapses in front of the home of a peasant couple by the name of Niekolawitz. There she is cared for and sheltered. She recuperates until the end of spring at which time she slips away in the early morning and wanders the countryside in search of the Polish Underground, eventually stumbling on a group of partisans. This group supplies her with falsified papers establishing her Polish identity as Maria Kvasigroich. She is instructed to obtain employment with a German mail unit further east with the intent of stealing travel documents for partisan use.

June 24, 1942—A partial liquidation takes place at Janowska labor camp. Thousands of Jews are executed.

July 8, 1942—A second liquidation occurs at Janowska in which seven thousand Jews are murdered.

Summer, 1942—Nina works temporarily for a female official directing the German military postal unit in Dnepropetrovsk. She soon gains a more secure position under the direction of Herr Zgoda.

November 4, 1942—War shifts in favor of the allies, with British victory at El Alamein. By the 19th the Russians launch a strong counter-offensive against German forces at Stalingrad.

June 21, 1943—Although the Nazis encounter resistance from those Jews remaining in the L'vov ghetto, it is ultimately liquidated.

June, 1943—Josef Morecki has by now made his way to Romania and is working in the Zmerinka ghetto. Many of the residents here have been spared deportation, and Jews living there are eventually liberated by advancing Soviet forces.

October, 1943—Dnepropetrovsk is liberated by the Soviets. Nina's military postal operation is moved to Zaporozje.

November, 1943—Nina's unit is moved to Vinnica for four to six months. The outfit is then transported to Ghivan, close to the Romanian border.

December, 1943—Nina turns twenty-three on the 24th of this month. On the 31st she leaves her job working for the Germans in the middle of the night, escaping to Zmerinka, a small town in Romania. She finds shelter with Maria Nikolajvna, who is caring for granddaughter Erichka. Nina provides for them all by doing odd jobs.

January–June, 1944—As the Allied bombing intensifies, the German army begins its retreat, and Nina gains employment with a Soviet medical unit. When her identity comes into question, Russian officials allow her to continue working under close surveillance.

Once the Russians gain control of Zmerinka, Nina is introduced to Josef Morecki, who has been drafted into the Russian army. He is later sent west to continue fighting in Berlin.

May 15, 1944—Nazis begin to transport as many Hungarian Jews as possible to Auschwitz while the Red Army advances from the east.

June 6, 1944—Allies land at Normandy, creating a second front.

June 8, 1944—The Hungarian government, reacting to pressure from Sweden, the Red Cross, and the Vatican, halts deportations of Jews.

July 8, 1944—Assassination attempt on Adolf Hitler fails.

July 27, 1944—L'vov, Poland, is liberated by the Red Army.

July, 1944—Advancing further west to follow Red Army troops, Nina's mobile medical unit passes very close to L'vov. Nina escapes from her Soviet employers at this time in order to search for any surviving family members. She reunites with Hania, who worked for the Grütz family before the war. Nina is given shelter and a number of family photographs the former servant was able to scavenge during the Nazi takeover. She eventually makes her way back east to register with the United Nations Relief and Rehabilitation Administration in an effort to locate missing family members.

January, 1945—As the Soviet army advances, Nazis begin to force remaining Jews on death marches toward Germany. By the 28th the Red Army liberates Auschwitz-Birkenau. Remaining concentration camps are liberated throughout the spring.

April 30, 1945—After retreating to his Berlin bunker with mistress Eva Braun and remaining staff, Hitler commits suicide. His last official proclamation accuses international Jewry for Germany's defeat.

May 2, 1945—The Red Army takes control of Berlin. By the 8th of May, Germany surrenders to the Allied army. All labor and concentration camps have been liberated; however, many survivors die from illness brought about by starvation and exhaustion.

June, 1944–end of 1945—Nina and Josef are reunited, marry in Warsaw, and join a group of Jewish refugees making their way to Austria. The small band of couples travels west for over a month. They are assigned an apartment in Vienna for a short time, and then continue to Salzburg to the Displaced Persons camp run by U.S. troops where they stay for over a year. Nina falls ill with a number of consecutive ailments while Josef arranges for their eventual departure to America. The Moreckis apply for travel papers in Munich, and by March 19th they leave the port of Bremen aboard an old U.S. military ship put back into service to transport refugees.

May 6, 1947—Josef and Nina Morecki arrive at Ellis Island in New York City. Nina's Aunt and Uncle Messing arrange for the immigrants to stay temporarily in a small hotel room in the city. They very quickly find permanent accommodations with Max and Rose Banner. Both

Nina and her husband find work and begin to save as much of their paychecks as possible.

October 12, 1948—Nina gives birth to her first daughter, Roselyn.

May 6, 1950—Nina and Josef welcome their second daughter, Carol.

1959—The Morecki family relocates to California, eventually purchasing a home in the Los Angeles suburb of Beverly Hills.

1971—Josef makes a career change from exporting to running the Hotel St. Moritz in Hollywood, California. Within the year he has made the hotel a success; however, at this time he is diagnosed with high blood pressure which advances to heart disease.

March, 1971—Josef experiences his first heart attack.

March, 1972—Josef suffers a second heart attack. To prevent another, possibly fatal attack, he undergoes a quadruple bypass operation.

1973—The Moreckis, along with daughter Carol and her husband Chris, finally make a pilgrimage to The Holy Land, Israel.

1974—Nina convinces her husband to officially retire.

Early 1988—Josef is diagnosed with cancer of the colon.

May, 1988—Josef passes away.

July, 1988—Nina moves to Carpinteria, California, to stay with her oldest daughter, Roselyn.

1990—Nina falls and breaks her arm while taking a walk through Carpinteria. She undergoes several weeks of physical therapy. After recuperating she takes on volunteer work and becomes friendly with a group of women who attend the local Lutheran church. Nina later moves into her own apartment in nearby Santa Barbara.

1993—Nina meets Masa, who convinces her to share her wartime experiences with Mrs. Elisabeth Chowning's students at Carpinteria High School. After Mrs. Chowning retires Nina continues to speak for Mr. Casey Roberts' class at the same school.

Spring, 1995—The students in Mrs. Chowning's Advanced Placement English class assist Nina in compiling her wartime experiences, which are written up by Alice White in the form of an open letter to young people.

Fall, 1996—Nina meets history professor Dr. Harold Marcuse and begins to speak to his students studying the Holocaust at the University of California, Santa Barbara.

Fall, 1998—Nina meets Colette Waddell, a U.C.S.B. student, during a speaking engagement.

August 5–9, 1999—Nina returns to her hometown of L'vov, now part of the Ukraine, with Dr. Marcuse and her daughter Carol.

April, 2002–March, 2005—Colette conducts interviews with Nina about her life.

L'vov Statistics—Jewish Population

Before World War II, L'vov, hailed as "the Vienna of the East," was also known for its Jewish community, the third largest in Poland. The general population of L'vov numbered around 315,000—110,000 of whom were Jews.

Jewish refugees fleeing from persecution caused the Jewish population in L'vov to swell by an additional 100,000.

Beginning in June of 1941, Ukrainian nationalists, encouraged by the Nazis, led a number of vicious pogroms that lasted two months and resulted in the deaths of some 6,000 Jews.

In the fall of 1941, Nazi troops rounded up the majority of Jews in L'vov and forced them into a ghetto sealed with barbed wire. 5,000 elderly and disabled Jews were murdered in the process.

It was also during this year that the Janowska labor camp was created in order to use the Jews as slave labor. At least 200,000 Jews were eventually executed when deemed unfit for further work. Tens of thousands were processed through the ghetto and Janowska for deportation to an extermination camp in Belzec, Poland.

When the L'vov ghetto was liquidated in **July of 1943,** only a small number of Jews were able to escape through the city's sewers and to the nearby woods.

By 1989, 12,800 Jews remained living in L'vov; however, their numbers dropped considerably after the fall of Soviet rule.

By 1992, only 8,500 Jews remained in L'vov.

Nina Grütz-Morecki

(Born 1920)

FAMILY TREE

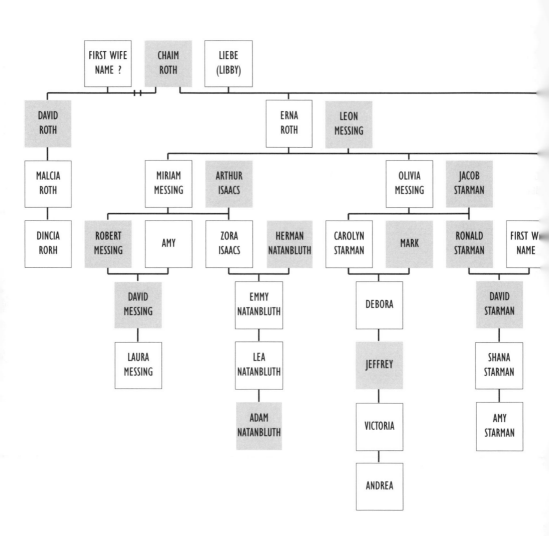

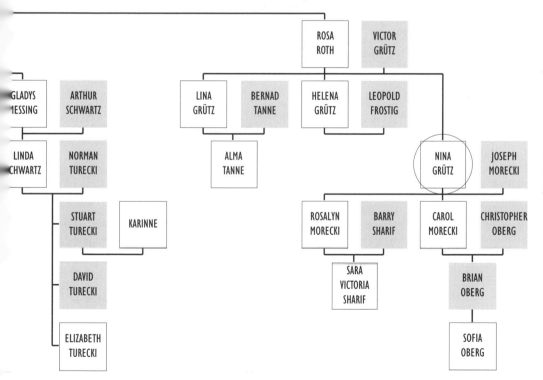

Glossary of Terms

Aktion—This Germanic term meaning "action" was used by the Nazis to identify periodic round-ups of Jews by force. Special teams within the German army coordinated these operations in order to collect Jews for labor or transport to concentration camps, or outright execution.

Aryan—In Nazism this term described a non-Jewish Caucasian, especially one of Nordic type.

Bar mitzvah—The age at which a boy becomes religiously responsible for his acts; and by extension, the ceremony celebrating his achieving that status, and generally held around his thirteenth birthday.

Bolsheviks—A member of the Communist, radical Marxist party that seized power in Russia.

Displaced Persons—Those millions of Europeans, Jews, and non-Jews, who, by the war's end, had been forced out of their homes, both by Nazi decrees and by the overall effects of the war.

D.P. Camp—Temporary shelter for "Displaced Persons" left homeless from World War II. Refugees remained in camp until more permanent housing could be found or immigration to other countries arranged.

Einsatzgruppen—Special mobile units organized by the Reich Security Main Office for the elimination of the Nazis' enemies in countries occupied by them. Primarily responsible for the large-scale massacres of the

Russian Jews, communists and intellectuals during Operation Barbarossa, 1941, and for the slaughter of Poles throughout the war years.

Gentile—A person who is not a Jew, specifically a Christian.

Gestapo—The German state secret police directly under the control of Himmler from 1936.

Ghetto—The quarters of European towns in which Jews were compulsorily required to reside in the Middle Ages. This system was resurrected by the Nazis following their takeover of Poland.

Ghetto benches—Seating designated for Jewish University students. The Nuremberg Laws, anti-Jewish policies and legislation of Nazi Germany beginning in 1933, had far-reaching effects, and called for the increased segregation of Jews from the general populace. The 'ghetto benches,' in which Jews were forced to take seats at the very back of university lecture halls, were a direct result of that segregation.

Gymnasium—A college-preparatory school in some European countries.

Judenrat—German term meaning 'Jewish Council' that was used to describe the Jewish representative body established by the Nazis in various ghettos and communities. The purpose behind their establishment was to provide the Nazis with vital administrative and supervisory assistance and to implement Nazi decrees.

Molotov-Ribbentrop Pact—Named after the respective Foreign Ministers of the Soviet Union who negotiated with Hitler in 1939. The result was this non-aggression treaty in which Stalin agreed that, in the event of war, Russia would not challenge Nazi troops marching into the western parts of Poland, so long as the Soviet Army were allowed to advance into the eastern region.

Numerus clausus—The policy enforced throughout parts of pre-war Europe in which Jewish attendance to particular universities was severely limited to a chosen few.

Pogrom—An organized act of violence against minority groups, particularly Jews, that often results in the massacre of the targeted population.

Polytechnicum—A prestigious architectural school in eastern Poland where the students were known to be especially anti-Semitic.

Shiksa—A female non-Jew, usually of the Christian faith. The way in which the term is used in Nina's narrative implies that this particular type of woman seduces eligible Jewish men.

Synagogue—A building or place of meeting for worship and religious instruction in the Jewish faith.

Torah—The first five books of the Hebrew Scriptures that holds the entire body of religious law and learning for Jews.

Zionism—An organized movement of world Jewry for the reconstitution of a Jewish state in Palestine, now concerned with supporting the state of Israel.

Zloty—Polish currency.

Bibliography

Andelin, Helen B. *Fascinating Womanhood*. Santa Barbara: Pacific Press, 1963.

Banas, Josef. *The Scapegoats: The Exodus of the Remnants of Polish Jewry*. London: Weidenfeld and Nicolson, 1979.

British Medical Journal. 1999; 319: 478–483.

Bussell, Harold. *Sermon at El Montecito Presbyterian Church*. October 10, 2005, Montecito, California.

Cala, Alina. "The Image of the Jew in Polish Folk Culture." Jerusalem: Magnes Press, 1995. 234 pp. In *Jews and Gender, the Challenge to Hierarchy*, edited by Jonathan Frankel, "History and the Social Sciences." 341–343. Oxford: Oxford University Press, 2000.

Chapnik, Liza. "The Grondo Ghetto and its Underground, A Personal Narrative." In *Women in the Holocaust*, edited by Dalia Ofer and Lenore J. Weitzmann, 110–112. London: Yale University Press, 1998.

Clayman, Charles B., M.D. *American Medical Association Encyclopedia of Medicine*. New York: Random House, 1989.

Cooper, Leo. *In the Shadow of the Polish Eagle*. Chippenham: Antony Rowe, Ltd., 2000.

Duffy, Michael. "Who's Who: Josef Pilsudski." Updated Sunday, 9
    March, 2003. Accessed on
    http://www.firstworldwar.com/bio/pilsudski.htm on December
    15, 2005.

Greenville, J.A.S. *A History of the World in the Twentieth Century.*
    Belknap Press: Cambridge, 1997.

Gutman, Yisrael. "Polish Antisemitism Between the Wars: An
    Overview." In *The Jews of Poland Between Two World Wars,*
    edited by Yisrael Gutman, Ezra Mendelsohn, Jehuda Reinharz
    and Chone Shmeruk, 293. Hanover & London: University Press
    of New England, 1990.

Heck, Alfons. *The Burden of Hitler's Legacy.* Frederick: Renaissance
    House Publishers, 1998.

Hertzberg, Arthur, contributing editor. *The Zionist Idea: A Historical
    Analysis and Reader.* MacMillan, 1972. Jewish Publication
    Society of America, 1997.
    http://www.amazon.com/gp/product/0827606222/ref=olp_prod
    uct_details/103-5977076-
    8429417?%5Fencoding=UTF8&v=glance&n=283155

Hospice at Home, Inc. Bereavement Program. *Hope for Bereaved
    Handbook.* Syracuse: Hope for Bereaved, 1998.

"How To Be A Good Wife." From a 1950's home economics textbook.
    http://www.wolfbane.com/jazz/goodwife.htm. Updated March
    26, 1997. Accessed October 10, 2005.

Huberban, Rabbi Shimon. *Kiddush Hashem: Jewish Religious and Cultural
    Life in Poland During the Holocaust.* New Jersey: KTAV
    Publishing House, Inc., 1987.

Hyman, Paula E. "Two Models of Modernization: Jewish Women in the
    German and the Russian Empires." In *Jews and Gender, the
    Challenge to Hierarchy.* Edited by Jonathan Frankel, 49–50.
    Oxford: Oxford University Press, 2000.

Isaacson, Judith Magyar. *Seed of Sarah.* Chicago: University of Illinois Press, 1991.

"Jews and Zion." http://encyclopedia.thefreedictionary.com/Zionism. Under "The Jews and Zion" and "Establishment of the Zionist Movement." Accessed December 15, 2005.

Klag, Michael J., M.P.H., editor-in-chief, *Johns Hopkins Family Health Book.* New York: Harper Collins Publishers, 1999. 817?818.

Korzec, Pawe. Anti-Semitism in Poland as an Intellectual, Social, and Political Movement." In *Studies on Polish Jewry, 1919–1939.* Edited by Joshua Fishman, 13–43. New York: Yivo Institute for Jewish Research, 1974.

Landau, Ronnie S. *The Nazi Holocaust.* Chicago: Ivan R. Dee, 1994.

Langer, Lawrence L. "Gendered Suffering? Women in Holocaust Testimonies." In *Women in the Holocaust.* Edited by Dalia Ofer and Lenore J. Weitzman, 360. London: Yale University Press, 1998.

Levin, Don. *The Lesser of Two Evils.* Philadelphia: The Jewish Publication Society, 1995.

Marcus, Joseph. *Social and Political History of the Jews in Poland, 1919–1939.* Berlin: Mouton Publishers, 1983.

Ofer, Dalia. "Gender Issues in Diaries and Testimonies of the Ghetto, The Case of Warsaw." In *Women in the Holocaust.* Edited by Dalia Ofer and Lenore J. Weitzman, 4–8, 149, and 103–105. London: Yale University Press, 1998.

Patek wrist watches. Tic-tock.com. http://www.tic-tock.com/PatekPhilippeWristWatchContemporary.htm. Accessed September 30, 2005.

Pinchuk, Ben-Cion. *Shtetl Jews under Soviet Rule, Eastern Poland on the Eve of the Holocaust.* Cambridge: Basil Blackwell, Inc. 1990.

Roark, James L. et al. *The American Promise.* Boston: Bedford Books, 1998.

Shirer, William L. *The Rise and Fall of the Third Reich.* New York: Fawcett Crest, 1992.

Tec, Nechama. "Women among the Forest Partisans." In *Women in the Holocaust.* Edited by Dalia Ofer and Lenore J. Weitzman, 223–229. London: Yale University Press, 1998.

Unger, Michal. "The Status and Plight of Women in the Lodz Ghetto." In *Women in the Holocaust.* Edited by Dalia Ofer and Lenore J. Weitzman, 125 and 130–134. London: Yale University Press, 1998.

Vago, Lidia Rosenfeld. "One Year in the Black Hold of Our Planet Earth, A Personal Narrative." In *Women in the Holocaust.* Edited by Dalia Ofer and Lenore J. Weitzman, 276. London: Yale University Press, 1998.

Weitzman, Lenore J. "Living on the Aryan Side in Poland." In *Women in the Holocaust. Edit*ed by Dalia Ofer and Lenore J. Weitzman, 189, 197–198, 203–215. London: Yale University Press, 1998.

Wells, Leon. *The Janowska Road.* Washington, D.C.: Holocaust Library, 1999.

Woods, William. *Poland: Eagle in the East.* New York: Hill and Wang, 1968.

Wynot, Edward D. "The Polish Peasant Movement and the Jews, 1918–1939." In *The Jews of Poland Between Two World Wars.* 36–43, edited by Yisrael Gutman, Ezra Mendelsohn, Jehuda Reinharz and Chone Shmeruk, Hanover & London: University Press of New England, 1990.

End Notes

CHAPTER I

1. Marcus, *History of the Jews*, vii.
2. Ibid., 65.
3. Ibid., 73.
4. Ibid., 146.
5. Ibid., 154.
6. Ibid., 154.
7. Hyman, "Two Models of Modernization," 49-50.
8. Korzec, "Anti-Semitism in Poland," 37, 39.
9. Ibid., 21.
10. Marcus, *History of the Jews*, 29.
11. Ibid., 30.
12. Hyman, "Two Models of Modernization," 49-50.
13. Marcus, *History of the Jews*, 65.
14. Ibid., 13.
15. Ibid.
16. Korzec, "Anti-Semitism in Poland," 43.
17. Cooper, *In the Shadow of the Polish Eagle*, 49, 61.
18. Marcus, *History of the Jews*, 20.
19. Ibid., 21.
20. Korzec, "Anti-Semitism in Poland," 13, 14.
21. Ibid., 14.
22. Cala, "Image of the Jew," 341-342.
23. Marcus, *History of the Jews*, 146.
24. Cooper, *In the Shadow of the Polish Eagle*, 36-37.
25. Klag, *Johns Hopkins Family Health Book*, 817-818.
26. Cooper, *In the Shadow of the Polish Eagle*, 54.

CHAPTER 2

1. Marcus, *History of the Jews*, 87.
2. Ibid., 92-93.
3. Ibid., 25.
4. Wynot, "Polish Peasant Movement and the Jews," 36.
5. Shmeruk, "Hebrew-Yiddish-Polish: A Trilingual Jewish Culture," 294
6. Wynot, "Polish Peasant Movement and the Jews," 43.
7. Ibid., 37.
8. Marcus, *History of the Jews*, 317.
9. www.TheFreeDictionary.com, "The Jews and Zion," 1, and "Establishment of the Zionist Movement," 2.
10. Ibid.
11. Marcus, *History of the Jews*, 160.
12. Cooper, *In the Shadow of the Polish Eagle*, 56-57.
13. Ibid., 49.
14. Ibid., 61.
15. Levin, *Lesser of Two Evils*, 26.
16. Cooper, *In the Shadow of the Polish Eagle*, 56, 57, 60.

CHAPTER 3

1. Huberband, *Kiddush Hashem*, 8, 11-12.
2. Ibid., 12.
3. Ibid., 12-13.
4. Levin, *Lesser of Two Evils*, 4.
5. Ibid., 70.
6. Wells, *Janowska Road*, 44.
7. Ibid., 4.
8. Levin, *Lesser of Two Evils*, 4.
9. Ibid., 8.
10. Ibid., 9.
11. Ibid.
12. Ibid., 73.
13. Pinchuk, *Shteltl Jews Under Soviet Rule*, 43, 44, 52.
14. Ibid., 8.
15. Greenville, *History of the World*, 268-269.
16. Wells, *Janowska Road*, 43.
17. Levin, *Lesser of Two Evils*, 34.

CHAPTER 4

1. Wells, *Janowska Road*, 45.
2. Ibid., 45-48.
3. Chapnik, "Grondo Ghetto," 112.

4. Landau, *The Nazi Holocaust*, 195.
5. Cooper, *In the Shadow of the Polish Eagle*, 94
6. Huberban, *Kiddush Hashem*, 44.
7. Wells, *Janowska Road*, 92.
8. Ofer, "Gender Issues," 149.
9. Wells, *Janowska Road*, 60.
10. Isaacson, *Seed of Sarah*, 55
11. Woods, *Eagle in the East*, 20.
12. Shimon, *Kiddash Hashem*, 45.
13. Woods, *Eagle in the East*, 24
14. Landau, *The Nazi Holocaust*, 171.
15. Ofer, "Gender Issues," 105.

CHAPTER 5

1. Woods, *Eagle in the East*, 23.
2. Ibid., 17-18.
3. Kaplan, "The Jewish Response to the Third Reich: Gender at the Grassroots," 82-83.
4. Ofer, "Gender Issues," 103-105.
5. Wells, *Janowska Road*, 136.
6. Weitzman, "Living on the Aryan Side in Poland," 197.
7. Woods, *Eagle in the East*, 29.
8. Chapnik, "Grondo Ghetto and Its Underground," 112-114; Unger, "Status and Plight of Women," 125, 130.
9. Unger, "Status and Plight of Women," 134.
10. Ibid., 131.
11. Weitzman, "Living on the Aryan Side," 198.
12. Woods, *Eagle in the East*, 27.
13. Landau, *The Nazi Holocaust*, 204.
14. Ibid., 24.
15. Ibid., 47.
16. Landau, *The Nazi Holocaust*, 167, 169.
17. Vago, "One Year in the Black Hold," 276.
18. Huberban, *Kiddush Hashem*, 36.
19. Woods, *Eagle in the East*, 52.
20. Wells, *Janowska Road*, 113.
21. Ibid., 113-115.
22. Landau, *The Nazi Holocaust*, 173-174.

CHAPTER 6

1. Landau, *The Nazi Holocaust*, 167-169.
2. Wynot, "Polish Peasant Movement," 37.

3. Woods, *Eagle in the East*, 24.
4. Chapnik, "Grondo Ghetto," 110-111.
5. Woods, *Eagle in the East*, 28.
6. Isaacson, *Seed of Sarah*, 167.
7. Tec, "Women among the Forest Partisans," 223.
8. Woods, *Eagle in the East*, 22-23.
9. Ofer, "Gender Issues," 8.
10. Ibid., 4.
11. Ibid., 213-214.
12. Weitzman, "Living on the Aryan Side," 215.
13. Cooper, *In the Shadow of the Polish Eagle*, 128.
14. Weitzman, "Living on the Aryan Side," 213.
15. Ibid., 189.
16. Ibid., 209.
17. Shirer, *Rise and Fall of the Third Reich*, 1311-1313.
18. Heck, *Burden of Hitler's Legacy*, 155.

CHAPTER 7
1. Shirer, *Rise and Fall of the Third Reich*, 1345, 1351.
2. Weitzman, "Living on the Aryan Side," 209-211.
3. Heck, *Burden of Hitler's Legacy*, 116, 132, 143.
4. Woods, *Eagle in the East*, 99-100.
5. Ibid., 61.

CHAPTER 8
1. Cooper, *In the Shadow of the Polish Eagle*, 194-195.
2. Baumgarten, "As Families Remember: Holocaust Memoirs and Their Transmission," 274.
3. Wells, *Janowska Road*, 263.
4. Baumgarten, "As Families Remember," 275.
5. www.tic-tock.com, "Philippe Wrist Watches."
6. Weitzman, "Living on the Aryan Side," 203.
7. Tec, "Women among the Forest Partisans," 228-229.
8. Woods, *Eagle in the East*, 100.
9. Wells, *Janowska Road*, 280.
10. Ibid.
11. Ibid., 274.

CHAPTER 9
1. Wells, *Janowska Road*, 328.
2. Ibid.
3. Ibid., 112.
4. Klag, *Johns Hopkins Family Health Book*, 884.

5. Ibid., 892.
6. Ibid., 459.
7. Woods, *Eagle in the East*, 46-47.
8. Roark, *American Promise*, 1075.
9. Ibid.
10. Ibid., 1073-1074.
11. Ibid., 1077.

CHAPTER 10

1. Langer, "Gendered Suffering?", 360.
2. www.wolfbane.com, "Good Wife," 1.
3. Andelin, *Fascinating Womanhood*, reference www.wolfbane.com.
4. Klag, *Johns Hopkins Family Health Book*, 795.
5. Clayman, *Encyclopedia of Medicine*, 514.
6. Klag, *Johns Hopkins Family Health Book*, 1022.

CHAPTER 11

1. "British Medical Journal," 478-483.
2. Baumgarten, "As Families Remember," 268.

EPILOGUE

1. Bussell, "Sermon at El Montecito Presbyterian Church."

www.ColetteWaddell.com